A QUEST FOR A MORE STABLE WORLD ECONOMIC SYSTEM

A QUEST FOR A MORE STABLE WORLD ECONOMIC SYSTEM
Restructuring at a Time of Cyclical Adjustment

Edited by

Lawrence R. Klein
University of Pennsylvania, USA

KLUWER ACADEMIC PUBLISHERS

Dordrecht / Boston / London

Distributors for North America:
Kluwer Academic Publishers
101 Philip Drive
Assinippi Park
Norwell, Massachusetts 02061 USA

Distributors for all other countries:
Kluwer Academic Publishers Group
Distribution Centre
Post Office Box 322
3300 AH Dordrecht, THE NETHERLANDS

Library of Congress Cataloging-in-Publication Data

A Quest for a more stable world economic system: restructuring at a
  time of cyclical adjustment / edited by Lawrence R. Klein.
       p.   cm.
    Based on papers from the International Symposium on a Quest for a
More Stable World Economic System organized by the International
Institute for Advanced Studies (Kyoto).
    Includes index.
    ISBN 0-7923-9389-9 (alk. paper)
    1. Economic policy--Congresses. 2. Economics--History--20th
century--Congresses. I. Klein, Lawrence Robert.
HD87.Q47 1993
338.9--dc20   93-25699
                                                          CIP

Printed on acid-free paper.

Printed in the United States of America.

Dedication

This volume is in memory of our respected colleague

Christopher Ian Higgins
Secretary, Department of the Treasury
Canberra, Australia

who contributed so much to the success of the symposium but passed away soon
after the occasion of our meeting.

TABLE OF CONTENTS

INTRODUCTION

ACKNOWLEDGEMENTS

The International Institute for Advanced Studies (Kyoto) organized the International Symposium on A Quest for a More Stable World Economic System, under the sponsorship of the Ministry of Education, Science, and Culture of Japan.

The staff members of the Institute, particularly Marie Matsui, were very helpful with organizing symposium details and the preparation of the manuscript for publication.

The international committee that planned the symposium program were

Lawrence R. Klein, University of Pennsylvania (Chairman)
Chikashi Moriguchi, Osaka University (Vice-Chairman)
Akihiro Amano, Kobe University
Koichi Hamada, Yale University
Christopher I. Higgins, Treasury of Australia
Herbert S. Levine, University of Pennsylvania

In addition Professors Moriguchi and Amano were assisted for local arragnements by

Charles Y. Horioka, Osaka University
Kazuhiro Igawa, Kobe University
Yoshiyasu Ono, Osaka University

The authors were, of course, presenters of papers at the Symposium. Also there were several participants in the discussions who came from various universities in Japan. They contributed greatly to the open discussions. I mention, in particular, Sadayoshi Ohtsu of Ryukoku University, Kyoji Fukao of Hitotsubashi University, Yusuke Onitsuka of the University of Tokyo, and Tsuneaki Sato of Nihon University.

Invited participants from academic centers in Japan also contributed significantly to the general discussion. They were

Kenn Ariga, Kyoto University
Kanemi Ban, Osaka University
Mitsuo Ezaki, Kyoto University
Hidekazu Eguchi, Hitotsubashi University
Saburo Fukui, Kyoto University
Toshihiko Hayashi, Osaka University
Shinichi Ichimura, Osaka International University
Kazuhito Ikeo, Kyoto University
Kazuo Ogawa, Kobe University
Michihiro Ohyama, Keio University
Michio Okamoto, Director, I.I.A.S. (International Institute of
    Advanced Studies)
Azuma Okuda, Chairman, Board of Trustees, I.I.A.S.
Mitsuo Saito, Tezukayama University
Hirofumi Shibata, Osaka University
Soichi Shinohara, Doshisha University
Toshiaki Tachibanaki, Kyoto University
Toshihisa Toyoda, Kobe University

I would like to thank the following companies for their support.

- ASAHI CHEMICAL INDUSTRY CO., LTD.
- Daiwa House Industry Co., Ltd.
- The Kansai Electric Power Co., Inc.
- Kinki Nippon Railway Co., Ltd.
- Kobe Steel Limited
- Matsushita Electric Works, Ltd.
- MATSUSHITA ELECTRONIC INDUSTRIAL CO., LTD.
- Nippon Shinyaku Co., Ltd.
- OBAYASHI CORPORATION
- SEKISUI HOUSE, LTD.
- SHIMADZU CORPORATION
- SHIONOGI & CO., LTD.
- Sumitomo Metal Industries, Ltd.
- SUMITOMO DENSETSU CO., LTD.
- Sumitomo Metal Industries Ltd.
- Takara Shuzo Company Limited
- TAKEDA CHEMICAL INDUSTRIES LTD.
- TANABE SEIYAKU Co., Ltd.
- TOYOBO CO., LTD.
- WACOAL CORP.

The preparation of this volume for publication has been done at the University of Pennsylvania, relying heavily on the efforts of Beverly Ann Meyers.

PREFACE

In the autumn of 1990 there was a sense of change taking place in the world economy. Readiness for war was occurring in the Middle East and a recession was already underway in a few major countries. The forces of reform and political re-shaping were visible in Eastern Europe and the Soviet Union. We economists, gathering in Osaka, Japan, under the auspices of the International Institute for Advanced Studies (Kyoto) could recognize that the Cold War was over and that politico-economic restructuring would take place among the powers in the Warsaw Treaty Organization.

Much has happened since the latter part of 1990 to affect international economic stability. The events of that period were both positive and negative for economic stability, but our concern was weighted towards the negative side. Our charge and sponsorship was scholarly, and the papers from the learned contributors to the symposium and this resulting volume used the many tools of economic analysis to try to understand the ongoing developments.

In the intervening period, while this volume was being prepared and edited, we did not change our viewpoints in any fundamental way, and we can take satisfaction in the way our symposium either relates to the unfolding sequence of events in a substantive sense or provides a framework in which to study these events.

The setting and support for the Symposium came from Japan. Many of the participants were from the Pacific Basin, but also from North America and Europe, including the Soviet Union. It was not our intent to try to analyze every international issue that we could see on the horizon, but I do believe that we focused on several important matters, and have ideas about them to put to printed page.

The International Institute for Advanced Studies is a new organization in Japan and this is their first excursion into economic studies. I can only hope that it lays a foundation for future efforts, in our field of study, by the Institute.

Lawrence R. Klein

A QUEST FOR A MORE STABLE WORLD ECONOMIC SYSTEM

1. RESTRUCTURING AND ARMS REDUCTION IN THE WORLD ECONOMY

L. R. Klein
Department of Economics
University of Pennsylvania
3718 Locust Walk
Philadelphia, PA 19104-6297
USA

ABSTRACT. This "keynote" chapter describes the international economic setting prevailing in late summer, 1990. The uncertainties of the military operation in the Gulf, together with economic reform in Europe, both West and East, gave rise to concern about the health of the international economy. Recession was under way or about to begin in some countries, and a general world slowdown was already being felt. This particular set of circumstances made international coordination of economic policy difficult. But after the prevailing cyclical correction, it was felt that the world economy could cope with restructuring in many countries and take advantage of pending technological improvements to embark on a new expansion in the final decade of the 20th century.

1. INTRODUCTION

When the ideas developed in this chapter were first germinating towards the end of 1989, everything seemed to be going in a favorable direction for the world economy. The basis for optimism rested on
- unification in Europe, including both the extension of the European Community and the eventual integration of Eastern bloc countries;
- the end of the Cold War;
- restructuring of economies in Eastern Europe and the Soviet Union;
- the potential realization of a Peace Dividend.

All these developments are continuing and remain as bases for optimism, especially for the medium term, but they have been displaced from the focus of attention by the crisis in the Persian Gulf.

Economists in particular felt good about the way that the world economy was moving early in 1990, because developments seemed to substantiate standard teaching about the laws of markets, industrial organization, economic incentives, and economic efficiency. In many respects, the economic direction represented a triumph of The Wealth of Nations over Das Kapital as a work that did better in surviving the test of time. This triumph was particularly fitting for the year 1990, which was the 200th anniversary of the death of Adam Smith. However, in terms of today's political spectrum, Smith's ideas were wide ranging and not all molded into the stereotype conservative message. In particular, Smith offered some very telling comments in support of a Peace Dividend and also of progressive income taxation, which are not in the typical conservative menu. At the same time, Karl Marx had nothing useful to say about how a socialist—planned economy ought to be operated, and his followers did little to advance economic science from that perspective.

Prior to the appearance of the Gulf Crisis, it was recognized that changes were taking place in the world economy that redistributed performance character- istics. North America had already begun to slow down by significant amounts; the Asia—Pacific region was shifting towards a more moderate although still vigorous growth path; and Western Europe was demonstrating the strongest growth characteristics. Investment in anticipation of economic unification was taking place at a rapid pace, unemployment was receding, and inflation was mainly in check.

The socialist countries were experiencing recession as a consequence of their restructuring. Some Latin American countries were still suffering from debt service burdens with hyperinflation; they too were in recession, with some restructuring, but they expected to recover, possibly to the extent that Chile and Mexico had.

When the world economy was seen as a whole, it was recognized that 1990 would be a year of slow growth, the experiencing of adjustment pains, and even recessions here and there, e.g., in Australia, Canada, and possibly the United States, not to mention some developing countries. But the general picture was one of short cyclical adjustment in preparation for a good decade of expansion to end the century.

The good prospects for the decade of the 1990s, after the present cyclical adjustment, remain intact even though the corrections for 1990—1992 are expected to be more severe. However, there are two specific developments that must be taken into account as a result of the present crisis. In the first place, the price of oil and other energy products will be higher than had previously been considered. Even for the medium—term projection made early in 1990 or in 1989, it had been expected that oil prices would begin to respond in an upward movement to supply—demand imbalances by mid decade. At the present time, Iraq has pressed for higher oil prices extremely forcefully from its position within OPEC. Iraq was not successful in doing this by argument, but its resort to force made the point; and it is now unlikely that prices will be rolled back to the levels that prevailed (under $20/barrel) in early 1990. This means effectively that the oil- price increases that were expected for approximately 1995 are already in place. Of course, it is possible that they could be pushed very high, depending on the military outcomes of the Crisis.

A second change concerns the distribution of income and wealth throughout the Arab world. It is unlikely that the concentration of gains in the hands of ruling families of Saudi Arabia, Kuwait, and the United Arab Emirates will be sustainable. Economic performance has been poor in the populous Arab countries, especially in those which are not major exporters of oil, and the populist views of Iraq for a more equitable sharing of oil wealth will gain some degree of credibility. A few Arab countries have been prosperous, and some have fared poorly. This situation will probably change, but the outcome depends on the resolution of the crisis situation.

There is one other side effect of the Gulf Crisis, namely, the treatment of guest workers. Vast members of Egyptians, Pakistanis, Indians, Bangladeshis, Thais, Filipinos and others from poorer countries in the region (and beyond) depended heavily on income that was remitted in significant amounts to home countries from the prosperous Gulf States, and this source has been cut off. The result is immediate hardship and an uncertain future. Again, the outcome depends on how the Crisis is settled.

2. THE CYCLICAL POSITION FOR 1990–1992

An economic slowdown or mild recession in the United States was already visible before the Crisis. Now we can look for a recession; it will probably be mild, but more severe than it would have been without the disruptions in energy markets.

During the 1970s, we learned a great deal about the role of energy in the modern industrial economy. The higher prices that prevailed after each oil shock acted as though they constituted a "tax" on the importing countries. Worse yet, the "tax" did not contribute to the domestic budget but was absorbed by the oil-exporting countries. In addition, the collections of oil based revenues were recycled throughout the world economy. Many people in the world financial community congratulated themselves on the alleged smoothness of the recycling mechanism, but in reality this recycling was accomplished to a large extent by making ill–conceived loans to developing and centrally planned economies. The result was the World Debt Crisis which put banks in the industrial world at risk. The Debt Crisis has not been resolved; it is a lingering problem for the world economy and stands in the way of achieving international balance on current accounts. This biased and unhealthy distribution of surplus and deficit positions throughout the world remains an obstacle to total recovery.

The higher prices for energy products dampened demand and generated large price rises. I believe that these price rises constituted inflation, but some economists prefer to classify them more benignly as shifts in relative prices. Higher prices lead to higher interest rates, lower investment, poorer growth, and severe burdens on indebted countries. Also, energy shortfalls or expensive energy can cause short–run bottlenecks in a roundabout production process. In the United States, these contributed greatly to the productivity slowdown of the 1970s. We spent the decade learning how to become more energy efficient, and this cut into labor productivity. The U.S. economy now is more energy efficient but has not gone as far as it should; however, it is in a better position to deal with the present escalation of energy prices.

Energy has other avenues of influence in the economy. Higher use taxes within the U.S. and other countries will contribute to additional pressures on inflation, and our entrance into the Crisis situation in a weak, indebted position complicates the adjustment process. The military buildup itself strains our fiscal position, leaving small margins for adjustment by monetary authorities.

One way to examine the impact of higher energy prices on the present cyclical position of the world economy is to simulate an international econometric model with higher oil prices and to compare the solution with a base case. A simple system for this purpose is a small interlinked trading model associating China, Japan, and the United States with the Rest–of–the–World (ROW).[1] This system was originally constructed in order to study various

---

[1]L.R. Klein, L.J. Lau, Shen Lisheng, Xu Leilei, and Yoshihisa Inada, "Quadrilateral Trading Patterns: China–Japan–USA and Rest–of–the–World," paper presented at ASSA meetings, Atlanta, GA, December, 1989.

bilateral problems among these individual countries and the ROW. In the present context, the main oil-exporting countries are in ROW. China is also an exporter on a modest scale, while the United States is a major importer. Japan, too, is an importer, being poorly endowed with many basic commodities.

A 20% oil-price increase, which is likely to turn out to be too small, leads to the following results:

1. ROW exports to the world rise by about 0.25% and then fall in 1993-1994 by 1.5% to 4.0%. The rise accrues to the oil exporters in the first instance, until the higher oil prices lead to a slowdown in other sectors and, therefore, a cutback in demand that reduces purchasing power in partner countries.

2. Japan, as a significant oil importer, loses a great deal of exports, reaching a cutback of almost 15% by 1994.

3. In contrast, China stands to gain — as much as 11.5% by 1994.

4. The United States fares reasonably well. Some customers cannot import as much as usual from the U.S., but U.S. gains on the export side, building up to nearly 3%.

5. The ROW import pattern has the same overall effects as in the export case. The import reduction is estimated at about 5.6% by 1994.

6. Japan should find itself importing more, as should China. China's imports are much larger than Japan's, and it seems quite natural that China should use enhanced oil revenues to import more and, it is hoped, to grow more vigorously. U.S. imports stay below base values in 1991 and 1992, but are expected to come back in a modest way in 1993-1994.

7. Among the countries and areas included in this model, prices are persistently higher by a very thin margin in the U.S. and China; ROW shows mixed results. Japan is expected to enjoy steadily falling (below baseline) prices.

8. In all countries, there is an expectation that GDP should rise steadily, year-by-year. All countries except Japan show output gains over the growing baseline path, as large as about 3.5% by 1991. The most impressive gains occur in ROW, where the bulk of the world's oil for export is located.

This is a familiar pattern in which exporting nations gain on the side of trade and production, while major importers lose. At a more detailed level, a similar scenario has been played out on the LINK system, which provides models for 80 countries or regions.

If oil reaches $30/barrel in 1991 (a higher figure than the 20% (increase) case just described), the LINK estimates show GDP growth falling by 60 basis points below the base case in oil importing developing countries, but by more than 100 basis points in advanced industrial economies. Total world trade should be down by as much as 130 basis points and the inflation rate up by 100 basis points. Services in the current account balances of affected developing countries should be off by $17 billion, and the trade balances of oil-importing developing countries should be off by $37 billion.

There is another immediate effect that will hurt many developing countries, especially those in the Gulf region: namely, many guest workers have left or have been sent home. These workers usually remit large balances to their families, and much of this income source has already vanished. To the extent that high prices lead to high interest rates, debt service burdens will rise.

A full and rounded simulation should be able to bring out many more effects that are associated with the present Gulf Crisis.

The LINK simulations include approximate values for the oil price that seems to be realistic; therefore, the present simulation based on oil at $30/barrel or even $40/barrel may soon stand as the new base case.

3. ARMS REDUCTION

The Persian Gulf crisis is not large enough to wipe out the favorable economic effects of arms reductions. The figures that were being assumed six months ago or more must be trimmed back as we think through security matters, but there should still be major cutbacks in the U.S. and Warsaw/Treaty military presence in Europe. The Cold War *is* over, and the U.S. defense budget should be able to be safely reduced by as much as $40 billion. In addition, talks are under way for eliminating or reducing U.S. armed-force presence in South Korea, Japan, and the Philippines.

The military response to the invasion of Kuwait showed the important need for regular troops, naval ships, and aircraft carriers. This highly mobile force was put together in just two months. The need for Star Wars or other exotic weapons systems has diminished, and the present preoccupation with very expensive facilities/equipment is not warranted; therefore, some cuts can be made apart from closing overseas bases.

Before the Gulf Crisis, it was felt that armament-expenditure cuts could, with enhanced revenues, bring the U.S. internal budget deficit towards balance, possibly reaching that state by mid decade. Three things that stand in the way of reduction in the *level* of budget deficit in the United States are as follows:

1. Financial failures, especially of the Savings & Loan or thrift institutions, are adding most unusual sums to the prevailing deficit. The budgetary losses, if properly evaluated, could amount to $500 billion in due course. Some of the costs are taken "off budget," but they nevertheless remain in terms of their adverse effects on the macroeconomy.

2. Large expenditures for the military operation in the Middle East will partially offset budgetary gains that could result from programs of arms reduction. These need not obliterate gains from arms reduction, but they will of necessity reduce the gains that we were hoping for in the early summer. It should be noted, however, that all the military costs in the Persian Gulf area will not be a burden for the United States, even though we organized the mobilization and deployment of troops. Saudi Arabia, the Kuwait government in exile, and other Gulf states will be in a position to help with the financial costs, even to the point of contributing to those countries who lost remittances or inexpensive energy fuels. It is generally expected, however, that Arab aid from the Gulf area will not last indefinitely. Many of the sources of help may fade in a year or less.

3. World recessionary tendencies, whether we are technically in a recession or simply participating in a very slow economy, make for increased budgetary deficits. Higher transfer payments and fewer tax collections cause government books to go into states of imbalance, mainly on the pessimistic side.

Some of these undesirable events will hit other countries as well; recessionary tendencies have a way of growing.

But the present business-cycle situation is not permanent. Cycles typically rise and fall or come and go. They are, by their very nature, temporary phenomena. There is every reason to expect that the present tendencies are not preludes to total world collapse, as in the 1930s, but simply the normal or average cyclical movement that has been typical of capitalist societies ever since the industrial revolution. Downturn, recession, reaching bottom, and then recovery are the usual cycle phases, and they should be taken care of by 1992 at the latest. When the world economy embarks on its new expansion, it is likely to grow strongly towards the end of this century.

4. OPTIMISM ABOUT TREND EXPANSION

After 1992, or possibly one year later, we can look for economic recovery, and there are solid bases for believing that this expansion will be very strong, possibly even stronger than the corresponding expansions of the 1960s or 1980s.

Europeans think that the Gulf Crisis is only a temporary obstacle that will soon fade away, allowing the world to turn again to the attraction of one Europe — without walls. Both tariff walls and the Berlin Wall (or the Iron Curtain wall) will be reduced or removed. Under these circumstances, all the long-run benefits of cooperation in the enhanced Common Market will prevail and will serve to lift the growth rate of member countries. Foreign investment from Japan and North America, joining that of Western Europe, should help to propel the new expansion. In addition, the new technologies are just beginning their period of intensive use, which should contribute substantially to growth.

People have learned to live with oil shortfalls and inflationary pressures. There is every reason to believe that people will eventually pull together in a rational way — not as U.S. politicians behave, in their confrontation with one another for votes.

Many new technologies, including microcomputing, biotechnology, robotics, modern medical techniques, expansion of telecommunications, are just beginning to realize full exploitation in business. These developments and breakthroughs will not be trouble free, but they should be able to serve well in starting and maintaining the next, upwards, cyclical swing.

5. SOME OBSTACLES

Expansion should be resumed, financed in part by a Peace Dividend, but improvement will not be easy. Some of the major obstacles are as follows:
    1. continuation of the LDC debt pressures;
    2. unmanageable population growth, especially in those developing areas where it is not considered to be so serious; and
    3. the possible appearance of protectionism and trade wars. The GATT is working towards another end, that of multilateral free trade, but the world is congregating into three main blocs — in Western Europe (the EEC), in North America (US/Canadian free trade zone), and in the Pacific Basin. There will be a struggle between the polar advocates and the truer free traders, but in the end trade should grow well, even though the ideal or optimal trade system is not selected.

A successful transition to restructured economies in Eastern Europe and the Soviet Union still holds much promise. The transition period is proving to be more difficult than was originally presumed by the advocates of reform in the East. They are now finding the road to expansion very complex, but after recessions of two or three years at most, these economies should be ready to grow.

6. SOME POLICY OPTIONS

After expansion began in November 1982 in the U.S. and a bit later in Japan and Western Europe, the policy recommendations for macroeconomic stability seemed to be fairly obvious and accepted across a broad spectrum of economic thinking: the United States, which was being propelled by extremely large public-sector deficits, should revert to more prudent fiscal policy and offset the restrictive aspects of this move by more liberal (easier) monetary policy. Such a combination, it was argued, would maintain the momentum of upswing and make conditions easier for debt burdened developing countries through lower interest rates. The appropriate policy for other major industrial countries would therefore be to ease monetary and fiscal policy, thereby stimulating their economies in order to bring their expansionary movements into line with those of the United States.

This proposal was called policy coordination, and would have been an excellent policy mix; had it been adopted, it would have made the present adjustment process easier, particularly in the United States. Other coordinating policies that would have helped were quick agreement with GATT proposals for further trade liberalization under the Uruguay Round. Such coordination would also have led to better exchange-rate stability and would have set up the workings for a world monetary system on a more lasting basis.

As things worked out, the U.S. policy mixture became more perverse and deteriorated badly. Lax regulation in the financial sector aggravated the problems. Europe was changed and partly surprised by the coming down of "walls" in two directions: the trade-barrier walls between European nations in the drive for the Single Market and the "Iron Curtain" walls separating East from West. European stimulus was achieved, to a large extent, by investment planning for January 1, 1993, when the extended Common Market is expected to come into operation. Western Europe also faced the problem of financing economic reform in Eastern Europe, especially in Germany. In any event, fiscal stimulus is now uncalled for in Western Europe, and some degree of inflation fighting is needed, through tighter monetary policy, to deal with the supply of financial capital to Eastern Europe. Japan, too, has trade and inflation pressure. In summary, restrictions prevail for the use of monetary policy. If the old prescriptions for a policy mix no longer prevail, and we need to follow new lines for policy coordination, what form should this coordination take? Should there be specific adaptations to the crisis in the Persian Gulf?

Policy coordination and cooperation should be the central theme of policy now. In backing the UN resolutions and support for the embargo and a form of military intervention in the Middle East, we have a form of cooperation, but more on the side of politics and strategy. There is, however, an economic component: countries that cannot supply military support for one reason or another are supplying some degree of financial support. Also, in agreeing to meet for more and more consideration of the Uruguay Round at the ministerial meeting in Brussels in December 1990, we have a form of coordination.

Policy coordination at the present time should emphasize maintenance of economic stability without worldwide recession. The United States, Canada, Australia are near or in recession; they need interest-rate relief for stabilization purposes. (In the case of the U.S., this could offset budget cutting.) In this respect, the Peace Dividend is important for military spending reductions even if the Gulf Crisis limits the amounts of arms reduction. The United Kingdom and some other countries in Western Europe, where growth has slowed in 1990, could also have interest-rate cuts. In Germany, however, the strength of demand stands in the way of monetary easing; here, government spending, and lending or transfers to East Germany, the USSR, and other countries in Eastern Europe would indicate that fiscal easing mixed with some degree of monetary tightness is appropriate. Interest rates have already gone up in Germany and in Japan; these two surplus countries should try to prevent further rises in rates at this time, but both are probably not in a position to lower rates.

These policies are all transitional in preparation for the next expansionary wave, which ought to be able to get under way on a broad international basis if the Gulf Crisis can be settled in the near future.

2. JAPAN'S ECONOMIC STRUCTURAL ADJUSTMENTS AND THE WORLD ECONOMY

Chikashi Moriguchi
Institute of Social and Economic Research
Osaka University
6-1, Mihogaoka
Ibaraki, Osaka 567
Japan

ABSTRACT. Structural adjustments have taken different forms in modern Japanese economic history. The poor resource base of Japan necessitated structural adjustment in the form of energy policy to adjust to the oil shocks. Industrial policy was used for energy conservation and for shifting the industrial base away from heavy energy using processes towards a high-technology orientation that consumed less energy.

The trading patterns of Japan also reveal structural adjustments. The services accounts shifted in favor of tourist outflows and international capital investments of strong yen balances that returned earnings inflows. The rise in land prices was instrumental in contributing to the "big bubble" that affected domestic investment as well as real consumption. Industrial policy has changed to deal with conditions after the "bubble" through deregulation, privatization, reduced working hours, and new forms of international competition.

There is an asymmetry between the speed of adjustments in tradable and nontradable sectors of the Japanese economy. The chapter analyzes the reasons lying behind this asymmetry. It indicates that policy problems will have to shift from macroeconomic measures to domestic institutional and structural aspects in order to enhance adjustment speed in the domestic sector.

1. INTRODUCTION

"Economic structural adjustments" is a keyphrase for many countries in this decade. Starting from Japan, it propagated to the U.S. through Japan-US negotiations, called "SII talks." Trailing in the modernization of the economy, the USSR realizes that a huge gap of unfinished structural adjustments must be bridged to catch up with the Western market-oriented economies. In the arena of European economic integration, economic structural adjustment has its own positive meaning that, among other things, implies integration of taxation and monetary systems as well as vast industrial structural changes.

Structural change is another side of economic development. Economic growth itself produces endogenous driving forces of structural change: from compositional changes in industry and employment structures to changes in demography and other socioeconomic characteristics that include the savings behavior of people. As Joseph Schumpeter emphasized, entrepreneurial innovation brings out structural changes through a process of creative destruction.

In the past two decades of world economic development, the major driving forces of structural change were 1) energy price shocks, 2) currency realignments, and 3) technological development centering around micro- and optoelectronics. One might add innovation of monetary policies in fighting inflation, which brought down primary commodity prices worldwide and contributed to the cumulative debt of many ambitious developing economies.

Some of these may be endogenous shocks, in the sense that the high economic growth up to the early 1970s produced scarcity of primary commodity supplies. But this chapter will not discuss whether some of the shocks are endogenous or not, but rather the impacts and outcomes that were brought forth by the "shocks" and the effects (negative as well as positive) of policies that intervened. The phrase "economic structural adjustments" seems to have a positive implication, involving policy efforts by various entities in private as well as public sectors.

Japan is considered to be a country where public policies have been conducted successfully, leading the economy toward a growth path that can get along well with substantial changes in relative prices in one form or another. It is an interesting observation that Japan, as compared to the U.S., has experienced much larger relative price changes of various sorts, let alone energy price changes. Since Japan lacks some of the most basic natural resources, it is natural that the country has been exposed to large price shocks from outside.

As Saxonhouse has pointed out, a biased endowment of natural resources tends to produce a larger change in trade structure in a Heckscher–Ohlin world.[1] Japan is a good example. However, when we look at some of the domestic endogenous prices, such as the wage rate relative to the capital goods price, we learn that they have shown a more remarkable upward trend than in the U.S. The capital goods price came down relative to consumer prices much faster than in the U.S. (see figure 1). This also might indicate that trade structure changes on a larger scale and that business fixed investment tends to concentrate in growing export industries in Japan (electronics and machinery).

Japan's public policy that is related to its industrial development is called industrial policy. In a narrow sense, industrial policy can be defined as the public policy adopted by MITI, which aims at a certain direction of trade and industrial structural changes.

In the early 1970s, industrial policy aimed at energy conservation and environmental protection. The long-run objective was to change Japan's industrial structure from one dominated by energy-intensive smokestack industries to a new one that largely consisted of high-tech-oriented clean-machinery industries.

In the early 1980s, Japan's number-one priority for public policy was a stringent fiscal policy aimed at rebalancing Japan's larger budget deficit by the end of 1990. It was not an industrial policy, but it was a single-minded structural adjustment policy by the fiscal authority. It then coincided with the disinflation policy of Prime Minister Thatcher of Britain and President Reagan of the U.S. A low-growth anticipation prevailed in Japan, which necessitated the fiscal authority's further efforts for reducing public spendings, thus bringing about a self-fulfilling process of low growth (see figure 2).

---

[1]Saxonhouse (1988).

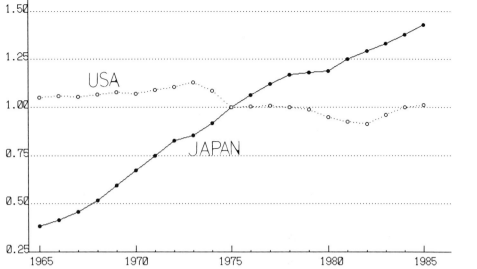

Figure 1. Average wage earnings divided by the deflator of fixed investment.
(Sources: for Japan — National Income Account, Annual Report (Economic Planning
Agency); for the USA — Economic Report of the President (Council of Economic
Advisors.)) 1975 = 1.0.

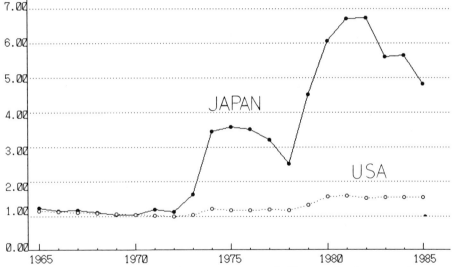

Figure 2. Oil price divided by investment deflator in Japan and average fuel
price divided by investment deflator in the U.S. 1970 = 1.0

But a positive industrial policy was under way at the same time; it was an
extended line for development of high-tech machinery industries. The focus
became clearer as early as 1980. Microelectronics technology development was
about to show its great potentiality in full scale. Development of the
semiconductor industry was one of the most exciting stories of industrial
development. The machinery industry was busy developing numerically controlled

machine tools, industrial robots, flexible manufacturing systems, and then later computer–integrated manufacturing systems.

2. JAPAN AND THE U.S. FACING INDUSTRIAL STRUCTURAL ADJUSTMENTS

In the latter half of the 1980s, primary commodity prices continued to be stagnant. After a cycle of 20 years, the relative price of energy and other primary commodity prices returned to historical low values comparable to the early 1970s (or in some cases comparable to the years prior to the Great Depression).

During these two decades of structural adjustment, Japan's industrial structure has completely adjusted to the new situation. One might say that it has conducted an overadjustment to high energy prices through technological development; energy conservation and hence potentially severe constraints on carbon dioxide emission are likely to be cleared in the future.

Meanwhile, in this 20–year cycle, the U.S. economy trailed behind Japan. The U.S. economy has ample room for energy conservation efforts; however, its industry has not yet adjusted to the lowered value of the dollar so as to bolster its export competitiveness. The U.S. economy looked all right when oil prices dropped back to the old price range and oil supply was plentiful. However, when another oil crisis came, the U.S. showed its weakness in the form of high import dependency on oil more than in Japan's case. The U.S. is still struggling with twin deficits. It is unquestionable that the U.S. should have done something about cutting its budget deficit effectively when the economy was enjoying successive years of economic expansion under the Reagan administration in its second term. But instead the U.S. simply let foreign investors finance the budget deficit.

This is not to say that Japan is well ahead of the U.S. in the productivity of major industries. We know that the U.S. still leads Japan in many industrial sectors, measured by the absolute level of labor productivity. In the dynamic contemporary world, however, international competition is a matter of comparative advantage. In the present context, what matters is a comparative speed of economic structural adjustment. Japan's exportable–goods sector managed structural adjustment rapidly and maintained a leading role in the international market of growing machinery industry products. Meanwhile the traditional, domestic, nontradable sector must still implement its long–overdue structural adjustments, particularly in distributive industries.

This chapter will review the economic structural adjustment policy of Japan and will discuss some of the reasons why we see so much asymmetry in the speed of industrial adjustment between the tradable goods and the domestic nontradable goods sectors.

3. RECENT TRENDS IN JAPAN'S MACROECONOMIC BALANCES

Despite the slow response in the domestic sector, the macroeconomic performance of the Japanese economy since the Plaza Agreement of 1985 has been remarkable (see figure 3). In the framework of national income accounts, the net exports of goods and services were reduced from ¥14.53 trillion (1986) to ¥8.43 trillion last year. In terms of percentage of GNP, it was a drop from 4.4% to 2.15%. It is expected to drop further to 1.8% in 1990.

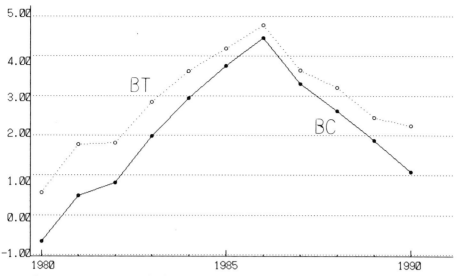

Figure 3. Japan's trade balance and current account balance as % ratio to GNP: 1980–1990.

Japan's imports increased by nearly ⅔ in the four-year period from 1985 to 1989. Among overall goods imports, manufactured imports increased by more than 2.5 times in dollar value. In 1989 the manufactured imports occupied more than half of total imports. The ratio was only 31% in 1985.

The historical increase in manufactured imports can be explained by the following three factors: 1) relative price declines because of a high yen rate, 2) imports from the overseas factories run by Japanese firms, 3) various measures to open the import market.

The last factor (or factors) includes such things as lower tariffs, gradual abolition of the import quota system, and deregulation that had controlled free entry in import business. Consumers' access to imported goods has been visibly widened during the past five years. The estimated price elasticities of import equations turn out to be larger in magnitude as we add more recent observations to the sample period.

The high yen rate drove many domestic firms overseas, since they could not compete against cheap imported goods. During the same period Japan's outstanding value of direct foreign investment increased from $83.6 billion to $253.9 billion — almost a threefold increase. Imports from overseas operations are concentrated in textile products, processed food, and semiprocessed nonferrous metal products.

This trend of increasing manufactured imports is not likely to be reversed even if the yen rate drops in the future. The process of Japanese corporate firms' deployment over the world has just begun.

A structural change in invisible trade is also occurring. In the service trade there are two remarkable items of expansion. One is payments abroad by Japanese tourists. This year the number of visits abroad made by Japanese citizens will exceed 10 million, and overseas spending per tourist, which is already the highest internationally, is still rising, partly because of more generous limits on the amount of tax-free purchases and partly because of higher purchasing power. As a matter of fact, tourism is a growing business in many

Asian nations now. The second item is a surge of income receipts from abroad that simply reflects the expansion of Japan's overseas investment.

These two growing items of invisible trade are offsetting factors in computation of the invisible trade balance. So far, net imports of tourism dominate net receipts of investment income. We think the present trend will prevail as long as the U.S. interest rates are kept low.

Then what about Japan's domestic saving-investment (S-I) balance? If its external imbalance is decreasing, then domestic excess saving must have begun to shrink too. Table 1 shows the recent trend of S-I balances in the private and public sectors of Japan.

Table 1. Japan's Saving-Investment Balance (% ratio of GNP)

	Household[a]	Corporate Firms	General Government	Overseas
1980	9.1	−5.7	−4.0	0.7
1985	9.8	−5.6	−0.8	−3.8
1988	8.5	−6.8	1.5	−3.2
1990	9.1	−10.6	3.0	−1.5

[a] Household includes unincorporated firms.

Several interesting points can be mentioned. First, even though private consumption expenditures and housing investment were strong, household savings also expanded. This explains why a decrease in the S-I balance for the household sector was slight. Taking income growth into account, we see that the saving ratio did not decline. A survey of worker households indicates that the saving ratio went up. In his chapter in this book, C. Horioka predicts that Japan's saving ratio will unquestionably decline in the future, but this will begin well beyond the year 2000.

Nonfinancial corporate firms expanded fixed investment and borrowing from external sources. But a remarkable change in the saving-investment relation is seen in the general government sector. A shortage of saving in the public sector was relatively large in 1980, but it had already shrunk to 0.8% by the mid-1980s. Central government efforts for fiscal rebalancing and growth of social security contributions produced sizable excess saving in the public sector by 1988.

4. THE BIG BUBBLE AND REAL DEMAND

Housing investment became strong when land prices in Tokyo began to rise. First came new housing starts, brought about by those who sold land/houses in downtown Tokyo and planned to move to the nearest suburbs. A boom of condominium construction followed, and the land-price increase spread to other major cities. Land-price inflation and a stock market boom continued from 1987 through 1989. Huge capital gains resulted: in the three-year period 1986-1989, total savings of 106 trillion yen were realized by private households, while the increase in the total value of their assets (financial assets plus real estate) was 700 trillion!

Financial foundations of corporate firms were strengthened for the same reason and were supported by the upward revisions in growth expectations. Business fixed investment now occupies nearly 20% of GNP. The ratio was 16% in 1985. Housing starts jumped to the level of 1.7 million units, close to a historical high of 1973, from a stagnant 1.3 million in 1985.

The public sector was no exception in the enjoyment of capital gains from the bubble. Then there began a demand switching policy, in the midst of a vicious circle of low growth, low tax revenues, and more spending cuts to balance the budget. The Ministry of Finance (MOF) was quite reluctant to switch to an expansionary policy at the beginning. But what actually followed was joyful for MOF, since the beginning of strong growth with asset inflation produced a sudden increase in tax revenues. In addition, the privatization of NTT brought in a large amount of money through stock sales to the public. The public sector gained much from the bubble!

Naturally, when this historical monetary easing took place and a real estate boom emerged, huge loans were supplied to those who speculated in the land market. Some of the real estate investors went into the stock market to earn capital gains. A recent incident resulting in resignation of the Chairman of Sumitomo Bank revealed that a cycle of bank-loan- financed real estate (and stock market) transactions is profitable if the cycle of growing loans is maintained. During the past five years, in spite of an extraordinary monetary expansion, the inflation rate did not accelerate at all. A high yen rate and freer imports absorbed most of the inflationary pressures. Prices of goods and services were stable, and the price of real estate, which has limited flexibility of supply under the present taxation scheme, simply absorbed speculative pressures.

Did that large amount of capital gains from financial and land assets affect consumer spending positively? The answer is yes, and it seems to have occurred in nonworker households that have relatively large amounts of these assets. An aggregate consumption function with household net assets as one of the explanatory variables was estimated, with a positive and significant coefficient. According to the estimate, ¥600 trillion in capital gains should have an additional ¥24 trillion impact on consumption expenditures over the long run.[2] Additional information indicates that spending on luxury goods as well as on fine arts and jewelry was notable in this period. Then an overall consumer spending expansion followed, with the multiplier impact of overall economic expansion.

Now, after a collapse of the stock market since the beginning of 1990, a capital loss of almost ¥100 trillion must have taken place in the portfolio of households (the total loss was approximately ¥300 trillion). If the asset effect works symmetrically, it will have a negative impact of ¥1.7 trillion. Almost 1% of current total consumption spending will have to be subtracted.

---

[2]The maximum likelihood estimate of the asset effect was .0054 for the shortrun (impact effect) and the adjustment speed is .11 per quarter. This should have a ¥16 trillion impact by the end of the first three years, under the assumption that ¥200 hundred trillion in capital gains were added for three years. That is to say, the level of consumption expenditures will be 8% higher than the level without any capital gains.

5. HISTORICAL ASPECTS OF ECONOMIC STRUCTURAL ADJUSTMENTS

Japan's macroeconomic policy as initiated by Prime Minister Nakasone was a new concept in the sense that a macroeconomic policy was strongly associated with "microscopic" structural adjustments. It was also new in the sense that Japan proclaimed its intention to reform its own socioeconomic structure in international society as a measure to redress its macroeconomic imbalance. This policy opened the way for a bilateral negotiation between Japan and the United States, through which both sides tried to intervene in some of the "domestic" problems of the other that are traditionally considered to be associated with a country's national sovereignty.

Steps toward an economic structural adjustment (ESA) policy started when Mr. Nakasone organized a special committee for studying structural impediments that might be blocking a swift adaptation of the Japanese economy to a new equilibrium. The committee, chaired by the late Mr. Maekawa, submitted a list of structural impediments to the Prime Minister in April 1986. In June, Nakasone proclaimed the economic structural adjustments policy at the Economic Summit held in Tokyo. As the Maekawa committee's official name, "Study Committee on Economic Structural Adjustments for International Cooperation," suggests, the Government considered ESA policy as a measure to reduce the trade surplus primarily through liberalizing imports and increasing domestic demand.

In the fall of 1986, a special committee on ESA was set up officially as an instrument of the Economic Deliberation Council, an economic advisory council to the Prime Minister to continue the work of the Maekaea committee. In the Spring of 1987, it released Guideline to Economic Structural Adjustments, an official document (based on a nationwide consensus) that was called a New Maekawa Report. It clarified the following points as major ESA policy targets:

1.   deregulation of distributive, banking, and transport industries; free entry of foreigners to the public bidding on construction contracts;
2.   strengthening of land policy; implementation of tax policy on farmlands in urban districts;
3.   acceleration of manufactured imports; and
4.   shorter work hours.

The goals of the first and the third categories were attained relatively fast. In particular, manufactured imports greatly expanded, mainly due to market forces produced by the high value of the yen.

Shorter work hours, however, and deregulation — for example, of the Large-Scale Retail Store Law (LSRSL) — are far from the goals. Land policy is being discussed belatedly now after the extraordinary price explosion is over! These topics will be discussed later from the viewpoint of industrial organization.

From 1988 to 1989, Japan's economic recovery turned out to be a long-lasting expansion with a surprisingly high rate of business fixed investment, housing investment, and strong consumption expenditures. All these have been pushed upward by capital gains. In the case of business fixed investment, an expanding stock market supplied a huge amount of low-cost capital to corporate firms through equity finance.

The goal of ESA policy was accomplished not by the policy itself, but rather by the unexpected effect of expanding asset values held by the private sector. After Nakasone retired following five years in power, Takeshita (who took over) had to resign when the big Recruit scandal was disclosed.

Even though Nakasone's period was abruptly finished with the development of a political scandal, his term should be evaluated by his achievement in the public-policy area, which sought administrative reform and privatization of public corporations, notably the national railway systems and NTT. Also, he sought a way to make a visible contribution to international cooperation in policy coordination among the Summit member countries. Now ESA is an established policy in the international world. The World Bank prescribes a menu of needed ESA to individual countries under study. Perhaps it will have to prescribe a menu for the USSR in the near future.

6. LONG WORKING HOURS AND CHARACTERISTICS OF COMPETITION IN JAPAN

The long working hours of Japanese workers became one of the hot issues in the Maekawa Report (see figure 4). Overall rough estimates indicate that workers in Japan put in 2100 to 2200 hours a year, on average, while the corresponding figure is 1900 for American workers and less than 1700 for German workers.

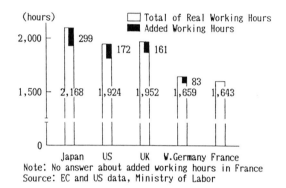

Figure 4. Working hours in major industrial powers (1985–1987).

Working hours are a rather difficult matter for international comparison. They vary among industries in which the relative population of regular workers, male or female, varies. A growing population of part-time workers in service sectors gives a misleading impression that average working hours are becoming shorter. Figure 4 is based on the Ministry of Labor statistics of working hours for regular factory workers.

Yet Japanese workers do tend to work, or at least tend to stay at the workplace, for longer hours than European and American workers. In addition, however, some other pieces of evidence indicate that Japanese workers are working longer than the above statistics show. White-collar workers tend to work long hours, and it is reported that some of their overtime work is not fully paid.

Basically, contracted weekly working hours in Japan are now about 40 to 42, as compared with 35 in Germany. A large difference in working hours between Japan and Germany cannot be explained by the difference in contracted working hours. One hundred hours difference should be explained by two factors: 1) difference of overtime working hours and 2) difference of paid no-work days that are actually "consumed" by workers.[3]

The Maekawa Report recommended to the government to take up the issue of shorter working hours as one of the targets of ESA. The report may seem to agree tacitly with criticisms made by foreign governments about long working hours as a potential source for Japanese industry to overproduce and to dump products abroad. But a primary reason was that it anticipated that shorter working hours will provide more leisure time for workers and hence stimulate consumption expenditures!

What has happened to working hours in Japan since the Maekawa Report? As the economic recovery developed into a strong expansion from 1987 to 1988, firms responded to rising demand for products by extending overtime working hours of employees. Employees are willing to accept such work. As indicated by several surveys on factory workers' preferences regarding "more leisure or more income?", most workers, particularly those who are over 30 and have family responsibilities, prefer more income to more leisure.[4] The government campaigned for shorter working hours through the shift to "five working days a week". In 1987 the public sector and banking sector partially shifted by taking two Saturdays off monthly working days. But statistics show that total working hours have nevertheless not been reduced. In the banking sector, average overtime hours were extended to make up for the loss of Saturdays.

As the economic expansion turned out to be long-lasting and business firms anticipated that a real labor shortage was coming, the rate of increase in employment went up in 1989 and total working hours came down slightly. But the use rate of paid holidays is not increasing.[5] When we look into small firm situations for this question, we learn that a wide gap exists in working hours between large and small firms. Small firm employees tend to work longer with lower wage rates. The five-day week system had long been established at the factories of large firms in Japan.

The wage differential between large and small firms was a symbol of the "dual structure" thesis in the 1960s. It vanished throughout the 1970s when the Japanese economy shifted from a labor-abundant to a labor-shortage economy. However, during the stagnant years from 1980 to 1986, a wage differential appeared again. Basic underlying factors are also reflected in the differences of working hours. It is said that the introduction of the "just-in-time" (or

---

[3]Perhaps a difference of 200 hours between American and German workers could be attributed to the difference of contracted weekly hours.

[4]The most frequently cited reason for this preference was that they need to work more for income to pay back housing loans. Young workers are different. Their job turnover rate is high, and they tend to prefer a higher hourly wage and no overtime work. A relatively steep age profile of wages seems to underline this contrasting attitude toward the income leisure tradeoff.

[5]Traditionally, unmarried female workers tend to take all paid holidays, while male workers who are more tightly knitted into the management system of firms cannot do so.

Kanban) system has widened the gap of working conditions between the parent company and its subcontractors.

7. CHARACTERISTICS OF JAPANESE-STYLE COMPETITION

Given the process of development (or nondevelopment) of a policy of shorter working hours, it is practically impossible for the public authority to pursue this policy rigidly -- for instance, by introducing measures to force firms to cut overtime work and to force employees to consume their paid holidays fully.[6] The problem is how to enforce these measures for small firms, which have long been protected by a public authority; such a policy will go against their anticipations. One might ask, "Why not let them exit from competition?" Actually, if competition among firms is conducted on the basis of a common wage rate and common working conditions monitored by an industry-wide labor union, competition will eliminate less efficient firms. But this story does not apply to Japan.

In Japan, competition in an industry is being "fought" by many firms which are not equally competitive. Less efficient firms can survive competition in the following manner. Each firm is run on the basis of agreements, made by the management and the company union, that accept existing differentials of wage and other working conditions between the company in question and other competitors. The profit rate of that company should be lower than its more efficient competitors and so should the stock price. The most efficient firm refrains from pursuing an aggressive strategy that might eliminate other lesser competitors (possibly by restraints from the antimonopoly law and administrative guidance by MITI that fears "disorder").

Thus it is likely that more firms are engaged in the Japanese domestic market than are engaged in the U.S. market, where wage differentials among firms do not exist or are smaller if they exist. Competition tends to be keen, since workers have incentives to work harder for improving their company's competitive positions. Competition for the sake of a relative share of market is serious, and room for tacit agreement among a few oligopolistic competitors is small.

This comparative model of competition has been stated in literary style, but it can be presented in a mathematical model. Each competitor's production function is homogeneous of degree of t ($t > 1$). There are N firms engaged in market competition, producing similar products. The efficiency of a firm is determined by the individual market shares of firms. The wage rate paid by each firm varies, however. Smaller firms share the cost of low efficiency by accepting lower wage rates and lower profit rates than the larger competitors.

Industry as a whole can improve total efficiency by mergers, but this might lead to a stagnation of research and development, with lower efficiency in the long run. Besides, the life time employment system of Japan helps deter mergers. Mergers of corporate firms are possible only under an agreement between management and an employees' union that lifetime employment be guaranteed. Many

---

[6]Some suggest the following measures: 1) raise the overtime wage premium from the present 25% to 50%, 2) set maximum overtime hours and prohibit excess overtime work by law, and 3) force firms to "buy back" the unconsumed paid holidays from employees.

merger proposals have turned out to be unworkable because the opposition of labor unions, who feared an infringement on their "job rights," played a crucial role. Instead of rejecting mergers, a union tends to accept worsening of working conditions in exchange for lifetime job security.[7]

8. ASYMMETRY OF SPEED OF STRUCTURAL ADJUSTMENT

The above-mentioned characteristics of competition in Japan can explain well why Japanese firms adapt so swiftly to a growing market. Non-price competitiveness is strong and based on joint efforts by management and labor, who share risks and rewards of growth.

The same set of characteristics can also explain why the adjustment speeds of Japanese firms are so low in the face of a declining market. None of the competing firms exits easily from competition, and they tend to prepare for long endurance of hard times. In this situation of "structural depression," MITI usually intervenes, and a "depression cartel" is organized in order to mitigate cutthroat price competition as an exceptional case of the Anti-Monopoly Act. The cartel guarantees to competing firms a certain period of time in which to down-size productive capacity. Mergers are encouraged, while free entry of domestic or foreign firms is restricted. This case applies to many domestic nontrade sectors of Japan. Banking, distributive, and agricultural industries are typical examples.

This policy tends to protect most firms in the cartel from potential competition in Japan, giving an excess profit from which an institutional rent is created. Excess profit tends to be distributed to employees (including executive managers) in the form of high wages and salaries, with good expense accounts and other fringe benefits. Thus the overhead cost of an employee becomes higher, and there is a strong pressure for existing employees to work harder and longer. Demand for expansion of employment is weakened.

Thus, we have to realize that shortening of working hours for Japanese workers is equivalent to changing the basic style of competition among firms and the so-called lifetime employment system. On the other hand, Masahiko Aoki, Kazuo Koike, and other economists who have studied the universal legitimacy of Japanese-style labor relations are now developing a J-firm theory. (See Aoki, 1988, 1989.) They emphasize the importance of joint risk-bearing by management and labor, with banks monitoring its performance.

However, an important task remains in explaining and analyzing competitive dynamics among J-firms within the framework of the new theory. One can argue that in the long run, market forces penetrate, and therefore, slow adjustments of Japanese domestic sectors will be completed anyway. The J-firm model will be effective only in explaining medium-term dynamic structural adjustments. It will remain to be seen in the future whether this view is correct.

---

[7]Professor L. R. Klein once pointed out (1977) that the lifetime employment system is one of the major sources of Japan-U.S. trade frictions. Reportedly he claimed that the system tends to produce an overtly expansionary export practice by Japanese firms, since they do not pay "due attention" to short-term profit and tend to be more concerned with expanding market share.

REFERENCES

Aoki, Masahiko (1988). _Information, Incentives, and Bargaining in the Japanese Economy_ (Cambridge: Cambridge University Press,).

Aoki, M. (1989). _Information and Organization of Japanese Firm_ (in Japanese) (Tokyo: Toyokeizai Shinposha).

"Guidepost of Economic Structural Adjustments: A Report of Special Subcommittee on ESA" (1987). Economic Deliberation Council, Tokyo.

Moriguchi, Chikashi (1988). _Changing Japanese Economy: Challenge and Response after the High-Growth Era_ (in Japanese) (Tokyo: Sobunsha).

Moriguchi, Chikashi (1989). "Driving Forces of Economic Structural Change: The Case of Japan in the Last Decade," in W. Krelle (ed.), _The Future of the World Economy (IIASA)_ (New York: Springer-Verlag).

Moriguchi, Chikashi (1989). "Economic Structural Adjustments and Macro-economic Balance of Japan," _Rivista Internationale di Scienze Economiche e Commerciali_, February.

Saxonhouse, Gary (1988). "Comparative Advantage, Structural Adaptation, and Japanese Performance," in Inoguchi and Okimoto (eds.), _The Political Economy of Japan Vol.2: The Changing International Context_, (Stanford, CA: Stanford University Press).

"Official Document of Japan-U.S. Economic Structural Adjustments Negotiation" (1990). MITI.

3. EDITORIAL COMMENTS — 1

The first session of this conference studied trade patterns in the world economy and trade-related policies, i.e., policies about institutions of trade, such as GATT; the theory of ironing out trade frictions, e.g., as between the U.S. and Japan or between other countries and Europe; or trade problems of developing countries. In this session, much attention was devoted to stability of the international economy and how it might be improved or generally affected by international monetary policy. Policies for money supply, interest rates, and exchange rates were also considered.

A natural tool for study of international conflict or cooperation is the methodology of game theory. Different countries and different institutions are the players. The game-theory models are obviously greatly simplified and do not generally lead to neat, definitive answers, yet they seem to provide economic theorists with an insightful way of looking at problems.

In this session, there was a good blend of pure theory and statistical information on institutional structure and theory. New thinking on the subject of international trade and finance was brought to bear on all the problems discussed, and all these persepectives were relevant to this conference with its aim of finding ways to improve world economic stability.

The passage of time since the conference in 1990 has not marred the relevance of the chapters below that arose from this session.

4. INTERNATIONAL NEGOTIATIONS AND DOMESTIC CONFLICTS: A CASE FOR COUNTERLOBBYING[1]

Koichi Hamada
The Economic Growth Center
Yale University
27 Hillhouse Avenue
New Haven, CT 06510

ABSTRACT. International economic negotiation should not be considered as a simple game between delegates who represent the "national interest" of the countries they belong to, but as a two-level game or as the layers of two kinds of games: one with diplomatic negotiations and the other between interest groups within a country (Putnam, 1988). This chapter attempts to formulate trade disputes concerning tariff rates as a two-level game. In contrast to the rent-seeking literature, where lobbying activities exhaust the rent, we assume that some part of lobbying expenditures is transferred to the government agent. It is shown that counter-lobbying, that is, lobbying across the national border, will often be beneficial to the consumer interest in both countries engaging in international trade.

1. INTRODUCTION

At the turn of the decade of the 1990s, the world has already experienced several dramatic changes in international political and economic relations. The Berlin Wall has melted, and the two Germanys have been united; the market principle is being introduced seriously in the Soviet Union as well as in Eastern European countries; and for the first time since the end of World War II, the United States and the Soviet Union have cooperated in the Security Council of the United Nations to act with regard to the invasion of Iraq into Kuwait.

In order to cope with the new challenges resulting from these changes in the world economic and political scene, we need to improve the existing policy tools and cooperation devices, and, at the same time, to explore the policy tools and cooperation devices from a different perspective.

Those who participate in international negotiations for achieving policy cooperation or agreement on an international regime are supposed to represent their national interests. However, they engage in negotiations within a complex network of concurring and conflicting interests. The same trade bill affects different groups of citizens differently. Trade liberalization benefits consumers and, indirectly, export industries, but it inflicts damage on the competing import industries. Negotiators are always aware of these

---

[1]This work is partially supported by a grant from the Matsushita International Foundation. I appreciate comments by Kyoji Fukao, Masahiro Okuno, Yoshiyasu Ono and Toshihiko Watanabe.

conflicting domestic interests. If they are politicians, they attempt to attain their objectives in terms of the probability of their reelection and their campaign funds. If they are high-ranking bureaucrats or diplomats, they attempt to improve their prestige, enhance the interest of the sectors of which they are in charge, and perhaps enhance their reputations in international diplomacy.

This chapter considers the relationship between international economic conflicts and domestic conflicts. "Domestic conflicts" means the conflict of economic and political interests among various groups within a country. Such interests include industries and different bureaus of the government. The representative of a country who participates in international negotiation is situated upon various layers of domestic conflict of interests. In this sense, the game of international economic, and often political confrontation can be regarded as a two-level game (Putnam, 1988). Following Putnam, let us call the game of international negotiation as level I, and that of domestic plays in each country as level II.[1]

In general, for a scheme of international economic cooperation to be agreed upon by participating countries, the scheme should be attractive enough to be adopted by each participant, or the status quo situation made so intolerable that the move to any cooperative scheme is welcomed by each participant. However, each negotiator is conditioned by the domestic structure of political and economic interest groups. Each negotiator may have his or her own personal preference, but his or her decision is made on the ordering strongly conditioned by the existing political or economic conflicts surrounding him or her. In the terminology of Putnam (1988), the negotiator can choose only from the win-set, that is, the set of all possible diplomatic agreements that would "win" or gain the necessary majority among the domestic constituents, and the game situation in which the international negotiation is placed can be characterized as a two-level game. Level I consists of an international negotiation game in which negotiators from various countries gather, hoping to reach a certain international agreement. Level II consists of a domestic game in which voters, interest groups, lobbyists, politicians, bureaucrats, ministers, diplomats, and the negotiator are the players. The nature of the first level of the game, that is, the game concerning domestic interests, differs from country to country, from time to time, and depends crucially on the constitutional structure of the country.

In addition the framework of the two-level game approach, the importance of incentive compatibility of any possible decisions made by the players, particularly at the level-I game, must be stressed. The discussions below should be supported by documentation of historical experiences and anecdotes and sharpened by analytical tools of economists and game theory. It is hoped that this chapter, however incomplete, will serve the purpose of facilitating intellectual communication among political scientists, game theorists, and economists.

The next section examines the conceptual structure of the two-level game

---

[1]In Section 3, we introduce counterlobbying across national borders. Then the level-II game is played internationally. Moreover, if the negotiator himself (or herself) tries to influence the public opinion of the other, then this definition of the level-I and level-II game could be found to be too restrictive.

following Putnam (1988), and shows how it interacts with the concept of incentive compatibility. Section 3, introduces a simple partial—equilibrium model of lobbying and counterlobbying in order to illustrate the structure of two—level games. It will be found that cross—country counterlobbying may produce a favorable effect on world economic welfare. According to Choate (1990), Japan spends about $400 million in Washington just for counterlobbying to halt the U.S. protective measures. Thus counterlobbying is a serious matter. Section 4 illustrates the implications of the strategic concepts by using the example of the current trade conflict between the United States and Japan. Trade issues give many interesting applications of these concepts. Section 5 sketches other examples of the application of the two—level game.

2. THE STRUCTURE OF INTERNATIONAL TRADE CONFLICTS

In this section, the conceptual structure of the two—level game is presented through the example of a trade conflict. In trade conflicts one finds a typical case of the two—level game, because the conflict among different domestic groups is conspicuous relative to other examples (such as macroeconomic policy coordination and the coordination of tax systems, where the nature of domestic conflicts is more subtle).

In the discussion of trade conflicts, people often use the phrase "the national interest": The American automobile industry or the American computer—chip industry should be defended for the sake of the American "national interest"; Japanese agriculture should be defended for the sake of the Japanese "national interest"; and so forth. In most of the cases of trade disputes and negotiations, trade protection or trade liberalization resulting from negotiation benefits one group of people and harms another group of people in a participating country. American producers of automobiles can be protected and benefited by the voluntary export restraints (VERs) on the part of Japan, but American consumers, businesses using cars, and automobile import dealers will be hurt. Similarly, Japanese farmers will lose much by the liberalization of rice imports, but Japanese urban consumers can be benefited. Thus the interests of consumers of a country often coincide with that of the export sector in its trading partner. In our particular example, the coincidence of interest crosses over the Pacific.

Negotiators, who are usually from governments, engage in the level—I game based upon some domestic conflicts, that is, the level—II game within the countries that they "represent." The forms of "representing" differ from country to country and from time to time. The difference comes from the difference in political systems, that is, whether the country is ruled by a presidential system or by a parliamentary system. It also comes from the nature of political equilibrium within each country. The political voice of interest groups is usually transmitted by voting, as well as by lobbying activities, but its relative significance differs from country to country. In one situation, some consensus on trade policy is needed prior to international negotiation; in another, the result of an international negotiation could be internally ratified later.

Reflecting upon the complex nature of domestic economic conflicts, there exist several alternative ways of formulating the process of economic policy—making in the domestic scene. Becker (1984) proposed pressure—group equilibrium following work by Stigler (1975) and others. In Becker's formulation, a pressure group spends money to influence the government in such a way that the transfer of income from the opposing group should take place for the advantage of the group. However, since the transfer of income cannot be realized by a pure poll tax and accordingly realized by distorting taxes and subsidies, the Nash equilibrium exhibits the undesirable property that the society loses from the Paretian state not only because of duplicated and ineffective lobbying efforts of pressure groups, but also because of the loss due to distortion caused by the transfer payments.

Similar but more trade-oriented theory is the rent-seeking or directly unproductive, profit-seeking (DUP) equilibrium developed by Krueger (1974), Bhagwati and Srinivasan (1980), Bhagwati (1982), Findley and Wellisz (1982), and others. According to this theory, as long as rent and government revenues emerge from quotas, monopolists or oligopolists in the import-competing industries and other lobbyists will compete to increase their share of the rent or revenue by spending on directly unproductive activities. In the most extreme form of the theory, resources equal to the total amount of rent are assumed to evaporate due to these rent-seeking activities. Legal expenditures that certainly do not produce material benefits except for the satisfaction of litigious feeling of the participants could be a good example. In most of the cases, however, rent seekers are competing interindustrywise or intra-industrywise with each other, and the lobbying technology is subject to decreasing marginal productivity. Thus it seems reasonable to assume that only a part of rent evaporates. Intramarginal lobbyists then gain rentseekers' surplus.

The concept of the pressure-group equilibrium can be regarded to be slightly more general than that of rent-seeking, because the former can be applied to the case of (generally distorting) transfers of income between groups.[2] On the other hand, the latter theory is developed in such a way as to be naturally imbedded in the political economic disputes regarding trade.

In some countries, lobbying activities take the form of disguised or illegal transfers of income to politicians or to bureaucrats. Could these transfers be classified as lobbying expenses to evaporate, that is, indirectly unproductive activities? The answer is yes, as long as the politicians who receive funds spend them for their election campaign (useless parades or banquets that have little to do with genuine consumer satisfaction), and as long as the bureaucrats who accepted some benefits spend them in order to realize certain types of policies that they were requested to promote. The answer is definitely no, however, if politicians and bureaucrats use the funds as incre-ments of income to be used for their consumption. Thus there is room to discuss "the bribery-corruption equilibrium," apart from the rent-seeking equilibrium. This bribery-corruption equilibrium may be regarded as a special case of pressure-group equilibrium.

Needless to say, politicians are always motivated by the domestic political consequences of international economic policy, namely, by the consideration of how his election outcome will be affected by their policy decisions. So behind a pressure function in these alternative formulations of domestic conflicts are hidden specific sets of assumptions. In particular, the behavior of politicians and the executive branch, including bureaucrats, will

---

[2]The DUP equilibrium is a more general concept than the rent-seeking equilibrium.

be affected, depending on whether the political system is a presidential system or a parliamentary system. In the United States, which adopts a presidential system, diplomatic decisions and international economic policies can be made by the Executive Branch more or less independently, but are later ratified or endorsed by the Congress. In Japan, which adopts a parliamentary system, those decisions and policies can hardly be made until some consensus is found between the politicians or bureaucrats that represent the opinion of a certain pressure group and those that represent the opinion of another. Thus at the table of negotiations, and particularly at its earlier stage, the Japanese negotiator usually does not have the authority to commit himself only. On the other hand, the U.S. negotiator has the authority to commit herself or himself, but the decision is subject to the ratification or practical ratification by the Congress. As will be discussed, this asymmetry does not necessarily work against Japanese negotiators.

Here the element of time or timing becomes important. First, when a negotiator who depends upon domestic consensus negotiates with another who can commit herself or himself for an agreement, the latter is more often irritated by the slow and even procrastinating attitude of the former. Thus the latter, frustrated, often appeals to ultimatum or threat measures combined with the deadline — determined unilaterally by the latter. For the country of the former negotiator, it is relatively easy to implement the contents of the agreement, once it is made, because national consensus has been made before committing to the agreement. On the other hand, for the other country, reaching an agreement in an international negotiation does not mean that the nation ultimately commits itself to the agreement. The former nation behaves as if it were equipped with more patience, or a lower rate of time discount.

Secondly, it is difficult to draw the standard game tree in this two-level game. At first sight it appears simple because in the former country, a domestic game of consensus takes place prior to the international negotiation, while in the latter, formal or informal ratification follows the international negotiation. However, the timing of international negotiation as well as the timing of consensus-making or ratification is not predetermined. The timing itself is endogenously determined by the strategic moves of participants. The timing of reaching international agreement is a decisive factor for the ultimate payoffs. The timing of achieving consensus in a nation is closely related to the timing of elections, which are decision variables for the incumbent government in some countries and given exogenously in others. Even though this situation is not formalized in this chapter, some analogy from the game of attrition might be useful.

The international commitment itself can be classified into two categories. The first is agreement on a set of rules, such as the GATT or its amendment, the Charter of IMF, or intervention rules in the exchange-rate market. As emphasized elsewhere (Hamada, 1985), the game of agreeing on a set of rules or regime is a two-stage game that consists of the game of agreeing on a set of rules, and that of playing under the agreed rules. The concept of subgame perfectness (or time consistency) can be applied here. When the participants agree on a set of rules, they compare the most plausible outcomes under these rules and decide what rule is most desirable for them. Also, the ongoing rule is most likely to continue in the absence of agreement. Thus, the game of agreeing on a rule has the character of "the battle of the sexes." Here, time is again important. Policy games are played repetitively through time, while the game of agreeing on a rule yields the outcome at the instant when a regime or a change of regime is agreed on by the participating countries. Choosing an appropriate time for agreement itself is a strategic choice.

Let us return from the two-stage game to the two-level game. Here the fact that a negotiator is bound by domestic political constraints often helps rather than obstructs the attainment of a desirable outcome of the international game (Putnam, 1988). Of course, too many constraints at home will limit the probability of reaching an agreement, by contracting the feasible set from which a negotiator can choose, namely, the win-set. However, as long as the win-set of the negotiator of the home country has some intersection with the win-set of the negotiator of the other, the negotiator may be able to achieve a better solution because he, or she, cannot give in to the other country's demand that is outside his or her win-set.

Here it is important for a country to create its positive self-image in the mind of the people of the other country and to persuade them of the merits or rationales of the trade proposal that the country aims to win by the negotiation. In a more general sense, diplomacy is a game of creating a convenient image — true or false — upon the other country's public. In this particular example of trade negotiation, a country can broaden the win-set of the other country by influencing public opinion of the other country. The U.S. Government, the American Embassy in Tokyo, and American Information Centers in Japan all attempted to build the image that trade liberalization is good for Japanese consumers.

3. A SIMPLE ANALYSIS OF LOBBYING AND COUNTER-LOBBYING

Let us present a model of international trade with cross-country lobbying activities. For simplicity, a simple partial-equilibrium framework is utilized, but the analysis in terms of general equilibrium would not be difficult and would yield similar conclusions.

Let us consider a two-country world where many goods are traded. Suppose that the X-good sector is at issue and that the home country imports X.

There are three policy instruments available: 1) a tax by the home country on X,
2) a quota by the home country, and 3) voluntary export restraints (VERs) at the foreign country at the request of the home country.

1. In the case of a tariff, the home country gains tariff revenue but loses consumers' surplus (the Harberger triangle).

2. In the case of a quota, the home importers gain monopoly rent but consumers lose surplus. Even though points 1 and 2 are equivalent in the purely economic sense, the political economy aspects can be quite different. In this case of a quota, the government can sell the right to a quota.

3. In the case of VERs, even though the loss of consumers' surplus is identical, a rent is obtained by the foreign exporters or by the foreign government that rations quotas to exporters. (See Ono, 1989 for a different view.)

Let us begin with the case where the amount of tariff to be taken by the negotiator is given, for example, at the level of maximizing tariff revenue or at the level of an optimal tariff.

Let us assume, following Brock and Magee (1978, 1979), that the probability that the tariff is realized depends on the levels of contributions by various agents of the economy. Let g be the amount that the i'th agent spends on a political contribution:

$$\pi = \pi \ (g_1, \ g_2, \ \ldots, \ g_k) \ . \tag{1}$$

A special form of this probability function is that the probability of enactment of a tariff depends on the sum of individual contributions (see also McMillan, 1986):

$$\pi = \pi \left(\sum_{i=1}^{k} g_i \right) . \tag{2}$$

Thus, the benefit to agent i, who is risk neutral, is written as

$$b_i = \pi(g_1, \ \ldots, \ g_k)s_i - g_i \ . \tag{3}$$

Given the amount of benefit s_i that is promised by a specific tariff proposal, agent i will choose to contribute g_i such that

$$\frac{\partial \pi}{\partial g_i} s_i - 1 \le 0 , \tag{4}$$

where strict inequality implies $g_i = 0$. In other words, agent i will contribute a positive amount g_i in such a way that the expected marginal benefit of a political contribution equals its marginal cost.

Before proceeding to the analysis, we should notice the following properties of this influence function.

1.   If the number of agents is large, and if only the total amount of contributions count, as in equation (2), then there is more room for free riders because many small agents will be able to enjoy the benefit without participating in the lobby. Of course, this temptation will be curtailed if each participant enjoys benefits directly related to his (her) contribution. Namely,

$$b_i = \pi \left(\sum_{i=1}^{k} g_i \right) s_i + \beta(g_i) - g_i .$$

2.   If the marginal increase in probability with respect to g_i — namely, $\partial \pi / \partial g_i$ — is decreasing, and is accordingly lower than the probability divided by g_i (or the "average" probability), then the expected value of benefits for a lobbyist will be larger than the amount of contribution g_i. For, from inequality (4) with equality,

$$\frac{\pi}{g_i} s_i > \frac{\partial \pi}{\partial g_i} s_i - 1 \tag{5}$$

or

$$\pi s_i > g_i \ .$$

This indicates that there is a lobbyists' surplus or whenever lobbying activities exhibit decreasing marginal productivity with respect to the amount of contribution.

A simplifying assumption often made in the rent-seeking literature is that the total monopoly (or protection) rent evaporates because of unproductive behavior. The assumption is based on the presumption that free entry to the lobby will in the long run exhaust the total rent. In theory, this prescription may be all right, but it is hard to conceive that during the time span we are considering, the new entry to the industry as well as to the lobbying group takes place so quickly and so smoothly.

3. The amount of economic loss to the society can be measured by the total cost of lobbying $\sum_{i-1}^{k} g_i$ and the expected deadweight loss expressed by the Harberger triangle. Part of the expenditure on lobbying may be disguised or may even be in the form of explicit transfers to politicians and bureaucrats, so that the expenditure may be classified not as a social loss, but as transfers. If politicians use these for campaign funds, as they often do, these funds will be regarded as unproductive. Therefore, the higher the possibility of free riding, the lower will be the social cost of lobbying and the better will be social welfare.

4. One can introduce the possibility of counterlobbying. Counterlobbying, or the pressures for free trade, comes from foreign as well as domestic sources. If we have counterlobbyists from the foreign country, then the probability function will become

$$\pi(g_1, g_2, \ldots, g_k; g_1^*, g_2^*, \ldots, g^*) \tag{1}$$

such that

$$\frac{\partial \pi}{\partial g_i} > 0, \; \frac{\partial^2 \pi}{\partial g_i^2} < 0 \text{ for } i - 1, \ldots, k$$

and

$$\frac{\partial \pi}{\partial g_j^*} > 0, \; \frac{\partial^2 \pi}{\partial g_j^{*2}} > 0 \text{ for } j - 1, \ldots, k^*.$$

A question that would lead to a crucial difference in the consequence of lobbying is whether or not an increased level of foreign counterlobbying expenditure increases the marginal effectiveness of lobbying activities at home. That is, what is the sign of the following cross derivative:

$$\frac{\partial^2 \pi}{\partial g_i \partial g_j^*} \; ?$$

If there is opposition from foreign countries, a marginal increase in lobbying activities for protective measures may become less effective or at most as effective as before. This would imply

$$\frac{\partial^2 \pi}{\partial g_i \partial g_j^*} \leq 0. \tag{6}$$

In a certain case, the foreign counterlobbying may enhance the nationalism of politicians, and accordingly could increase marginal effectiveness:

$$\frac{\partial^2 \pi}{\partial g_i \partial g_j^*} > 0 . \tag{6A}$$

Since this case seems to be a rarity, we will proceed with assumption (6) instead of assumption (6A).

Given the framework of the model, let us consider how lobbying pressure can influence the degree of protection. Here, we assume that the national strategy is restricted to the tariffs, that the level of the tariff rate is already chosen, and that only the probability of realizing the designated level of tariff is affected by lobbying and counterlobbying. Several cases are conceivable as to how the lobbying activities are organized.

1. There is a unified organization of import-competing industries, and that is the only agent that engages in lobbying.

Then i = 1, and the activity of that organization can be reduced to maximizing the benefit

$$\max : \quad \pi(g)s - g$$

where g (without subscript) indicates lobbying by the association. The marginal condition is

$$\pi'(g)s = 1 , \tag{7}$$

from which we derive the result that there is rent-seekers' surplus.

2. If each firm in the import-competing industry lobbies separately, then the i'th firm will maximize, with respect to g, the benefit $\pi(g_1, \ldots, g_h)s_i - g_i$.

$$\frac{\partial \pi}{\partial g_i} s_i = 1 \tag{8}$$

is satisfied for the internal equilibrium and rent-seekers' surplus emerges.

Let us compare this condition with the optimal condition for the industry as a whole. The expected surplus for the industry is:

$$\pi(g_i, \ldots, g_k) \sum_{i=1}^{k} s_i - \sum_{i=1}^{k} g_i ,$$

so that

$$\frac{\partial \pi}{\partial g_i} \sum_{i=1}^{k} s_i = 1 . \tag{9}$$

Comparing conditions (8) and (9), one can conclude that the expenditures by individual agents fall short of the optimum for the industry. Of course, this is a desirable outcome from the social point of view, because the smaller that rent-seeking activities are, the smaller will be the waste from unproductive activities and smaller the deadweight loss of the Harberger triangle.

3.   There can be the possibility of counterlobbying.   Counterlobbying could come   from   foreign   exporters,   domestic   exporters,   or   perhaps   domestic consumers.   There is no need to explain why foreign exporters complain. Domestic exporters may counterlobby because protection of imports at home can be a trigger for protectionism abroad.   Domestic consumers have a strong cause for lobbying.   However, because the cost of protection is distributed to so many consumers, they may not effectively build a coalition.   If they cannot build a coalition, then free—rider logic applies, and each consumer will not consider lobbying as an effective means to resist.

Let   us   now   consider   the   simplest   case   in   which   domestic   firms   are represented by a single agent and there is only one foreign lobbyist.   Then the domestic lobby maximizes

$$\pi(g, g^*)s - g,$$

where g and g* are, respectively, the expenditures by the domestic lobby and foreign lobby.

The first order condition is

$$\frac{\partial \pi}{\partial g}s - 1 . \tag{10}$$

Since we have assumed

$$\frac{\partial^2 \pi}{\partial g \partial g^*} \leq 1, \tag{11}$$

the amount of lobbying by the domestic lobby is expected to be smaller than the no—lobby situation.

On the other hand, the foreign counterlobby will attempt to minimize

$$\pi(g, g^*)s^* + g^*,$$

where g* is the loss of profits for the foreign export industry.   The first-order condition is given by

$$\frac{\partial \pi}{\partial g^*}s^* - -1, \tag{12}$$

where $\partial \pi / \partial g^*$ is negative.

Under assumption (11) for the cross derivative, one could draw the home-reaction curve (RR in figure 1) of g with respect to g*, and the foreign-reaction curve (R*R* in figure 1) of g* with respect to g.

It is easy to see that RR has a negative slope while R*R* has a positive slope.[3]

---

[3]From inequality (11) and equality (12), one obtains as RR

$$\frac{dg^*}{dg} - \frac{\pi_{gg}}{\pi_{gg^*}} .$$

The intersection of RR and R*R* gives the Nash equilibrium of the domestic import-competing industry and the foreign export industry.

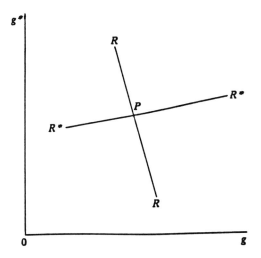

Figure 1. Home-reaction curve and Foreign-reaction curve.

From figure 1, one can see that the level of domestic lobbying will be reduced. If we compare this solution with the joint profit maximization solution for both the domestic import-competing and the foreign export industry, then by evaluating the joint profit at the Nash equilibrium $(\hat{g}, \hat{g}*)$, which satisfies equations (10) and (12), we obtain

$$\frac{\partial}{\partial g}[\pi(g,\ g*)(s-s*) - (g+g*)]\Big|_{\substack{g\ -\ \hat{g} \\ g*\ -\ \hat{g}*}} - \frac{\partial \pi}{\partial g}(s-s*) - 1 - \frac{\partial \pi}{\partial g}s* < 0$$

and

For R*R*,

$$\frac{dg}{dg^*} - - \frac{\pi_{gg*}}{\pi_{g*g*}},$$

where $\pi_{gg} - \dfrac{\partial^2 \pi}{\partial g^2}$, $\pi_{gg*} - \dfrac{\partial^2 \pi}{\partial g \partial g*}$, $\pi_{g*g*} - \dfrac{\partial^2 \pi}{\partial g*^2}$.

The signs of slopes come from the conditions

$$\pi_{gg} < 0,\ \pi_{gg*} < 0 \text{ and } \pi_{g*g*} > 0.$$

$$\frac{\partial}{\partial g*}\left[\pi(g,\ g*)(s-s*)\ -\ (g+g*)\right]\Big|_{\substack{g\ =\ \hat{g} \\ g*\ =\ \hat{g}*}}\ =\ \frac{\partial\pi}{\partial g*}(s-s*)\ -\ 1\ -\ \frac{\partial\pi}{\partial g*}s*\ <\ 0.$$

This implies that both g and g* are excessive from the viewpoint of the coalition between the domestic import-competing industry and the foreign export industry. They compete in lobbying activities.

From the standpoint of national welfare, the home country will gain by counterlobbying because it reduces the lobbying activity in the home country. Thus, if we can reduce lobbying expenditures as well as the expected deadweight loss from protection, the foreign country will also gain because the lobbyist gains the rent seekers' surplus, and the deadweight loss to the foreign country will also be reduced.

Of course, counterlobbying could come not only from foreign producers, but also from the domestic industry that uses the import goods as input, the domestic export industry, or the consumers' union. The domestic export industry may be afraid that the heavy protection of the import industry will trigger retaliatory action against the export product from the home country by the foreign country. The analysis of the effect of counterlobbying on the level of lobbying activities and the national welfare remains the same.

We have sketched the interaction of lobbying and counterlobbying in the level-II game, that is, the game of sectoral interests. Given this structure, what will be the nature of the level-I game, that is, the game of international negotiation?

The strategic structure of the level-I game will first depend on the nature of the political institutions between level-II players and level-I players. Let us assume here for simplicity that both of the chief negotiators are politicians and interested in getting popular votes. The votes they collect can be a function of the amount of lobbying money, which can be given to politicians as campaign contributions, and the general economic welfare expressed by the national welfare. Or, in some rare cases, the negotiators may be motivated to build cooperative relationships to abide by international law or the charter of international limitations and agreements. Under this assumption, one would be able to find a subgame perfect solution. The simplest framework is that the negotiator announces the tariff rate by which he maximizes the number of votes. Further research is needed to formalize this game more rigorously, but the following factors seem to be important as determinants of the degree of protection.

First, an important element that influences both the strategic structure and the outcome is the timing of plays or decisions in these two levels of the game. In some countries like Japan, the resolution of level-II conflicts takes a long time and irritates the counterpart. On the other hand, in the United States, the negotiator is given a freer hand in deciding the strategy in level-I games, but the decision is not necessarily bound to be satisfied in level-II games.

Secondly, the negotiator will find his situation more flexible if there are more than one kind of good in dispute. If a country exports X but imports Y, then the negotiators have the possibility of a tradeoff between the tariff rate on X in the foreign country and the tariff rate on Y in the home country.

Finally, this type of analysis tells why VERs are popular in many industries and in many countries. Compare the two situations, one with a tariff by the importing country and another with the equivalent VERs by the exporting country. The only difference between the two situations is whether the rent is acquired by the exporter's government or by exporters. (See Ono, 1989, for a different view.) The shift of rent from the importing country to the exporting country does affect government revenue, but does not affect producers' surplus in the importing country. It often increases producers' income (producers' surplus and rent) in the exporting country. Thus, incentive compatibility is well satisfied for the producers in both countries. This is certainly the reason why VERs are popular, but, at the same time, why VERs are dangerous for healthy observance of the principle of free trade in the GATT. It is such an easy temptation!

4. ILLUSTRATION: THE PROCESS OF U.S.-JAPAN ECONOMIC RELATIONS

Let us illustrate the above conceptual framework by using as an example the process of trade issues between the U.S. and Japan. There is a long history of trade disputes between the two countries. The commodities at issue have shifted from time to time — from textiles, to transistor radios, to TVs and VCRs, to automobiles, and to semi-conductors on the export side; and from grapefruit, to oranges, to beef, to rice on the import side. But one can find some common patterns in these negotiation processes.

The commodities that Japan exported, which were mostly manufactured products, met with protests, objections, and political pressures on the U.S. Congress. The U.S. government responded to these political pressures through Congress. At the beginning, the Japanese government usually assumed the attitude that concessions would be impossible. After a while, the Japanese government persuaded most of the firms, or the association in the sector at issue, to agree on some kind of voluntary export restraints (VERs). It is well known that VERs leave the monopoly rent to the exporting sector, while for a tariff the monopoly rent is captured by the government of the importing country. VERs and various Ordinary Market Arrangements (OMAs) leave room for participating firms to capture the rent, and perhaps give the government the authority or power to distribute the rent. (See, again, Ono, 1989, for a different view.) Here the incentives for rent-seeking activities emerge. As argued in the previous section, these activities do not necessarily exhaust the monopoly rent. Always some rent-seekers' surplus should remain. Therefore, potential incentives for adopting VERs and OMAs existed on the part of firms and perhaps some branches of Ministries — for example, the Ministry of International and Trade and Industry. Potentially, consumers lose consumers' surplus because of the higher domestic price of the export product. This author has never heard, however, any complaints from Japanese consumer organizations against VERs or OMAs.

In the United States, consumers of textile products and electronic products often voiced their interest. In particular, users of computer chips were helpful in fighting against the protective measures taken or conceived by the U.S. government.

For the commodities that Japan imported, which consisted mostly of food and agricultural products, postwar history started with very restrictive and often prohibitive protective measures such as tariffs and quotas. As the balance of current accounts of the United States deteriorated, the import barriers of Japan against these products were strongly criticized by the United States. The attitude of the Japanese government was to postpone the agreement as much as possible, following Tokugawa Iyeyasu's "wait and see" attitude. The government needed to wait during the time the consensus between import competitors and other groups in Japanese society were gradually formed. Losers should be compensated or at least persuaded to give unwilling consent.

Strangely enough, Japanese consumers' groups do not welcome import liberalization of food. Many times they petitioned against the liberalization of agricultural products (see Hamada and Nakajo, 1986). Either they are unaware of the merit of liberalization of import, or, in spite of knowing it, they feel that they should share the view with farmers for mutual fellowship. In any case, the lobbying activities by consumer organizations are difficult to analyze for the reasons explained in the previous section. In the Japanese case, the difficulty is reinforced by the attitude of consumer groups.

Activities of the American Embassy in Tokyo and of American Information Centers often attempt to influence public opinion for their advantage. It seems that some mass media people were educated, perhaps at receptions at the embassy, about the merit of trade liberalization of food and agricultural products. Surprisingly, however, the public opinion expressed by the polls in Japan did not turn much against the United States even after the designation of Japan as the Section 301 country of the Trade Act and the initiation of Structural Impediments Initiative (SII) talks. In local papers, anti-American opinions are strongly expressed in editorials, as Atsushi Kusano (1990) has documented. The absence of anti-American feeling is probably helped by public relations activities on the part of American people. The Japanese government then can take the "wait and see" attitude, and watch the gradual change in public opinion towards more consumer-oriented attitudes. A decade ago, even suggesting import liberalization of beef and leather was almost taboo. Suggesting rice import was inconceivable. Nowadays the import of rice has become a frequent topic for debate.

On the other hand, Japanese companies seem to spend a large amount of money on lobbying (Choate, 1990). Many former government officials are working for Japanese companies and government-related agencies, if not for the Japanese government itself. It seems, that more effort could be made on the part of the Japanese to influence the public opinion of the United States if Japan would like to broaden the win-set of the American counterpart for the advantage of the Japanese negotiator. Unlike Japan, where a consumers' movement is working against its own advantage, American consumers seem at least to have been aware of the need to protect their genuine interests, and of the harm of protectionism. Therefore, the public relations activities by Japanese agencies may well be accepted effectively.

Thus the overall pattern of U.S.-Japan negotiations is as follows. With reference to the manufacturing exports of Japan, American import competitors complain to Congress and the Administration first. Then Congress starts drafting protectionist legislation, and the American representative starts negotiating with Japan. Meanwhile, the Japanese Government and industrial organizations start lobbying in the United States. The negotiation often reaches a stalemate; then the U.S. appeals to or threatens to appeal to some drastic measure, such as Section 301. The American government announces very restrictive measures for Japanese exports. Gradually, firms in the Japanese export sector at issue give in and reluctantly obey the rationing rule accommodated by the MITI. Firms are unhappy because they cannot freely export to the United States, but they can tolerate the VERs or OMAs because most of the monopoly rent will belong to the exporting firms.

This ends the "pure" economic story. Behind it, however, many other things may be hidden. For example, the monopoly rent is captured by exporting industries in VERs. It is then more likely that X-efficiency in the sense of Leibenstein (1966) may be impaired if a group of existing export firms continue to be rationed and enjoy monopoly rent. VERs are a good compromise in the short run, but they may deteriorate incentive mechanisms within exporting firms in Japan. In the long run, there is a risk that Japanese export industries will be spoiled because of indulgence in VERs.

For import goods, American producers and farmers complain that the Japanese market is too closed. For those industries where the government does not intervene by protective measures, informed administrative guidance may be enough to open the Japanese market. According to newspapers, the government itself encourages or "guides" for flexible pricing. This would surprise the students of price theory who learned that prices will adjust depending on excess demand if they are not constrained. In most sectors where the Japanese market is closed, government interventions such as the Large Scale Retailers Act exist; import quotas are used for some agricultural products; prohibition of imports is used in the case of rice. Also, for the pricing of goods and services in the government, related sectors such as air transportation are used. In the past, international telephone service was overly protected.

While the Japanese negotiator is earning time, and while strong demand from the United States is reported in newspapers and televisions, the domestic game continues to settle the conflict of interests in Japan. Very slowly and reluctantly, interest groups representing the highly protected sector give in. This process is promoted not so much by the enlightened consumer movement as by the pressure from exporting sectors that are under the threat of retaliatory import restriction in the United States. Also under the present circumstance, where most of protected goods are consumption goods for people, the interest of manufacturing sectors in general favors the import liberalization of agricultural products. Japanese import-competing industries mostly succeed in adjusting their production methods gradually in such a way that they can survive under foreign competition.

There is an asymmetry between the way the Japanese respond to trade conflicts and the way the Americans do. After the postwar period, the Japanese took the Americans to be their good uncle, if not their master. The Japanese resist foreign pressure at the initial moment, but they try at the same time to adjust themselves to American demand or requests. On the other hand, there is little effort from the side of Americans to adjust themselves or accommodate Japanese demand. Americans are interested in the management style in Japan only for the sake of competing or beating Japan and not for the sake of accommodating Japanese demand for exports. This asymmetry is most obvious in the case of SII talks. The American Government demanded that the Japanese Government adhere to a long series of requests, starting with the abolition of the Large Scale Retailers Act, publication of the minutes of the breakfast meeting of "Keiretsu" group, to the expansion of fiscal expenditures over ten years for the future. On the other hand, Japanese suggestions were taken as little more than jokes.

The consequence of this asymmetry is not necessarily beneficial to the United States. Japanese retail industry will certainly increase its efficiency in the near future, and even Japanese agriculture may turn into a competitive sector. The success of persuading the Japanese in the SII talks may lay the groundwork for an increase in Japanese competitiveness in the long run.

5. OTHER APPLICATIONS

Before recent developments in the Soviet Union and Eastern Europe occurred, attention was focused on the high savings rates of Japan, West Germany, and some Newly Industrialized Economies (NIEs), on the one hand, and the low savings rate of the United States, on the other. The low savings rate of the U.S. household sector and the large deficit of the federal budget were often blamed, as the cause of a large deficit of the United States in the current account of the balance of payment and resulting increased net indebtedness. Moreover, the high savings rate of Japan was a target of the Strategic Impediments Initiative (SII) talks between the United States and Japan. Needless to say, the present world is not yet rich enough to make savings redundant. The important questions were whether the United States could afford to run a large deficit for some years to come, and how to find channels of savings from high saver countries to less developed countries (LDCs), where funds do not flow smoothly due to the loss of creditworthiness after the debt crisis.

Now a new investment opportunity has opened in East Germany — a name that will soon vanish, in Eastern Europe, and in the Soviet Union. One should not be concerned with the high savings rate of West Germany or Japan. The world requires new capital formation and accordingly sources of funds.

What then is the strategic structure of the savings game? At the level-I game, governments react in the Cournot fashion, each assuming that the government expenditures of other countries as given will lead to a Pareto-inferior equilibrium with excessive government expenditures (Hamada, 1986). The domestic political environment in many countries tends to encourage more spending. Constituents wish to benefit from further spending. Therefore, unless the ideology favoring a balanced budget and small government prevails, the outcome of the level-II game may lead to a Pareto-inferior solution.

Of course, what is lacking is not merely physical capital accumulation. As the "new" growth theory emphasizes, human capital formation and learning-by-doing effects are important. Technical, medical, and educational assistance would, in most cases, lessen economic tension, as would the flow of funds, like direct investments. It is even more nonsensical to blame the "excess" savings after the recent dramatic changes in world political economy.

In the policy coordination problems of interest rates and intervention, there are subtle conflicts at the level-II game. Suppose the Federal Reserve (or the central bank) is more stabilization oriented than the Treasury (or the Ministry of Finance); then the degrees of price stability and employment stability should depend upon the power relation between them.

In these examples, the intensity of the level-II game is not as high as in the level-II game of trade and restriction. However, it still holds true that any policy coordination scheme or plan for reforms in the international regime needs to be incentive compatible.

6. CONCLUDING REMARKS

In this chapter, it has been argued that the two-level game is the most relevant framework for understanding international economic conflicts and that trade disputes are clear examples of the interaction between domestic and international conflicts. In a partial equilibrium framework, it is shown that the existence of counterlobbying from foreign as well as domestic sources is likely to reduce the lobbying cost and the deadweight loss.

Many unsolved questions remain. Empirically, we have to know more about lobbying cost, its effectiveness, and the amount of money that is really unproductively spent. Theoretically, we have to study how the formulation sketched here can be related to the literature of strategic tariff equilibrium (Okuno-Fujiwara and Ueda, 1989), connected games (Alt, Putnam, and Shepsle, 1988; Alt and Eichengreen, 1989), and norm equilibria (Okuno-Fujiwara and Postlewaite, 1988; Milgrom, North, and Weingast 1990).

REFERENCES

Alt, J. and B. Eichengreen (1989). "Parallel and Overlapping games: Theory and Application to the European Gas Trade," Economics and Politics 1(2), 97-117.

Alt, J., R. D. Putnam, and K. A. Shepsle (1988). "The Architecture of Linkage," mimeo, Harvard University.

Bhagwati, J. N. (ed.) (1982). Import Competition and Response, NBER, (Chicago: University of Chicago Press).

Bhagwati, J. and T. N. Srinivasan (1980). "Revenue-seeking: A Generalization of the Theory of Tariffs," Journal of Political Economy 88, 1069-1081.

Becker, G. S. (1984). "A Theory of Competition Among Pressure Groups for Political Influence," Quarterly Journal of Economics 98, 371-400.

Brock, W. A. and S. P. Magee (1978). "The Economics of Special Interest Politics: the Case of the Tariff," American Economic Review: Papers and Proceedings 68, 246-250.

Brock, W. A. and S. P. Magee (1979). "Tariff Formation in a Democracy," in J. Black and B. Hindley (eds.), Current Issues in International Commercial Policy and Economic Diplomacy (London: Macmillan), pp. 1-9.

Choate, P. (1990). Agent of Influence: How Japan's Lobbyists in the United States Manipulate America's Political and Economic System (New York: Knopf).

Denzau, A., W. Riker, and K. Shepsle (1985). "Farquharson and Fenno: Sophisticated Voting and Home Style," American Political Science Review 79, 1117-1135.

Findlay, R. and S. Wellisz (1982). "Endogenous Tariffs, the Political Economy of Trade Restrictions, and Welfare," in J.N. Bhagwati (ed.), Import Competition and Response, NBER (Chicago: University of Chicago Press), pp. 223-238.

Hamada, K. (1985). Political Economy of International Monetary Interdependence (Cambridge, MA: MIT Press).

Hamada, K. (1986). "Strategic Aspects of International Fiscal Interdependence," Economic Studies Quarterly 37, 165–180.

Hamada, K. and Y. Nakajo (1986). "Trade Issues and Consumer Interests: The Japanese Experience" (with Yoshiro Nakajo), in the Proceedings of the Symposium Consumer Policy and International Trade (Paris: OECD), pp. 57–76.

Kennedy, P. (1988). The Rise and Fall of the Great Powers (New York: Random House).

Krueger, A. O. (1974). "The Political Economy of Rent–Seeking Society," American Economic Review 64, 291–303.

Kusano, A. (1990). "Chiho kara mita Nichibei Masatsu (Japan–U.S. trade conflicts from the standpoint of local regions in Japan)," Ushio 369, 110–127 (in Japanese).

Leibenstein, H. (1966). "Allocative Efficiency vs. X–Efficiency," American Economic Review 56, 392–415.

McMillan, John (1986) Game Theory in International Economics (Chur, Switzerland: Harwood Academic Publishers),

McMillan, J. (1990). "The Economics of Section 301: A Game–Theoretic Guide," Economics and Politics 2(1), 45–57.

Magee, S. P., W. A. Brock, and L. Young (1989). Black Hole Tariffs and Endogenous Policy Theory (Cambridge, England: Cambridge University Press).

Milgrom, P. R., D. C. North, and B. R. Weingast (1990). "The Role of Institutions in the Revival of Trade: The Law Merchant, Private Judges a n d the Champagne Fairs," Economics and Politics 2(1), 1–23.

Okuno–Fujiwara, M. and A. Postlewaite (1988). "Social Norm in Random Matching Games," mimeo, University of Tokyo.

Okuno–Fujiwara, M. (1989). "On Labor Incentives and Work Norm in Japanese Firms," Journal of Japanese and International Economies 3, 367–384.

Okuno–Fujiwara, M. and K. Ueda (1989). "Industry Specific Interests and Trade Protection: A Game Theoretic Analysis," mimeo, University of Tokyo.

Ono, Y. (1989). "Orderly Marketing Arrangement in the Context of the GATT Regime," mimeo, Osaka University.

Putnam, R. D. (1988). "Diplomacy and Domestic Politics: the Logic of Two–Level Games," International Organization 42(3), 7.

Stigler, G. J. (1975). Citizen and the State (Chicago: University of Chicago Press).

5. GLOBALIZATION AND THE DESIGN OF INTERNATIONAL INSTITUTIONS

J. Eaton
Department of Economics
Boston University
279 Bay State Road
Boston, Massachusetts 02215
U.S.A.

ABSTRACT.   Current arrangements governing international trading relationships are under attack in both academic and policy circles.   There is concern that a multilateral system of free and open trade, to the extent that it ever existed, is degenerating into a system of preferential trade among regional blocks.   This chapter reviews evidence from the 1980s indicating that, while export patterns do reveal some regional bias, this bias did not grow over that period.   Recent work in trade theory is then reviewed, with the conclusion that these theories mostly reinforce rather than diminish the orthodox case for free trade.   They also suggest, however, why national governments may be unwilling to pursue laissez-faire unilaterally. Areas where the current system appears to be failing are then enumerated and three reasons for failure are suggested.   The world economy seems to be best served if multilateral arrangements, when they are made, have open membership.   Rules-based trade agreements are preferable to arrangements with quantitative targets.

1. INTRODUCTION

The pending conclusion of the Uruguay Round of the General Agreement on Tariffs and Trade (GATT) raises questions about the extent and direction of future economic integration.   Until now, trade policies and other policies affecting trade have been an overwhelmingly national concern.   GATT has provided a framework for the major market-oriented industrial nations of the world, along with anyone else willing to abide by its rules, for promoting freer and more open trade with one another.   A fundamental goal of the GATT treaty was to incorporate the principles of multilateral reciprocity and nondiscrimination into the conduct of trade policy.   As measures toward accomplishing this goal, GATT has overseen a series of negotiations to cut barriers, requires its members to extend most-favored-nation status toward each other, and specifies sanctions that members can impose on each other for violating GATT terms.

But to what extent GATT can succeed in achieving an economically integrated world economy, or even whether such a goal is desirable, has been called into question.

On an intellectual level, international economists during the 1980s have developed a number of new theories of trade in which trade patterns emerge not from natural comparative advantage or differences in endowments, but because of government policies or historical accident. These theories have been interpreted by some as justifying various forms of trade intervention.

On a practical level, a number of observers have questioned how successful GATT has been, and whether the world economy is capable of sustaining further economic integration. Several developments, in particular, have generated these doubts.

One is the emergence of areas of economic integration (i.e., free trade areas, customs unions, and common markets) within the GATT community. Aside from the European Economic Community, which is scheduled to become much more integrated during the coming decade, the United States has entered into free trade agreements with Israel and Canada, and similar bilateral or trilateral agreements with other countries are under discussion. Such areas violate the principles of multilateralism and nondiscrimination, but are explicitly permitted by the GATT charter (although they are subject to restrictions and require GATT approval).

The theory of customs unions tells us that such arrangements can divert as well as create trade.[1] While the first effect is generally beneficial, the second is likely to lead to inefficiency.[2] To the extent that these arrangements have led to the growth of regional trade at the expense of global trade, then, they are likely to have reduced welfare.

A second development is the tendency of GATT members to act outside the GATT framework by pursuing trade policies bilaterally, or by unilaterally imposing conditions on particular trading partners, which are enforced with the threat or actual implementation of unilateral sanctions. The "voluntary export arrangements" between the United States and Europe as importers and various other countries (particularly in Asia) as exporters are examples of the first. "Super 301," "Special 301," and other amendments to the U.S. Trade Act embodied in the U.S. Omnibus Trade and Competitiveness Act of 1987 are examples of the second. These provisions call upon the United States Government, in particular the United States Trade Representative, to restrict imports from countries found to engage in certain practices specified in the legislation.

These ad hoc unilateral and bilateral measures, as well as formal regional trading areas, constitute trade barriers between the major industrial regions.

The next section of this chapters examines the extent to which trade among the major industrial regions does appear to be biased toward trade within regions rather than between them. There does appear to be some regional preference in

---

[1]Viner's classic piece (1950) provides the original discussion. See Kowalczyk (1990) for a review of more recent contributions to the literature, which typically assume a situation of perfect competition. Kiyono (1989) extends results on customs unions to situations in which competition is imperfect.

[2]Economic integration creates trade to the extent that the removal of trade barriers against regional partners causes imports from partners to replace domestic production. In this case, production has shifted from a high cost (domestic) source to a lower-cost source (the partner), so that world production has become more efficient. However, economic integration diverts trade to the extent that imports from regional partners replace those from outside the region. In this case, production has shifted from a low cost source outside the region to a higher-cost source inside the region, so that world production patterns become less efficient.

trading relationships, but intraregional trade does not appear to be diverting trade between the major industrial regions.   Furthermore, no trend is found toward regional integration away from interregional integration during 1983–1988.

Section 3 examines recent trade theories in terms of their implications for trade intervention. These theories, if anything, reinforce the case for free and open trade, but also suggest why a regime of global free trade may be much harder to achieve than what orthodox trade theory would suggest.

Section 4 turns to specific areas in which the current world trading system is experiencing difficulty. Lack of harmonization of policy is often responsible.

Finally, Section 5 considers different approaches that have been suggested for modifying the world trading system. A basic conclusion is that further global integration can best be served by open, multilateral arrangements. Furthermore, these arrangements should specify and enforce rules of behavior for national governments rather than specify trade targets, i.e., attempt to "manage" trade. In many areas, internationalization, rather than just harmonization, of government activities would not only solve trade problems but also achieve substantial economies of scale.

2. TRADE PATTERNS IN THE 1980s: ARE REGIONAL TRADING BLOCKS FORMING?

To provide a portrait of trade patterns of the 1980s, two years have been chosen as a focus: 1983, the beginning of the recovery from the 1982 recession, and 1988, the most recent year for which comprehensive data are available. The industrial world has then been divided into three major geographical regions: "Greater" Asia, divided between Japan and other Asian countries, henceforth just "Asia"; North America, consisting of the United States and Canada; and the European Community.[3] Tables 1 through 5 and figures 1 through 3 present data on export amounts from Asia and Japan, North America (the United States and Canada), and the European Community. Tables 9 and 10 present export data as a ratio to the GNP of the country of origin.

2.1 Basic Trends In Overall Exports From The Industrial Countries

One fact is clear: Trade between the major regions, and within the major regions, grew substantially, in the 1980s, both absolutely and relative to GNP. Growth in exports from the Asian countries is most dramatic. Japan is the only unit that actually experienced a decline in exports as a share of GNP between the two years, from 12% to 10%, reflecting a relative decline in exports both to the United States and to the rest of the world. In contrast, exports as a share of GNP from other Asian countries grew from 20% to 32%. (Not surprisingly, regions that consist of many small countries, Asia and the European Community, and Canada, a small country, have larger export ratios than Japan and the United States.)

---

[3]Export data are from the International Monetary Fund's <u>Direction of Trade Statistics Yearbook, 1990</u>, while GNP data are from the World Bank's <u>World Tables</u>, <u>1989–1990</u>. The IMF's definition of Asia, which excludes the Middle East, has been used. The data do not distinguish internal exports of the European Community from EC exports to the rest of the world.

2.1.1.   Is There a Regional Bias? To what extent do export data show evidence of a bias toward trade within regions versus trade between regions? Figures 1 through 3 show that, for each region, the region itself is the largest destination for exports (assuming that most EC exports to the EC and rest of the world (ROW) are in fact to the EC). However, there does not appear to be any trend toward regional trade away from interregional trade. Exports to other major regions for the most part grew just as fast as exports within each region. In particular, greater Asia grew significantly not only as a source of exports but as a destination for exports from other regions: it has been the fastest growing market for both North America and the European Community.

Another feature revealed by a comparison of export levels in the two years is the growth of both intraregional trade and trade between the major industrial regions relative to exports to countries outside these regions: relative to trade among the industrial countries, North-South trade is languishing.

A better sense of the extent to which regional biases appear in export patterns can be ascertained by comparing the actual destinations of exports with what would occur if the share exported to each destination were proportional to the destination's GNP. Tables 1 through 8 and figures 4 through 11 compare actual exports with the level of exports that would occur if the source had exported the same total amount but its distribution among destinations was proportional to the GNP of those destinations.[4]

As shown in table 1 and figure 4, for Asia and Japan together, exports to the rest of the world and to North America were roughly comparable to what would be predicted by the relative GNPs of these destinations. Exports to the EC are much lower, however, compensated for by a higher level of exports to Asian destinations themselves.

Tables 4 and 5 and figures 7 and 8 decompose these figures by source and destination.   Exports from Asian nations including Japan to Asian nations other than Japan are the reason for the disproportionately high level of intrablock trade within Greater Asia. Exports from other Asian nations to Japan are about what relative GNP would predict. Both Asia and Japan export somewhat less to Canada, the United States, and the rest of the world than what relative GNP would predict, and only about half of what relative GNP would predict to the EC.

Table 2 and figure 5 perform the equivalent exercise for exports from North America.   For the region as a whole, exports to Greater Asia and within the region absorbed about what relative GNP would predict. As with Asia, the EC bought less than what its GNP share would predict. For North America, however, the difference is made up by relatively higher exports to the rest of the world.

Tables 6 and 7 and figures 9 and 10 decompose North American exports by source and destination. Aggregation in fact disguises the relative significance of trade across the U.S.-Canada border, which for each country is much more than what relative GNP shares would predict.[5]

---

[4]Rounding error sometimes causes actual and predicted levels to sum to different magnitudes.

[5]Aggregation hides the importance of intraregional trade because of the asymmetry between the relative sizes of Canada and the United States, as the following hypothetical data illustrate: Imagine that Canada had a GNP of 0,

Disaggregation continues to show, however, that the EC absorbed much less of U.S. or, in particular, of Canadian exports than what its relative GNP would indicate. It also reveals that the approximate correspondence between actual and predicted exports from North America to Greater Asia is the consequence of higher–than–predicted U.S. exports to Asia, offset by lower–than–predicted U.S. exports to Japan and Canadian exports to either Asia or Japan.

Finally, tables 3 and 8 and figures 6 and 11 compare actual and predicted exports from the EC. Intracommunity trade and exports to the rest of the world absorb a disproportionate share of EC exports. Hence both North America and Greater Asia receive proportionately much less than what their relative GNP shares would predict. Disaggregating the destinations of EC exports indicates that the shortfall is particularly great for EC exports to Japan and North America, and least pronounced for EC exports to other Asian countries.

Overall, these data do suggest that export patterns from the major industrial regions are biased toward other destinations within that region. As mentioned, however, from a welfare perspective a regional bias (to the extent that it is based on preferential trading arrangements at all) is detrimental only to the extent that regional trade occurs instead of interregional trade. If interregional trade occurs in addition to regional trade, then a regional bias is probably advantageous.

2.1.2. Has Intraregional Trade Created Trade or Diverted Trade? To provide some indication of whether intraregional trade has crowded out trade between regions, have been calculated; exports by destination and overall as a share of the total GNP of the source, the results for the major geographical regions appear in table 9 and on a more disaggregated basis in table 10.

Note that the regions with the greatest amount of intraregional exports are also those that export the most overall, i.e., high exports to destinations within the region are associated with a high level of exports generally. Asian exports to destinations outside Asia, Canadian exports to destinations other than the U.S., and European exports to Asia and North America are typically as high or higher, relative to GNP, than exports from sources that export relatively less to destinations within their own region (Japan and the United States). This finding, while not definitive, suggests that intraregional exports occur in addition to, rather than instead of, trade between regions.

2.2. Basic Trends

The data suggest four essential features about trade among the major industrial regions during the 1980s.

---

while the U.S. and the rest of the world each had a GNP of 10. The U.S. exports 4 to the rest of the world and 2 to Canada, while Canada exports 2 to the U.S. and 0 elsewhere. Intraregional exports are 4, as are exports from the region as a whole to destinations outside. These amounts are proportional to the relative GNPs of the two regions. On a disaggregate basis, however, relative GNPs would predict a 0 level of U.S. exports to Canada, instead of the actual level of 2, and exports elsewhere at 6, instead of the actual level of 4. Similarly, Canada's exports of 2 would be divided between the U.S. and the rest of the world, rather than all flowing to the U.S.

1. Trade among the major industrial regions has grown both absolutely and, to a less pronounced extent, relative to GNP.

2. Trade within and among the industrial regions has grown relative to trade between these regions and the rest of the world.

3. Countries tend to trade more with other countries within their region, both absolutely and compared with what relative GNP shares would predict. The bias toward intraregional trade does not appear to have grown during the 1980s, however.

4. The relatively greater importance of trade within regions compared with that between regions does not appear to have occurred at the expense of interregional trade, but rather in addition to it.

While trade among the industrial nations grew substantially during the 1980s, the welfare implications of this trade, and the prospects for continued growth in interregional trade, have been questioned both by some academic economists and by those in the political sphere. Academic arguments questioning the desirability of unilateral or multilateral free trade have been made, while there are various unilateral, bilateral, and multilateral initiatives to reform radically the world trading system. The academic arguments will be considered first.

3. "NEW TRADE THEORY" AND THE "NEW PROTECTIONISM"

During the 1980s a number of academic economists developed explanations for trade based not on traditional notions of national comparative advantage arising from differences in endowments or differences in relative productivities. Rather, these new theories assigned much greater importance to government policy and to scale economies.

To a large extent, these theories actually strengthen the orthodox case for unilateral and multilateral laissez-faire. Some theories, however, may justify, from a national perspective, some type of government intervention.

The justifications fall into three categories. First, intervention can create rents for the country. Second, it can shift existing rents earned by foreigners to the home country. Third, intervention can be a punishment for undesirable intervention abroad.

3.1. The Rent-Creating Argument for Protection: John Stuart Mill

The rent-creating argument for protection is actually an old one, having been made by John Stuart Mill in 1858. By restricting its imports (through a tariff or quota, for instance), a country that is a large purchaser of the imported good in the world market can drive down its world price, thus taking advantage of its monopsony position. (An equivalent argument applies to restrictions on exports if the country is a major supplier to the world market).[6]

It is worth noting that Mill's argument does not extend to voluntary export restrictions (VERs), which have become a popular form of protection in the last

---

[6]The argument assumes, of course, that the importing or exporting industry is not already monopolized. Otherwise, its behavior would internalize the country's market power.

two decades. Since VERs specify that exporting countries apply the restriction, whatever rents are generated by the consequent difference between world and domestic prices become monopoly rents for the exporting countries rather than monopsony rents for the importer. From a national welfare perspective, VERs can never be preferred to a tariff or domestically imposed quota.[7]

The optimal–tariff argument for protection, as well as the rent–shifting arguments discussed below, applies only at the national level. Protection is harmful to the trading partner and makes the global allocation of resources less efficient. Pursuit of nationally optimal policies by all countries can thus be mutually destructive: that is, all countries could be better off with no intervention than with a situation in which each country unilaterally pursues nationally optimal policies.

3.2. New Trade Theories and Profit–Grabbing Intervention

Rent–shifting, or profit–grabbing, arguments for intervention are more recent, and arise in situations in which markets are already imperfect, either because of concentration or because of increasing returns to scale.

3.2.1. Grabbing A Foreign Rival's Market.
One justification for government intervention is provided in a classic paper by Brander and Spencer (1985). They show that an export subsidy can confer gains to a nation with an exporting firm competing with a foreign firm. Their argument makes the following assumptions: 1) firms are Cournot (i.e., quantity–setting) rivals; 2) the government can commit itself to a subsidization policy prior to the output decisions of the firms in question; and 3) subsidization does not cause the government of the foreign firm to subsidize as well.

Under these assumptions, a subsidy moves the domestic firm toward a position as a Stackelberg leader: by lowering its marginal cost of exporting, it exports more, causing its foreign rival to export less. By causing its rival to retreat from the market, the firm earns a larger share of the monopoly rents generated in the export market.

The Brander–Spencer result is very sensitive to its assumptions, however. For one thing, if firms are Bertrand (i.e., price–setting) competitors, an export tax rather than subsidy is the preferred policy. For another, for the two countries as a whole export subsidization is a negative–sum game: not only does it shift rents, it destroys them. Both countries would prefer a situation of no subsidization to one in which both subsidized.[8] Finally, the assumption that governments are better at committing to tax policies than firms are at committing to quantity levels is questionable. In the opposite case, in which firms commit to output quantities before governments choose subsidies, a policy of subsidiza- tion can very well be welfare reducing from a national perspective.

---

[7]Hamilton (1988) calculates that VERs on clothing averaged US$.5 billion during 1982–1983, "with around 80 percent of this total being transferred from the United States, and approximately two-thirds of the total rent going to Hong Kong" (p. 221).

[8]See Eaton and Grossman (1986).

3.2.2. Grabbing a Foreign Supplier's Profit. A second profit-shifting argument for intervention, this time for import tariffs, was made by Katrak (1977), who showed that, with linear demand, a tariff shifts rents from a foreign monopolistic supplier to the importer. Again, this argument assumes that the importing government has an ability to commit to a tax rate for a longer period than the supplier can commit to a price. Moreover, under different assumptions about domestic demand, an import subsidy rather than a tariff can be an optimal policy.[9]

3.2.3. Exploiting Scale Economies to Expand Market Share. Imperfect competition and the consequent rents generated motivate both of these arguments for rent-grabbing intervention. A third argument relies on the presence of some (static or dynamic) economies of scale, such as those that might emerge from "learning-by-doing."

With constant returns to scale, trade occurs because of differences between countries, in their endowments or relative productivities, for example; countries that are identical have no reason to trade with each other. With increasing returns, however, there are gains from trade between two absolutely identical countries. The problem, however, is that the outcome is unlikely to be symmetric: the country that specializes in the industry in which increasing returns are more important is likely to do better, since it can exploit the cost advantage associated with scale.[10]

Intervention may thus be justified to capture industries in which scale economies are important. Krugman (1984) provides a particular example in which, by protecting a home market, a government can increase its home firm's export profits. The reason is that protection gives the home firm a larger home market. This increases its overall scale of production and lowers its cost in the foreign market. Domestic protection acts just like an export subsidy, and is nationally advantageous under the assumptions of the Brander-Spencer (1985) analysis, e.g., Cournot competition and no retaliation.

This argument, like the others, applies only at the national level. Independent pursuit of nationally optimal policies is a negative-sum game globally. All countries might prefer a situation with no intervention to one in which all intervene.

To summarize, the new trade theories do not imply that trade intervention benefits the world as a whole. On the contrary, imperfect competition and increasing returns imply that the costs of intervention can be much greater than what orthodox analysis would suggest. Trade restrictions not only interfere with natural comparative advantage but also enhance monopoly power and prevent the exploitation of scale economies.

What the new trade theories do point out is the strength of the incentive to intervene from a purely national point of view. These theories explain much better than orthodox analysis why the political pressure for intervention can be so strong.

---

[9]See Brander and Spencer (1984).

[10]See, for example, Eaton and Panagariya (1979) and Ethier (1982).

3.3. Intervention to Discipline: Game—Theoretic Considerations

Given the strength of this pressure, how, if decisions about trade intervention are made by sovereign governments, can a world trading order give governments an incentive to pursue globally optimal rather than nationally optimal policies?

Military intervention is, of course, one means by which a government can extend its sovereignty beyond its borders.   Iraq's invasion of Kuwait was justified on exactly these grounds: Iraq wanted to restrict Kuwait's oil output in order to generate more monopoly rents for itself.

Fortunately, conflicts over trade policy rarely lead to military conflict. What does occur, however, is that countries may change their trade policies in response to changes in trade policies elsewhere.   A third argument for intervention, then, is not to create or to shift rents, but to punish other countries for intervening.

For this reason, trade liberalization is often pursued on a reciprocal basis, either bilaterally or multilaterally.   Bilaterally, nations may agree to reduce tariffs against each others' goods, or not to subsidize exports to one another.   The implicit threat enforcing such an agreement is that, if one country violates it, so will the other.   Bilateral reciprocity was the primary means of negotiating tariff reductions before World War II and the free trade agreement between the United States and Canada.

Unless bilateral arrangements are extended to encompass the whole world, however, there is no guarantee that they can achieve a better outcome than no agreements at all.   Trading blocks rather than individual countries may then become the units engaging in trade policies, and large trading blocks are likely to find intervention unilaterally more desirable than small countries.[11]

GATT is an attempt to provide a reciprocal, multilateral arrangement for reducing intervention.   GATT, however, has no enforcement capability of its own. Instead, it allows signatories to deviate from GATT rules to punish other countries for doing so.   Signatories may, for instance, impose "substantially equivalent" retaliation against other members who impose the escape clause.[12] Members may also impose countervailing duties against countries that subsidize exports.

An alternative to a bilateral or multilateral approach based on reciprocity is a unilateral one in which a country restricts trade as response to policies in another country.   The 301 provisions of the U.S. Trade Act, as amended by the Omnibus Trade and Competitiveness Act of 1988, represent one such unilateral approach.

These multilateral, bilateral, and unilateral arrangements have not managed to prevent a number of international disputes or "trade frictions."   These areas of major concern will be discussed below.

---

[11]See, for example, the hypothetical calculation in Krugman (1989).

[12]Ono (1989) analyzes the implications of the retaliation provision of the escape clause and shows why it may have led to the prevalence of VERs in recent years.

4. SOURCES OF "TRADE FRICTION"

GATT has traditionally focused on explicit barriers to trade in manufactures. Until recently it has not attacked barriers to trade in agricultural goods and services, and it has done little about internal policies, rather than border measures, that are possible sources of "artificial" comparative advantage, i.e., comparative advantage emanating from policy rather than natural differences in endowments or relative productivity. Nevertheless, nations can use internal policies, as much as border measures and subsidies, to create or to grab rents.

GATT's limitations in each of the areas enumerated below have become sources of dispute among industrial countries. In many cases GATT members are trying to resolve these disputes with bilateral and unilateral measures rather than through multilateral channels.

4.1. Trade in Agricultural Commodities and Services

Until the Uruguay Round, GATT negotiations have ignored trade in agriculture and services. Trade in these categories is significantly affected not only by border measures, but by other domestic policies such as government commodity programs, insurance, and regulations.

In agriculture there are, in each of the major industrial regions, long-standing policies that are highly protectionist and that receive the vehement support of special interest groups. The Japanese ban on rice imports, the common agricultural policy of the EEC, and the United States sugar quota system and water programs for farmers are examples. There are also significant export subsidization programs in the EEC and United States. McDonald (1990) estimates that liberalization of trade in agriculture would generate a world welfare gain of about US$22 billion annually.

Service exports are a major component of trade that has not been, for the most part, subject to international agreement. In the case of services, the U.S. prohibition of foreign entry into domestic transportation has already been a source of friction. Expanding trade in financial and banking services will at some point require the harmonization of bank regulation and monetary policies.[13]

4.2. Foreign Direct Investment

While the United States has been a major source of direct foreign investment for the rest of the world, it has recently become a major recipient of investment from Western Europe and Japan. Lack of harmonization of regulatory and anti-trust policies of different countries is likely to create artificial sources of comparative advantage that generate inefficiencies.

---

[13]The U.S. experience with the Latin American debt crisis illustrates how national banking regulation and government deposit insurance (explicit or otherwise) can create a (disadvantageous) artificial comparative advantage. A combination of lax regulation and government deposit insurance made the United States a low-cost intermediary. The U.S. Government has now found itself bearing much of the downside risk associated with the LDC debt crisis.

4.3. Macroeconomic Policy

Lack of harmonization of monetary and fiscal policies is another source of friction. These policies affect overall trade balances, which are themselves a current source of friction.

Furthermore, differences in tax policies have major implications for competitiveness and trade flows. National differences in tax rates and tax bases are obvious sources of artificial comparative advantage.

4.4. Global Public Goods

A major function of a government is to provide "public goods." These are goods that are either "nonrival," in that their use by one party does not infringe upon their use by another, or "nonexcludable," in that, once they are provided, it is impossible to keep others from using them. Some goods are globally public. Since many nations may benefit from expenditure on such goods by any single country, a free rider problem arises. Three particular areas in which such global public goods are creating international tensions will be discussed below.

4.4.1. Peacekeeping. The recent crisis in Iraq dramatized the potential seriousness of disputes about how to allocate the cost of an effort to enforce treaties and to defend borders.

4.4.2. Environmental Regulation. Environmental issues can be a source of international tensions for at least two reasons. For one thing, many activities degrade the global environment. National governments, acting on their own, have little incentive to limit pollution to the optimal extent, and different governments may perceive different degrees of self-interest in achieving a global solution. Recent protocols halting the use of chlorofluorocarbons were a multilateral effort to protect the ozone layer that successfully overcame significant differences in national opinion. A consensus about how much to restrict emissions of greenhouse gases to forestall global warming has yet to be achieved.

Another source of friction is the differences in national policies toward the environment that affect the competitive position of local firms in global markets. This has been an issue in the debate about Mexico's entry into the North American Free Trade Agreement. The extent to which differences in environmental policies constitute a natural rather than artificial source of comparative advantage is subject to debate.

4.4.3. Research and Development. The benefits of research and development, both basic and applied, are often global. The two types of activity differ, however, in how they are usually encouraged and in the nature of the international conflicts that they are likely to create.

Applied research and development typically leads to the development of new products. Innovation of this type is usually encouraged by intellectual property rights, which give the innovator a temporary monopoly over the use of the innovation. Intellectual property is currently a national concern subject only to very limited constraint by multilateral international agreements.[14]

Extending protection of U.S. intellectual property globally has been a major concern of the United States. According to Maskus (1990) the United States earned $10.7 billion in royalties and license fees abroad in 1988, generating a surplus of $8.7 billion on this account. The U.S. Omnibus Trade and Competitiveness Act of 1984 unilaterally extends protection of U.S. intellectual property offshore, both through its amendment to Section 337 of the Trade Act, which bans imports found to infringe upon U.S. intellectual property, and more broadly though "Special 301," which seeks to affect policies toward intellectual property protection abroad.[15]

A particular concern is that policies toward intellectual property, like the other policies discussed so far, can serve as a source of artificial comparative advantage. A foreign firm that does not pay a royalty on a patent or copyright that a domestic firm must pay is, other things equal, at a competitive advantage. Countries can thus use policies toward intellectual property for trade-related purposes.

Basic research, unlike applied research and development, often does not lead directly to a new product or process that the innovator can sell to recover the cost of his effort. For this reason basic research often requires government funding. When more than a single country benefits from the research, a public goods problem at the international level obviously arises. However, with the exception of institutions like CERN, multilateral funding for basic research is rare.[16]

5. SEEKING SOLUTIONS

Current arrangements for overseeing national policies seem to suffer from three basic defects. One is the limited domain of current multilateral institutions. A second is the limited enforcement power of these institutions. A third is the lack of transparency of national policies.

---

[14]The Paris convention, administered by the World Intellectual Property Organization, governs patent protection. It requires only that foreigners be provided national treatment in the assignment of intellectual property rights, and does not set minimum standards for protection. The Berne Convention governing copyrights also requires nondiscrimination, but says little about the level of protection that its parties must provide. National policies toward patents and copyrights do in fact vary widely between countries.

[15]Threatened 301 actions are perceived to have strengthened intellectual property protection in several Asian countries.

[16]The recent exchange between the United States and Japan about paying for the Texas supercollider is an example of a dispute arising over the funding of basic research with potentially global implications. The issue is not funding, however, but also the direction that research should take.

5.1. The Limited Domain of Existing Multilateral Arrangements

Clearly GATT and other multilateral arrangements have not harmonized national policies to the extent that they no longer achieve national gain at the expense of world welfare. As long as countries perceive that they are harmed by the policies of other countries, they will find that intervention on their part, either to offset the effect of foreign policy or to retaliate against it, is economically and morally justifiable.

The Uruguay Round attempted to expand the GATT framework to incorporate a much wider range of issues. Its success will do much to alleviate this source of concern. In the meantime, countries are pursuing bilateral arrangements with regional partners to achieve deeper integration than what the GATT mechanism currently provides.

The danger is that deeper integration within regions will lead to more protection for the region as a whole from outside, for the reasons given by Krugman (1989). A further danger is that bilateral arrangements will be perceived as a substitute for global arrangements. One way to avoid the formation of protectionist regional blocks is to insist that any arrangement involving any group of countries be "open" in that, as with GATT, any country willing to abide by the rules of the agreement would be able to join. A country's policies, not its location, should matter.

5.2. The Limited Enforcement Power of International Institutions

As mentioned, GATT relies on individual parties to enforce its terms, and sanctions are specified only for a limited range of violations. Unilateral U.S. arrangements specify a wider range of violations, and call for stiffer penalties. For a multilateral arrangement to be effective, it must be able credibly to threaten sanctions with the appropriate deterrent capacity. The protocols limiting chlorofluorocarbon emissions, for example, call for trade sanctions against nonparties that do not abide by the terms of the agreement. This arrangement has already persuaded some nonparties to implement these terms.[17]

5.3. The Opaqueness of National Policies

Domestic regulatory, procurement, and tax policies and systems of intellectual property protection are much harder for a foreign or international body to monitor or to evaluate than border measures such as tariffs. Such policies may, for example, emanate as much from custom and convention as from codified law. As a consequence, international agreements that specify rules of conduct may be difficult to apply and enforce.

This problem in enforcing international rules and agreements has led some to advocate the abandonment of rules-based arrangements, such as GATT and 301, in favor of results-based arrangements — that is, arrangements that require other countries to achieve specific quantitative trade targets rather than to modify laws or practices. U.S. Representative Gephart, for example, has indicated that the United States Trade Representative should seek to eliminate

---

[17]See Parson (1991).

54

the U.S.–Japanese bilateral trade deficit, rather than to change particular practices in Japan. In academic circles, Dornbusch (1990), while criticizing the nature of the target that Gephart specifies, advocates that a target "be set for the growth rates of Japanese imports of U.S. products. ...Additionally, the U.S. should employ automatic sanctions forceful enough to demonstrate to the Japanese that adjustment is required."

Dornbusch correctly maintains that there is absolutely no argument for focusing on the bilateral trade balance. Trade that is bilaterally balanced fails to exploit fully the gains from trade among the countries of the world. Also correct is his assertion that the U.S. overall trade deficit and the Japanese surplus are the consequences of macroeconomic phenomena rather than of trade policy. But he does not explain why the level of Japanese imports from the United States is an appropriate concern for U.S. policy. Natural comparative advantage could dictate that Japan import even less from the United States than it does now. The targets that he advocates may simply provide a form of protection for U.S. firms.

A more promising solution is to internationalize those activities where harmonization and transparency are at issue. A patent or copyright system, for instance, need not be a national endeavor, but could be administered and enforced internationally. Internationalizing such activities would confer the additional benefits of eliminating duplication of effort and realizing economies of scale.

6. SUMMARY

During the 1980s trade among the major industrial regions grew more rapidly than trade generally. While GATT has provided a multilateral, largely nondiscriminatory framework that has fostered expanded trade in manufactures, there are reasons to worry that subsequent economic integration will be more regional than global in character.

One reason is the increased importance of regional trading units scheduled for the 1990s, particularly the further integration of the European Community and the implementation of the North American Free Trade Agreement.

A greater threat, however, is the inability of current multilateral arrangements to resolve trade frictions that are beyond the purview of existing multilateral arrangements. In areas where strong multilateral oversight is lacking, individual countries are seeking unilateral or bilateral solutions to international differences. The danger is that these routes will lead to regional segmentation and retaliation that not only blocks further integration of the global economy, but also reverses the gains that were achieved in the last three decades.

REFERENCES

Brander, James A. and Barbara J. Spencer (1984). "Tariff Protection and Imperfect Competition," in H. Kierzkowski (ed.), Monopolistic Competition and International Trade (Oxford: Clarendon Press), pp. 194–206.

Brander, James A. and Barbara J. Spencer (1984). "Export Subsidies and International Market Share Rivalry," Journal of International Economics 18, 83–100.

Dornbusch, Rudiger W. (1990). "The SII Talks are a Joke," The International Economy, February/March, pp. 47–49.

Eaton, Jonathan and Arvind Panagariya (1979). "Gains from Trade under Variable Returns to Scale, Commodity Taxation, Tariffs and Factor Market Distortions," Journal of International Economics 9, 481–501.

Eaton, Jonathan and Gene M. Grossman (1986). "Optimal Trade and Industrial Policy under Oligopoly," Quarterly Journal of Economics 101, 383–406.

Ethier, Wilfred J. (1982). "Decreasing Costs in International Trade and Frank Graham's Argument for Protection," Econometrica 50, 243–268.

Hamilton, Carl B. (1988). "Restrictiveness and the International Transmission of the 'New Protectionism,'" in R.E. Baldwin, C.B. Hamilton, and A. Sapir (eds.), Issues in US–EC Trade Relations (Chicago: The University of Chicago Press), pp. 199–227.

Katrak, H. (1977). "Multinational Monopolies and Commercial Policies," Oxford Economic Papers 29, 283–291.

Kowalczyk, Carsten (1990). "Welfare and Customs Unions," unpublished manuscript, Dartmouth College.

Krugman, Paul R. (1984). "Import Protection as Export Promotion: International Competition in the Presence of Oligopoly and Economies of Scale," in H. Kierzkowski (ed.), Monopolistic Competition and International Trade (Oxford: Clarendon Press), pp. 180–193.

Krugman, Paul R. (1989). "Is Bilateralism Bad?" National Bureau of Economic Research Working Paper No. 2972.

McDonald, Bradley J. (1990). "Agricultural Negotiations Late in the Uruguay Round: Ten Scenarios for the Eleventh Hour," presented at the NBER International Seminar on International Trade: Analytical Issues and Developments in the Uruguay Round, August.

Maskus, Keith E. (1990). "Normative Concerns in the International Protection of Intellectual Property Rights: Implications for the Uruguay Round," presented at the NBER International Seminar on International Trade: Analytical Issues and Developments in the Uruguay Round, August.

Ono, Yoshiyasu (1989). "VERs and the Escape Clause," unpublished manuscript, ISER, Osaka University.

Parson, Edward A. (1991). "Stratospheric Ozone and CFCs: International Institutions," unpublished manuscript, JFK School of Government, Harvard University.

Viner, Jacob (1950). The Customs Union Issue, Carnegie Endowment for the Peace, New York.

TABLE 1

EXPORTS FROM ASIA AND JAPAN

US$ BILLION

DESTINATION	YEAR	ACTUAL	PREDICTED
ASIA AND	1983	119.8	66.2
JAPAN	1988	242.2	145.3
NORTH	1983	94.0	112.5
AMERICA	1988	193.6	208.4
EEC	1983	42.4	86.0
	1988	94.3	176.8
ROW	1983	74.6	66.2
	1988	101.5	101.1
TOTAL	1983	330.8	330.8
	1988	631.6	631.6

TABLE 2

EXPORTS FROM NORTH AMERICA

US$ BILLION

DESTINATION	YEAR	ACTUAL	PREDICTED
ASIA AND	1983	57.4	55.4
JAPAN	1988	102.3	100.4
NORTH	1983	92.0	94.2
AMERICA	1988	151.1	144.1
EEC	1983	54.1	72.1
	1988	84.7	122.2
ROW	1983	73.7	55.4
	1988	98.5	69.9
TOTAL	1983	277.2	277.2
	1988	436.6	436.6

TABLE 3

EXPORTS FROM THE EEC

US$ BILLION

DESTINATION	YEAR	ACTUAL	PREDICTED
ASIA AND	1983	35.4	119.7
JAPAN	1988	77.1	244.9
NORTH	1983	52.9	203.6
AMERICA	1988	101.7	351.4
EEC	1983		155.7
	1988		298.1
ROW	1983		119.7
	1988		170.4
EEC AND	1983	510.4	275.4
ROW	1988	885.9	468.5
TOTAL	1983	598.7	598.7
	1988	1064.7	1064.7

TABLE 4

EXPORTS FROM ASIA

US$ BILLION

DESTINATION	YEAR	ACTUAL	PREDICTED
ASIA	1983	47.9	14.7
	1988	108.9	25.7
JAPAN	1983	31.9	20.2
	1988	55.9	58.7
USA	1983	44.4	57.0
	1988	90.8	113.6
CANADA	1983	2.7	5.5
	1988	6.2	11.0
EEC	1983	22.9	47.8
	1988	47.2	102.6
ROW	1983	34.0	36.8
	1988	57.6	58.7
TOTAL	1983	183.8	183.8
	1988	366.6	366.6

TABLE 5

EXPORTS FROM JAPAN

US$ BILLION

DESTINATION	YEAR	ACTUAL	PREDICTED
ASIA	1983	40.0	13.3
	1988	77.4	22.1
USA	1983	43.3	51.4
	1988	90.2	98.0
CANADA	1983	3.6	5.0
	1988	6.4	9.5
EEC	1983	19.5	43.1
	1988	47.1	88.6
ROW	1983	40.6	33.2
	1988	43.9	50.6
TOTAL	1983	147.0	147.0
	1988	265.0	265.0

TABLE 6

EXPORTS FROM THE USA

US$ BILLION

DESTINATION	YEAR	ACTUAL	PREDICTED
ASIA	1983	28.4	23.4
	1988	51.4	32.4
JAPAN	1983	21.9	32.2
	1988	37.7	74.0
CANADA	1983	38.2	8.8
	1988	69.2	13.9
EEC	1983	48.4	76.0
	1988	75.9	129.5
ROW	1983	63.6	58.5
	1988	86.2	74.0
TOTAL	1983	200.5	198.9
	1988	320.4	323.8

TABLE 7

EXPORTS FROM CANADA

US$ BILLION

DESTINATION	YEAR	ACTUAL	PREDICTED
ASIA	1983	3.2	6.3
	1988	6.2	8.4
JAPAN	1983	3.9	8.7
	1988	7.0	19.1
USA	1983	53.8	24.5
	1988	81.9	37.0
EEC	1983	5.7	20.5
	1988	8.8	33.5
ROW	1983	10.1	15.8
	1988	12.3	19.1
TOTAL	1983	76.7	75.9
	1988	116.2	117.1

TABLE 8

EXPORTS FROM THE EEC

US$ BILLION

DESTINATION	YEAR	ACTUAL	PREDICTED
ASIA	1983	26.8	47.9
	1988	53.0	74.5
JAPAN	1983	8.6	65.9
	1988	24.1	170.4
USA	1983	47.9	185.6
	1988	88.7	330.1
CANADA	1983	5.0	18
	1988	13.0	31.9
EEC	1983		155.7
	1988		298.1
		510.4	
		885.9	
ROW	1983		119.7
	1988		170.4
TOTAL	1983	598.7	592.7
	1988	1064.7	1075.3

TABLE 9

EXPORTS AS A SHARE OF SOURCE GNP, BY DESTINATION
REGIONAL BLOCKS

DESTINATION

SOURCE	YEAR	ASIA & JAPAN	NORTH AMERICA	EEC	ROW	TOTAL
ASIA &	1983	0.06	0.04	0.02	0.03	0.15
JAPAN	1988	0.07	0.05	0.03	0.03	0.17
NA	1983	0.02	0.02	0.01	0.02	0.07
	1988	0.02	0.03	0.02	0.02	0.08
EEC	1983	0.01	0.02	0.18		0.22
	1988	0.02	0.02	0.20		0.24

TABLE 10

EXPORTS AS A SHARE OF GNP, BY DESTINATION
COUNTRY DISAGGREGATION

DESTINATION

SOURCE	YEAR	ASIA	JAPAN	USA	CANADA	EEC	ROW	TOTAL
ASIA	1983	0.05	0.03	0.05	0.00	0.02	0.04	0.20
	1988	0.10	0.05	0.08	0.01	0.04	0.05	0.32
JAP	1983	0.03		0.04	0.00	0.02	0.03	0.12
	1988	0.03		0.03	0.00	0.02	0.02	0.10
USA	1983	0.01	0.01		0.01	0.01	0.02	0.06
	1988	0.01	0.01		0.01	0.02	0.02	0.07
CAN	1983	0.01	0.01	0.17		0.02	0.03	0.24
	1988	0.01	0.02	0.19		0.02	0.03	0.26
EEC	1983	0.01	0.00	0.02	0.00		0.18	0.22
	1988	0.01	0.01	0.02	0.00		0.20	0.24

FIGURE 1: EXPORTS FROM ASIA AND JAPAN
BY REGION, 1983, 1988

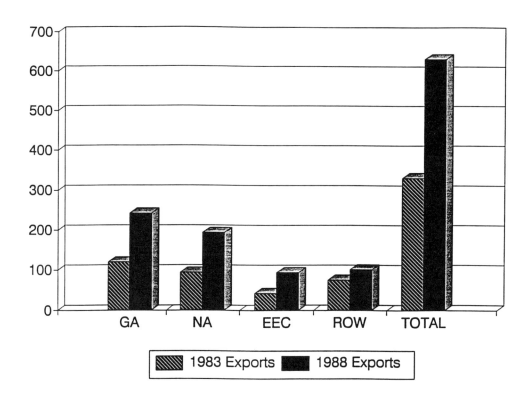

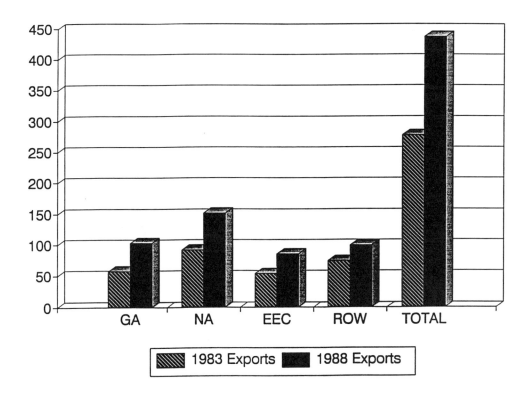

FIGURE 2: EXPORTS FROM NORTH AMERICA
BY REGION, 1983, 1988

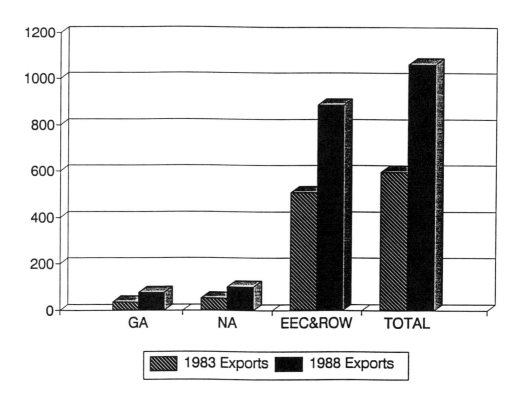

FIGURE 3: EXPORTS FROM THE EEC
BY REGION, 1983, 1988

FIGURE 4: EXPORTS FROM ASIA AND JAPAN
1988, ACTUAL AND GNP PREDICTED

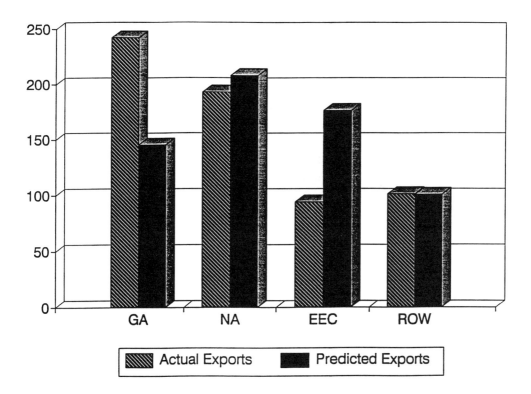

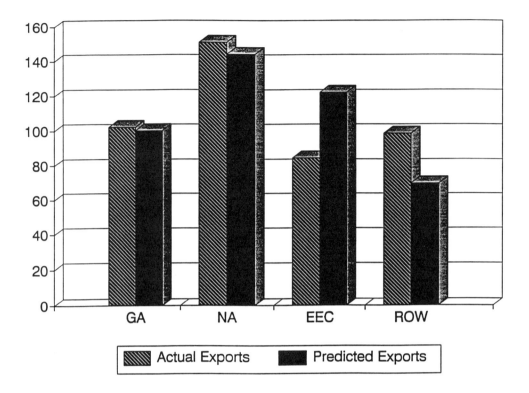

FIGURE 5: EXPORTS FROM NORTH AMERICA
1988, ACTUAL AND GNP PREDICTED

FIGURE 6: EXPORTS FROM THE EEC
1988, ACTUAL AND GNP PREDICTED

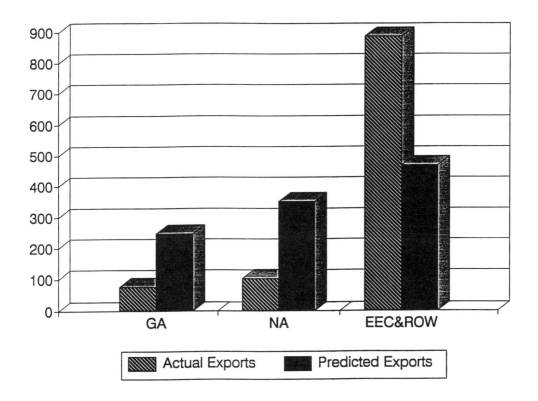

68

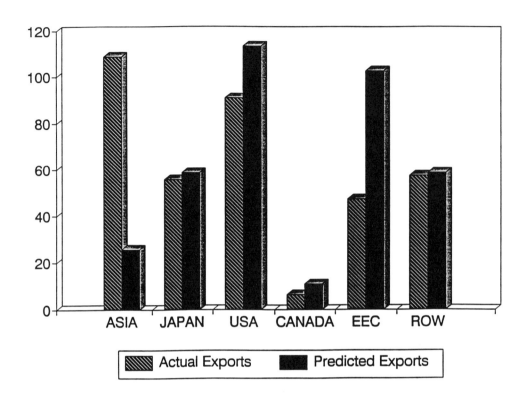

FIGURE 7: EXPORTS FROM ASIA, 1988
ACTUAL AND GNP PREDICTED

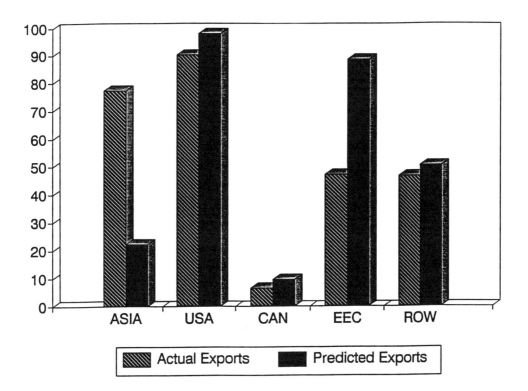

FIGURE 8: EXPORTS FROM JAPAN, 1988
ACTUAL AND GNP PREDICTED

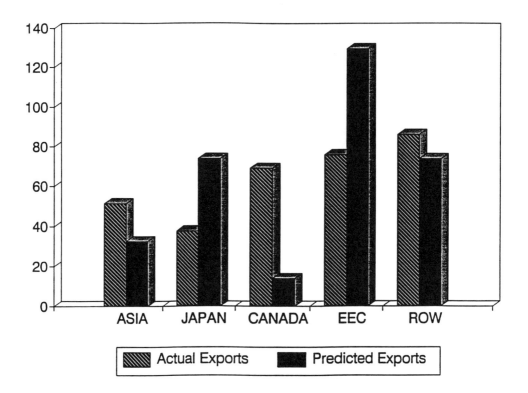

FIGURE 9: EXPORTS FROM THE USA, 1988
ACTUAL AND GNP PREDICTED

FIGURE 10: EXPORTS FROM CANADA, 1988
ACTUAL AND GNP PREDICTED

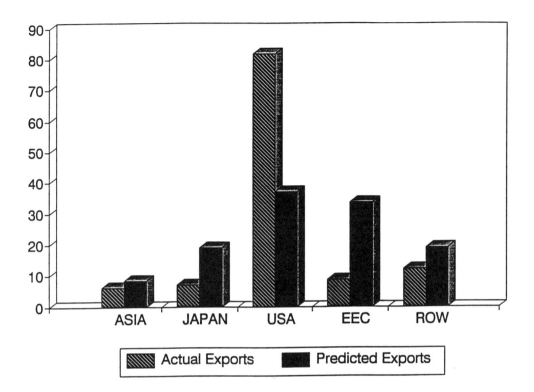

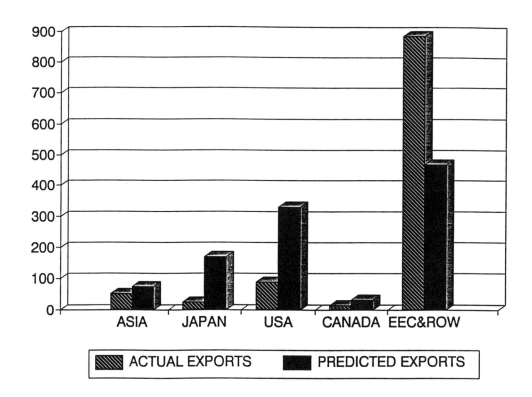

FIGURE 11: EXPORTS FROM THE EEC, 1988
ACTUAL AND GNP PREDICTED

6. MONETARY POLICY REGIMES, CENTRAL BANK COMMITMENTS, AND INTERNATIONAL POLICY COOPERATION

Masahiro Kawai
Institute of Social Science
University of Tokyo

and

Hideaki Murase
Faculty of Economics
Yokohama National University

ABSTRACT. This chapter develops a formal, game-theoretic model to analyze the importance of monetary policy regimes and central bank commitments in international policy games in a world economy of two interdependent countries. In particular, it examines the welfare implications of the choice of monetary policy instruments, the ability of monetary authorities to commit themselves to policy targets, private-sector responses and initiatives in international policy games, and international monetary policy cooperation. Important elements of the model are the strategic interactions between the monetary authority and the private sector and the policy interactions between the two countries' monetary authorities.
Earlier versions of this chapter were presented at the 1989 Annual Meeting of the Japan Association of Economics and Econometrics and at a seminar at the Australian National University. The authors thank to Takatoshi Ito, Yoshiyasu Ono, Kyoji Fukao, participants in the above meeting and seminar, and those who participated in this symposium.

1. INTRODUCTION

Let us consider four monetary policy regimes: the money-supply regime, the exchange-rate regime, the fixed exchange-rate system, and the interest-rate regime. The money-supply regime, where the authorities use the money supply as a policy instrument, is the one most commonly studied in the literature. The exchange-rate regime, where one authority controls the exchange rate and the other authority uses the money supply as its policy instrument, is essentially a managed exchange-rate system. A special case of this regime is the fixed exchange-rate system, in which one authority pegs the exchange rate while the other controls the money supply. The exchange rate regime and the fixed exchange-rate system appear appropriate to study such international monetary arrangements as the Bretton Woods System and the European Monetary System. The interest-rate regime, where one authority controls the interest rate and the other controls the money supply, the exchange rate, or the interest rate, has not been adequately investigated in the literature, mainly because it usually yields model indeterminacy.

For each monetary policy regime, four types of international policy games are examined: (A) a game where both countries' monetary authorities can credibly commit themselves to policy targets, (B) a game where only one country's monetary authority can credibly commit itself to a policy target, (C) a game where neither authority can credibly commit itself to a policy target, and (D) a game where the private sector has the power to commit itself to its choice variables. The relationship between the two authorities is symmetric in games A, C, and D and asymmetric in game B. The asymmetric game B is useful for the study of the role of the credible center country in an international monetary system but has not been carefully investigated in the literature. Game D is taken up in this chapter, since it makes the model determinate under the interest rate regime.

The organization of the chapter is as follows. Section 2 sets up the two-country macroeconomic model consisting of the monetary authorities and the private sector and explains these agents' objectives. Sections 3, 4, 5, and 6 examine the money-supply regime, the exchange-rate regime, the fixed exchange-rate system, and the interest-rate regime, respectively. Noncooperative and cooperative solutions are obtained in each regime. Section 7 discusses the implications of our results, and section 8 summarizes the conclusions.

2. THE MODEL

In this section, we present a formal model and explain the types of monetary policy regimes and international policy games that will be examined. The model is kept sufficiently simple so that decision rules of the agents and policy outcomes can be compared across different types of monetary policy regimes and international policy games.

2.1. The Two-Country Model

The model is a straightforward extension of the closed macroeconomic framework of wage contracting by Kydland and Prescott (1977) and Barro and Gordon (1983a,b) to a two-country world macroeconomic framework. Its structure is similar to those of Rogoff (1985), Turnovsky and d'Orey (1986), Canzoneri and Henderson (1988, 1991), and Giavazzi and Giovannini (1988, 1989). The model abstracts from stochastic shocks, uncertainty, and pertinent dynamics. The economies are described at their steady state and are assumed to be symmetric in size and structure. These abstractions and simplifications are made in order to sharply focus on the issues of monetary policy regimes, policy commitments, and interactions among authorities and private agents in a simple one-shot game framework.[1] The model is presented as follows:

---

[1] If stochastic shocks were present, a case could be made for discretionary monetary policy. Though our model does not leave any room for discretion, its implication could be obtained straightforwardly (but with a large amount of algebra) as is done by Rogoff (1985) and Giavazzi and Giovannini (1989) in a similar framework.

$$m - q = \phi(y + p - q) - \lambda i, \qquad \text{[Home Money Market Equilibrium]} \qquad (1)$$
$$y = \alpha y - \sigma(i - q^e + q) + \delta(s + p^* - p) + \beta(y^* - y),$$
$$\text{[Home Goods Demand]} \qquad (2)$$
$$y = \gamma(p - q^e) - \epsilon(s + p^* - p), \qquad \text{[Home Goods Supply]} \qquad (3)$$
$$q = \theta p + (1 - \theta)(p^* + s), \qquad \text{[Home General Price Index]} \qquad (4)$$
$$m^* - q^* = \phi(y^* + p^* - q^*) - \lambda i^*, \qquad \text{[Foreign Money Market Equilibrium]} \qquad (5)$$
$$y^* = \alpha y^* - \sigma(i^* - q^{*e} + q^*)$$
$$\qquad - \delta(s + p^* - p) - \beta(y^* - y), \qquad \text{[Foreign Goods Demand]} \qquad (6)$$
$$y^* = \gamma(p^* - q^{*e}) + \epsilon(s + p^* - p), \qquad \text{[Foreign Goods Supply]} \qquad (7)$$
$$q^* = \theta p^* + (1 - \theta)(p - s), \qquad \text{[Foreign General Price Index]} \qquad (8)$$
$$i - i^* = s^e - s, \qquad \text{[Uncovered Interest Rate Parity]} \qquad (9)$$

where

m = nominal money supply in logarithmic form,
y = real output, measured as a deviation from the natural rate level and expressed in logarithmic form,
p = the price of home goods in logarithmic form,
q = the general price index in logarithmic form,
q^e = the expected general price index in logarithmic form,
i = the nominal interest rate, expressed in natural units,
s = the spot exchange rate, measured as units of home currency per unit of foreign currency and expressed in logarithmic form,
s^e = the expected exchange rate in logarithmic form.

Foreign variables are expressed with asterisks (*) and home variables without. The Greek letters are positive constants.

Equations (1) and (5) describe the money market equilibrium conditions in the two countries. The money balances on the left-hand side and the output on the right-hand side are deflated by the country's general price index, q or q^*.

Equations (2) and (6) represent goods demand in the two countries. Goods demand depends on consumption, αy, investment, $- \sigma(i - q^e + q)$, and net exports, $\delta(s + p^* - p) + \beta(y^* - y)$. Note that the real interest rate, which affects investment inversely, is defined as the nominal interest rate, i, minus the expected rate of inflation in general price indices, $q^e - q$. Business firms undertaking investment form expectations, q^e.

Equations (3) and (7) define goods supply in the two economies in terms of standard Lucas supply functions adjusted for imported inputs. Each economy is assumed to be specialized in the production of a distinct good. Since labor and imported inputs are used for production in each country (Daniel, 1981), the supply of output is postulated to depend positively on the inverse of the real wage the firm faces, $p - q^e$,[2] and negatively on the relative price of imported

---

[2]With explicit time-scripts, the real interest rate in equation (2) and the inverse of real wages in equation (3) would be expressed, respectively, as $i_t - (q^e_{t+1/t} - q_t)$ and $p_t - q^e_{t/t-1}$, where $q^e_{t/t-1}$ is the expectation of q_t as of time $t-1$. In the steady state without permanent inflation, $q^e_{t+1/t} = q^e_{t/t-1} = q^e$.

inputs, s + p* − p. Here q^e is interpreted as the nominal wage determined by the negotiations between labor and management.[3]

Equations (4) and (8) define the general price index in the two countries. The expressions embody the assumption that θ and $1 - \theta$ $(-1 \leq \theta \leq 1)$ are fixed expenditure shares spent on domestic and imported goods.

Equation (9) is the usual uncovered interest−rate parity condition, which reflects the assumption of perfect substitutability between home and foreign bonds. It states that the differential between home and foreign nominal interest rates, i − i*, equals the expected rate of depreciation of the spot exchange rate, s^e − s.[4] The expected spot exchange rate, s^e, is nothing but the forward exchange rate, due to the assumed absence of an exchange risk premium.

Equations (1) to (9) contain nine endogenous variables and two policy instruments, y, y*, p, p*, q, q*, i, i*, m, m*, and s. In this model, 2 of the 5 variables, i, i*, m, m*, and s, will be chosen as policy instruments by the home and foreign monetary authorities.

2.2. The Maximization Problems of the Authorities and the Private Sector

The home and foreign monetary authorities' objectives are to maximize, respectively,

$$U = y - \tfrac{1}{2}\omega q^2, \quad U* = y* - \tfrac{1}{2}\omega q*^2, \quad \omega > 0, \tag{10}$$

---

[3]The underlying assumption here is that nominal wages are sticky. An alternative assumption would be to make nominal wages indexed fully and automatically to the general price indices, q, so as to keep labor's real wages constant. The latter assumption, however, would not bring out the important question of wage negotiators' nominal wage formation, which is one of the main issues of this chapter.

[4]With time−scripts, again, the expected rate of change in the spot exchange rate would be expressed as $s^e_{t+1/t} - s_t$. In the steady state without permanent depreciation or appreciation, $s^e_{t+1/t} = s^e$.

by setting their respective monetary policy variables.[5] The parameter ω is a constant, relative weight attached to the price objective and assumed to be the same for the two authorities.

For the sake of expository convenience, we consolidate home and foreign private agents into one private sector and regard them as a single decision maker. The objective of the private sector as a whole is to maximize

$$V = - \mu_1 (q - q^e)^2 - \mu_2 (q* - q*^e)^2 - \mu_3 (s - s^e)^2, \quad 0 < \mu_j < 1, \quad \Sigma\mu_j = 1 \quad (11)$$

by setting the values of q^e, $q*^e$, and s^e.[6] That is, the private sector maximizes the negative of a weighted average of the squared differences between the actual general price indices and their expectations, $(q - q^e)^2$ and $(q* - q*^e)^2$, and the squared difference between the actual spot exchange rate and its expectation, $(s - s^e)^2$. The price expectations q^e and $q*^e$ are formed both by business firms who decide on investment and by labor and management who negotiate on wages. Since s^e is interpreted as the forward exchange rate, it is thought of as determined by exchange market traders.[7]

2.3. Monetary Policy Regimes and International Policy Games

We examine four monetary policy regimes, depending on what variables are chosen as policy instruments by the monetary authorities. First is the money–supply regime, where both the home and foreign authorities use the money supply, m and m*, as their policy instrument. This is the regime commonly studied in the literature. Second is the exchange–rate regime, where one authority uses the exchange rate, s, and the other uses the money supply, m or m*, as policy instrument. This regime may be called the "managed exchange–rate system"

---

[5]These objective functions are standard in the literature; see Kydland and Prescott (1977) and Barro and Gordon (1983a). Another standard type is

$$U = - \nu(y - \bar{y})^2 - \nu_2 q^2, \quad \bar{y} > 0, \quad 0 < \nu_j < 1, \quad \Sigma\nu_j = 1,$$

which is used by Barro and Gordon (1983b). The fundamental results of this chapter do not hinge on which form of the objective function is chosen. Some minor change arises under the interest–rate regime (see footnote 18).

[6]It turns out that the parameter values μ_j do not affect the results.

[7]This formulation of the private agents' objectives is a direct extension of Backus and Driffil (1985) and others. Alternatively, home and foreign private agents may be regarded as separate decision makers who solve their respective maximization problems independently of each other: home business firms and wage negotiators may be assumed to maximize $- (q - q^e)^2$, foreign business firms and wage negotiators to maximize $- (q* - q*^e)^2$, and global exchange–market traders to maximize $- (s - s^e)^2$, each taking other agents' decision variables as given. Under this alternative formulation, the essential conclusions of this chapter remain intact.

(Giavazzi and Giovannini, 1989) and involves an essential asymmetry in the choice of policy instruments between the two authorities. Third is the fixed exchange-rate system, where one country's authority unilaterally pegs the exchange rate to the other country's currency by setting s = 0. This system is a special case of the exchange rate regime. Last is the interest-rate regime, where one authority controls the interest rate and the other controls the money supply, the exchange rate, or the interest rate. The interest-rate regime has typically been ignored in the literature, mainly because of the indeterminacy problem it faces. (See Sargent and Wallace, 1975; McCallum, 1981; and Canzoneri, Henderson, and Rogoff, 1983.) This chapter proposes a type of game, game D below, that makes the model determinate even under the interest-rate regime.

For each monetary policy regime, we consider four different types of games, depending on who can act as a leader, i.e., can make credible policy commitment, in an international policy game:

A: The home and foreign monetary authorities are leaders and the private sector is a follower in the sense that the former two can credibly commit themselves to their respective policy targets, to which the latter responds optimally.

B: The home monetary authority is a leader and the foreign monetary authority and the private sector are followers, in the sense that the former can credibly commit itself to its policy target, while the latter two, acting as Nash-Cournot players with each other, respond optimally to the home authority's policy target.

C: No leader exists in international policy games in the sense that both authorities and the private sector play a Nash-Cournot game.

D: The private sector is a leader and the home and foreign monetary authorities are followers in the sense that the former credibly sets its expectations of general price indices and exchange rates, to which the latter two respond optimally.

Here, the concept of commitment is defined in terms of the agent's ability to assume leadership in setting its choice variable.

The relationship between the two monetary authorities is symmetric in Games A, C, and D and asymmetric in game B. The exchange rate regime in game A or B may be called the Target Zone System, since exchange-rate targeting is assumed fully credible. Game B is appropriate to study the role of the credible center country in an international monetary system. A version of the money supply regime in game C is often alleged to approximate the current flexible-rate system. Game D describes the situation where the private sector (such as the labor union) has the power to set its choice variables (such as the nominal wage rate) as a leader and the monetary authorities act as followers. Such a game is taken up here, since it generates determinate solutions under the interest-rate regime.

In each game, the two monetary authorities may or may not cooperate when controlling their policy instruments and, thus, noncooperative and cooperative solutions are obtained and compared (see the pioneering work of Hamada, 1985). At the outset of model analysis, the expectations variables, q^e, q^{*e}, and s^e, are not assumed to be rational, in the sense of consistency with the model, but they turn out to be model-consistent in equilibrium. Hence, $q = q^e = m$, $q^* = q^{*e} = m^*$, and $s = s^e = m - m^*$ in equilibrium, and the monetary authorities cannot keep output systematically above its natural rate. The implication is that the private sector always achieves its highest (bliss) level of utility, and the authority's utility depends inversely on the squared money-supply level.

3. THE MONEY-SUPPLY REGIME

In the money-supply regime, the home and foreign authorities control the money supply as their policy instrument. Given that m and m* are policy variables, the solution to equations (1) to (9) can be expressed as

$$y = \Psi_1(m - q^e) + \Psi_2(m^* - q^{*e}) + (\lambda\Psi_1 - \sigma\Psi_3)(s^e + q^{*e} - q^e), \qquad (12a)$$

$$y^* = \Psi_2(m - q^e) + \Psi_1(m^* - q^{*e}) - (\lambda\Psi_1 - \sigma\Psi_3)(s^e + q^{*e} - q^e), \qquad (12b)$$

$$q = q^e + \Pi_1(m - q^e) + \Pi_2(m^* - q^{*e}) + (\lambda\Pi_1 - \sigma\Pi_3)(s^e + q^{*e} - q^e), \qquad (12c)$$

$$q^* = q^{*e} + \Pi_2(m - q^e) + \Pi_1(m^* - q^{*e}) - (\lambda\Pi_1 - \sigma\Pi_3)(s^e + q^{*e} - q^e), \qquad (12d)$$

$$s = s^e + A_1[(m - q^e) - (m^* - q^{*e})] + (\lambda A_1 - \sigma A_2 - 1)(s^e + q^{*e} - q^e), \qquad (12e)$$

where

$$\psi_1 = \frac{\gamma}{2}\left[\frac{\sigma}{\Delta_1} + \frac{2\delta + \sigma(2\theta - 1)}{\Delta_2}\right] > 0,$$

$$\psi_2 = \frac{\gamma}{2}\left[\frac{\sigma}{\Delta_1} - \frac{2\delta + \sigma(2\theta - 1)}{\Delta_2}\right] \gtrless 0,$$

$$\psi_3 = \frac{1}{2}\left[\frac{\gamma\lambda}{\Delta_1} + \frac{\gamma[\lambda + 2(1 - \theta)(1 - \phi)] + 2\epsilon(1 + \lambda)}{\Delta_1}\right] > 0,$$

$$\pi_1 = \frac{1}{2}\left[\frac{\sigma}{\Delta_1} + (2\theta - 1)\frac{2\delta + \sigma(2\theta - 1) + 2\epsilon(1 - \alpha + 2\beta)}{\Delta_2}\right] + (1 - \theta)A_1 > 0,$$

$$\pi_2 = \frac{1}{2}\left[\frac{\sigma}{\Delta_1} - (2\theta - 1)\frac{2\delta + \sigma(2\theta - 1) + 2\epsilon(1 - \alpha + 2\beta)}{\Delta_2}\right] - (1 - \theta)A_1 \gtrless 0,$$

$$\pi_3 = \frac{1}{2}\left[\frac{\lambda}{\Delta_1} + (2\theta - 1)\frac{\lambda + 2(1 - \theta)(1 - \phi) - 2\epsilon\phi}{\Delta_2}\right] + (1 - \theta)A_2 \gtrless 0,$$

$$A_1 = \frac{2\delta + \sigma(2\theta - 1) + (1 - \alpha + 2\beta)(\gamma + 2\epsilon)}{\Delta_2} > 0,$$

$$A_2 = -\frac{(1 - \phi)(2\theta - 1) + \phi(1 + \gamma + 2\epsilon)}{\Delta_2} < 0,$$

$$\Delta_1 = \gamma\lambda(1 - \alpha) + \sigma(1 + \lambda + \gamma\phi) > 0,$$

$$\Delta_2 = (1 + \lambda + \gamma\phi)[2\delta + \sigma(2\theta - 1)] + (1 - \alpha + 2\beta)\{\gamma[\theta + 2(1 - \theta)(1 - \phi)] + 2\epsilon(1 + \lambda)\} > 0.$$

3.1. Game A: Home and Foreign Monetary Authorities as Leader

Game A represents the case where the home and foreign monetary authorities act as Stackelberg leaders vis-a-vis the private sector. They become leaders by virtue of the assumed ability to credibly commit themselves to their money—supply targets.[8]

In order to solve the game, we must first obtain the private sector's optimal response to m and m*. The private sector maximizes V as defined by equation (11) over q^e, q^{*e}, and s^e, using equations (12c), (12d), and (12e) and taking m and m* as given. The first—order conditions are

$$q^e = m, \quad q^{*e} = m^*, \quad s^e = m - m^*, \tag{13}$$

which also satisfy the second—order condition for maximization. The private sector gives full credibility to the home and foreign monetary authorities by way of setting reaction functions (13) and acting as a Stackelberg follower. The two monetary authorities, as Stackelberg leaders, take the private sector's optimal response (equations (13)) into consideration and select the target money supplies, m and m*. They may or may not cooperate in selecting m and m*.

When the home and foreign monetary authorities do not cooperate, they solve the following maximization problems:

$$\underset{(m)}{\text{Max}} \ U, \text{ subject to equations (12), (13), given } m^*,$$

$$\underset{(m^*)}{\text{Max}} \ U^*, \text{ subject to equations (12), (13), given } m.$$

That is, the authorities maximize U over m and U* over m*, respectively, taking each other's policy variable as given, subject to the economic structure (equations (12)) and the private—sector optimal response (equations (13)). The first—order conditions of these maximization problems yield the noncooperative solution

$$m = q = q^e = 0, \quad m^* = q^* = q^{*e} = 0, \quad s = s^e = 0.$$

This means that all agents achieve their highest level of utility, which is zero.

When the home and foreign monetary authorities cooperate, they are assumed to jointly maximize the collective utility:

---

[8]This game can be best understood by considering the following three steps:

1. The home and foreign monetary authorities announce their money—supply targets, m and m*, respectively.

2. The private sector takes m and m* as credibly given and sets the expected general price indices (q^e and q^{*e}) and the expected spot exchange rate (the forward exchange rate, s^e) as optimal responses to the announced m and m*.

3. The home and foreign monetary authorities actually implement the announced money—supply targets, m and m*.

This interpretation of game A in the money supply regime is consistent with the "credibility" concept discussed in a static closed—economy framework by Kydland and Prescott (1977) and Barro and Gordon (1983a,b). It is also consistent with the "precommitment" or "reputation" concept discussed in a dynamic two—country framework by Oudiz and Sachs (1985) and Currie, Levine and Vidalis (1987). The well-known problem with this game, however, is that it is not time consistent.

$$\underset{(m,m*)}{\text{Max}} \tau U + (1 - \tau)U*, \text{ subject to equations (12), (13)}.$$

Here τ and $1 - \tau$ $(0 < \tau < 1)$ are the weights attached to home and foreign utilities, respectively. If the authorities can find the range of τ yielding bargains that dominate the noncooperative outcome and, thus, satisfy individual rationality, then they would have an incentive to strike bargains and coordinate monetary policy with each other.[9] In symmetric games with symmetric policy instruments such as the case under consideration, $\tau = \frac{1}{2}$ is a natural candidate value of the bargain. The cooperative solution is obtained from the first-order conditions of this collective maximization problem:

$$m = q = q^e = 0, \quad m* = q* = q*^e = 0, \quad s = s^e = 0,$$

which turns out to be independent of the value of τ. The solution again attains the highest level of utility, zero, for all players.

Note that rational expectations prevail (i.e., $q = q^e$, $q* = q*^e$, $s = s^e$) in equilibrium, and the money supply–solutions are the same and zero regardless of whether the home and foreign monetary authorities cooperate. The utility levels of the authorities and the private sector are the highest possible so that Pareto optimality is ensured. The implication is that when the two authorities can credibly commit themselves to money–supply targets, they can achieve the maximum welfare no matter whether they cooperate or not. This is interpreted as an ideal case for Milton Friedman's classic advocacy for flexible exchange rates.

3.2. Game B: Home Authority as Leader

In game B, the home authority credibly commits itself to a money–supply target, to which the foreign authority and the private sector respond optimally. In responding to the home authority's money–supply target, m, the foreign authority sets $m*$ and the private sector sets q^e, $q*^{e,}$ and s^e, as Nash–Cournot players with each other and as Stackelberg followers vis-à-vis the home authority. Taking the optimal responses of the foreign authority and the private sector into consideration, the home monetary authority sets m as a Stackelberg leader. The home and foreign authorities may or may not cooperate when setting m and $m*$.

When the two authorities do not cooperate, the solution can be obtained by the following two procedures. First, the reaction functions of the foreign monetary authority and the private sector are derived from their respective maximization problems,

$$\underset{(m*)}{\text{Max}} U*, \text{ subject to equations (12), given } m, q^e, q*^e, s^e,$$

$$\underset{(q^e,q*^e,s^e)}{\text{Max}} V, \text{ subject to equations (12), given } m, m*.$$

---

[9]A Nash bargaining game would be an alternative formulation of policy cooperation. In asymmetric monetary policy regimes (such as the exchange–rate regime) or asymmetric international policy games (such as game B), however, Nash bargaining solutions are extremely complicated and often difficult to obtain. Our formulation is much easier to work with.

That is, they maximize the objective functions over their respective choice variables, with all other players' choice variables as given. The first-order conditions of these maximization problems yield

$$m* = q*^e = q* = -\frac{\psi_1}{\omega\pi_1}, \quad q^e = m, \quad s^e = m - \frac{\psi_1}{\omega\pi_1}. \tag{14}$$

These are the reaction functions of the foreign monetary authority and the private sector, expressed as functions of m.

Second, the home monetary authority sets m to maximize its own utility subject to equations (14), that is,

$$\underset{(m)}{\text{Max}} \; U, \text{ subject to equations (12), (14).}$$

This maximization problem yields the noncooperative solution,

$$m = q = q^e = 0, \quad m* = q* = q*^e = -\frac{\psi_1}{\omega\pi_1}, s = s^e = -\frac{\psi_1}{\omega\pi_1}. \tag{15}$$

Hence, in equilibrium the home authority's and the private sector's utility levels are zero, while the foreign utility is $-(1/2\omega)(\Psi_1/\Pi_1)^2$.

The concept of policy cooperation in Game B may appear paradoxical at first sight, since the home authority acts as a leader and the foreign authority, together with the private sector, acts as a follower. Policy cooperation is, however, well defined because the two authorities can maximize the collective utility, keeping the leader–follower relationship intact.[10] Consider the following two procedures to obtain the cooperative solution.

First, the reaction functions of the foreign monetary authority and the private sector are derived from

$$\underset{(m*)}{\text{Max}} \; \tau U + (1 - \tau)U*, \text{ subject to equations (12), given m, } q^e, q*^e, s^e,$$

$$\underset{(q^e, q*^e, s^e)}{\text{Max}} \; V, \text{ subject to equations (12), given m, m*.}$$

Note that the foreign authority maximizes the collective utility over m*, taking all other players' choice variables as given. The private sector's maximization problem is the same as before. The first-order conditions of these two maximization problems yield

$$m* = q*^e = \frac{1}{1 - \tau} \left(\frac{(1 - \tau)\psi_1 + \tau\psi_2}{\omega\pi_1} - \tau\frac{\pi_2}{\pi_1}m \right), \quad q^e = m, \tag{16}$$

$$s^e = m - \frac{1}{1 - \tau} \left(\frac{(1 - \tau)\psi_1 + \tau\psi_2}{\omega\pi_1} - \tau\frac{\pi_2}{\pi_1}m \right).$$

---

[10]This chapter defines policy cooperation as the two authorities' maximization of the collective utility $\tau U + (1 - \tau)U*$. Since the authorities are not required to maximize the collective utility <u>simultaneously</u>, it is possible to argue that this definition is unsatisfactory and that policy cooperation in game B should be identical to that in game A. However, our definition produces some interesting results and deserves attention.

Second, the home authority's maximization problem is

$$\underset{(m)}{\text{Max}}\ \tau U + (1 - \tau)U^*, \text{ subject to equations (12), (16).}$$

From the first-order condition of this maximization problem, we obtain the cooperative solution:

$$m = q = q^e = \frac{\pi_2[(1 - \tau)\psi_1 + \tau\psi_2]}{\omega[(1 - \tau)\pi_1^2 + \tau\pi_2^2]}, \quad m^* = q^* = q^{*e} = \frac{\pi_1[(1 - \tau)\psi_1 + \tau\psi_2]}{\omega[(1 - \tau)\pi_1^2 + \tau\pi_2^2]},$$

$$s = s^e = \frac{(\pi_2 - \pi_1)[(1 - \tau)\psi_1 + \tau\psi_2]}{\omega[(1 - \tau)\pi_1^2 + \tau\pi_2^2]}. \tag{17}$$

It is straightforward to show that individual rationality requires

$$\tau = \frac{\psi_1}{\psi_1 - \psi_2},$$

because otherwise a bargain would not be struck by both authorities. (It is easily shown that $\Psi_1 > \Psi_2$ and $\tau > \frac{1}{2}$.) Note that in this game the relationship between the home and foreign authorities is asymmetric and, hence, $\tau = \frac{1}{2}$ does not constitute a Pareto-dominant bargain. Moreover, if $\Psi_2 \geq 0$, then τ exceeds or equals unity, but a bargain will still be struck. The weight τ can exceed unity because in this three-player game, unlike in two-player games, the cooperative and noncooperative games do not share the same utility possibility frontier.[11] With $\tau = \Psi_1/(\Psi_1 - \Psi_2)$, the cooperative solution is

$$m = q^e = q = 0, \quad m^* = q^{*e} = q^* = 0, \quad s = s^e = 0.$$

This solution, therefore, ensures maximum utility for every player.

To summarize game B, the home authority, which is credibly committed to a money supply target, achieves the highest utility in the absence of international policy cooperation. The foreign authority, which lacks policy credibility and therefore suffers from inefficiency without international policy cooperation, can achieve the maximum welfare by making a collective decision with the credible home authority. Hence, for an authority lacking credibility, policy cooperation with a credible authority can be a substitute for establishing credibility.

3.3. Game C: No Leadership

Game C represents the case where the monetary authorities cannot credibly commit themselves to policy targets. The monetary authorities behave as Nash-Cournot players vis-à-vis the private sector.

---

[11]When $\psi_2 > 0$, by setting $\tau = \psi_1/(\psi_1 - \psi_2) > 1$ the foreign authority can achieve the maximum utility despite the negative weight attached to U* in the collective utility. This peculiar result obtains because the utility possibility frontiers are not comparable between the noncooperative and cooperative cases.

When the authorities set money supplies noncooperatively, they maximize U over m and U* over m*, respectively, by taking as given each other's money supply and the private sector's expectations:

$\underset{(m)}{\text{Max}}$ U, subject to equations (12), given m*, q^e, q^{*e}, s^e,

$\underset{(m*)}{\text{Max}}$ U*, subject to equations (12), given m, q^e, q^{*e}, s^e.

The first-order conditions of these maximization problems are

$$q = q* = \frac{\psi_1}{\omega \pi_1},$$
(18)

which constitute the authorities' reaction functions. The private sector's reaction function has already been derived in equations (13). Therefore, the noncooperative solution with no leadership is obtained by combining equations (18) and (13):

$$m = q = q^e = \frac{\psi_1}{\omega \pi_1}, \quad m* = q* = q^{*e} = \frac{\psi_1}{\omega \pi_1}, \quad s = s^e = 0.$$
(19)

This is the solution under the typical laissez-faire flexible exchange-rate system often studied in the literature. It indicates that the money supply is excessive in a laissez-faire flexible exchange-rate system, but not as much as in the case of a closed economy model.[12]

When the home and foreign monetary authorities coordinate their money supplies, while playing a Nash-Cournot game vis-à-vis the private sector, they jointly solve

$\underset{(m,m*)}{\text{Max}} \tau U + (1 - \tau)U*$, subject to equations (12), given q^e, q^{*e}, s^e.

The first-order conditions of this maximization problem yield

$$q = \frac{\pi_1[\tau\psi_1 + (1 - \tau)\psi_2] - \pi_2[\tau\psi_2 + (1 - \tau)\psi_1]}{\omega\tau(\pi_1^2 - \pi_2^2)},$$
(20)

$$q* = \frac{\pi_1[\tau\psi_2 + (1 - \tau)\psi_1] - \pi_2[\tau\psi_1 + (1 - \tau)\psi_2]}{\omega(1 - \tau)(\pi_1^2 - \pi_2^2)},$$

which constitute the authorities' joint reaction functions. The private sector's reactions are given, again, by equations (13). Hence the cooperative solution is obtained from equations (13) and (20):

$$m = q = q^e = \frac{\pi_1[\tau\psi_1 + (1 - \tau)\psi_2] - \pi_2[\tau\psi_2 + (1 - \tau)\psi_1]}{\omega\tau(\pi_1^2 - \pi_2^2)},$$

$$m* = q* = q^{*e} = \frac{\pi_1[\tau\psi_2 + (1 - \tau)\psi_1] - \pi_2[\tau\psi_1 + (1 - \tau)\psi_2]}{\omega(1 - \tau)(\pi_1^2 - \pi_2^2)},$$
(21)

---

[12]Our model is reduced to a closed-economy model if $\delta = \beta = \epsilon = \theta - 1 = 0$. In this case, a noncooperative game between the monetary authority and the private sector yields the money supply level of $\frac{\gamma}{\omega}$, which exceeds $\frac{\psi_1}{\omega\pi_1}$.

$$s = s^e = \frac{(1 - 2\tau)(\pi_1\psi_2 - \pi_2\psi_1)}{\omega\tau(1 - \tau)(\pi_1^2 - \pi_2^2)}.$$

In order to find the range of τ that satisfies individual rationality, cooperative and noncooperative solutions must be carefully defined and compared. The cooperative and noncooperative solutions to be compared are not equations (19) and (21), but equations (18) and (20). That is, the comparison requires that private-sector expectations be fixed (see Carraro and Giavazzi, 1991). The task then is to find the range of τ that ensures individual rationality, i.e.,

$$U^c \geq U^n \text{ and } U^{*c} \geq U^{*n},$$

where U^c and U^{*c} are the home and foreign authorities' utility levels given equations (20) and U^n and U^{*n} are those given equations (18). Since private-sector expectations are fixed, the game is effectively reduced to a two-player game, and such a range of τ between zero and unity always exists. A simple example is $\tau = \frac{1}{2}$, which makes sense because the economic structure, the type of game, and the choice of policy instruments are all symmetric between the two countries. Therefore, each authority has sufficient incentive to coordinate money supply once private-sector expectations are held constant. However, this does not mean that policy cooperation brings about a Pareto-superior outcome.

It can be shown that the money supply level of at least one country under cooperation must exceed the level under noncooperation.[13] This means that international policy cooperation cannot be Pareto dominant and may be Pareto inferior. For example, when $\tau = \frac{1}{2}$, both authorities' welfare levels under cooperation are $-\frac{1}{2\omega}\gamma^2$, which are lower than those without cooperation, since $\gamma^2 > (\Psi_1/\Pi_1)^2$. Generally, both authorities cannot simultaneously be made better off by international monetary policy coordination, and may actually be made worse off. This is similar to the result noted by Rogoff (1985) and Currie, Levine, and Vidalis (1987).

The reason why international policy cooperation cannot be Pareto dominant, although each authority has a sufficient incentive to cooperate for a given set of private-sector expectations, is provided by Carraro and Giavazzi (1991). Without policy coordination, each monetary authority attempts to reduce the

---

[13]Let the home and foreign money supply solutions under cooperation be

$$m^c = \frac{\pi_1[\tau\psi_1 + (1 - \tau)\psi_2] - \pi_2[\tau\psi_2 + (1 - \tau)\psi_1]}{\omega\tau(\pi_1^2 - \pi_2^2)},$$

$$m^{*c} = \frac{\pi_1[\tau\psi_2 + (1 - \tau)\psi_1] - \pi_2[\tau\psi_1 + (1 - \tau)\psi_2]}{\omega(1 - \tau)(\pi_1^2 - \pi_2^2)}.$$

When $\tau = \frac{1}{2}$, it is easy to see that $m^c = m^{*c} = \frac{\gamma}{\omega}$, which exceeds $-\frac{\psi_1}{\omega\pi_1}$, a noncooperative solution. When $0 < \tau < 1$, m^c is a monotonically decreasing function of τ and m^{*c} is a monotonically increasing function of τ. Then it is straightforward to show that $m^{*c} < \frac{\gamma}{\omega} < m^c$ for $0 < \tau < \frac{1}{2}$ and that $m^c < \frac{\gamma}{\omega} < m^{*c}$ for $\frac{1}{2} < \tau < 1$. Since $0 < \frac{\psi_1}{\omega\pi_1} < \frac{\gamma}{\omega}$, the cooperative money supply solution of at least one authority exceeds the noncooperative solution.

general price index by appreciating the real exchange rate, thereby importing low prices from abroad at a small output cost. When both monetary authorities attempt to do this, the equilibrium is characterized by low levels of money supply. However, under policy coordination, there is no incentive to competitively appreciate the real exchange rate and so the game's outcome is determined mainly by strategic interactions between the authorities and the private sector. As in the Barro–Gordon [1983a, b] closed–economy model, such interactions give rise to excessive money supplies without raising output, thus reducing the authorities' welfare.

3.4. Game D: Private Sector as Leader

In game D, the private sector acts as a leader and the home and foreign monetary authorities act as followers in the sense that the former commits itself credibly to the price and exchange rate expectations, to which the latter two respond optimally. This game represents the situation where the private sector has the ability to credibly set its expectations of prices and exchange rates (such as the labor union making credible nominal–wage commitment) and the monetary authorities act as followers. The authorities may or may not cooperate.

It turns out that the solutions of game D, whether noncooperative or cooperative, are identical to those of game C. This is essentially because the private sector always sets $q^e = m$, $q^{*e} = m^*$, and $s^e = m - m^*$ so that its leadership does not affect its own or the authorities' behavior. The implications for international policy coordination are also the same as those of game C.

4. THE EXCHANGE–RATE REGIME

The exchange–rate regime is asymmetric, in the sense that one country's authority uses the exchange rate and the other country's authority uses the money supply as their policy instruments. The authority controlling its own money supply assumes that it cannot affect the exchange rate, whereas the authority controlling the exchange rate believes that it can directly affect the general price index at a small output cost. This is essentially a "managed exchange–rate system." If the authority controlling the money supply credibly commits itself to a money–supply target, the regime may approximate the European Monetary System (EMS). In the EMS, the center country, Germany, adopts a credible money–supply policy and the peripheral countries attempt to stabilize their exchange rates with occasional realignments. If the authority controlling the exchange rate credibly commits itself to an exchange–rate target, the system may be called the "Target Zone System."

When the home authority controls the money supply, m, and the foreign authority controls the exchange rate, s, the solution to equations (1) to (9) can be expressed as

$$y = (\Psi_1 + \Psi_2)(m - q^e) - \frac{\psi_2}{A_1}(s - s^e)$$

$$+ [\lambda\Psi_1 - \sigma\Psi_3 + \frac{\psi_2}{A_1}(\lambda A_1 - \sigma A_2 - 1)](s^e + q^{*e} - q^e), \qquad (22a)$$

$$y^* = (\Psi_1 + \Psi_2)(m - q^e) - \frac{\psi_1}{A_1}(s - s^e)$$

$$- [\lambda\Psi_1 - \sigma\Psi_3 - \frac{\psi_1}{A_1}(\lambda A_1 - \sigma A_2 - 1)](s^e + q^{*e} - q^e), \qquad (22b)$$

$$q = q^e + (\Pi_1 + \Pi_2)(m - q^e) - \frac{\pi_2}{A_1}(s - s^e)$$

$$+ [\lambda\Psi_1 - \sigma\Pi_3 + \frac{\pi_2}{A_1}(\lambda A_1 - \sigma A_2 - 1)](s^e + q^{*e} - q^e), \qquad (22c)$$

$$q^* = q^{*e} + (\Pi_1 + \Pi_2)(m - q^e) - \frac{\pi_1}{A_1}(s - s^e)$$

$$- [\lambda\Psi_1 - \sigma\Pi_3 - \frac{\pi_1}{A_1}(\lambda A_1 - \sigma A_2 - 1)](s^e + q^{*e} - q^e), \qquad (22d)$$

where Ψ_1, Ψ_2, Ψ_3, Π_1, Π_2, Π_3, A_1, and A_2 have been defined previously. If, on the other hand, the home authority controls the exchange rate and the foreign authority controls the money supply, the solutions can similarly be found.

4.1. Game A: Home and Foreign Monetary Authorities as Leader

When the home and foreign monetary authorities credibly commit themselves to the exchange rate and the money supply, and the private sector reacts to the authorities' committed policies, the outcome turns out to be completely identical to that of game A of the money-supply regime. This implies that when both authorities' policies are fully credible, the money-supply and exchange-rate regimes are effectively the same. Both can achieve the highest welfare levels regardless of the presence or absence of international policy cooperation. A switch in the home and foreign policy instruments does not affect the conclusion, again, due to the underlying symmetry of the two economies.

4.2. Game B: Home Monetary Authority as Leader

In game B, the home monetary authority commits itself credibly to its policy target (the money supply, m, or the exchange rate, s), and the foreign authority and the private sector respond optimally to the home authority's committed policy target. This case is quite interesting, because both the choice of monetary policy instruments and the structure of the game are asymmetric between the home and foreign monetary authorities.

Let us first take up the case where the home authority controls the money supply, m, acting as a Stackelberg leader, and the foreign authority controls the exchange rate, s, acting as a Stackelberg follower together with the private sector. In this case the noncooperative and cooperative solutions are the same as those of game B of the money-supply regime. Hence, as long as the leader authority controls its money supply (m), the choice of the follower authority's policy instrument (whether m* or s) does not matter. The implications for international policy coordination are also the same: it can be beneficial to the follower, without worsening the leader's welfare, because it amounts to virtually providing with the follower some policy credibility.

Next, let us consider the case where the credible home authority controls the exchange rate, s, and the noncredible foreign authority controls the money supply, m*.

The noncooperative solution is obtained in two procedures. First, the foreign authority maximizes U* over m* and the private sector maximizes V over q^e, q^{*e} and s^e by taking each other's choice variables and the exchange rate, s, as given. The first-order conditions of these maximization problems yield

$$m* = \frac{\gamma}{\omega}, \quad q^e = s + \frac{\gamma}{\omega}, \quad q^{*e} = \frac{\gamma}{\omega}, \quad s^e = s. \tag{23}$$

Second, the home monetary authority maximizes U over s subject to equations (23), which yields the noncooperative solution,

$$m = q = q^e = 0, \quad m* = q* = q^{*e} = \frac{\gamma}{\omega}, \quad s = s^e = -\frac{\gamma}{\omega}.$$

This means that the home authority achieves the maximum welfare, while the foreign authority's welfare level is very low at $-\frac{1}{2\omega}\gamma^2$.

In the case of policy cooperation, the foreign authority maximizes $\tau U + (1 - \tau)U*$ over m* and the private sector maximizes V over q^e, q^{*e} and s^e, each taking the other's choice variables and the exchange rate, s, as given, which yields

$$m* = \frac{\gamma}{\omega} - \tau s, \quad q^e = \frac{\gamma}{\omega} + (1 - \tau)s, \quad q^{*e} = \frac{\gamma}{\omega} - \tau s, \quad s^e = s. \tag{24}$$

Second, the home authority maximizes $\tau U + (1 - \tau)U*$ over s subject to equations (24), which results in the cooperative solution,

$$m = q = q^e = \frac{\gamma}{\omega}, \quad m* = q* = q^{*e} = \frac{\gamma}{\omega}, \quad s = s^e = 0.$$

The cooperative solution turns out to be independent of τ and reduces the level of home welfare from zero to $-\frac{1}{2\omega}\gamma^2$. This is the same as the foreign welfare level, which is unchanged from the noncooperative case. Therefore, policy coordination between the two authorities is Pareto inferior in this three-player game.

4.3. Game C and Game D

In games C and D, both monetary authorities lack policy credibility and, hence, cannot behave as leaders. The private sector acts as a leader in game D, but not in game C. The solutions in these two games turn out to be the same. Only the result for game C is presented here on the assumption that the home authority controls m and the foreign authority controls s. The choice of policy instruments by the home and foreign authorities can be reversed with the corresponding changes in welfare due to the symmetric relationship between the authorities.

Without policy cooperation, the home authority, the foreign authority, and the private sector maximize U over m, U* over s, and V over q^e, $q*^e$ and s^e, each taking all other players' choice variables as given, subject to equations (22). These maximization problems yield the noncooperative solution,

$$m = q = q^e = \frac{\gamma}{\omega}, \quad m* = q* = q*^e = \frac{1}{\omega} \frac{\psi_1}{\pi_1}, \quad s = s^e = \frac{\pi_1\psi_2 - \pi_2\psi_1}{\omega\pi_1(\pi_1 + \pi_2)}.$$

Since $\gamma^2 > (\Psi_1/\Pi_1)^2$, the home authority's welfare level falls short of the foreign level.

When the two authorities cooperate, they jointly maximize $\tau U + (1 - \tau)U*$ over m and s, taking the private-sector expectations, q^e, $q*^e$, s^e, as given. The private sector maximizes V over q^e, $q*^e$ and s^e, taking m and s as given. These maximization problems yield the cooperative solution identical to that of game C of the money-supply regime, namely, equations (21). The welfare outcome under cooperation is similar to the case of the money-supply regime: international policy coordination does not raise, and may in fact reduce, both authorities' welfare.

5. THE FIXED EXCHANGE–RATE SYSTEM

This section discusses a special case of the exchange-rate regime, that is, the case where one country's authority fixes the exchange rate unilaterally against the other country's currency and the latter authority controls the money supply.[14] Since, by assumption, the authority fixing the exchange rate does not optimize, this regime is treated separately from the exchange-rate regime of the previous section. If the authority controlling its money supply can credibly commit itself to a money-supply target, the system may approximate the Bretton Woods System. Under the Bretton Woods System, the center country, the United States, committed itself to a credible money-supply policy and the peripheral countries pegged their exchange rates against the U.S. dollar (McKinnon, 1992).

In this section, exchange rate pegging may or may not be considered as credible.

When the home authority controls the money supply and the foreign authority fixes the exchange rate, the solution to equations (1) to (9) becomes identical to equations (22), the solution for the exchange-rate regime, except that s will have to be set equal to zero in equilibrium. When the home authority fixes the exchange rate and the foreign authority controls the money supply, the solution can similarly be obtained. In this system, U (or U*) and $\tau U + (1 - \tau)U*$ are maximized under noncooperation and cooperation, respectively, by the authority not fixing the exchange rate.

---

[14]This formulation of the fixed exchange rate system is similar to that of Canzoneri and Gray (1985).

5.1. Game A: Home and Foreign Monetary Authorities as Leader

When the home and foreign monetary authorities credibly commit themselves to targeting the money supply and fixing the exchange rate, and the private sector reacts to the authorities' commitments, the outcome is completely identical to game A of the money supply or exchange-rate regime. Hence, with fully credible policies, the authorities and the private sector can achieve the highest welfare regardless of whether the exchange rate is fixed, controlled, or flexible and whether or not international policy cooperation is present.

5.2. Game B: Home Monetary Authority as Leader

In game B, there are two possibilities: 1) the home monetary authority credibly commits itself to a money-supply target and the foreign authority simply sets s = 0, and 2) the home authority credibly commits itself to a fixed exchange rate (s = 0) and the foreign authority responds to the home authority's fixed rate commitment by controlling the money supply. The private sector responds optimally to the credible authority's chosen policy.

First, let us examine the case where the credible home authority controls its money supply, m, acting as a type of Stackelberg leader given that the noncredible foreign authority fixes the exchange rate by setting s = 0.[15]

The noncooperative solution is obtained when the home authority maximizes U over m, by taking into account the condition that the foreign authority sets s = 0 and that the private sector maximizes V over q^e, q^{*e}, and s^e, for a given set of policy variables, m and s. The cooperative solution is obtained when the home authority maximizes $rU + (1 - r)U^*$ over m, taking into account the condition that s = 0 and that V is maximized over q^e, q^{*e}, and s^e, given m and s.

Not surprisingly, both the noncooperative and cooperative games yield zero money supplies as policy solutions for the two authorities. That is, as long as the credible authority controls the money supply, the noncredible authority can effectively buy full credibility by completely abandoning its monetary policy and fixing the exchange rate.[16] Since there is only one policy instrument, m, it is no surprise that the noncooperative and cooperative solutions are the same.

Second, let us examine the case where the credible home authority sets s = 0, thereby fixing the exchange rate, while the noncredible foreign authority

---

[15]The assumption here is that, even though the foreign authority cannot credibly commit itself to exchange-rate pegging, it actually fixes the exchange rate without solving any optimization problem. However, if one takes the view that the fixed exchange-rate system can be maintained only by commitments (see Canzoneri and Henderson (1991, p.31), then he should focus on game A and/or the second case of game B. But this view fails to capture one of the most interesting results of this chapter: a monetary authority incapable of making a policy commitment can achieve the best outcome by fixing the exchange rate against the currency of a country that is credibly committed to a money-supply target.

[16]A similar conclusion has been reached by Giavazzi and Pagano (1988) in a noncooperative framework.

controls the money supply, m*. It turns out that the noncooperative and cooperative solutions are the same and lead to a very low welfare level of $-\frac{1}{2\omega}\gamma^2$. Hence, this type of a fixed rate system results in one of the worst welfare outcomes, and international policy coordination is not helpful at all in raising the authorities' welfare.

5.3. Game C and Game D

Since the solutions in games C and D turn out to be the same, only the result for game C is presented here on the assumption that the home authority controls m and the foreign authority sets s = 0.

When the monetary authorities do not cooperate, the home authority and the private sector maximize U over m and V over q^e, q^{*e}, and s^e, respectively, by taking all other players' choice variables and the exchange rate, s, as given. The foreign authority simply sets s = 0 without maximizing U*. The maximization problems together with s = 0 yield the noncooperative solution,

$$m = q = q^e = \frac{\gamma}{\omega}, \ m* = q* = q^{*e} = \frac{\gamma}{\omega}, \ s = s^e = 0.$$

The cooperative solution is the same as the noncooperative solution. Therefore, the fixed exchange-rate system for games C and D yields the lowest welfare that cannot be improved upon by international policy cooperation.

6. THE INTEREST-RATE REGIME

When at least one authority uses the interest rate as a monetary policy instrument, the regime is called the interest-rate regime. The other authority may control the money supply, the exchange rate, or the interest rate. The interest-rate regime has not been seriously examined in the literature, presumably because it is subject to the indeterminacy problem as discussed by Sargent and Wallace (1975), McCallum (1981), and Canzoneri, Henderson and Rogoff (1983) in closed-economy rational-expectations models. This section argues that the indeterminacy problem disappears if the private sector can assume leadership.[17] Therefore, game D is of particular interest to us.

If both the home and foreign monetary authorities use the interest rates, i and i*, as their policy instruments, the solution to equations (1) to (9) can be expressed as

$$y = \Sigma_1 i + \Sigma_2 i* + \Gamma(s^e + q^{*e} - q^e), \tag{25a}$$

$$y* = \Sigma_2 i + \Sigma_1 i* - \Gamma(s^e + q^{*e} - q^e), \tag{25b}$$

$$q = q^e + \Omega_1 i + \Omega_2 i* + \Lambda(s^e + q^{*e} - q^e), \tag{25c}$$

$$q* = q^{*e} + \Omega_2 i + \Omega_1 i* - \Lambda(s^e + q^{*e} - q^e), \tag{25d}$$

---

[17]Similarly, private-sector leadership would eliminate the indeterminacy problem in closed-economy rational-expectations models.

$$s = s^e - i + i*, \tag{25e}$$

where

$$\Sigma_1 = \tfrac{1}{2}[\Psi_1(\tfrac{1}{B} - \tfrac{1}{A_1}) + \Psi_2(\tfrac{1}{B} + \tfrac{1}{A_1})],$$

$$\Sigma_2 = \tfrac{1}{2}[\Psi_1(\tfrac{1}{B} + \tfrac{1}{A_1}) + \Psi_2(\tfrac{1}{B} - \tfrac{1}{A_1})],$$

$$\Omega_1 = \tfrac{1}{2}[\Pi_1(\tfrac{1}{B} - \tfrac{1}{A_1}) + \Pi_2(\tfrac{1}{B} + \tfrac{1}{A_1})],$$

$$\Omega_2 = \tfrac{1}{2}[\Pi_1(\tfrac{1}{B} + \tfrac{1}{A_1}) + \Pi_2(\tfrac{1}{B} - \tfrac{1}{A_1})],$$

$$\Gamma = \lambda\Psi_1 - \sigma\Psi_3 - \frac{\lambda A_1 - \sigma A_2 - 1}{2A_1}(\Psi_1 - \Psi_2),$$

$$\Lambda = \lambda\Pi_1 - \sigma\Pi_3 - \frac{\lambda A_1 - \sigma A_2 - 1}{2A_1}(\Pi_1 - \Pi_2),$$

$$B = - \frac{\sigma + \gamma(1 - \alpha)}{\Delta_1} < 0,$$

and Ψ_1, Ψ_2, Ψ_3, Π_1, Π_2, Π_3, A_1, A_2, and Δ_1 are as defined previously. If the authorities use different combinations of policy instruments, the solutions can be rewritten accordingly.

6.1. Game A, Game B, and Game C

In games A, B, and C, the private sector acts either as a follower taking monetary policy commitments as credible or as a Nash–Cournot player against the authorities. Then, it is easily confirmed that the model does not yield determinate solutions, although the home and foreign general price indices, q and q*, can be determined.[18] The reason for this indeterminacy is similar to that given by Sargent and Wallace (1975), that is, the model cannot determine both expected exchange rates and expected prices. There is nothing to anchor price and exchange-rate expectations under the interest-rate regime. However, the indeterminacy problem disappears if the private sector acts as a Stackelberg leader, because private-sector leadership provides a necessary anchor.

6.2. Game D: Private Sector as Leader

In game D, the private sector as a leader sets the expectations, q^e, q^{*e}, s^e, and the authorities respond passively but optimally to the expected prices and exchange rates. Here we focus our exercise on the case where both authorities use the interest rates, i and i*, as policy instruments.

---

[18]Our specification of the authorities' objective functions allows q and q* to be determined. However, if the objectives took the form suggested in footnote 5, q and q* would remain indeterminate.

In the absence of policy cooperation, the home and foreign authorities maximize U over i and U* over i*, respectively, taking each other's interest rate and private-sector expectations as given, which yields

$$q = q* = \frac{\Sigma_1}{\omega\Omega_1}. \tag{26}$$

Next, the private sector maximizes V over q^e, q^{*e}, and s^e, taking the authorities' reactions (equation (26)) into account. This yields the noncooperative solution,

$$m = q = q^e = \frac{\Sigma_1}{\omega\Omega_1}, \quad m* = q* = q^{*e} = \frac{\Sigma_1}{\omega\Omega_1}, \quad s = s^e = 0.$$

In the presence of policy cooperation, the monetary authorities' joint behavior is to maximize $\tau U + (1 - \tau)U*$ over i and i*, taking q^e, q^{*e}, and s^e as given. The joint maximization yields expressions identical to equations (20). The private sector then maximizes V over q^e, q^{*e}, and s^e subject to equations (20), which yields the cooperative solution identical to the solution under the money supply and exchange rate regimes, i.e., equations (21).[19]

Comparison between the cooperative and noncooperative solutions indicates that international policy cooperation does not raise, and may in fact reduce, both authorities' welfare levels. This is again similar to the conclusion reached by Rogoff (1985) and explained by Carraro and Giavazzi (1991).

When the authorities use different combinations of policy instruments, the solutions can be obtained similarly. Though not shown here (but summarized in table 1, to be discussed in the next section), it is noted that the use of the interest rate as a policy instrument may achieve higher welfare levels than the use of the money supply, and that the use of the exchange rate is less efficient than the use of the interest rate or money supply.

7.   IMPLICATIONS OF THE MODEL

A number of interesting results have emerged from the analytical exercise in the preceding sections. The results are summarized in table 1. The first column of the table indicates the type of international monetary policy game to be played, and the second column identifies policy instruments used by the monetary authorities. In games A, C, and D, where the authorities' mutual relationship is symmetric, switching the home and foreign policy instruments should yield the

---

[19]The cooperative solution is

$$m = q = q^e = \frac{\Omega_1[\tau\Sigma_1 + (1 - \tau)\Sigma_2] - \Omega_2[\tau\Sigma_2 + (1 - \tau)\Sigma_1]}{\omega\tau(\Omega_1^2 - \Omega_2^2)},$$

$$m* = q* = q^{*e} = \frac{\Omega_2[\tau\Sigma_1 + (1 - \tau)\Sigma_2] - \Omega_1[\tau\Sigma_2 + (1 - \tau)\Sigma_1]}{\omega(1 - \tau)(\Omega_1^2 - \Omega_2^2)},$$

$$s = s^e = \frac{(1 - 2\tau)(\Omega_1\Sigma_2 - \Omega_2\Sigma_1)}{\omega\tau(1 - \tau)(\Omega_1^2 - \Omega_2^2)},$$

which can be shown to be identical to equations (21).

corresponding money-supply solutions. The third and fourth columns report, respectively, the noncooperative and cooperative solutions for the money supply. The private sector's utility is at its bliss, i.e., $V = 0$, in all cases and therefore is not reported in the table. The authorities' welfare is $- \frac{1}{2}\omega$ times the squared quantity of the money supply.

7.1. Game A

When both the home and foreign authorities can credibly commit themselves to their policy targets and, hence, act as leaders vis-à-vis the private sector, they attain the highest utility levels. Game A satisfies "optimality" regardless of what policy instrument is chosen and whether or not monetary policy is internationally coordinated. With fully committed policies and credibility, policy interdependence across countries disappears in our simple framework and, therefore, the welfare outcome does not depend on the type of monetary policy instruments chosen (except in the interest-rate regime, which yields the familiar problem of indeterminacy) or on the extent of international policy coordination. The problem with game A is that it lacks "time consistency" à la Kydland and Prescott (1977), in the sense that the monetary authorities are tempted to renege on policy announcements when the private sector acts in the expectation that the announced policy will be implemented. (However, the possibility of defection by the authorities may be eliminated in a Barro-Gordon (1983a, b) type of repeated game.)

7.2. Game B

When only the home authority can credibly commit itself to a policy target, while the foreign authority cannot, the former behaves as a leader and the latter as a follower. Then, in the absence of international policy cooperation, the home authority committed to a money-supply target achieves the highest utility. If the foreign authority abandons its independent monetary policy and fixes the exchange rate against the currency of the home country committed to a money-supply target, it can also achieve the highest utility. Such a fixed exchange-rate system à la Bretton Woods ensures that a noncredible authority can buy full credibility by pegging the exchange rate. If the noncredible foreign authority controls the money supply or the exchange rate but does not peg the exchange rate, it achieves only a low level of utility. In this case, international policy coordination is useful to improve its welfare. That is, if the noncredible foreign authority cannot achieve a maximum level of utility when it acts on its own under the flexible or managed exchange-rate system, then it has an incentive to join international policy cooperation with the home authority committed to a money supply target. Some credibility can be bought through policy cooperation.

If the credible home authority controls the exchange rate and the noncredible foreign authority controls the money supply, then, in the absence of policy cooperation, the former's welfare is at its maximum level while the latter's welfare is at its lowest level. The foreign authority would be better off if the home authority used the money supply, rather than the exchange rate, as its policy instrument. Furthermore, there is no Pareto-dominant international policy coordination if the credible home authority controls the exchange rate.

Essentially, the private sector behaves so as to worsen the authorities' utility possibility frontier under such policy cooperation.

An even worse scenario is the case where the credible home authority fixes the exchange rate and the noncredible foreign authority controls the money supply. This case results in the lowest utility for both authorities, because the credible authority is not allowed to optimize and there is an undesirable convergence toward the policy of the noncredible foreign authority. No wonder we have not observed such an international monetary arrangement in the past.

To summarize game B, there are three ways in which the foreign authority lacking credibility can achieve the highest level of welfare. One obvious way is to build up its own reputation, acquire credibility, and change the type of game from B to A. A second way is to fix the exchange rate against the currency of the home country whose authority maintains a credible money-supply policy. Finally, it can make a collective decision with the home authority committed to a money-supply target. (However, international policy cooperation is harmful if the credible home authority is committed to an exchange-rate target.)

7.3. Game C

When no leadership is assumed by any player, the home and foreign monetary authorities achieve low levels of welfare (suboptimality) under the money-supply or exchange-rate regime. Note that, in spite of international policy cooperation always being preferable from both authorities' welfare viewpoint for a given set of private-sector expectations, their welfare levels cannot be higher simultaneously, and may, in the presence of international policy cooperation, be lower. Essentially, this is because private-sector expectations adjust in such a way as to raise the general price indices $(q, q*)$ when the two authorities cooperate. Policy cooperation exacerbates the excessive money supply and keeps the authorities' welfare below the level achieved in the absence of policy cooperation.

In this game, again, the money-supply regime (the laissez-faire flexible exchange-rate system) is preferable to the exchange-rate regime (the managed exchange-rate system). That is, each authority would be made better off if the counterpart authority controlled the money supply, rather than the exchange rate. Furthermore, exchange-rate pegging results in the worst outcome: when no authority has sufficient money-supply credibility, pegging the exchange rate does not raise welfare because it amounts to having only one authority and thus reduces the game to a Barro-Gordon (1983a, b) closed-economy game.

Comparison of game C with game B reveals that each authority has an incentive to unilaterally build up its reputation and policy credibility and move from game C to game B. The move is Pareto-improving, since it raises the mover's own welfare without worsening the other authority's welfare.

7.4. Game D

When the private sector has the ability to credibly set its price and exchange rate expectations and behaves as a leader vis-à-vis the monetary authorities, the interest-rate regime yields determinate solutions. This is because when the private sector commits itself to price and exchange-rate expectations, the authorities must validate them through accommodative money supplies. Effectively, this means that the regime provides an anchor for expectations. A second interesting result is that the use of the interest rate as a policy instrument may achieve a higher welfare than the use of the money supply and, hence, may be more desirable. Other results are similar to those of game C, namely, international policy cooperation can be Pareto inferior and controlling the exchange rate is less efficient than controlling the interest rate.

8. CONCLUDING REMARKS

This chapter has developed a formal, two-country model where monetary policy instruments, the authorities' ability to make policy commitments, and the private sector's responses and initiatives play crucial roles. It has discussed the welfare implications of monetary policy regimes, strategic interactions between the authorities and private agents, and policy interactions between the two countries' authorities.

The novelty of this chapter has been in an analysis of asymmetric monetary policy regimes (such as the exchange-rate regime and the fixed exchange-rate system), asymmetric games (such as game B), and the interest-rate regime. The new results can be summarized as follows. First, when both authorities are fully credible, they can enjoy the highest levels of welfare regardless of the type of monetary policy regime and international policy game. Second, when one authority can commit itself to a policy target and the other cannot, the former's welfare is always at its maximum regardless of whether it controls the money supply or the exchange rate. The best international monetary regime is a Bretton Woods-type fixed exchange-rate system, where the credible authority controls its money supply and the noncredible authority fixes the exchange rate unilaterally against the former's currency. Alternatively, international policy cooperation can also achieve the maximum welfare as long as the credible authority controls the money supply, rather than the exchange rate. Third, when one authority lacks policy credibility, the other authority has no incentive to fix the exchange rate. In this case, the latter would keep the noncredible authority's welfare from declining to a very low level by controlling the money supply, rather than the exchange rate. Fourth, when the private sector can act as a leader, the interest-rate regime not only has determinate solutions, but also may generate higher levels of welfare than does the money-supply regime.

These theoretical results may not be complete or general. The model does not take up other relevant issues such as uncertainty, shocks, aggregation, nonlinearities, dynamics, and imperfect and/or incomplete information. Despite such limitations, this chapter has demonstrated some useful welfare implications for different types of monetary policy regimes, central bank commitments, and international policy cooperation.

REFERENCES

Backus, David and John Driffil (1985) "Inflation and Reputation," American Economic Review, 75 (June), pp.530-538.

Barro, Robert J. and David B. Gordon (1983a) "Rules, Discretion and Reputation in a Model of Monetary Policy," Journal of Monetary Economics, 12 (July), pp.101-121.

Barro, Robert J. and David B. Gordon (1983b) "A Positive Theory of Monetary Policy in a Natural Rate Model," Journal of Political Economy, 91 (August), pp.589–610.

Canzoneri, Matthew B. and Jo Anna Gray (1985) "Monetary Policy Games and the Consequences of Non–Cooperative Behavior," International Economic Review, 26 (October), pp.547–564.

Canzoneri, Matthew B. and Dale W. Henderson (1988) "Is Sovereign Policy Making Bad?," in Karl Brunner and Alan Meltzer, eds., Carnegie–Rochester Conference Series on Public Policy, 28, pp.93–140.

Canzoneri, Matthew B. and Dale W. Henderson (1991) Monetary Policy in Interdependent Economies, (Cambridge, Mass.: MIT Press).

Canzoneri, Matthew B., Dale W. Henderson and Kenneth S. Rogoff (1983) "The Information Content of the Interest Rate and Optimal Monetary Policy," Quarterly Journal of Economics, XCVIII (November), pp.545–566.

Carraro, Carlo and Francesco Giavazzi (1991) "Can International Policy Coordination Really Be Counterproductive?," in Carlo Carraro, Didier Laussel, Mark Salmon and Antoine Soubeyran, eds., International Economic Policy Co–orination (Oxford: Basil Blackwell), pp.184–198.

Currie, David, Paul Levine and Nic Vidalis (1987) "International Cooperation and Reputation in an Empirical Two–Block Model," in Ralph C. Bryant and Richard Portes, eds., Global Macroeconomics: Policy Conflict and Cooperation (New York: St. Martin's Press), pp.75–121.

Daniel, Betty (1981) "The International Transmission of Economic Disturbances under Flexible Exchange Rates," International Economic Review, 22 (October), pp.491–509.

Giavazzi, Francesco and Alberto Giovannini (1988) "The Role of the Exchange–rate Regime in a Disinflation: Empirical Evidence on the European Monetary System," in Francesco Giavazzi, Stefano Micossi and Marcus Miller, eds., The European Monetary System (Cambridge and New York: Cambridge University Press), pp.85–107.

Giavazzi, Francesco and Alberto Giovannini (1989) "Monetary Policy Interactions under Managed Exchange Rates," Economica, 56 (May), pp.199–213.

Giavazzi, Francesco and Marco Pagano (1988) "The Advantage of Tying One's Hands: EMS Discipline and Central Bank Credibility," European Economic Review, 32 (June), pp. 1052–1082.

Hamada, Koichi (1985) The Political Economy of International Monetary Interdependence (Cambridge, Mass.: MIT Press).

Kydland, Finn E. and Edward C. Prescott (1977) "Rules Rather than Discretion: The Inconsistency of Optimal Plans," Journal of Political Economy, 85 (June), pp.473–492.

McCallum, Bennet T. (1981) "Price Level Determinacy with an Interest Rate Policy Rule and Rational Expectations," Journal of Monetary Economics, 8 (November), pp. 319–329.

McKinnon, Ronald I. (forthcoming 1992) "The Rules of the Game: International Money in Historical Perspective," Journal of Economic Literature.

Oudiz, Gilles and Jeffrey Sachs (1985) "International Policy Coordination in Dynamic Macroeconomic Models," in Willem H. Buiter and Richard Marston, eds., International Economic Policy Coordination (Cambridge and New York, Cambridge University Press), pp.274–319.

Rogoff, Kenneth (1985) "Can International Monetary Policy Cooperation Be Counterproductive?," Journal of International Economics, 18 (May), pp.199–217.

98

Sargent, Thomas J. and Neil Wallace (1975) "'Rational' Expectations, the Optimal
    Monetary Instrument, and the Optimal Money Supply Rule," <u>Journal of
    Political Economy</u>, 83 (April), pp.241–254.
Turnovsky, Stephen J. and Vasco d'Orey (1986) "Monetary Policies in Interdepen-
    dent Economies with Stochastic Disturbances: A Strategic Approach," <u>Economic
    Journal</u>, 96 (September), pp.696–721.

7. SUMMARY BY PROFESSOR G. BASEVI OF SESSION 1: "SUSTAINABLE WORLD ECONOMIC GROWTH: A NEW DIMENSION OF ECONOMIC POLICY COOPERATION"

1. DISCUSSION OF KOICHI HAMADA'S CHAPTER "INTERNATIONAL NEGOTIATIONS AND DOMESTIC CONFLICTS: A CASE FOR COUNTERLOBBYING"

Professor Y. Ono's main comments addressed three aspects of Hamada's chapter. The first is the nature of the two-level game used for analyzing policymaking, on the one hand, and the pressures to influence policymakers, on the other hand. The second deals with extensions of the analysis from tariffs to other means of protection. The third concerns the assumption that free trade is an optimal policy, relative to which alternative policies must be compared.

With reference to the first aspect, Ono pointed out that Hamada's specification of the game as one in which Congressmen are the leading players and lobbying groups are the followers is a particular case of a more general setup, in which the institutional ruling of the game is endogenously determined, so that the two levels of the game are related. In fact, while Hamada's chapter is limited to the analysis of only one level in the game, it is clear that politicians' actions respond to other players' actions, in so far as politicians are the representatives of these players. In a similar model dealing with an oligopolistic situation, Ono analyzed a more general setup in which leader-follower roles are chosen on the basis of the payoffs of the game. While his approach was too general to allow description of the game by a choice tree, it could be narrowed down to manageable dimensions by specifying an institutional setting with players' precommitments. The importance of precommitments was indeed mentioned in Hamada's chapter, but their generation remained exogenous.

With reference to the second aspect, Ono expressed the opinion that the traditional distinction, according to which rents accrue to the Government of the importing country in the case of tariffs, to importers in the case of quotas, and to exporters in the case of VERs, was too simple. In fact there are theoretical and empirical cases in which the distinction between quotas and VERs is blurred, in so far as exporters are able to capture part of the rent also with quotas. Hamada's analysis is mainly concerned with tariffs, but he also commented on these other means of protection; extending the analysis to them should therefore take into account that the traditional distinction is not always the correct one to make.

With reference to the third aspect, Ono underlined the fact that Hamada's analysis is based on the assumption that free trade with no lobbying is optimal. However, tariffs and other protective means are used in practice to offset sectoral costs of adjustment. While these means of intervention are theoretically inferior to others that directly compensate for adjustment costs, their presence is enough to make free trade a suboptimal policy. Moreover, as Ono demonstrated in some of his work, world welfare may be increased by import restrictions under an oligopolistic industrial structure. Indeed, rather than assuming that the total amount of monopoly rent is given, as in Hamada's chapter, lobbying activities may themselves increase that amount and therefore influence the world welfare ranking of the protected situation relative to free trade.

In a final comment, Ono pointed out that different conclusions could be reached than those indicated by Hamada, with regard to the effect of counter-lobbying. In fact, if we admit that well-established exporters and importers may both have an interest in keeping import restrictions if they share in the resulting rents, whereas potential exporters and importers may be interested in lifting them in order also to take part in the rent, then lobbying in support of existing trade arrangements may also take place in the foreign country, as may counterlobbying in the domestic country. A case in point seems to have been the negotiations between the U.S. and Japan about U.S. citrus exports.

Professor K. Fukao wondered why, in considering the influence of foreign counterlobbying on the attitude of domestic politicians, Hamada dismissed as rare the case in which this might enhance the nationalism of politicians and thus be countereffective. On the contrary, Fukao believed that such enhancement may very well be the result of Japanese counterlobbying in the United States.

Another point made by Fukao was similar to the one made by Ono in his first comment. Fukao too believed that Hamada's analysis might be enriched by considering the interrelations between the two levels of the game. More specifically, he underlined that in Putnam's work, on which Hamada builds his analysis, the negotiating stand of the politicians is reinforced by a noncooperative attitude of the lobbyists.

In answering to the discussants' comments, Hamada agreed with Ono that making the share of benefits to the lobbyists depend on their lobbying adds interest to the model. He also thought that this would avoid the free-rider problem.

With reference to scale economies and other departures from the assumptions of the classical trade model, Hamada admitted that his results were limited and agreed that it would be interesting to examine how they would be affected by the "new international trade theory" approach.

Finally, Hamada recalled that in his chapter he endorsed Putnam's point, and expected that the results of his own analysis would be enriched by ongoing research on the interrelationship between the two levels of the game.

2. DISCUSSION OF JONATHAN EATON'S CHAPTER: "GLOBALIZATION AND THE DESIGN OF INTERNATIONAL INSTITUTIONS"

Ono expressed his appreciation of how neatly Eaton's chapter summarizes and emphasizes the applicability of new trade theories to current international economic issues, particularly to changes in the trade structure of the three main world economic blocks. He then provided comments on three main points.

The first one was essentially the same he had just made with respect to Hamada's chapter, i.e. that the conclusions may radically change when, in a world of oligopolistic firms, the free-trade situation is no longer considered as the optimal reference point.

The second comment was on the relation between environmental and trade policies. He thought that the approach to them was not new: well-established traders are tempted to hide behind environmental protection agreements in order to keep newcomers from competing away their advantage. This happened with the whaling business, and it may happen again with regulations against CO_2 emissions, at least according to the developing countries. In this case it would be necessary for developed countries to come in and help with either financial or technological transfers.

The third comment was on the atemporal nature of Eaton's chapter. Ono suggested that trade policies affect the rate of interest and its time profile. Thus they would affect the financial situation of debtor and creditor countries, and this requires a dynamic model for adequate treatement. With such a model Ono had obtained some results that are very different from those derived from a-temporal models.

Fukao made two comments on Eaton's chapter. The first was on the regional trading blocks. He pointed out that, in contrast to North America and the European Community, which are both identifiable by internal free-trade agreements, "Greater Asia" is not bound by specific trade preferences. However, he observed that Japan discriminates by selectively opening the domestic market to countries in which Japan's direct investment is particularly significant — a point recently noticed by Krugman, and on which Fukao asked Eaton's opinion.

The second comment was on the need to consider the option of free capital movements in addition to that of free international trade. Fukao asked for Eaton's opinion regarding this additional dimension and how it should be incorporated in institutional arrangements of economic relations among countries and blocks of countries.

In responding to the comments, Eaton said that he did not have an opinion about Krugman's observation on how Japan preferentially treats some countries. He also acknowledged the validity of Fuako's other comment although he pointed out that the free trade agreement between the U.S. and Canada has not been implemented as yet.

Eaton recognized that importance of freeing capital movements is on the same level as that of freeing trade. However, this raises the problem of harmonizing banking regulations: failure to deal with this issue has generated many of the problems with the U.S. role in the financial crisis of the 1970s.

Eaton also accepted the relevance of Ono's criticism regarding the issue of optimal intervention in the presence of domestic distortions. However, he expressed the opinion that trade policies are usually not the best means for correcting those distortions.

In the general discussion that followed Eaton's replies, Nerb raised the possibility that in a world of few regional blocks, coalitions may be formed that would widen the distance from free trade. He asked Eaton whether he thought that a new GATT would be required to correct for such a development.

Igawa underlined that, in the spirit of Eaton's chapter — where it is advocated that GATT should deal with direct investment, trade in services, and other modern fields of international economic relations— attention should be given also to the reality of multinational corporations.

Horioka, while expressing strong interest in Eaton's methodology, observed that transportation costs might further contribute to his model of trade among regional blocks.

In answering these additional comments, Eaton did not have a definite opinion on the need for a new institution or a stronger GATT. However, he thought that a positive approach would be to keep regional institutions open to new membership. He also thought that a valuable characteristic of GATT, as well of other successful international organizations, was that, although open, they also require new members to meet certain standards.

On the issue of multinationals, again GATT may indeed be too wide and diverse to tackle it adequately. However, a smaller organization made up of the main trading blocks should not be an excuse for them to become detached from the body of the other trading nations: developing countries must continue to evolve towards participation in a world open trading system.

As for methodology, Eaton thought that, although important, transport costs could hardly explain the differences in trade patterns among the three main regional blocks.

3. DISCUSSION OF MASAHIRO KAWAI AND HIDEAKI MURASE'S CHAPTER: "MONETARY POLICY REGIMES, CENTRAL BANK COMMITTMENTS AND INTERNATIONAL POLICY GAMES"

Fukao expressed his general appreciation of Kawai and Murase's chapter, particularly for its analyses in great detail of the results of a game between monetary authorites and the private sector under alternative international monetary arrangements. He then made three comments.

The first concerned the objective function of private agents with regard to exchange rate formation. Fukao thought that the microeconomic foundation of this part of the objective function was not given: it was not clear to what group of agents the category of exchange-rate setters referred, as opposed to firms and workers that are identified as price and wage setters. It is not clear whether the expected exchange rate is indeed an expectation or a strategic variable. Suppose s^e is a strategic variable. Then Fukao wondered why the private sector should want to minimize $(s^e - s)$. On the other hand, suppose s^e is an expectation. Since s^e denotes the expected spot exchange rate of the next period, and s denotes the spot exchange rate of the present period, there is no reason why $(s^e - s)$ should be minimized. In any case, the results are at odds with the usual rational expectations model, where expectations are such that spot exchange rates for the period to which expectations refer are forecasted at their equilibrium level, evaluated on the basis of the current information set, so that the current spot exchange rate is set, for given expectations, by uncovered interest-rate parity. Contrary to this, an undesirable result of Kawai's specification is that this parity requires the domestic and foreign interest rates to be always equal.

The second comment addressed the fact that in Kawai and Murase's chapter the private sector's objective functions are maximized up to the bliss point, regardless of the nature of the monetary regimes and the kind of game, while the public authorities are unaffected by regime changes. This eliminates interactive effects in the game. Such an interaction could be introduced, in an open economy, by specifying an objective function that involves the terms of trade: improvements of the terms of trade would raise real wages, thereby leading to a higher economic welfare of domestic agents. Conflicts of private interests between the two countries would then arise, and it would be possible to compare the effects of changes in monetary regimes on private welfare.

The third comment was also related to the analysis of Hamada's chapter. In Kawai and Murase's model, a monetary authority plays two games simultaneously: one with the country's private sector, the other with the foreign monetary authority. Interestingly, the nature of one game affects the outcome of the other. As has been pointed out by Rogoff, if the two authorities cooperate, then welfare will be lower than in a noncooperative case; this is because of the time-inconsistency problem, which is made more serious by collusion among monetary authorities. From the viewpoint of the two-level games, another interesting question is how cooperation between one authority and the private sector affects the game between the two authorities. Fukao wondered whether it would be possible that a country having an uncooperative private sector obtains stronger bargaining power in international negotiations, as suggested in Putnam and Hamada's works.

Ono provided various comments, mainly related to the nature of the objective functions and the selection of the games. He first wondered how it could be assumed that foreign and domestic private sectors are merged into a single decision maker. This is equivalent to assuming cooperation between the two sectors, which seems unreasonable. Yet this assumption strongly affects the conclusions that are reached, such as the fact that in game A it does not matter whether the two monetary authorities cooperate or not.

Ono then suggested that, rather then enumerating various games and the derived results, the model should endogenize the selection of regimes. Optimization may lead to selection of regimes through commitment by the monetary authorities, much as in Hamada's chapter. In fact Ono noted that, Kawai and Murase consider which game is preferable to monetary authorities. This indicates that the games, and the underlying regimes, can be chosen by them.

In the general discussion that followed, many additional comments were raised.

Hamada asked about the meaning that should be attributed to the several occurrences of infinity symbols in the payoff matrix.

Higgins raised a question about the game in which the private sector is the leader and the home and foreign monetary authorities are followers, in the sense that the former sets its expectations about wages and exchange rates, to which the latter responds optimally. He suggested that, with analogy to the phenomenon studied in the U.S. bond market, a stabilizing influence may be played by the private sector also through its expectations in the interest-rate market.

Ohyama objected to the assumption in the chapter that the private sector is considered as just one agent: this makes it difficult to understand why a representative Government would have an objective function that is completely different from that of the private sector. In Henderson and Canzoneri's model the private sector is divided into more than one agent: workers, firms, etc., each with their own objective function. The Government may then more reasonably be assumed to have its own different objective function. A second comment related to the notion of credibility: Ohyama questioned that the first-mover advantage could be made equivalent to the notion of credibility.

Basevi raised a question related to Ohyama's intervention. He suggested that the Government sector could also be considered as being made up of more than one agent, each with a different objective function. Besides referring to some of his work in this direction, he cited as an example the current situation in Europe, where countries dealing with Germany and the process of European monetary unification have to consider that at least two German authorities are in charge: the Government and the central bank. They do not always appear to have the same objective function or to act cooperatively in playing the game of German and European unification.

Klein also commented on the private sector's objective function, which involves domestic and foreign prices, plus the exchange rate. This seems too much, considering that, in equilibrium, purchasing-power parity and interest-rate parity do not allow freedom to set exchange rates in addition to price targets. In relation to the effects of monetary authorities' intervention following the Plaza and Louvre agreements, Klein recalled that all they probably did was to keep the path of dollar depreciation that was already under way. He suggested that, in most cases, authorities can do little more than maintain a steady market.

Onituka raised the issue of credibility and suggested an evolutionary approach to it. Given its credibility, a Government enforces certain policies, with various results; but these results affect credibility. Thus, in the case of Germany, the experience of hyperinflation generated a stubborn defence of anti-inflationary policies by German monetary authorities, which now makes it easier for them to carry out their policies.

Pauly provided a technical comment on authorities' objective function. The weight of prices could go close either to zero or to infinity, but then games C and D would imply equivalent strategies, and he asked for an interpretation of this.

In replying to the discussants and the general comments, Kawai defended the specification of the objective function in the light of rational expectations. He did not think that it was inconsistent with equilibrium purchasing power and interest parity either, since it is expected exchange rates and prices that are specified in the objective function, and these need not be always at their long-run equilibrium level.

With reference to Ono's comments and others' discussion of the credibility issue, he agreed that the choice of the regime and game could be endogenized, but he suggested that the model is already highly complex, and a dynamic game model would be required for that purpose.

On Hamada's comment about infinity in the payoff matrix, Kawai suggested that any high number would do the job: the two monetary authorities cannot both choose the exchange rate, so the regime does not determine the system. On Higgins' point, he clarified that price expectations are built into interest rates, so that the suggestion is indeed already considered in the model.

On Klein's comment, Kawai agreed and suggested that, rather than trying to stabilize exchange rates, authorities should aim at maintaining stable markets. He then agreed that the question raised by Onituka was an important one, but it required again a more dynamic setting of the model in order to be studied.

Finally, Kawai submitted that, in order to consider fiscal authorities separately, as suggested by Basevi, even more games should be modeled. This could be done, but with much work.

While the first session was not purely theoretical, there was emphasis on game theory and international trade theory for understanding the underlying concepts and objectives involved in improving the world economy. The second session, on the other hand, approached the common objectives of this conference in a different way—from the side of institutional arrangements, recent history, and statistical analysis.

A few major themes run through this entire conference. Prominent among these are the changes taking place in Europe—steps toward realization of a single market in Western Europe, integration of Eastern Europe into the economy of the West, and the tendency towards polarization of the world economy into three major blocks, one of these being the Asia—Pacific block. Given the sponsorship and locale of the meetings, it is only natural that a good deal of attention should be paid to economic performance in the Asia—Pacific countries. All these themes were taken up in session 2.

The chapter by Gernot Nerb deals with German unification, which is an important special case of East—West integration in Europe. Christopher Higgins concentrated on the emergence of a cohesive economic center in the Asia—Pacific region and presented an authoritative picture of the emerging institutions, which are not yet at the point of constituting an official trading zone, such as the Common Market in Europe or the North American Zone between Canada and the United States, but are certainly closer to becoming a polarized region than in the past.

Yasukichi Yasuba traces the recent history of East Asia's economic development, with special reference to the position of Thailand, which he examines in an interesting way as a patrimonial state. He covers the Asian NIEs, Asean, and China in his chapter.

The chapter by John Helliwell, Alan Chung, and Ardo Hanssan (which was presented by the senior author) is an econometric simulation study of the concept of convergence (catch–up) in the explanation of comparative growth performance among both industrial and Asian developing countries. The findings so far are not definitive, and the evidence is only slight in support of the hypothesis that countries move towards the economic achievement of major leaders in a region. In this sense, Helliwell et al. did not find much evidence of tripolarity, which is a popular concept at the present time.

9. EFFECTS OF GERMAN UNIFICATION ON THE EUROPEAN INTEGRATION PROCESS

Dr. Gernot Nerb[1]
ifo Institute for Economic Research
West—Germany

ABSTRACT. Political and economic effects of German unification are considered with respect to European integration. Politically, German unificaiton provides support for cooperation between the EC and the former East Bloc countries. Economically, unification lends concreteness to the goal of an "all—European economic region." The institutional, attitudinal, and organizational problems of unification are discussed. Bundesbank and other economic policies are considered for dealing with the transitional issues.

1. THE POLITICAL DIMENSION

On the political level the founders of the European Community had more in mind than merely a free trade zone. The long—term goal was and still is a European economic and currency union combined with cooperation in foreign and defense policies via the democratic bodies of the Community. As developments in the past 30 years have shown, political unification has encountered problems. The partial surrender of national rights of sovereignty is a very painful process. In order to advance the European Community at least in the economic sphere, the EC 1992 single—market project was started in 1985. Because of goal—oriented action, a strict schedule, good marketing, and support from the German—French axis, this project has turned into a success story that few would have dreamed of before 1985.

In this phase where European politics has concentrated almost exclusively on 1992, the German question has suddenly emerged. Initial plans for a gradual adjustment of the two parts of Germany have been swept away by political realities and expectations. The reaction of the European partners, especially France and Britain, was at first one of irritation or shock. This, however, was short—lived. Demoscopic polls in France and Britain, and in other EC countries, were instrumental in dispelling initial reservations vis-à-vis German unification. The polls indicated sympathy towards German unification. Delors and the EC Commission in Brussels, with the full support of the West German Government, seized this opportunity and insisted that German unification be bound to the accelerated process of European political integration. This was the

---

1Dr. Nerb is head of the Department for Business Surveys, Investment Analyses and Entrepreneurial Behavior of the ifo Institute. From 1984 to 1987 he was an economic adviser to the EC Commission.

prevailing tone at the EC special summit in Dublin in April 1990. The Federal Republic showed, for example, a previously unexpected readiness to compromise on the question of the European Monetary Union, thus placing the ball in the court of the other EC countries. Today it can indeed be maintained that the German question has accelerated the process of political integration in Europe and has not—as many initially expected—slowed it down. A typical statement in this connection was made by Italy's Ambassador Marcello Guidi: "It would be a mistake to believe that competition or even incompatibility exists between European integration and German unification. I am convinced that the Bonn Government, in full awareness of the interdependency of these two processes, will act both for national and European union, for the one would have no chance of success without the other. If it is true that a unified Europe would make no historical or geographical sense without Germany, then it is also true that the unification of Germany outside of the European context would not have the same chances of success; it would lack above all the ideological basis that its success could build on."

German unification has not only accelerated the process of integration in the EC but has also led to a more rapid rethinking of the European position vis-à-vis the former Eastern Bloc than would otherwise have been the case. Even if EC membership for individual East European countries is not currently on the agenda, signs are emerging of accomodations that would have been unimaginable not long ago. In the meantime the EC has signed cooperation agreements with nearly all East European countries, and there is a strong consensus for turning these cooperation agreements into a form of association. What form this will take is not yet clear. Plans, however, call for solutions that would go far beyond the normal trade and cooperation agreements. The clear advantages of association agreements are an almost completely free exchange of goods and extensive freedom of movement for labor, as well as considerable financial support from the EC. Signals are already coming out of Brussels that the EC budget must be noticeably expanded in order to meet these added responsibilities. In addition, Eastern Europe would also have access to credits from the European Investment Bank and the European Coal and Steel Community. There is also talk of common investment in traffic routes and other infrastructural measures.

Even though an institutionalized political dialogue has been promised, the EC Commission still wants a passage written into such association agreements that they are sui generis and not an initial step towards a later, quasi-automatic, full EC membership. Here Brussels has learned from the painful experience of the Turkish agreement. The European Community thus intends to offer all East European reform states the closest political and economic relations possible outside of full membership. The status of "reform state" will only be given to countries that have implemented the essentials of a market economy prior to the association agreement. This includes above all the freeing of prices, the introduction of the free choice on occupation, the admission and promotion of private property, the achievement of currency convertibility, and the adherence to GATT rules, as well as the wide-scale adoption of EC law in the areas of competition and environment. In advance of future association agreements, the EC Commission will continue its coordinating function by the PHARE assistance programs of the group of industrial countries (G 24).

In short, it can be stated that the political dimension of German unification has provided a new thrust to the process of European integration and has considerably accelerated the political and economic cooperation between the EC and the former East Bloc countries. Finally, the question of defense in Europe is clearly on the agenda. In contrast to the failed attempt to form a European defense union there is now a greater chance for a solution within a reshaped NATO.

2. THE ECONOMIC EFFECTS

What can be said about the economic effects of the German unification on the EC? The territorial expansion of the Federal Republic has increased the population of the present Community by about 5% and EC GNP by about 3%. These figures indicate that there are no dramatic changes for the EC due to the integration of the GDR.

The calculations of various economic models indicate that economic growth in the Federal Republic as a result of the GDR effect will permanently increase by about 1% and in the EC by about 0.25%. The OECD in Paris is somewhat more skeptical here and anticipates no additional growth effect in Europe due to increasing interest rates directly and indirectly caused by German unification. But more important than these global effects are the economic impacts of unification on selected economic areas.

Of great importance is the question whether the huge financial resources necessary for bailing out the GDR economy can be raised on the capital market without further increases in interest rates. A higher level of interest rates would make investment in German financial securities more attractive and would thus instigate capital imports. The danger of a crowding-out process to the detriment of other countries that are dependent on capital imports could not be ruled out. In order to counter such an unwise development, the Deutsche Bundesbank correctly believes that cutting public expenditure in West Germany is absolutely essential in order to curb credit demand. This is especially to take place in the form of significant reductions in the defense budget but also in subsidies (such as aid to the regions bordering the GDR and to West Berlin). The poorer alternative to a prudent expenditure policy would be tax increases; these must in any case be introduced very carefully so that the attractiveness of Germany as a production location does not suffer too much. Internal studies of the European Commission have reached conclusions similar to those of the Deutsche Bundesbank. If major price increases were to result from a too-strong private and public demand, the action suggested is a consistent course of monetary restrictions and an upward revaluation of the D-Mark in the EMS.

Nevertheless, there is a note of concern in the EC about whether the Bundesbank, in the face of strongly increasing unemployment in East Germany, would have the strength for a restrictive policy that would ultimately worsen the situation on the labor market. If no consistent monetary policy in Germany were to emerge, the D-Mark could lose some of its function as key currency in the EMS. The question is then whether another currency, such as the French Franc, could take over this function. Ultimately, the whole EMS would suffer if Germany were to abandon the stability course. These are all, of course, hypothetical considerations; at the moment these dangers have not become real. But in any case this scenario should be cause enough for a prudential guidance of German fiscal policy, for Germany's and Europe's sake.

Another topic of much discussion is the impact of German unification on the European Regional Development Fund. In simplified terms, the receiver countries of European structural assistance, especially Spain, Ireland, Portugal, Greece, and (Southern) Italy, fear that this EC fund will be plundered by the former GDR. In order to assuage such fears, the German Government gave assurances from the outset that it would raise the necessary financial means for East Germany. Although this suggestion was well intended, the Commission in Brussels received it with mixed feelings. Brussels' concerns are based on the motto, "Whoever pays the piper calls the tune"; the Commission fears that Germany, for example in the case of assistance regulations, would not keep to the relatively strict EC rules, thus creating a precedent on which other EC countries could orient themselves. For this reason the solution that is emerging is preferable; according to it, the former GDR would only be fully included in the EC Regional Development Fund program after 1993, but would also already have access to structural funds in the context of a planned special agreement for the years 1991 to 1993. For this transitional arrangement it is assumed that the ex-GDR is primarily to be assigned to the type of EC problem regions termed "objective 2" (i.e., older industrialized regions undergoing structural change, such as the Ruhr area or Weser–Ems, etc.) and that only a small part would be termed "objective 1," i.e., underdeveloped regions.[2]

Precisely how the allocation into "objective 1" and "objective 2" will take place for the ex–GDR––a decision that is also important for the maximum amounts of assistance allowed––has not yet been definitely decided. It can be assumed, however, that the region of the former GDR will receive nearly 1 billion ECU in the years 1991, 1992, and 1993 (i.e., more than DM 2 billion) from the EC Regional Development Fund, of which about 15% will be "objective 1" funds. The Regional Development Fund, according to preliminary plans of the EC Commission, will have a volume of nearly DM 28 billion in 1991; nearly two thirds of this fund, i.e., more than DM 17 billion, is reserved for "objective 1" regions.

No other EC region, however, is to suffer financial losses from EC support for the former GDR. How the increased budget funds are to be raised is not clear at the moment. In estimating the additional financial needs, the increased revenue for the EC from the share of the value–added tax that is collected in the ex–GDR must be taken into consideration. According to model calculations by the EC, this would mean a net transfer from Brussels to the ex–GDR of about DM 1 billion for the year 1991 and about DM 2 billion in 1992.

More important in terms of volume for the ex–GDR is the so–called Agricultural Guarantee and Guidance Fund. Here, payments of between DM 3 and 4 billion can be expected in 1991. Since the total volume of the guarantee fund is more than DM 60 billion in 1991, the envy of the other EC countries over the new recipient East Germany is not justified.

In the context of anticipated agricultural assistance, a more fundamental look can be taken at the integration of East German agriculture into the

---

2In order to be assigned to the problem regions termed "objective 1," real per capita GNP cannot exceed 75% of the EC average. Due to insufficient statistics in the ex–GDR, it cannot be clearly determined which GDR regions would fulfill stipulation. For this reason the allocation is largely political. This also applies for the stipulations of the Regional Development Fund and for the "objective 2" areas. Here, the criteria of a certain level of unemployment in the past applies. Previously, however, the GDR had no major unemployment apart from the hidden unemployment, which is hard to measure statistically.

European agricultural system. In East German agriculture, there will have to be a fundamental change from the previous quantity orientation of the planned economy to a locational and cost orientation, as well as an adjustment to quality and demand in a market economy. Ecological requirements will be assigned a much higher value than previously. The key factor of the economic new beginning, however, is the inevitable reform of prices. From the EC perspective, the main problem is that the East German farmers produce a surplus of grain, milk, and sugar—precisely those products of which the EC already has too much.

With the help of export subsidies, East Germany is now to export unsalable agricultural products to Eastern Europe and the Soviet Union. This is meant to reduce the short-term sales problems of East German agriculture and at the same time not burden the EC market with its quantity quotas, guaranteed prices, and export subsidies.

Even though such an assistance program with export subsidies is understandable in light of the current emergency situation in East German agriculture, the reverse side must not be overlooked. The more that domestic and EC producers can protect themselves from the uncomfortable consequences of integration via the present price intervention system, the higher the cost will be for the consumers and taxpayers.

3. CONCLUSIONS

German unification and the collapse of the centrally planned economic systems of Eastern Europe have introduced an unprecedented dynamism into the European integration process. It is important now to take advantage of this opportunity and to introduce institutional improvements in the European Community, especially to enhance the status of the European Parliament. At the same time it is important to draw the reforming countries of the former East Bloc closer to the EC by means of association agreements and to ease their adjustment difficulties by opening markets and by financial assistance. A central issue is the question of security in Europe; here a solution, which will best take place within a newly conceived NATO, seems closer than ever before.

The utopian goal not long ago of an "all-European economic region" has become a concrete objective of practical policy as a result of the radical political and economic reforms in the countries of Central and Eastern Europe. The various forms for approaching an all-European economic region can be characterized as follows:[3]

1. The EC, whose attractiveness has considerably promoted reform policies in Central and Eastern Europe and without which this reform may not have been possible, must strengthen its own structure and power in its own interest and also in order to play a convincing role in the formation of the "all-European economic region." On January 1, 1993, the new constitutional structure of the EC must take effect.

---

[3]These points are based on a lecture given by G. Krenzier, EC General Director of Foreign Affairs, in Munich on September 14, 1990, "Die EG und der Wandel in der UdSSR und in Mittel- und Osteuropa."

2. The long-term goal of the EC in structuring its relations to its neighbors is the "all-European economic region" based on a market economy with an all-European free-trade zone as its essential element.

3. In EC relations to EFTA countries, with whom free trade has already been achieved, the realization of the European economic region, i.e., home-market-like relations, is intended by January 1, 1993.

4. With the countries of Central and Eastern Europe, which for some time will not be in a position to conduct free trade on a reciprocal basis, association agreements will be negotiated to gradually achieve this goal and also to introduce the gradual realization of the free movement of services, capital, and labor. The EC will quickly and completely open its market to products from Central and Eastern Europe in the framework of association and free trade agreements. The GDR foreign trade obligations vis-a-vis the Comecon countries and Yugoslavia, which were transferred to the EC after German unification, will function as an additional force for a rapid and comprehensive opening of the EC market for these states.

5. The EC is strongly supporting the reform policies in the Soviet Union with the goal of helping the Soviet Union in its transition to market-based structures and including it as an active partner for a future "all-European economic region."

In terms of the economic effects of German unification on other EC countries, the positive aspects predominate. The partner countries anticipate being able to increase their exports to Germany by 2%, on average. The growth stimulation in Europe will be paralleled by the often-demanded decline of the German current-account surplus. Possible negative aspects are rising interest rates resulting from the large borrowing needs. As already discussed, a properly coordinated monetary and fiscal policy can limit this danger.

The major question is how quickly the transitional problems from a command to a market economy can be overcome in East Germany. A repetition of the economic miracle in postwar West Germany will be difficult for the following reasons:

1. The currency in the ex-GDR (i.e., the D-Mark) is overvalued in terms of the local economic conditions, and in addition is fully convertible, which was not the case for the initial years of the Federal Republic.

2. In terms of total economic productivity for manufacturing and services, wages in the former GDR are higher than in other industrial countries, whereas West Germany started out with a clear wage-cost advantage in comparison with other industrial countries.

3. For the above two reasons the profit situation of East German enterprises is likely to be worse in the short and medium term than was the case for West German firms after the war.

4. The question of property ownership is much more complicated than in post-war West Germany.

5. The inhabitants of East Germany have a greater freedom of choice, i.e., they can move to richer regions (in the Federal Republic or anywhere in the European Community) without major difficulty.

On the other hand, the former GDR—unlike postwar West Germany—has the advantage of being able to adopt proven techniques and a different know-how relatively quickly by means of East-West enterprise cooperation or mergers.

The decisive factor, however, will be the attitude of the East German population. At the moment, an enthusiasm for a new beginning is still lacking in the East. The faintheartedness of many in the former GDR coupled with a lack of information on the market economy is curbing the readiness to make a new beginning in so far as doing so involves risks.

To bank on the "free market forces" taking their own course thus means underestimating the supply-conditioned bottlenecks (especially in the infrastructure) and also overestimating the readiness of the population for a new beginning (e.g., a change of residence or profession, setting up new companies, and so forth). Pioneer firms à la Schumpeter are much scarcer in the former GDR than in the West, which is not surprising; such behavioral patterns were neither in demand nor rewarded during the past 40 years in the GDR. At present, preserving vested interests, even though modest in comparison to the West, seems to have the highest priority in East Germany. If a new attitude does not emerge soon, the danger exists that a new "Mezzogiorno" will arise in the ex-GDR territory, which, similar to Southern Italy, will swallow billions of dollars of assistance and subsidies without affecting self-sustaining economic growth. Here, there is also a potential for conflict within the EC that should not be underestimated. As long as it can be assumed that EC aid from the Regional Development Fund is a relatively short-term transitional support for East Germany, the solidarity of the traditional "have-nots" in the EC—above all Portugal, Greece, Ireland, and parts of Spain and Southern Italy—can be expected. But as soon as it is apparent that the massive support for the Eastern German regions is becoming a permanent condition, we can anticipate intensified competition for help from the Regional Development Fund, which could develop into an explosive issue for the European Community.

In light of these considerations, it was justified to create clear tax incentives for private investment in the former GDR, and parallel to this by means of massive public infrastructure investment (roads, telecommunications, sewage treatment facilities, etc.) not only to create new jobs but also to improve the framework conditions for private investments. Only in this way is there a chance for creating the economic impetus in East Germany that is necessary in order to achieve largely self-sustaining growth after about two years. Important for this aim is a gradient in assistance between the former GDR and the West German regions bordering on the GDR (which has been as much as 23% of taxable investment subsidies). This was achieved by an increase in the assistance rates for the former GDR to a maximum of about 33%[4] and by a gradual elimination of border-region assistance. With investment assistance of a maximum of about 33%, East Germany would be on equal terms with regions in a similar economic situation, such as Ireland and Spain, but far removed from the maximum assistance rates of up to 75% of the investment amount in several EC "objective 1" regions, e.g., in Portugal.

To the extent that the border-region assistance is eliminated, the subsidies to East Germany could also be reduced. This process must be accompanied by an employment agreement between companies and unions to ensure that future wage increases do not surpass productivity but even remain below this level in the initial phase in order to create additional investment

---

4Investing companies can receive at maximum a 23% premium from the so-called "Betriebsverwaltungsbüros" in the new federal states. These offices also decide whether a firm receives the full premium or only a part. While the 23% premium is taxable, firms can apply for an additional investment premium of maximum 10%, which is tax free.

incentives. In order to achieve these concessions from the unions, corresponding profit-sharing models must be created.

The attractiveness of East Germany as a location for production could also be considerably increased if the unions and employers indicated a readiness to tolerate longer machine running times and with this a decoupling of personal working time from plant production time.

The organizational integration of the former GDR into the EC has made much progress. A document of more than 200 pages was prepared in Brussels and presented at the end of August 1990. It contains complete instructions for transferring EC laws and regulations to the former GDR after formal unification. Approximately 80% of all EC regulations can be applied directly in East Germany without transitional provisions. The number of exceptions is smaller than originally assumed. In particular for food, chemicals, certain cosmetics, and pharmaceuticals, temporary transitional periods are envisaged, most of which will expire in 1992; consequently, with the beginning of the single European market in 1993, there will be no more exceptions for the ex-GDR territory. The GDR products listed in the transitional regulations that do not conform with EC stipulations can continue to be sold in East Germany after unification but not in the other EC countries. In the case of agricultural products, foreign trade (e.g., 3000 GDR trade agreements with third countries, primarily with former Comecon states), and environmental protection, this ambitious goal of "1992" will not be achievable. Here intensive and lenthy negotiations will be necessary.

The main principle will not be changed that Brussels is responsible for foreign trade agreements and for concluding trade agreements – not the individual national states. But renegotiating all present supply commitment agreements will probably not be possible, since some of them extend beyond the year 2000. Products imported in the ex-GDR from the former Comecon countries were tax-free in 1991 and will also be in 1992 in so far as they are consumed or processed in East Germany. At the same time, the EC Commission has indicated that the special conditions in the bilateral trade agreements between the ex-GDR and the former Comecon states could be included in the association agreements that the EC has proposed to the Eastern European states.

With reference to the environment, plans call for the application in a few years of the rulings for air pollution (e.g., large power plants) and almost all rulings on water quality, as well as setting limits for air pollutants. In general, the adjustment period that began from the point of unification was one year longer than originally agreed upon for West Germany. For the construction of new industrial facilities, however, the EC norms applied immediately.

10. ASIA–PACIFIC ECONOMIC DEVELOPMENT

C. Higgins
Secretary, Australian Treasury
Canberra
Australia

Sadly, Dr. Higgins passed away suddenly on 6 December 1990.
Work underlying this chapter was undertaken in the International Economic
Conditions Section of the Australian Treasury.

1. INTRODUCTION

The harmonization of global regionalisms is an important issue that has been
given added urgency by several recent and prospective developments that prompt
concern that the world may be evolving into inward–looking regional economic
groupings.
These developments include the process to create a single European market by
1992; the recently completed U.S./Canada free–trade agreement; indications that
the GATT Uruguay Round will not be able to reduce substantially nontariff
barriers to trade; and the tendency toward the more widespread use of unilateral
discriminatory trading action.
Many observers have expressed concerns that protectionism will continue to
grow under a new guise of regionalism and that world trade and economic growth
will suffer as a result.
How to ensure that regional cooperation is consistent with nondiscriminatory principles and is outward–looking is an issue of paramount importance. This
chapter will discuss the Asia–Pacific region from this perspective, including:
1. economic development in Asia–Pacific countries and the emergence of
   an integrated economic region;
2. the reasons underlying the economic strength of the Asia–Pacific
   region, the potential benefits of further regional integration and
   cooperation for all economies, and the costs of "closed" regionalism; and
3. mechanisms developing in the Asia–Pacific to advance regional
   development and open multilateral economic relations—in
   particular, the Asia–Pacific Economic Cooperation (APEC) forum.
Such mechanisms point to how regionalism can be "harmonized," facilitating
the emergence of open and competitive economies as the basis for stronger and
sustained world growth.

2. DEVELOPMENT OF THE ASIA–PACIFIC REGION

The present core of the Asia–Pacific region includes
- the industrialized economies of the U.S., Canada, Japan, Australia, and
  New Zealand;

- the newly industrializing economies (NIEs) of the Republic of Korea, Taiwan, Hong Kong, and Singapore; and
- the other developing Asian nations of Malaysia, Thailand, the Philippines, Indonesia, Brunei (ASEAN), and China.

We often hear the Asia-Pacific region described as "the most dynamic region in the world economy"—so often, in fact, that the expression risks losing its impact. It is worth pausing for a moment to reflect on what this phrase actually means.

At one level, we can identify the dynamism of the region in terms of a number of individual success stories. Last year, for example, seven economies in the region achieved real growth of more than 6%.

At another level, we can see the region's dynamism in terms of various rapidly changing and expanding relationships—that is, in terms not only of growth and development but also of trade, direct investment and other capital flows, technology, tourism, changes in the structure of economies, and growing intraregional linkages.

2.1. Economic Growth and Size

Real GNP growth for the region in the 1980s averaged around 3.5% per annum, compared with 2.75% for the industrialized countries (see tables 1 and 2).

- At the same time, inflation has been relatively low in most cases, while employment and investment growth has been strong.
- The region's trade volumes increased by 6.5% in the 1980s compared with an increase in world trade of 4.5%. Comparisons from the mid–1980s to recent years, where available, are set out in table 3.
- The greatly expanded trade and productivity of the region have improved economic well-being (per capita output) at a faster rate than in other regions (see table 1).
  Figures 1 and 2 show the resulting shift in the share of global economic activity towards the Asia-Pacific.
- The region accounted for around 45% of world output in 1987 (the latest data available) compared with around 38% in the late 1960s.
- This reflects the outstanding growth performance of a number of Asian countries. In particular, Japan and the dynamic economies of Hong Kong, Singapore, South Korea, and Taiwan have more than tripled their share of the growing world economy in the last 20 years.
- The Asia-Pacific region is currently responsible for around 38% of world trade (see figure 3). This share has grown by about five percentage points in the last 20 years, particularly reflecting the growth of Japanese and Asian trade.
- The relative position of the Asia-Pacific should continue to expand. The sheer size of the population of the region indicates its productive and demand potential. By the turn of the century, the Asia-Pacific will make up well over half the world's economy—some estimates are as high as 55%.

2.2. Asia-Pacific Economic Interdependence and Linkages

What we have seen with the emergence of the Asia-Pacific region is a clear case of interconnected economic development and structural adjustment. The picture is one of complementary economies, substantial and growing economic linkages, and increased interdependence, based on growing economic strength and dynamic comparative advantages.

As Japan emerged during the 1960s, North America and Australasia provided a market for Japan's output as well as the raw materials it required. The NIEs concentrated on moving from subsistence and agricultural production into labor intensive manufactures.

More recently, as Japan moved into capital—and technology—intensive production, it has become an increasingly important source of demand in the region, including for manufactures and tourism. The NIEs began to move into areas of industry and trade that Japan had occupied, receiving investment and technology from Japan and elsewhere. Other ASEAN nations and China are now expanding their light manufactures, with the NIEs providing an increasing source of demand and investment for these economies.

Structural change has not been limited to the East Asian economies. The industrialized economies have also adapted to changing economic patterns, including greater competition. The natural resources and markets of North America and Australasia are an important and complementary component of the industrialization process of the other regional economies, and they have been important sources of investment, technology, and advanced services.

Regional economic growth and specialization have produced an intensive, multilayered network of trade and other economic ties.

2.3. Trade

A high proportion of trade in the Asia–Pacific is intraregional trade reflecting the complementarity between economies in the region.

- The proportion of intraregional trade has increased significantly in the last ten years, rising for the region as a whole from 54% in 1978 to 65% in 1988 (see figure 4).
  - Every major country category has also increased its share of intra-regional trade in the ten years to 1988.
- The NIEs and other ASEAN countries, China, Japan, and Australasia are the most heavily involved in intraregional trade (table 4). Nevertheless, North America is an important point in the triangle of trade that has emerged with Japan and the NIEs. Trade across the Pacific for countries such as Australia is also vitally important.
- Structural adjustment in the region has changed the pattern of intra-regional trade in recent years.
  - For many years, Asia–Pacific trade relationships were based on vertical trade, commonly the exchange of manufactures for raw materials and food.
  - Vertical trade has continued to expand and will remain important because of the varying resource endowments, labor costs, and technology of economies in the region.
  - Vertical trade has, however, been joined by an increasing element of horizontal trade in a broad range of goods, particularly between the NIEs and ASEAN countries on the one hand and Japan and the U.S. on the other.

2.4. Investment

Another factor enabling rapid economic growth in the Asia-Pacific is the high level of foreign direct investment including, more recently, increased intra-regional investment.

Direct investment has added to the growth in aggregate capital formation and has also facilitated the transfer of technology and management skills. Much direct investment has stimulated economic restructuring, intraregional trade, and a higher degree of regional integration. For the investing economies, direct foreign investment provides the opportunity for better returns for funds and other resources.

Intraregional investment makes up a large component of total investment flows in the Asia-Pacific region (see table 5).

- At the end of 1988, the stock of U.S. foreign direct investment was around US$ 327 billion, with more than US$ 100 billion or around one third received by other countries in the Asia-Pacific region.
- At end-September 1989, the stock of Japanese foreign direct investment totalled around US$ 217 billion, of which around US$ 140 billion or 64% was invested in other Asia-Pacific economies.
- Foreign direct investment by the newly industrializing economies is relatively small but growing dramatically. The vast majority of this investment is in countries in the Asia-Pacific.
- At end-June 1989, the stock of Australian foreign direct investment abroad totaled over A$ 28 billion, with over 40% invested in other Asia-Pacific economies. Of foreign investment in Australia, more than half comes from other Asia-Pacific economies.

The pattern of intraregional investment has also evolved over time. Previously, the larger and more developed economies (initially the U.S. but then also Japan) have invested in the NIEs. More recently, the NIEs have themselves become capital exporters, with the ASEAN nations receiving a great deal of this investment.

2.5. Other Linkages

Other linkages within the Asia-Pacific region have also expanded in recent years:

- The region includes some of the world's largest financial centers, particularly in the U.S. and Japan, while other cities—Singapore, Hong Kong, and Sydney—are major regional centers.
- While immigration has not been high in some Asia-Pacific countries, it is very important for others, and regional migration/labor flows have increased. For instance, in 1989 Australia received some 130,000 settler arrivals, of whom more than half were from other Asia-Pacific nations. The U.S. and Canada are also receiving increasing numbers of migrants from within the region.
- Trade in education services has expanded, and significant numbers of students from within the region have enrolled in higher and other tertiary educational institutions in the U.S., Canada, Australia, and elsewhere.
- Finally, the region's tourism has grown substantially over the past two decades. The vast majority of Asia-Pacific tourism is intraregional, accounting for more than three fourths of total tourism (see table 6).

It is clear that economies in the region have greater linkages among themselves than they have with economies outside the region. In some respects, the region is also more economically integrated than others. For example, whereas intra-Asia-Pacific trade accounts for 65% of the region's total trade, the comparable figures for the EC and the U.S./Canada are 60% and 30% respectively.

2.6. Prospects for the Asia-Pacific

The prospects for continued growth of the Asia-Pacific region remain favorable.

- The latest forecasts indicate Asia-Pacific real GDP growth in 1990 and 1991 could be as high as 5%. While this is somewhat lower than the growth experienced in much of the 1980s, it is still around twice the estimates of average world GDP growth (see figure 5 and table 7). Inflation, however, is forecasted to pick up and to rise more quickly than in the industrialized countries.
- While these forecasts were compiled prior to recent developments in the Persian Gulf, and the impact of these events on the region and the world is a source of uncertainty, it is not likely that the relative performance of the Asia-Pacific will suffer substantially.
- Some commentators have also suggested that the increased demands for investment and savings, associated with the transition of Eastern European countries to market economies, will divert activity and investment from the Asia-Pacific region. The extent to which this occurs, however, should not be major, since it is becoming increasingly clear that in many Eastern European countries the transition to market economies will occur over a long period.

  The potential for increased regional trade and investment is large, because
- Asia-Pacific economies are progressively expanding intensive trade ties with a number of economies in the region;
- the potential for specialization flowing from different comparative advantages is only starting to be realized; and
- the region has rising populations and living standards.

3. ASIA-PACIFIC REGION - THE BASIS FOR GROWTH

The strong economic growth in the Asia-Pacific has not been accidental. While owing something to the prolonged expansion of the global economy, it also owes much to regional developments and has, in turn, contributed to that global expansion.

3.1. Lessons of History

The Asia-Pacific economies are conspicuous in their willingness to engage in trade around the globe, forsaking the insular focus that is common elsewhere. They have not waited for opportunities to come to them, but have sought to forge their own niche in world markets.

In earlier stages of development, some of the more dynamic Asia-Pacific economies engaged in extensive import protection and closely regulated their domestic financial markets. In addition, the Chinese economy has, of course, been highly directed and regulated.

However, there has been steady movement through many countries in the region towards a policy framework that accords a more important place to outward-looking commercial, industrial, and financial policies and that relies primarily on market forces to ensure efficiency in resource allocation decisions.

A strong outward orientation has allowed these countries to specialize in areas of comparative advantage and has underpinned their strong growth and closer regional integration.

A high level of internal flexibility with an absence of substantial impediments to factor mobility, as well as hard-working and increasingly well-educated workforces has also contributed to growth. This is reflected in the declining share of the economy/population engaged in primary production in the fastest-growing economies, while the shares in industry and services have risen (see table 8).

The flexibility and adaptiveness of the Asia-Pacific economy has been enhanced by efforts to liberalize trade and capital flows. To give some examples of recent reductions in barrier protection:

- The Republic of Korea has reduced average tariff levels from 60% in 1970 to 28% in 1984.

- Indonesia reduced its effective rate of assistance to manufacturing from 137% to 58% in the late 1970s and has continued to reduce protection more recently.

- Japan has recently disbanded prohibitive restrictions on a number of food items, most notably beef, and has loosened controls on public construction projects.

- Australia and New Zealand have both recently announced widespread and substantial reductions in tariffs.

Meanwhile, some of the region's more dynamic performers opened up their economies long ago. Hong Kong, for example, maintains a completely free trading regime, while Singapore has virtually negligible import barriers.

The lessons of the economic history of the region therefore suggest that the Asia-Pacific countries should continue the development of open and competitive economies if they are to maintain their dynamic economic growth.

3.2. Regionalism and Multilateralism

It is clear that the Asia-Pacific has gained from increased regional integration based on appropriate and increasingly open market-oriented policies. The transformation of the Asia-Pacific into a distinct economic region is therefore one step towards the ideal of greater integration of the world economy based on market forces and comparative advantages, and towards enhanced world economic growth based on open nondiscriminatory multilateral policies.

Regional integration or cooperation that is inward oriented and protection-ist not only holds back the growth of that region's economies but also of the world economy more generally.

An example of an appropriate regional approach to trade is the Closer Economic Relations (CER) Agreement between Australia and New Zealand.[1] The CER is outward—looking and seeks to foster trade liberalization not only between the two countries but vis-à-vis all countries. Thus the liberalization of trade between the two countries has taken place against the backdrop of significant global reductions of trade barriers in both countries.

The benefits of CER are wider than an expansion of trade between Australia and New Zealand, important though that is. They also arise from the structural changes in the two economies that have been facilitated by CER and because they help pave the way for reducing protection more widely.

The European Community (EC)—which is aiming to develop a single unified market by 1992—is a prominent trade arrangement in the global arena. The nature of the external policy of the EC following the achievement of a single market is not clear at this stage, and some analysts have expressed concern that it might not be outward—looking, citing the Common Agricultural Policy (CAP) as an example.

As with CER, the logical step to accompany/follow the removal of internal barriers within the EC is to reduce substantially the external trade barriers, including domestic economic policies, which disrupt international trade flows. While such reforms will benefit world output, trade, and growth, the main beneficiaries will be EC consumers. That it is in the interests of the EC to do so is graphically highlighted in a recent study.

The study—"Western Trade Blocs — Game, Set or Match for the Asia—Pacific and the World Economy" by Stoeckel, Pearce and Banks of the Centre for International Economics in Canberra—examines the impact on the world economy of barriers to trade. It uses a methodology of linked general equilibrium models. Consistent with work elsewhere, including that by the World Bank, the study finds enormous potential gains from trade liberalization (see figures 6 and 7). Hopefully, the EC will recognize those gains in determining its policy approaches. This topic will be further discussed below.

3.3. Mechanisms for Asia—Pacific Regional Cooperation

As the interdependence of the Asia—Pacific region has been increasingly recognized, political mechanisms to advance its development further have emerged.

There are several mixed public—private bodies—including the Pacific Economic Cooperation Conference (PECC)—which have stimulated greater cooperation in the Asia—Pacific. The recently formed Asia—Pacific Economic Cooperation (APEC) forum is a comprehensive mechanism for cooperation between governments of the region as a whole. It has the prospect of lifting Asia—Pacific economic relations to a new plane.

---

[1]Another encouraging example among Asia—Pacific countries of outward—looking liberalization is the recent Structural Impediments Initiative (SII) agreed between the U.S. and Japan. Both countries are likely to benefit substantially from the implementation of their respective SII undertakings, but no other country will be made worse off.

4. ASIA-PACIFIC ECONOMIC COOPERATION (APEC)

The APEC forum was established following a proposal raised by the Australian Prime Minister in a speech during his visit to Korea in January 1989.

The first Ministerial Level Meeting (MLM) was held in Canberra in November 1989. The second MLM will be held in Seoul in October 1991, with further meetings envisaged in Thailand in 1992 and in the U.S. in 1993.

The grouping includes the U.S., Canada, Japan, Australia, New Zealand, the Republic of Korea, and the ASEAN countries. It is hoped that China, Hong Kong, and Taiwan will participate at the MLM in Seoul.

Since its inception the APEC process has had as its guiding principles:

- a commitment to open dialogue and consensus between the countries involved, with equal respect for the views of all participants, while recognizing the social and economic diversity of the region;
- a commitment to cooperation that will not lead to closed or inward-looking trading arrangements;
- a commitment to complement and draw on existing organization including ASEAN; and
- participation to be assessed on the basis of economic linkages, not ideology.

A full list of the underlying principles of APEC, which were agreed upon at the first APEC MLM in November 1989, is found in the appendix to this chapter.

APEC does not operate to promote an Asia-Pacific trading and financial bloc, but has embraced the principles of multilateralism. It emphasizes complementarity, interdependence, and comparative advantage as a means of maximizing growth and economic welfare. It has been agreed that the results of regional cooperation through APEC should not damage third parties.

APEC is thus a clear example of regional cooperation that aims to promote freer economic flows not only among the countries involved but also throughout the world.

4.1. Impediments to Growth

As noted earlier, there are concerns that some regional groupings will seek to maintain existing income levels and industries by stifling competition and sheltering behind costly import barriers and subsidies.

For the Asia-Pacific region, recent developments in the European Community and North America are of critical concern, since these provide the final destination for a substantial portion of the exports from the Asia-Pacific region.

- In both of those regions there appears to be a lack of enthusiasm for at least some forms of structural change. In particular, new sources of imports and a decline in agriculture are not being accommodated.
    - The EC's CAP has taken Europe from being the world's largest importer of agricultural goods in the early 1980s to being its largest exporter at present. This refusal to accept comparative advantage is perhaps the greatest single challenge to the current world trading system.
- The other major challenge is the growth in protection.

-    Tariff levels around the world are on a continuing downward trend, and the GATT has made a major contribution to this welcome development.

-    However, there is a growing recourse to the use of nontariff barriers such as quotas, voluntary export restraints, and orderly marketing arrangements. For example, a recent World Bank study (Laird and Yeats, 1988) found that the share of the major developed countries' trade "affected" by nontariff measures had nearly doubled to 48% from the level of 20 years earlier.

These nontariff barriers now constitute a major impediment to the growth of world trade. And, given the outward-looking orientation of our region, impediments to world trade will mean impediments to Asia-Pacific economic growth.

The political attraction of such measures is that their effects are hidden from general public view and scrutiny. The costs are indirect and diffuse. Consumers are not aware how much such assistance is costing them. For this reason, there is a strong case to make trade policy measures and their effects more transparent.

In that context, Australia has been an early and strong supporter of the recent establishment of a Trade Policy Review Mechanism (TPRM) within the GATT. The TPRM was set up following the midterm review within the current Uruguay Round. This involves a process of review of the trade policies and practices of individual countries. It is hoped that the greater transparency that results will discourage recourse to complex measures such as nontariff barriers, in preference to less trade-distorting policies.

In addition to impediments to world trade, there are a number of impediments within the Asia-Pacific region itself that are hampering the process of international specialization of production and comparative advantage and the development of greater linkages. As in the world more generally, these include industry protection, barriers to investment and financial flows, and structural rigidities—measures that distort appropriate market signals and that limit the capacities of the Asia-Pacific economies to continue expanding their trade and growth.

The role of APEC in dealing with these impediments to world and regional growth and the scope for enhanced regional cooperation will be discussed shortly. However, before proceeding, it should be noted that much can be done at an individual-country level. For instance, in Australia, the Industry Commission plays an active role in structural and industry reforms in Australia by publicizing, through an open public-enquiry process, the cost of protection and the benefits of structural reform and trade liberalization. It provides a model that may be of interest to others.

4.2. APEC's Role

The fundamental objectives of APEC are the promotion of sustained growth and development of the regional and world economy and the overcoming of impediments to Asia-Pacific growth.

Regional exchanges carry forward the interests of Asia-Pacific economies by adding to our knowledge of policies, practices, and economic developments; by providing opportunities for discussion of policy matters among decision makers of regional economies; and by identifying common problems that can be better tackled from a coordinated, regional platform in broader international discussions. Some examples are cited below.

- The joint statement issued at the Singapore MLM sets out a strong position on the GATT Uruguay Round, indicating that a successful conclusion of the Round was the primary objective of APEC this year and noting that all countries had agreed to review their negotiating positions.
- This was followed by more specific discussions at a meeting of APEC Trade Ministers held in Vancouver last month, which made progress of this kind on a number of fronts.
- Beyond the Uruguay Round, it has been agreed that a continuing central theme of APEC will be the promotion of a more open trading system. This would include the exploration of reductions in trade barriers in the region, which, of course, would be consistent with GATT principles and not to the detriment of third parties.
- A permanent feature of APEC MLMs is a full discussion of economic developments affecting the region. APEC has also launched a number of specific work projects that aim to examine areas where regional co-operation can identify and solve common problems, and where countries can otherwise gain by the sharing of experience and information in specific areas.

The APEC work program currently includes projects involving a review of trade and investment data; trade promotion; expansion of investment and technology transfer in the region; human resources development; regional energy cooperation; marine resource conservation; and telecommunications. An additional three work projects are under consideration in the areas of transport, tourism, and fisheries.

The results of these work projects are still emerging, and the APEC process itself is still feeling its way. However, APEC shows considerable promise as a coherent regional body able to present the views of the Asia-Pacific and to influence outcomes that will benefit not only the countries of the region but also the world by virtue of its open, multilateral precepts.

4.3. "Open Regionalism"

This chapter has highlighted

- the dramatic growth and development of the Asia-Pacific region and the increasing interdependencies within the region;
- the basis for that growth—economic policies that seek to produce open and competitive economies; and
- the increasing regional economic cooperation that should help to maintain growth both within the region and the world more generally, provided that it is firmly based on the APEC model of "open regionalism."

It is to be hoped that the success of the Asia-Pacific region in this regard will encourage other major regional groupings to commit themselves clearly to an open market-oriented approach, not only in the context of the current GATT negotiations, but also in the longer term across a broad spectrum of economic policies.

APPENDIX: THE PRINCIPLES OF APEC

The nine principles of the Asia—Pacific Economic Cooperation (APEC) forum are as follows:

- the objective of enhanced Asia—Pacific Economic Cooperation is to sustain the growth and development of the world economy;
- cooperation should recognize the diversity of the region, including differing social and economic systems and current levels of development;
- cooperation should involve a commitment to open dialogue and consensus, with equal respect for the views of all participants;
- cooperation should be based on nonformal consultative exchanges of views among Asia—Pacific economies;
- cooperation should focus on those economic areas where there is scope to advance common interests and achieve mutual benefits;
- consistent with the interests of the Asia—Pacific, cooperation should be directed at strengthening the open multilateral trading system: it should not involve the formation of a trading bloc;
- cooperation should aim to strengthen the gains from interdependence, both for the region and the world economy, including by encouraging the flows of goods, services, capital, and technology;
- cooperation should complement and draw upon, rather than detract from, existing organizations in the region, including formal intergovernmental bodies such as ASEAN and less formal consultative bodies like the Pacific Economic Cooperation Conference (PECC); and
- participation by Asia—Pacific economies should be assessed in the light of the strength of economic linkages with the region, and may be extended in the future on the basis of consensus on the part of all participants.

TABLE 1: KEY INDICATORS FOR ASIA–PACIFIC ECONOMIES, 1980–1988
(Average per annum growth, percent)

	Real Output (b)	Real Output per capita	Consumer Prices (b)	Empl't (d)	Real gross fixed Invest. (b)
Industrialized Countries (a)					
Australia	3.2	1.7	8.5	2.1	3.3
Canada	3.0	2.1 (f)	6.6	1.8	5.5
Japan	4.1	3.4 (f)	2.6	1.0	4.8
New Zealand	2.3 (e)	1.7 (e)	12.5	0.2	3.7
United States	2.6	1.6 (f)	5.6	1.7	2.3
Total	3.1	2.20 (b) 2.17 (c)	4.8	1.5	3.3
Newly Industrializing Economies (g)					
Hong Kong	8.0	6.3	8.5	3.1	5.3
Korea, Rep. of	7.6	6.2	8.4	2.4	7.4
Singapore	6.9	6.4	2.8	2.2	6.4
Taiwan	7.5	6.2	4.4	2.6	5.6
Total	7.6	6.25 (b) 6.24 (c)	6.6	2.5	6.4
Other ASEAN (g)					
Brunei (j)	-1.4 (h)	-5.1 (h)	n.a.	4.9 (k)	n.a.
Indonesia	5.0 (h)	2.8 (h)	9.1	3.6 (h)	8.1 (h)(i)
Malaysia	5.4	2.6	3.8	2.9	4.5
Philippines	1.6	-0.9	15.5	3.1	-4.8
Thailand	6.2	4.1	5.8	3.5 (e)	5.4
Total	4.6	2.27 (b) 2.28 (c)	8.6	3.4	4.3
China (g)	9.3 (h)	8.0 (h)	7.1	3.3 (h)	11.2 (h)(i)
Total Asia–Pacific Region	3.5	2.55 (b) 5.71 (c)	5.0	2.9	3.7
Total Asia–Pacific Region – excluding China	3.3	2.35 (b) 2.58 (c)	4.9	2.3	3.4

(a) Source: IMF International Financial Statistics, Yearbook 1989.

(b) Groupings weighted by 1987 GDP/GNP estimates.

(c) Groupings weighted by 1987 population estimates.

(d) Groupings weighted by 1988 employment estimates.

(e) 1980 to 1986.

(f) Source: IMF World Economic Outlook, October 1990

(g) Source: ADB Key Indicators of Developing Member Countries of ADB, July 1989.

(h) 1980 to 1987.

(i) Deflated using GDP deflator.

(j) Source: World Bank Atlas 1988.

(k) 1982 to 1986.

TABLE 2: KEY INDICATORS FOR INDUSTRIALIZED COUNTRIES, 1980-1989 (a)
(Annual changes, percent)

	1980-89(b) Average	1980	1981	1982	1983	1984	1985	1986	1987	1988	1989
REAL OUTPUT											
United States	2.6	-0.2	1.9	-2.5	3.6	6.8	3.4	2.7	3.4	4.5	2.5
Japan	4.2	4.3	3.7	3.1	3.2	5.1	4.9	2.5	4.6	5.7	4.9
Germany	1.9	1.5	0.0	-1.0	1.9	3.3	1.9	2.3	1.7	3.6	4.0
INDUSTRIALIZED COUNTRIES	2.7	1.4	1.5	-0.3	2.7	4.9	3.4	2.6	3.5	4.3	3.3
WORLD	2.8	2.2	1.5	0.5	2.6	4.4	3.2	3.0	3.3	4.1	3.0
CONSUMER PRICES											
United States	5.5	13.5	10.4	6.1	3.2	4.4	3.6	1.9	3.6	4.1	4.8
Japan	2.5	8.0	5.0	2.7	1.9	2.3	2.0	0.6	0.1	0.7	2.3
Germany	2.9	5.5	6.3	5.3	3.3	2.4	2.2	-0.1	0.2	1.3	2.8
INDUSTRIALIZED COUNTRIES	5.6	11.8	10.1	7.5	4.9	4.7	4.2	2.4	3.0	3.3	4.4
GROSS FIXED INVESTMENT											
United States	2.1	-7.9	1.1	-9.6	8.2	16.8	5.3	1.0	1.9	5.6	1.6
Japan	5.3	-0.1	3.1	0.8	-0.3	4.9	5.8	5.8	10.4	12.6	11.0
Germany	1.5	2.8	-4.8	-5.3	3.2	0.8	0.1	3.3	2.2	5.9	7.2
INDUSTRIALIZED COUNTRIES	4.0	-1.5	-0.6	4.6	3.1	8.8	4.7	3.0	4.7	8.1	5.5
EMPLOYMENT GROWTH											
United States	1.7	0.5	1.1	-0.9	1.3	4.1	2.0	2.3	2.6	2.2	2.0
Japan	1.1	1.0	0.8	1.0	1.7	0.6	0.7	0.8	1.0	1.7	1.9
Germany	0.4	1.5	-0.6	-1.1	-1.4	0.2	0.8	1.4	0.7	0.7	1.4
INDUSTRIALIZED COUNTRIES	1.1	0.6	0.2	-0.6	0.5	2.1	1.4	1.7	1.8	1.8	1.8
UNEMPLOYMENT RATES (c)											
United States	7.3	7.2	7.6	9.7	9.6	7.5	7.2	7.0	6.2	5.5	5.3
Japan	2.5	2.0	2.2	2.4	2.7	2.7	2.6	2.8	2.8	2.5	2.3
Germany	7.0	3.3	4.8	6.7	8.1	8.1	8.2	7.9	7.9	7.7	7.1
INDUSTRIALIZED COUNTRIES	7.4	5.7	6.6	8.0	8.6	8.1	8.0	7.9	7.5	6.9	6.4

SOURCE: IMF World Economic Outlook, October 1990.

(a) Composites for the country groups are averages of percentage changes for individual countries weighted by the average U.S. dollar value of their respective GDPs over the preceding three years.

(b) Compound annual rate of change.

(c) Proportion of total labor force.

TABLE 3

WORLD TRADE VOLUMES, 1984–1989 (a)

(Annual changes, percent)

	Average 1984–89 (b)	1984	1985	1986	1987	1988	1989
World	6.5	8.6	2.7	4.9	6.7	9.1	7.4
Industrialized Countries	7.3	11.1	4.5	6.0	6.1	9.0	7.7
Asia–Pacific Region (c)(d)	NA	14.1	3.3	7.5	9.9	NA	NA
Industrialized Countries	NA	15.3	3.6	5.5	6.7	NA	NA
NIEs	NA	13.6	3.2	16.7	23.1	17.8	NA
Other ASEAN	6.7	-0.9	-1.8	3.2	7.6	14.2	19.4 (e)

SOURCES: IMF World Economic Outlook, October 1989, and International Financial Statistics, Yearbook 1989;
World Bank 'World Tables,' 1988–89; and Asian Development Bank 'Key Indicators,' July 1989.

(a) Averages of growth rates for exports and imports.
(b) Compound annual rates of change.
(c) Excluding China and Brunei.
(d) Groupings weighted by 1987 merchandise trade.
(e) Includes only imports data for the Philippines and exports data for the
     Philippines and Malaysia.

TABLE 4: TRADE IN ASIA–PACIFIC REGION

Country	Share of Exports going to Asia-Pacific Economies from ...		Share of Imports going to Asia-Pacific Economies from ...		Share of Trade with Asia-Pacific Economies	
	1978	1988	1978	1988	1978	1988
Japan	54.7%	66.7%	51.4%	62.8%	53.2%	65.1%
China	55.7%	69.9%	50.2%	65.3%	52.8%	67.4%
NIEs	64.6%	73.5%	69.8%	74.6%	67.4%	74.0%
Other ASEAN	75.3%	74.9%	65.5%	69.3%	70.9%	72.3%
North America	47.7%	59.2%	50.6%	62.3%	49.3%	60.9%
Australia and New Zealand	63.3%	67.8%	57.4%	65.9%	60.4%	66.9%
Total excluding Japan and North America	66.6%	72.6%	64.5%	71.3%	65.5%	72.0%
Total Asia-Pacific	54.3%	65.7%	54.2%	65.2%	54.2%	65.4%

TABLE 5: ASIA-PACIFIC FOREIGN DIRECT INVESTMENT

Major Investment Sources					Major Investment Destinations			
	Rank	Amount	%			Rank	Amount	%
United States (a)					United States (a)			
		(US$m)					(US$m)	
Investment in					Investment from			
– Canada	1	61244	18.7%		– Japan	2	53354	16.2%
– Japan	5	16868	5.2%		– Canada	4	27361	8.3%
– Australia	7	13058	4.0%		– Australia	7	5330	1.6%
– Hong Kong	8	5028	1.5%		– Total Asia-Pacific		86045	26.2%
– Indonesia	9	3006	0.9%		– Total		328850	
– Total Asia-Pacific		107549	32.9%					
– Total		326900			Canada (c)			
							(C$m)	
Japan (b)					Investment from			
		(US$m)			– United States	1	66337	73.2%
Investment in					– Japan	4	2340	2.6%
– United States	1	84985	39.1%		– Total Asia-Pacific		68677	75.7%
– Australia	3	10402	4.8%		– Total		90670	
– Indonesia	4	10142	4.7%					
– Hong Kong	6	7108	3.3%		Australia (d)			
– Singapore	9	3006	1.4%				(A$m)	
– Total Asia-Pacific		139954	64.4%		Investment from			
– Total		217180			– United States	2	19616	32.2%
					– Japan	3	5883	9.7%
Canada (c)					– Canada	4	2116	3.5%
		(C$m)			– New Zealand	6	2003	3.3%
Investment in					– Singapore	9	1131	1.9%
– United States	1	37836	71.2%		– Total Asia-Pacific		31653	51.9%
– Indonesia	3	1112	2.1%		– Total		60947	
– Australia	5	963	1.8%					
– Total Asia-Pacific		39911	75.1%		Japan (e)			
– Total		53173					(US$m)	
					Investment from			
Australia (d)					– United States	1	6268	49.0%
		(A$m)			– Hong Kong	6	390	3.0%
Investment in					– Total Asia-Pacific		8311	65.0%
– United States	2	4493	15.9%		– Total		12794	
– New Zealand	3	4357	15.4%					
– Hong Kong	5	1586	5.6%		Taiwan (f)			
– Total Asia-Pacific		11798	41.8%				(US$m)	
– Total		28237			Investment from			
					– Japan	1	2837	26.8%
					– United States	2	2713	25.6%
					– Hong Kong	3	1141	10.8%
					– Total Asia-Pacific		6691	63.1%
					– Total		10597	

(a) *Stock of Direct Investment as at end-1988.*
(b) *Stock of Direct Investment as at end-September 1989.*
(c) *Stock of Direct Investment as at end-1986.*
(d) *Stock of Direct Investment as at end-June 1988.*
(e) *Stock of Direct Investment as at end-March 1989.*
(f) *Cumulative Direct Investment 1952 to end-October 1989.*

TABLE 6

NUMBER OF TOURIST ARRIVALS IN THE ASIA–PACIFIC – 1987

	Total ('000s)	From Asia–Pacific Economies	
		%	('000s)
Australia	1785	65	1160
Canada	15017	88	13215
Brunei Darussalam (a)	201	96	193
China (b)	1728	71	1227
Hong Kong	4566	79	3607
Indonesia	1050	63	662
Japan	2155	77	1659
Korea	1875	92	1725
Malaysia (c)	1246	44	548
New Zealand	844	84	709
Philippines	795	83	660
Singapore	3679	72	2649
Taiwan	1761	91	1603
Thailand	3346	67	2242
United States (d,e)	29657	72	21353
Hawaii	5607	94	5271
TOTAL	75312	78	58482

SOURCE: PECC Pacific Economic Outlook 1990–1991

(a) *Figure for Brunei is a 1986 figure.*
(b) *Figures for China do not include overseas Chinese.*
    These numbers were not included due to the high volume of
    Hong Kong Chinese making frequent cross-border trips.
(c) *Figure for Malaysia is a 1988 figure.*
(d) *Figures for United States do not include Hawaii.*
(e) *Figures for United States only indicate arrivals by air.*

TABLE 7

WORLD ECONOMIC PROSPECTS
(Annual percentage changes)

	1989	1990	1991
REAL OUTPUT			
World	3.0	2.1	2.7
Industrialized countries	3.4	2.8	2.8
Developing countries	3.0	2.4	4.2
-Asia	6.0	5.1	5.8
-NIEs	5.5	6.6	5.7
Asia-Pacific region (a)	5.3	5.0	5.2
TRADE VOLUMES			
World	7.4	5.9	5.9
GROSS FIXED INVESTMENT			
Industrialized countries	5.5	3.3	5.3
INFLATION (CONSUMER PRICES)			
Industrialized countries	4.4	4.5	3.8
Asia-Pacific region (a)	6.5	6.1	5.5

SOURCES: All forecasts are from IMF World Economic Outlook, October 1990,
except for (a), which is from PECC Pacific Economic Outlook, April 1990.

TABLE 8

SECTORAL SHARES OF GDP:
ASIA-PACIFIC REGION

	Value added in Agriculture (% of GDP)		Value added in Industry (% of GDP)		Value added in Services (% of GDP)	
	1970	1987	1970	1987	1970	1987
Industrialized Countries						
Australia	6.05	4.06	40.50	32.15	53.45	63.79
Canada (a)	3.67	2.96	31.68	29.44	64.64	67.60
Japan	6.09	2.80	46.64	40.60	47.27	56.70
New Zealand (b)	12.60	8.41	31.47	15.07	55.92	76.52
United States	2.72	2.00	34.84	29.20	62.44	68.80
SUB TOTAL (WTD GDP)	3.42	2.39	36.59	32.86	59.98	64.79
	1970	1989	1970	1989	1970	1989
Newly Industrialized Countries						
Hong-Kong	2.20	0.40	36.50	28.80	61.40	70.90
Korea, Rep. of	28.00	9.00	22.40	45.20	49.60	45.80
Singapore	2.30	0.40	29.80	36.60	67.90	63.00
Taiwan	16.90	4.40	35.50	45.40	47.70	50.10
Other ASEAN						
Brunei	NA	NA	NA	NA.	NA	NA
Indonesia	46.00	20.50	20.90	40.30	33.10	39.30
Malaysia	32.00	20.20	24.70	41.00	43.30	38.70
Phillipines	28.80	26.90	29.40	33.10	41.80	40.00
Thailand	30.20		25.70	33.70	44.10	50.50
China	41.20	24.30	35.90	60.70	22.90	15.00
SUB TOTAL (WTD GDP)	36.21	15.25	32.46	48.63	31.33	35.18

SOURCES: ASIAN COUNTRIES: Asia Development Bank Outlook 1990, p.227.
OECD: Historical Statistics 1960-87 and National Accounts.

(a) Canadian data are 1986 data.
(b) NZ data are for 1971.

134

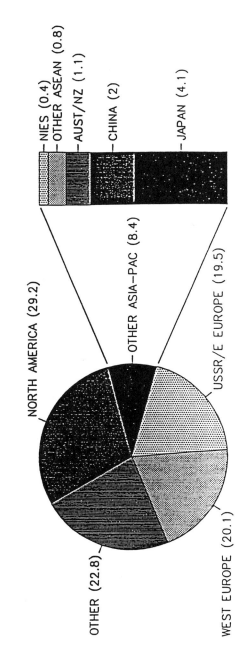

FIGURE 1

DISTRIBUTION OF WORLD GNP — 1967
(PERCENT) (a)

NIES (0.4)
OTHER ASEAN (0.8)
AUST/NZ (1.1)
CHINA (2)
JAPAN (4.1)

NORTH AMERICA (29.2)

OTHER ASIA-PAC (8.4)

USSR/E EUROPE (19.5)

OTHER (22.8)

WEST EUROPE (20.1)

(a)   Includes World Bank nonmember,
      nonreporting countries, such as the USSR.

FIGURE 2

DISTRIBUTION OF WORLD GNP – 1987
(PERCENT) (a)

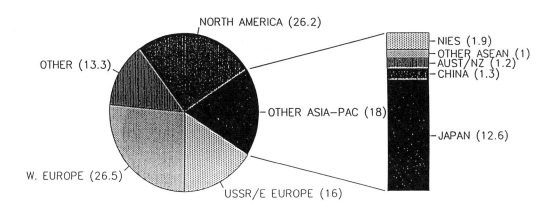

(a) Includes World Bank nonmember,
nonreporting countries, such as the USSR.

FIGURE 3

SHARE OF WORLD TRADE
(PERCENT)

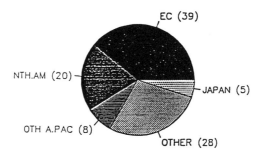

SHARE OF WORLD TRADE
1967

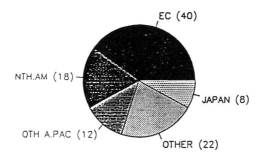

SHARE OF WORLD TRADE
1987

137

FIGURE 4

SHARE OF TRADE WITH ASIA–PACIFIC ECONOMIES
(PERCENT)

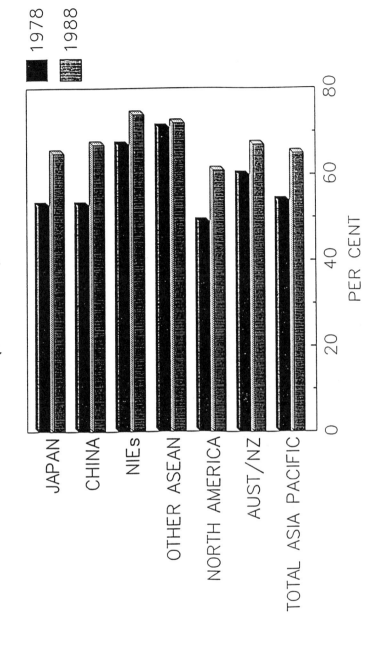

138

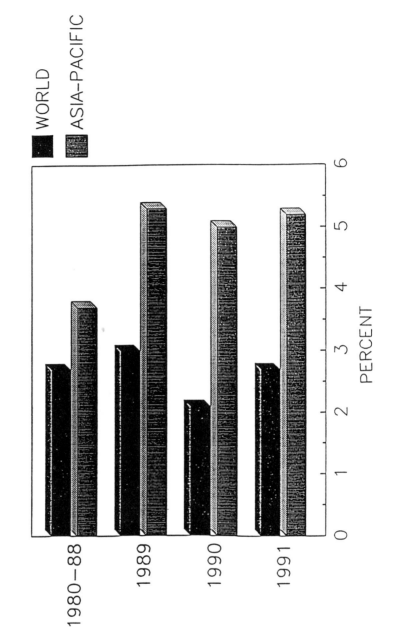

FIGURE 5

WORLD AND ASIA-PACIFIC OUTPUT GROWTH

139

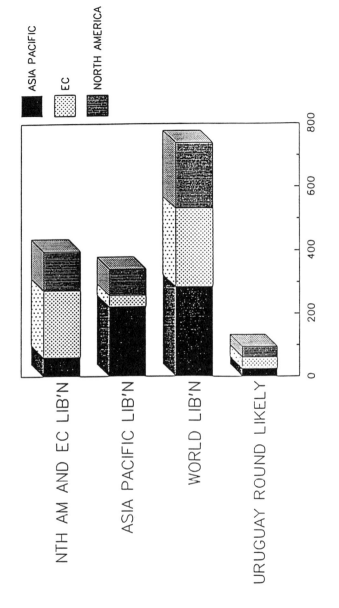

FIGURE 6

GAINS FROM TRADE LIBERALIZATION
CHANGES IN GDP IN 1988 US$ BILLION (a)

ASIA PACIFIC
EC
NORTH AMERICA

NTH AM AND EC LIB'N

ASIA PACIFIC LIB'N

WORLD LIB'N

URUGUAY ROUND LIKELY

0   200   400   600   800

Source: Centre for International Economics, 1990,
"Western Trade Blocs: Game, Set or Match for
Asia-Pacific and the World Economy?"

(a) Changes in the level of GDP after liberalization effects are fully worked through.

FIGURE 7

Payoff matrix from EC and North America protection or liberalization

Changes in GDP in 1988 US$ billion (a)

	North America protects (retaliates)		North America liberalizes	
EC protects ('fortress' Europe)	EC	−132	EC	42
	Asia–Pacific	−18	Asia–Pacific	38
	North America	−64	North America	53
		World −214		World 133
EC liberalises	EC	37	EC	211
	Asia–Pacific	7	Asia–Pacific	63
	North America	7	North America	124
		World 50		World 397

(a) Changes in the level of GDP after liberalization effects are fully worked through

Source: Centre for International Economics (1990)
"Western Trade Blocs: Game, Set or Match for Asia–Pacific and the World Economy?"
(An independent report commissioned by the Confederation of Asia–Pacific Chambers of Commerce and Industry.)

11. THE RISE OF EAST ASIA AND RECENT EXTERNAL SHOCKS

Yasukichi Yasuba
Osaka University
Department of Economics
1-1 Machikaneyama-machi
Toyonaka, JAPAN 560

ABSTRACT. In the last 10 to 20 years economic activity in the countries of East Asia, including China, rose very substantially. Whether government-guided or laissez-faire, these countries relied heavily on the market and prospered on the exports of manufactured goods. In the early phase of industrialization, most of these countries invited direct foreign investment on a massive scale. By the end of the 1980s, East Asia was the growth center of the world. Three major incidents between 1989 and 1991, namely, the crushing of the student movement for democracy in Beijing, the fall of Communism in Eastern Europe, and the resultant end of the Cold War—as well as the recent Gulf War—shook the world and East Asia as a part of it. These incidents, and particularly the latter two, will have long-lasting effects on the future of world history, but the position of East Asia as the growth center of the world will not be much affected.

1. INTRODUCTION

The rapid economic growth of the East Asian countries is, by now, well known. Four newly industrializing economies (NIEs), namely, Hong Kong, South Korea, Taiwan, and Singapore, grew at annual rates of around 10% in the Golden '60s. Other ASEAN nations were not far behind. What is remarkable is the continuation of this growth in later years which included two oil crises. ASEAN countries other than Singapore also accelerated their pace of growth in the 1970s. The decline of the rate of growth of world trade in the middle of the 1980s slowed down the growth of most countries, but they regained the status of fastest-growing countries by the latter half of the 1980s. Finally, China recorded a very fast growth after it changed its policy in 1978 and introduced a market mechanism.

This chapter will first survey the growth of the NIEs in East Asia. The industrial growth of "patrimonial" ASEAN states may be hard to understand, so this development will be explained, taking Thailand as a example. Then, the recent acceleration of Chinese growth will be described. Finally, the effect on these countries of recent shocks, political repression in China, democratization in Eastern Europe, and Iraq's invasion of Kuwait will be assessed.

2. NIEs

In the 1960s, free-trading Hong Kong started to grow rapidly due to machinery and entrepreneurs brought from the mainland. The rising number of manufactured exports, which consisted of textiles, apparel, plastic products, and toys went largely to industrial countries such as the United States, Japan, and Europe. The existence of disciplined low-wage workers made Hong Kong's exports highly competitive in foreign markets.

In other NIEs, the governments intervened more or less to promote exports. South Korea changed its policy of import substitution to export promotion in the early 1960s without lowering high tariff barriers on consumers goods, just like Japan. South Korea also followed Japan in subsidizing exportable goods.

In industry, South Korea imported capital goods from Japan and exported mostly light manufactured commodities to industrialized countries. Unlike Hong Kong and Taiwan, the Korean Government favored heavy industry from a relatively early period. Its Third Economic Development Plan, which started in 1973, mentioned iron and steel, nonferrous metals, petroleum, machinery, ship-building, and electronics as the six "strategic" industries and supported their growth.

In industry, Taiwan also started from import substitution and the introduction of direct foreign investment. Just like South Korea, it relied heavily on the import of capital goods from Japan and the export of light manufactures to the United States. Textiles, apparel, shoes, and light electric and electronic appliances became major export commodities. Huge firms did not emerge, in contrast to South Korea, because Taiwan did not support specific industries or firms through favorable credit rationing. It should be noted that the lessguided Taiwanese economy grew at about the same rate as the Korean economy. Big projects such as highways, railroads, ports, iron and steel, and petrochemicals were first started as public projects.

Government also played an important role in the growth of Singapore. Here, a major source of funding was the social security fund (Central Provident Fund), which was used for building of infrastructure, including apartments and the Jurong Industrial Park. Major industries were built by foreign firms and joint ventures. Since investment was not heavily controlled in Singapore, export industries ranged from labor-intensive textile, apparel, and plywood manufacture to capital-intensive refined oil, machinery, and shipbuilding.

As real wages became higher, the center of industry in the NIEs shifted to more capital-intensive or knowledge-intensive industries. Again in Hong Kong, government intervention was minimal. The recent growth of the exports of watches and electric appliances was a major event in this economy.

Singapore adopted a "high wage" policy to withdraw from labor-intensive sectors in the beginning of the 1980s. This policy, combined with the world recession in 1985, brought forth a zero growth rate in that year. This caused a rapid shift of the industrial structure from light to heavy industry, and the growth rate bounced back to 8.8% in 1987 and 11.0% in 1988.

Similar shifts can be observed in South Korea where electric appliances, shipbuilding, petrochemicals, iron and steel, and automobiles became major exports. South Korea was affected severely by the world recession in 1985. The vitality of the economy, however, was so strong that the growth rate exceeded 10% in 1986.

In Taiwan, reaction to world recession was similar, and the export of electronic components, color TVs, and cassette-recorders increased significantly. Rapid growth was resumed, just as in South Korea, to more than 10% by 1986.

Another recent feature of the economy in Taiwan was the creation of a huge current account surplus. The surplus became as large as 21.85 of GNP in 1986 and had to be consciously curtailed in the ensuing years.

To sum up, all the NIEs grew at such high rates under relatively (Korea) or completely (Hong Kong) liberal policy that all of them achieved a highly respectable level of income by 1988. Per capita GDP was $9230 for Hong Kong and $9100 for Singapore. Taiwan ($6070) and South Korea ($3530) were somewhat behind but were closing ground. Hong Kong and Singapore may now be included as industrial countries. Taiwan and South Korea will soon acquire that status.

3. THE DEVELOPMENT OF A PATRIMONIAL STATE: THAILAND

All the Southeast Asian nations, with the exception of Singapore, used to be patrimonial states. This section will explain how Thailand developed, even though many people thought that such a state would never become a high-income industrial country. In fact, a political scientist characterized the social change of Thailand in the century preceding 1970 as "modernization without development." Even J.C. Ingram, an economist, entitled his book on Thai economic history up to 1970 Economic Changes in Thailand rather than Economic Development of Thailand.

According to the thesis of the patrimonial state, the patrimony and politics of the authority were yet to be clearly separated. The ruling authority from time to time sold off part of their power to minority groups, usually Europeans and overseas Chinese, to make the best use of patrimony. "Tax farming" in which the authority sold off the right to tax, is the typical patrimonial way to run the state. Similarly, the ruling authority sold off various monopoly rights, the right to produce and sell a certain product, the right to organize gambling, and the right to dig a canal and to sell the land along it.

The ruling authority has maintained patrimony, while the Chinese and other foreigners managed their acquired concessions within the prescribed framework. Under the circumstances, however greatly patrimonial bureaucracy was modernized and however extensively the concessions were utilized, economic development never permeated the indigenous society.

The Europeans, the Chinese, and the indigenous people tended to live in separate places, with the first two in towns and the indigenous people in rural areas. The Europeans tended to run mines and plantations, and the Chinese were engaged in commerce, money lending, and land reclamation. Lower-class Chinese, who worked as manual laborers in mines, plantations, and construction sites, tried to climb the social ladder to become merchants, money lenders, and landowners. Through hard work, most of them succeeded, more or less, and went back to their homeland in China with some fortunes.

Even today it may be argued that the ASEAN states are still patrimonial states. Much of the industrialization before 1970 can be explained in terms of patrimonialism. Direct foreign investment for import substitution can be explained away as giving investment privileges and protection to foreigners in exchange for positions and shares in joint ventures and other gifts. The authority was satisfied with the transaction, and foreign interests did not have to try hard to innovate because they were protected from imports.

Moreover, protection removed the criteria for selecting the right industry, because any industry could become profitable if the government raised tariffs to the necessary height or banned the import of competing goods altogether.

Understandably, as did most other governments of developing countries, ASEAN governments chose "modern industries," which tended to be capital intensive, skill intensive, and large-scale in the first phase of industrialization.

Workers in joint-venture factories were not yet well educated in the 60s. They lacked punctuality and did not come to the factory after pay days until the money was exhausted. Absenteeism and turnover ratio were extremely high. Uninterested in work, workers never tried to improve production methods or help other workers, even when they were not busy. In other words, they were like legendary British workers in the mercantile period.

Unfortunately, the combination of such managers and workers did not produce good results. In the first place, the industries being promoted relied on resources that were scarce in developing countries, namely, capital and skill. As a result, not much employment was created, and the unemployed people had to work on marginal farms and urban informal sectors. People who were still less lucky had to be counted as unemployed. The real wages of unskilled workers did not rise at all.

Another feature of modern industry, that of its large size, worked against the policy of import substitution. While there were foreign imports to be replaced, domestic industry expanded production rapidly. This was what is called "the easy phase of import substitution." This phase had to come to an end eventually as the protected domestic industry came to occupy most of the market.

Fortunately, however, two important changes—improvement in human resources and change in policy—were taking place. Education and on-the-job training raised the quality of labor substantially. From 1974 the government began to improve the teacher-pupil ratio drastically, and the curriculum became more pragmatic. The enrollment ratio rose at all levels. By 1980, absenteeism and the turnover ratio of young workers improved substantially at factories. Workers' discipline and morale became higher, and they even started to be interested in technical improvement.

Education and research at tertiary levels also improved. The Faculty of Economics at Thammasat University, which had only one Ph.D. in 1970, now has more than 40 and it has exported many Ph.D.s to other universities. Empirical research, which was started at the end of the 1960s, became the main stream of economic research at universities. The graduates of the engineering schools, who used to sit in offices, now come down to the shop floor and engage themselves in repairing of machines and in assisting productivity improvement.

With this background, the government introduced a new Industrial Investment Law in 1972. The Law reduced tariffs and turnover taxes for export industries. It also exempted the corporate income tax for specified export industries. Finally, interest on export credit was lowered to encourage exports. In 1978, the Industrial Investment Law was amended. It reduced the price of electric power for large exporters. The rapid increase of the export of frozen food was promoted by this measure. Beginning in 1978, tariff rates were reduced on a number of imports. Probably more important was the devaluation of the baht. The baht was linked with the U.S. dollar at the rate of 20-21 baht per dollar for a long time, but this rate was changed to 23 baht per dollar in 1981 and to 27 baht per dollar in 1984. After the Plaza Accord, a 50% appreciation of the yen vis-à-vis the dollar benefited Thailand, whose currency was still pegged to the U.S. dollar.

Finally, Thailand declared that it would definitely seek to become an export-oriented country according to a plan adopted in the 1980s. Considering that Thailand was a resource-rich country, the plan stated that Thailand will aim to be a New Agro-Industrializing Country (NAIC). Actually, Thailand was no longer such a resource-rich country. This policy means that the Thai government will try to export manufactures, including processed food, in the future. With this in mind, it now allows 100% foreign-owned investment if the company in question is ready to export more than 80% of its product. This decision coincided with the appreciation of the yen, discussed earlier. With disciplined workers and pragmatic engineers, Thailand in the 1980s was ready to receive direct foreign investment in large quantities.

Direct foreign investment (approval basis) in promoted industries increased 67% in 1986, 460% in 1987, and more than 300% in 1988, compared with the same period one year earlier. Japan was the number-one investing country, followed by Taiwan. Industries covered had a wide range and included machinery, transport equipment, metal products, textiles, and frozen agricultural and fishery products. About three fourths of the Japanese investment was export oriented. Virtually all new investments were labor intensive.

Thailand in the 1960s was apparently dominated by rent-seeking "big shots." Even today we find them in large numbers, but there are also a number of younger managers who are interested in production and innovation. The most important implication of the switch from import substitution to export promotion is that the switch tends to weaken the basis of patrimonial tradition. In the case of import substitution, the authority can increase revenue by raising tariff rates and creating special privileges, which are given to the Chinese and other foreign capitalists in exchange for high-ranking positions, equity shares, and other types of rewards, as stated before. Under such arrangements, it is only natural for managers and workers not to feel obliged to make innovations.

In the case of export promotion, on the contrary, the government has to endure reduction of revenue and/or increase of subsidies. Even in this case it is possible to create vested interests by restricting the number of entrants, but it is not possible to increase revenues while creating special privileges, as in the case of import substitution. In any case, the Thai government has been inviting more exporting firms rather than restricting their entry. Under the circumstances, the managers are always forced to increase productivity in order to compete in the world market. This appears to be the most important reason why the export-oriented strategy is much more effective than the import-substitution strategy. This seems to explain the success of Thailand and other ASEAN countries in the 1980s.

In addition, exports from these countries are more labor intensive than imports. Hence the transformation of these countries from import-substituting economies to export-oriented economies must have meant substantial improvements in resource allocation.

I made surveys of Thai factories to measure the improvement in productivity and to find cause of such improvement in the period 1971-1981. The average growth rate of total-factor productivity in this period for the firms visited was 7.1% per year, which is extremely high. In Japanese joint ventures, average productivity grew at 10.3%, the highest. Indigenous firms recorded a reasonably high average rate of 7.6%. In Euro-American firms, the growth rate was the lowest, but even here it was a respectable 4.4%. Such high average growth rates of total-factor productivity can hardly take place in a predominantly patrimonial state. This is clear for Thailand, where the proportion of manufactures in total exports increased from 5% in 1970 to 53% in 1987.

4. OTHER ASEAN COUNTRIES

Similar transformations have taken place in other ASEAN countries. Indonesia gained from the Oil Crisis, but its growth rate became somewhat lower in the mid-1980s. Indonesia has never recorded a negative growth rate, however, and it regained a rate of around 5% by the end of the 1980s. Indonesia's strategy of shifting from oil to nonoil industry appears to be paying off. Manufacturing industry grew at an annual rate of 10%, and some manufactures such as plywood and apparel began to be exported. The attainment of self-sufficiency in rice should also be noted. Indonesia was traditionally an importer of rice and suffered from social unrest in bad harvest years. Irrigation, introduction of high-yield varieties of rice, and the increased input of fertilizer raised the yield of rice, and self-sufficiency was achieved by the mid-1980s. This is highly meaningful from the viewpoint of social stability.

Malaysia is also a resource-rich country, second only to Indonesia. Its major exports were petroleum, rubber, tin, and more recently palm oil. As the 1969 racial crush showed, the minority issue was a very important social problem for this country. The Chinese, who composed more than 30% of the total population, were usually engaged in commerce and money lending and occupied most of the important business positions in cities.

To reduce the discontent of the Malays, the government adopted what was called the "New Economic Policy," which was intended to raise the position of the Malayian citizens. One important component of the "New Economic Policy" was an assimilation policy in education. Only Malays could be used at all levels of education. This policy caused a brain drain, particularly at the college level. Another important component of the "New Economic Policy" was the raising of the proportion of Malays in capital and in professional and engineering positions in nonagricultural fields. Capital and professional proportions could not be raised easily, and the government set up many public enterprises to achieve this target. This policy tended to lower efficiency in nonagriculture. In the world-recession year of 1985, GNP growth was negative for the first time, and high growth could not be regained until 1988. In manufacturing, Malaysia also adopted an import-substitution policy at first, though its tariff level has never been high. Since the end of the 1970s, its trade policy has shifted to export promotion. This policy accelerated industrialization and economic growth, as was the case in other countries.

Another factor explaining economic recovery since 1987 was the increase of direct foreign investment wich increased (approval basis) 61% in 1986, 43% in 1987, and then more than 100% in 1988. The rapid influx of capital was caused by the appreciation of the yen, which promoted the emigration of Japan's labor-intensive industries to lower-wage countries. Capital also moved from Taiwan to Thailand and Malaysia. Taiwanese capital was even more labor intensive and small-scale than Japanese capital, so its benefit to employment and economic growth should be substantial.

The Philippines was once the richest country in Southeast Asia. Also, industrialization started at the earliest date in this country, pressed by deficits in the balance of payments. Import substitution proceeded rapidly and reached the end of the "easy phase of import substitution" by the end of the 1960s. Since then the Philippines has become more and more protectionist until it became probably the most protectionist country in Southeast Asia. The export promotion of manufactures was pushed haphazardly and the expansion of manufacturing exports was slow.

In the 1970s and 1980s, President Marcos made the Philippines's economic dynamism weaker by giving financial and other assistance to his cronies, who made little effort to innovate since they could make money using connections with the President. Partly due to the government mismanagement and partly because of the social unrest, the Philippines economy grew very slowly in the beginning of the 1980s. In 1983 the government had to declare a moratorium on all public debt and induced substantial negative growth in 1984 and 1985. With the flight of Marcos, the economy was given momentum again and grew at a rate exceeding 6% by 1988. Even though the political base of President Aquino is still weak as of this writing, economists believe that, if political stability is regained, the Philippines could maintain growth at 5% or thereabouts.

5. CHINA

Communist China nationalized most of the economy after the victory on the mainland. Although heavy industry, which was deemed strategically important, grew, other sectors tended to stagnate, because the price mechanism and inducement were removed. Assistance from the Soviet Union in capital and technology was also eventually terminated. The policy of keeping prices of agriculture commodities under control discouraged agricultural production. In the days of the Great Cultural Revolution, the economy was further neglected. Moreover, population grew at the rate of 3%, or thereabouts, and per capita output stagnated. In 1977, the per capita GNP of China was only $230, which was one of the lowest figures in the world.

Changes were introduced, first by the encouragement of late marriages and eventually by the restriction of the number of children per family to one. As a result, population growth was drastically controlled. Then from 1978, a modernization policy was initiated. Privatization was adopted in all agricultural sectors; the prices of agricultural commodities were raised; and the prices of agricultural inputs were generally reduced. The rural nonagricultural firms were made independent. Even though productivity was low, it started to rise rapidly. Also, the concept of the market mechanism was partially introduced into national manufacturing firms.

Internationally, China decided to open its doors to foreign firms. In 1980 three special free-trade zones were established, and in 1984, 15 more were opened. Trade and investment have increased at a very rapid rate since then. Output has also started to grow rapidly. In 1980–1987, real GNP increased at an average annual rate of 9.7%. The average annual growth rate of agricultural output was 7.4%, probably unprecedented in world history.

6. THREE INCIDENTS AND EAST ASIA

These East Asian countries' growth records are summarized in table 1. The year 1985 was a recession year, and in many countries the growth rate was zero or negative. The growth rate, however, picked up in one or two years to 10%, or thereabouts, in the NIEs and 3% to 5% in Indonesia and the Philippines. Malaysia's growth rate did not return to its previous high level until 1989. Thailand's growth proceeded remarkably. The growth rate was not negative in 1985, and it jumped to two-digit figures in 1986, 1987, and 1988 (see table 1).

Several significant incidents shook the world between 1989 and 1991. First, massive student demonstrations for democracy in Beijing were crushed in June 1989 by the military. Secondly, in autumn of 1989 the Communist governments in most of the Communist countries in Europe fell and were replaced by new regimes that were politically democratic and economically more market oriented, causing the end of the Cold War. By the end of 1991, even the Soviet Union seems to be disintegrating. Thirdly, Iraq invaded and absorbed Kuwait in 1990. The last incident not only invited economic and military containment of Iraq by most big countries of the world, but also raised the price of crude oil temporarily to the $30 to $40 range.

Table 1

Average Annual Growth Rate of Real GDP (%)

	1970–74	1975–79	1980–84	1985	1986	1987	1988*	1989*	1990*
Hong Kong	6.5	10.2	7.9	−0.1	11.9	13.8	7.4	4.5	4.0
South Korea	9.4	10.0	5.9	5.4	11.7	11.1	11.0	7.2	7.4
Singapore	11.5	7.4	8.5	−1.6	1.8	8.8	11.0	8.5	7.2
Taiwan	9.4	10.3	6.7	4.4	10.6	12.4	6.8	7.1	7.2
Indonesia	8.6	6.9	4.8	2.5	4.0	3.6	—	5.6	5.7
Philippines	5.6	6.4	1.4	−4.3	1.4	4.7	6.4	6.0	6.6
Malaysia	7.8	7.2	6.9	−1.9	1.2	1.2	5.2	6.9	6.1
Thailand	6.1	8.5	5.9	4.4	10.6	12.4	6.8	10.0	8.5
China	—	4.9	8.6	13.2	8.0	10.5	—	6.6	6.5

*Forecast
Source: Key Indicators of Developing Member Countries of ADB, July 1989, p. 9, and Pacific Economic Outlook 1989–1990, 1989, table 1.

The first incident is largely an internal affair for China, and even though the political implications may be large, the outside world, except for Hong Kong, will not be seriously affected. China is still pursuing an outward–looking economic policy, and the economic sanctions imposed by the Western countries are being lifted as China liberalizes its internal policy. The impact on Hong Kong may be more serious because there is now doubt about the "one country, two systems" policy. A massive drain of human resources may take place in the future. China will itself lower the speed of growth, but the damage is likely to be small if the country retains its outward–looking and market–oriented economic policy.

The second incident, the end of the Cold War, is likely to turn out to be one of the most important historical events in this century, and it may affect East Asia significantly in the long run. For the unification of Germany, West Germany agreed to extend credit amounting to $8.5 billion to the Soviet Union as the cost of stationing and evacuation of Soviet soldiers. The United States agreed to give stopgap food aid to the Soviet Union. Most other former Communist countries, which are in difficult economic conditions, have asked for the extension of a large amount of credit from the rich countries of the free world. Even Japan has promised to extend credit to some of these countries, just as former Prime Minister Kaifu agreed to help Poland and Hungary.

The end of the Cold War will bring a peace dividend to countries that formerly confronted each other. The amount of savings may be huge. The United States has already announced a plan to reduce military personnel by 440,000 (25%) by fiscal year 1995. Similarly, naval vessels will be reduced from 566 to 455, strategic bombers from 21 to 17 divisions, and intercontinental ballistic missiles from 950 to 500. As a result, military expenditure should become less than 4% of GNP by 1995. Such disarmament will affect most countries of the world as well. Japan will not be directly affected, however, because its defense expenditure is much smaller as a proportion of GNP than that of other countries. Also, the security conditions in Northeast Asia are not yet completely stable. In the long run, the end of the Cold War will bring other important political and economic changes in East Asia. Mongolia has already decided to move towards a market mechanism. The isolation of North Korea would force it to seek closer ties with South Korea and Japan. Vietnam is also trying to have more friendly relations with its neighbors. As a result, peace is likely to return to Cambodia.

The third incident, Iraq's invasion of Kuwait, had a number of effects on the world. First, the United States sent large military forces, including two aircraft carriers, to the Middle East to protect Saudi Arabia and other Gulf States and asked major countries of the world to join a coalition. The war ended swiftly and decisively in favor of the coalition. Japan, which is not in a position to send military personnel, was persuaded to donate $2 billion in funds. It also sent a small fleet of minesweepers to the Gulf after the end of the war.

Finally, the price of crude oil went up temporarily to the $35 to $40 range, and this affected all the countries of the world more or less. Japan was able to absorb the shock, as it did in 1980. Indonesia and Malaysia gained substantially as exporters of crude oil for the time being. The fragile Philippines stagnated because other large-scale national disasters hit the country at the same time.

Other countries withstood the direct effect of the oil shock, since their per capita consumption of oil was not very large. To most Asian countries, worldwide recession would be more important, as it was in 1985.

One factor in the Middle East stalemate is the return of Filipinos, Thais, and other migrant workers from Iraq and Kuwait. Since most of them are poor, unskilled workers, it will be difficult for the home countries to absorb them. The loss of remittances from migrant workers will also be a blow. Eventually, these workers will try to come back to the Middle East. They will also migrate to other countries in East Asia.

Even though there is no reason to be pessimistic about the future of the world economy, the restructuring of Eastern Europe, the sanctions against Iraq, and the rise of oil prices induced mild inflation in the short run. Since inflation was slowly rising in most East Asian economies, each government took stringent monetary and fiscal measures to combat inflation. As a result, growth rates became somewhat lower. We should, however, be impressed by the increased resilience of East Asian developing countries. As of the end of 1991, they are still growing robustly, despite the slowdown in Japan and the recession in the United States.

In the long run, the Eastern European transition will be over, and economic development will resume there. The Kuwait incident may bring peace in the Middle East. Disarmament will spread to most industrial countries, while developing countries will have learned a lesson from the blunder of Iraq. Economic growth will continue in East Asia. All the countries in the region, except Japan and possibly the Philippines, will grow at the rate of 6% to 8% per year, and East Asia will continue to be the growth center of the world.

12. TRIPOLAR GROWTH AND REAL EXCHANGE RATES: HOW MUCH CAN BE EXPLAINED BY CONVERGENCE?

John F. Helliwell and Alan Chung[1]
Department of Economics
University of British Columbia
Vancouver B.C. Canada V6T 1W5

ABSTRACT. We test for regional and global convergence of growth rates and levels of technical progress using data from the early 1960s through 1985 for nine Asian, fourteen European, two North American and two Australasian economies. For most countries, a model with the United States technology index as the target for convergence is preferred by the data. The exception is for the smaller European countries, where there is some evidence favoring the addition of a supplementary target based on the productivity levels of the four largest European economies. Overall, the evidence in favor of convergence is stronger among the Western industrial countries than among the Asian economies. In both groups of countries, a strong link is found between real per capita GDP and the real exchange rate, and this relationship applies even more clearly between the two groups of countries.

1. INTRODUCTION

In earlier papers, we and others have studied the hypothesis that convergence or catch-up has been an important factor in explaining the comparative growth performance of industrial countries over the past 30 years.[2] Our studies used the United States as the target for convergence, on the grounds that it had the highest level and slowest rate of growth of real GDP and productivity among the

---

[1]We are grateful for the research support of the Social Sciences and Humanities Research Council of Canada, and for the research collaboration of Ardo Hansson.

[2]Among the earlier empirical studies using convergence or catch-up to help explain international differences in post-1950 or longer-period growth rates are those by Denison (1967), Gomulka (1971), Abramovitz (1979), Maddison (1982), and Marris (1982).

sample of industrial countries.[3] We found that the evidence of convergence was stronger for productivity levels[4] for GDP or GNP per capita, and if purchasing power parities (PPPs) rather than market exchange rates are used to make international comparisons. This is what theory would suggest, since the convergence process relates primarily to techniques of production rather than income levels.

Earlier studies also showed that the evidence of convergence is stronger if the sample is restricted to a set of countries that all have sufficient "social capability" (Abramovitz, 1990), literacy levels (Rauch, 1989), or some other set of conditions necessary to permit a poorer country to "take off" (Rostow, 1978) into a process of sustained growth along a convergence path. The group of industrial countries in 1960 provides one such restricted set of countries for which the evidence of convergence is strong. Helliwell and Chung (1988) report data showing much stronger evidence of convergence among these industrial countries than among all countries together.[5]

In more recent work[6], we have extended our coverage to include data for eight Asian economies (Hansson and Helliwell, 1990), and in this chapter we combine these data with those for the OECD countries to consider some issues

---

[3]The first results (Helliwell, Sturm, and Salou, 1985) made use of data for the seven largest OECD countries (the G-7), and employed a three-factor, two-level, nested CES production structure embodying Harrod-neutral technical progress with convergence towards U.S. rates of productivity growth. As in our more recent work, the longer-term production structure was in turn nested within a model explaining the short-run output or factor utilization decision.

[4]Our central measure of productivity is the output per worker obtained by inverting a two-factor CES production function using total fixed capital and employment to produce real GDP. Dowrick and Nguyen (1989) also found that the convergence among OECD economies is clearer for productivity levels; they use gross investment rates as a proxy for capital deepening.

[5]De Long (1988) shows graphically, by adopting a mid-1800s sample of likely members of the "convergence club" (including Spain, Portugal, Chile, and Argentina) for which the evidence of convergence over the subsequent century is very weak, that there is a real danger of sample selection bias in favor of convergence if the sample is based on the countries that are most productive at the end of the sample period. Baumol, Blackman, and Wolff (1989) find that the evidence of convergence is strongest when the sample is restricted to the 16 countries with the highest initial per capita incomes, and becomes progressively weaker as the sample is extended to include poorer countries.

[6]Hansson and Helliwell (1990) uses a data sample including the same group of Asian economies that we use in this chapter, along with Canada and the United States. That paper also spelled out for those same economies the two-way linkages between convergence and real exchange rates, picking up a strand of the discussion on competitiveness in Helliwell and Chung (1988).

posed by the possibility of a tripolar global economy. Our sample now includes nine Asian economies (Japan plus the new eight), fourteen from Europe, and two from North America, plus Australia and New Zealand. The data for the Asian countries are not generally as complete and comparable as those for the OECD countries, thus limiting somewhat the range and power of the comparisons we are able to make. Thus our efforts must be treated as exploratory rather than conclusive.

What are the main issues to consider using the tripolar data? First and foremost, are there differences among the three poles in the convergence process? If the global economy has been evolving principally in regional blocs, and if the primary transfers of investment and technology are among countries in the same geographic area, then we might expect to find that poorer countries within a region might approach the norm or best practice for the region.

On the other hand, if the world economy is truly global, and the world stock of ideas and blueprints is as accessible as the nearest fax machine, then all countries could converge to the same frontier, which might be represented by the country with the highest productivity level or, more realistically, some multinational or global definition of best practice.

More generally, we might expect to find that countries within a region would have opportunities available from the world leader (or leaders) as well as from their own regional leaders.

We shall present our data and results in four further sections. First, we shall show comparable data for GDP per capita and measured productivity levels for the 27 countries in our sample. Then we shall present, in section 3, the results of our tests of alternative models for explaining productivity growth and convergence. Then, in section 4, we shall establish the links between productivity convergence and real exchange rates. This will be followed by a short concluding section.

2. COMPARING OUTPUT AND PRODUCTIVITY LEVELS AND GROWTH

In this section we present comparative data for real GDP per capita and measured productivity growth paths. In both cases we group countries with others in their region, and report both levels of GDP (in '000 constant 1980 international $ per capita)[7] and ratios to U.S. data (with the United States equal to 100).

The four panels of figure 1 show the levels of real per capita GDP, from 1960 to 1985, in the industrial countries. Although the series in figure 1 all show general upward trends punctuated by cyclical episodes, the narrowing of the income gaps between the United States and the other industrial countries can be seen more easily in figure 2, which shows each country's per capita GDP growth path relative to that in the United States. Even the relative data reveal substantial year-to-year variation, showing that cyclical experiences have been quite varied among the industrial countries. Underlying these shorter-term movements, there appears to be some broad convergence process in operation, with

---

[7]The data for real GDP and PPP exchange rates for the Asian economies are drawn from Summers and Heston (1988). The data sources for the industrial countries are described in the appendix, which also outlines the assumptions and methods used to estimate measured productivity growth paths for all economies.

154

the countries with the lowest per capita incomes in 1960 having the fastest per capita growth rates over the subsequent 25 years.

The data in figures 3 and 4 refine the comparative data by converting them into productivity measures, and thereby adjusting for international differences in labor-force growth, changes in unemployment rates, and rates of capital accumulation, all of which tend to create international differences in per capita incomes not directly related to the international convergence process.[8] The measured productivity paths continue to show substantial year-to-year fluctuations, since they still include the effects of short-term changes in output and utilization rates, but the visual impression of longer-term convergence is stronger for the productivity levels than for real GDP per capita.[9]

Figures 5 through 8 show the same data for the nine Asian economies, including Japan (repeated from the previous figures) plus Hong Kong, Indonesia, Korea, Malaysia, the Philippines, Singapore, Taiwan, and Thailand. Figure 5 shows the data for real GDP per capita, with figure 6 showing the same data relative to the United States. Figures 7 and 8 show the corresponding data for measured productivity levels. For both GDP per capita and for productivity, the evidence in favor of convergence is less uniform for the Asian economies than it is among the OECD countries. The nine countries seem to be divided into three groups of three countries each. The three richest countries—Japan, Hong Kong, and Singapore—had the highest incomes in 1960 (at between 20% and 30% of U.S. levels of GDP per capita), and had all converged to the 60% to 70% range by the mid-1980s. A middle group of countries, including Taiwan, Malaysia and Korea, started in the 10% to 15% range in 1960, and had reached 20% to 25% by 1985. A third group, including Indonesia, Thailand, and the Philippines, shows much less evidence of convergence, with real per capita GDPs in the 7% to 10% range in 1960 and in the 10% to 15% range in the mid-1980s. Perhaps this should be taken as evidence that the latter group of countries still lack some of the necessary characteristics of full membership in the "convergence club." In any event, we shall not be surprised to find, in the more formal tests reported in the next section, that the evidence for convergence is less consistent among the Asian economies than among the OECD economies.

---

[8]This is done by inverting an estimated underlying long-run CES production structure with constant returns to scale, common parameters and Harrod-neutral technical progress. The methods are described in more detail in the appendix. Tests supporting the constant-returns assumption, as opposed to the increasing-returns formulation recently stressed in theoretical contributions by Romer (1986) and Grossman and Helpman (1990), are reported in Helliwell and Chung (1990, pp. 5-6).

[9]This visual impression is supported by the cross-sectional equations estimated in section 3 of Helliwell and Chung (1988). These results show increases in the goodness of fit of the convergence hypothesis (taken to imply that subsequent growth rates will be higher for countries with initially lower levels of income or productivity) by moving from GDP to productivity, and again by moving from initial GDP to the initial productivity level to define the independent variable.

3. TESTING ALTERNATIVE TARGETS FOR CONVERGENCE

Our primary goal in this section is to see to what extent the geographic grouping of countries, which also coincides in most cases with stronger trade and invest- ment linkages, affects the structure of the convergence process. The data shown in the previous section were displayed relative to the United States, thereby implicitly treating that country as the target for the convergence process. However, given that in many industries the technology-leading firms are located in other countries, and that convergence in any event brings other countries closer to U.S. levels of productivity and per capita GDP, there is every reason to expect that U.S. technologies will not be the sole foreign source of ideas for converging countries.

To keep our estimation and reporting task manageable, we shall consider only a few simple alternatives to treating the United States as the technological leader. For all these tests, we shall generally treat the OECD and Asian countries as comprising separate data samples, thus recognizing differences in the quality of the data, as itemized in the appendix.[10] Our tests rely mainly on a two-stage process whereby we first estimate the key parameters of alternative models of longer-run technical progress, and then compare the models in terms of the relative goodness of fit of output or "factor utilization" equations (Helliwell and Chung, 1986) based on the alternative models of technical progress. The essential reason for this two-stage approach is that output and productivity growth have substantial short-term variations that may confound the direct estimation of the parameters of the longer-run convergence process, and in any event will make the goodness of fit of the first-stage equations a risky guide to the success of the alternative models of productivity growth. Thus our primary criterion for comparing the alternative models of productivity growth will be the goodness of fit of the output equations, which provide a combined test of the underlying production function (which embodies one of the specific hypotheses about technical progress) and the factors determining short-term cyclical departures from the production function. Since the assumed form of the output equation is the same for all of the alternative productivity models (although it differs for the Asian and OECD data samples, because of shortcomings in our data for the Asian economies), the output equations will serve to discriminate among the alternative models of technical progress.

We shall concentrate on five different models of technical progress. The first, which provides a handy benchmark against which the convergence models can be assessed, assumes that underlying Harrod-neutral technical progress takes place at a rate that differs by country but for each country does not change from one year or decade to the next. We can use the model-1 estimates of the average 1960-1985 productivity growth rates for each country, and use cross-sectional estimation to assess the extent to which the international differences in growth rates were negatively related to initial productivity levels, as required by the convergence hypothesis. This is done in table A11 in the appendix, which shows significant cross-sectional evidence of catch-up among the industrial countries and for the whole sample of countries, but not among the nine Asian economies,

---

[10]Japan is, of course, a member of the OECD as well as an Asian economy. For the purposes of our convergence estimates, it is included among the OECD countries rather than with the Asian group.

which in any event provide a very small sample. The evidence in favor of convergence is stronger if initial productivity levels are used instead of initial levels of GDP per capita.[11]

The second model, which is the first of four alternative convergence models we assess, treats the United States as the target for convergence, with the rate of convergence estimated separately for each country, and with each country equation having its own constant term, thus permitting convergence to take place towards a productivity growth rate that is equal to, but a productivity level that differs from, the corresponding values for the United States. In the third model, each country in Europe or Asia is assumed to converge to a productivity growth rate equal to that of a frontier defined by best-practice productivity growth within its own region, rather than by the U.S. path. For Europe, this regional frontier is defined by the employment-weighted aggregate productivity measure for Europe.[12] For Asia, the regional target is taken to be the Japanese productivity level.

In the fourth model, the target for convergence is taken to be a global frontier, defined by the employment-weighted average of the measured productivity values for all countries in the sample.[13] In the fifth and final model, there

---

[11]Other tests reported in table A11 also show the absence of economies of scale, although one of the four equations provides an indication that the larger industrial countries grew slightly faster than the smaller ones, after allowing for convergence. This effect is not significant, and in any event is much smaller than the convergence effect. The convergence coefficient is unaffected by the addition of the scale variable. This reflects the low correlation (0.22 for the OECD countries and -0.17 for the Asian countries) between 1960 country sizes and productivity levels. This evidence, combined with earlier tests (in Helliwell and Chung, 1990) indicating no economies of scale at the national level, tends to support continued use of our constant-returns specification, and to deemphasize the importance of technology transfer models (such as those of Romer, 1986) that rely on economies of scale at the national level (as opposed to those that may operate at the plant, firm, or industry level).

[12]We also experimented with using the German productivity index as a target, since Germany is the largest economy in Europe, as Japan is in Asia. However, the other European economies are much closer to Germany, in size and productivity level, than is true for the Asian economies relative to Japan, so we here treat the European frontier (which in any event is empirically superior to that for Germany) as the regional target for the European countries. The possibility of bias created by having countries chase a target that includes its own experience is avoided, since the equations include the previous year's values for both the regional frontier and its own measured productivity.

[13]There is a potential problem posed by this definition of a productivity target, since its level is below that in many countries. This problem is avoided by using a specification that includes a constant term, since any scalar displacement of the target path can be offset by an appropriate change in the constant term. Thus only the growth rate, and not the level, of the target path influences the level and rate of growth of the estimated target path for each of

are, for most countries, two targets for convergence: the United States and the regional leader.[14]

The specification and results of the alternative models, for both the technical progress and output equations, are described and tabulated in the appendix. In this section, we shall concentrate on some attempts to compare the goodness of fit of the alternative models. This is done in table 1, which shows nonnested tests of the predicted values of output derived from the five alternative models of technical progress. For this purpose, we use the C-test of Davidson and Mackinnon (1981), which uses the predicted values from two alternative models as independent variables in a test equation. In each pairwise test, the preferred model is that for which the predicted value obtains the higher coefficient in the test regression.

The test results are shown in table 1. Especially for the industrial countries, and to a lesser extent for the countries of Asia, the convergence models are preferred, to a statistically significant degree, to the "constant" case, in which productivity growth is different in each country but unchanging over time.[15] The margin of preference for the convergence models over the constant case is substantially greater for the industrial countries than for the Asian countries, averaging about 5:1 for the former and 2:1 for the latter.[16] As for the ranking among the convergence models, the results for the OECD countries and for the Asian economies show the global frontier case (model 4) to be inferior to all other convergence models. As is the case among the models that involve U.S. leadership, regional leadership, or some combination, there is a slight preference for U.S. over regional models, with some evidence favoring a combination of the two.

---

the converging countries.

[14]For Europe, this "regional leader" term was found to be relevant only for the smaller European countries, so it is included for all European countries outside the G-7. Thus Germany, Italy, France, and the U.K. have the United States as the target for convergence, while the smaller European countries have the United States (with country-specific coefficients) and the weighted-average European frontier (with a coefficient constrained to be equal for all country equations in which it appears) as the target.

[15]Our earlier papers (Helliwell and Chung, 1988, 1990) show that convergence models also dominate another frequently discussed alternative, where there is a productivity break for each country in the mid-1970s, with the rate after then being below the pre-1973 values.

[16]As can be seen from the test statistics reported in table 1, for the OECD countries all of the convergence models dominate the constant case at a high level of significance. For the Asian countries, only the U.S.-as-leader convergence model dominates at a 1% level of significance; for the other cases, the dominance is much less strong.

For the ranking among the nonglobal convergence models, there are some differences between the results for the OECD and the Asian countries. For the OECD countries, the regional frontier model (model 3) is the best of the convergence models relative to the constant case. However, pairwise comparisons among all the convergence models for the OECD countries shows both model 2 (which has the U.S. as leader) and model 5 (with the U.S. and regional leaders) to dominate the regional frontier model. A pairwise comparison of models 2 and 5 shows the best model for the OECD countries to be model 5, combining a U.S. target for each country with an additional European target for the smaller European countries.

For the Asian countries, all of the pairwise comparisons support the use of the U.S. as the target for convergence, although the margin of preference is not usually very great. For example, when the Japan-as-leader case is compared to the U.S.-as-leader case (model 3 vs. model 2), the margin of preference for the U.S. case is 60:40, and the difference is not statistically significant.

4. CONVERGENCE AND REAL EXCHANGE RATES

Research using recently developed data for real exchange rates based on PPPs has found a significant positive linkage between real per capita GDP and the real exchange rate.[17] Here we address two further questions relating to convergence and the regional or global structure of the world economy. First, if convergence is an important part of the comparative growth of the countries over the period we are studying, then we might expect to find a smaller dispersion of real per capita incomes and productivity levels as we move from the 1960s through the 1970s and into the 1980s and 1990s. We might also expect to find a corresponding drop in the spread of real exchange rates, to the extent that the link between real incomes and real exchange rates is fairly stable over time, and if there have not been other forces at work increasing the volatility of real exchange rates. Third, if the world economy is becoming more global, then we would expect to find the reductions in the disparity of real incomes, productivity, and real exchange rates to be taking place as much between regions as among countries within the same region.

Table 2 shows the cross-sectional standard deviations of real exchange rates, real per capita GDPs, and measured productivity levels for the 1960s, 1970s, and 1980s, for the OECD countries, the Asian countries, and for the entire sample of 27 countries.[18] For the same regions and countries we also show the cross-sectional correlation between real exchange rates and real per capita GDPs, and between real exchange rates and productivity levels.

---

[17]See Hill (1986), Heston and Summers (1988), and Hansson and Helliwell (1990).

[18]Each country observation is based on the average logarithmic value for the time period in question; i.e., for Japanese per capita GDP in the 1970s, the observation is equal to the mean value of the logs of real per capita GDP for the ten years 1970 to 1979. The average is taken over the years 1980 to 1985 for the 1980s, and from 1962 through 1969 for the 1960s.

For the OECD economies, the results do show a steady decline in the dispersion of real per capita GDP, and of measured productivity levels, from the 1960s to the 1980s, as the convergence hypothesis would suggest. The correlation between the real exchange-rate and real GDP increases over the same period, as would be expected if there were increases in the international mobility of goods and services. However, the standard deviation of the real exchange rate shows little evidence of falling over the decades. This suggests that there has been a growing volatility of real exchange rates for reasons other than convergence, and that this increased market volatility is roughly offsetting the decline in real exchange rate variability that would be expected from the convergence of real incomes. The correlation results show that the link between real exchange rates and convergence is more evident for the GDP link than for productivity.

As would be expected from our earlier results, there is much less evidence of convergence among the Asian economies; the standard deviation of real GDPs and real exchange rates shows some signs of rising rather than falling from the 1960s to the 1980s, indicating that the faster-growing countries are to some extent leaving the slower-growing countries behind. This in turn suggests that not all of the countries appear to have been equally well placed at the beginning of the period to be members of the "convergence club." If their potential has improved during the period, then evidence of convergence will become more apparent in the future, as the late starters join the convergence process. As for the link between the real exchange rate and real GDP, it remains strong throughout the period, as does that between measured productivity and the real exchange rate.

When the whole sample of countries is considered together, the correlations between the real exchange rate and real GDP and real productivity are substantially higher than within either group of countries. This reveals, as is shown in figures 9 through 12, that the OECD countries as a group have higher real incomes, higher productivity levels, and higher real exchange rates than the Asian economies. The regression lines shown in those figures also show that the relation between the groups is consistent with that for the OECD countries as a whole. This is fairly strong corroborative evidence for the idea that the real exchange rates of the Asian economies will rise to the extent that convergence takes place.

When we look at the evidence for the Asian countries as a group, moving from the 1960s to the 1980s, what does it reveal by way of convergence of real GDP and real exchange rates to those of the industrial countries? Table 3 shows real exchange rates, real per capita GDPs, and productivity levels for the OECD economies (including Japan), and for eight Asian economies (excluding Japan) for 1962 and 1985, the beginning and ending years for our data sample. At the bottom of the table are the ratios of the Asian to the OECD averages, for the same years. These figures show very strong evidence of convergence for the Asian countries as a group, with relative per capita GDP rising from 23% of the OECD average in 1962 to 46% in 1985. The productivity-ratio data also reveal convergence, but at a less rapid rate, showing the importance of high rates of relatively high capital accumulation and employment growth (relative to population) in these economies. The real exchange rates also show relative increases, from 55% to 60% of those in the OECD countries. These are smaller increases, relative to the convergence of per capita GDPs, than we found from our pooled regressions reported below, reflecting the fact that the relative real exchange rates shown in table 3 are in comparison to those in the OECD countries on average. This matters because the cross-sectional relation between real exchange rates and real GDPs has a steeper slope for the OECD countries than for the Asian countries, which means that the Asian countries have so far been catching up faster in GDPs than in real exchange rates, relative to the average of the OECD economies.

The estimated exchange rate equation based on 1980s cross-sectional evidence, and graphed in figure 12, suggests that over the longer term each 1% increase in a country's real income relative to the United States will be accompanied by a 0.5% increase in its real exchange rate. The relatively large standard errors of the exchange-rate equations also suggest that there is much at play, in addition to convergence, in the determination of real exchange rates. An interesting future line of research might be to test whether the combination of future convergence prospects and the link between real incomes and real exchange rates is sufficient to provide a significant aid to the notoriously difficult task of forecasting real and nominal exchange rates.

5. CONCLUSIONS

Is the world economy tripolar? Our preliminary results show only slight evidence of tripolarity. By this we mean that there is little evidence suggesting that low-income countries in a region move more toward the income and productivity levels of their regional leaders, rather than directly toward a more internation-al target. Our attempts to define some global productivity frontier to replace the United States as target country, however, have not met with success. Thus far, the evidence for Europe and Asia suggests that over the 1962 to 1985 period, the United States was the target for convergence, with some additional attraction in the case of the smaller European countries towards a European frontier. However, it is important to emphasize that the evidence is not strong enough to discriminate clearly between the alternative targets for convergence, and convergence itself is far from being the only factor affecting international differences in productivity growth. In addition, we should emphasize again that our Asian results are based on a smaller sample of countries and make use of less adequate data. We do not yet have adequate data for all the Asian economies, especially for capital stocks, prices, employment, and wage rates. Thus the derived output equations, which imbed the longer-term supply structure within a model of the shorter-term determinants of factor utilization, and which we use for our main tests of competing versions of the convergence hypothesis, are necessarily less satisfactory and less conclusive for the sample of Asian countries.

Turning to the results for real exchange rates, we first reviewed the evidence showing a strong positive link between productivity levels and real exchange rates, and then considered whether the evidence of convergence is strong enough, and the link between income and real exchange rates sufficiently close, to have produced a decline in the international variability of real incomes, productivity, and real exchange rates over the period from the 1960s to the 1980s. We found, for the OECD countries, that convergence has been a sufficiently important part of the growth process that there has been a decline in the dispersion of per capita GDPs and productivity levels from the 1960s to the 1980s. For the Asian countries, convergence has been apparent for some, and not for others, and there has not been a downward trend in the dispersion of real incomes and productivity levels moving from the 1960s to the 1980s. For both groups of countries, however, the standard deviation of the real exchange rate shows little evidence of falling over the decades. We took this to mean that increased volatility in the foreign exchange market is offsetting the decline in real exchange-rate variability that would otherwise be expected from the convergence of real incomes within each of the two groups of countries.

As between the two groups of countries, on the other hand, there has been a noticeable amount of convergence in real GDPs, in measured productivity levels, and in real exchange rates. This provides further support for convergence, and suggests that it has if anything been more important between regions than among countries within Asia.

In general, our results do not show much evidence of economic growth, transfer of technology, and exchange-rate linkages taking place within regional blocks in a tripolar world economy. There is substantial evidence of convergence, and some slight evidence of regional as well as U.S. leadership, but not much so far to support the notion of compartmentalized regional economies. Of course, if tripolarity is an emerging phenomenon, it will take make years to show up in the data with sufficient force to overthrow the evidence from the 1960s and 1970s. Thus it would be a mistake to stop looking for evidence of the importance and effects of regional groupings, since that evidence may only now be starting to appear.

REFERENCES

Abramovitz, M. (1979) "Rapid Growth Potential and its Realization: The Experience of Capitalist Economies in the Postwar Period." In E. Malinvaud, ed., Economic Growth and Resources (London: Macmillan) 1–30.

Abramovitz, M. (1990) "The Catch-up Factor in Postwar Economic Growth." Economic Inquiry 28: 1–18.

Baumol, W.J. (1986) "Productivity Growth, Convergence and Welfare: What the Long-Run Data Show." American Economic Review 76: 1072–85.

Baumol, W.J., S. Blackman and E.N. Wolff (1989) Productivity and American Leadership, The Long View. (Cambridge, Mass., MIT Press).

Baumol, W.J., and E.N. Wolff (1988) "Productivity Growth, Convergence and Welfare: Reply." American Economic Review 78: 1155–59.

Blades, D. and D. Roberts (1987) "A Note on the New OECD Benchmark Purchasing Power Parities for 1985." OECD Economic Studies 9: 153–84.

Davidson, R. and J.G. Mackinnon (1981) "Several Tests for Model Specification in the Presence of Alternative Hypotheses." Econometrica 49: 781–94.

De Long, J.B. (1988) "Productivity Growth, Convergence and Welfare: Comment." American Economic Review 78: 1138–54.

Denison, E. (1967) Why Growth Rates Differ. (Washington: Brookings Institution).

Dowrick, S. and D-T. Nguyen (1989) "OECD Comparative Economic Growth 1950–85: Catch-Up and Convergence." American Economic Review 79: 1010–30.

Grossman, G.M. and E. Helpman (1990) "Comparative Advantage and Long-Run Growth." American Economic Review 80:796-815.

Gomulka, S. (1971) Inventive Activity, Diffusion, and the Stages of Economic Growth. (Aarhus: Institute of Economics).

Hansson, A., and J. Helliwell (1990) "The Evolution of Income and Competitiveness in the North Pacific Rim." In F. Langdon, ed. Canada and the Growing Presence of Asia. (Vancouver: Institute for Asian Research) 17-40.

Helliwell, John F., and Alan Chung (1986) "Aggregate Output with Variable Rates of Utilization of Employed Factors." Journal of Econometrics 19: 597-625.

Helliwell, John F., and Alan Chung (1988) "Aggregate Productivity and Growth in an International Comparative Setting." Prepared for SSRC conference, Stanford University, October 1988. Forthcoming in B.G. Hickman, ed., International Productivity and Competitiveness (New York, Oxford University Press).

Helliwell, John F., and Alan Chung (1990) "Macroeconomic Convergence: International Transmission of Growth and Technical Progress." NBER Working Paper No. 3264 (Cambridge, National Bureau of Economic Research).

Helliwell, John F., Peter Sturm, Gerard Salou (1985) "International Comparison of the Sources of the Productivity Slowdown 1973-1982." European Economic Review 28: 157-91.

Heston, A. and R. Summers (1988) "What Have We Learned About Prices and Quantities From International Comparisons: 1987." American Economic Review 78 (2): 467-73.

Hill, P. (1986) "International Price Levels and Purchasing Power Parities." OECD Economic Studies 6: 133-59.

Maddison, A. (1982) Phases of Capitalist Development. (Oxford: Oxford University Press).

Marris, R. (1982) "How Much of the Slowdown was Catch-up?." In R. Mathews, ed., Slower Growth in the Western World. (London: Heineman) 128-144.

Rauch, J.E. (1989) "The Question of International Convergence of Per Capita Consumption: An Euler Equation Approach." NBER Summer Institute Paper. (Cambridge: National Bureau of Economic Research).

Romer, P.M. (1986) "Increasing Returns and Long-Run Growth." Journal of Political Economy 94: 1002-37.

Rostow, W.W. (1978) The World Economy: History and Prospect. (Austin: University of Texas).

Summers, R. and A. Heston (1988) "A New Set of International Comparisons of Real Product and Prices: Estimates for 130 Countries, 1950 to 1985." Review of Income and Wealth 34: 1-25.

APPENDIX

In this section, we first provide the main data sources for the OECD countries, followed by those for the eight Asian countries. We also describe the methods used to obtain the capital stocks for both the OECD and Asian countries. We then outline both the derivation of the productivity level measure and the estimation procedure used in the regressions reported in the appendix tables. Finally, we describe the output equation specification that is used in this chapter. The appendix tables containing the productivity and output equations for the various cases for the OECD and Asian countries follow. The tables including the cross-sectional evidence of convergence conclude this section.

Data Sources

Industrial Countries (including Japan). Data for this study were taken from:
IMF International Financial Statistics
OECD, Flows and Stocks of Fixed Capital, 1960–1985
OECD Standardized National Accounts [SNA], Vol I & II
OECD 1984, 1986 and 1987 INTERLINK supply block tapes for G–7 countries
OECD 1987 supply block tape for the smaller OECD countries
Sample period: 1960–1985
Most of the supply block data for this study were derived from the OECD National Accounts (denoted by SNA) as indicated below.
Square brackets indicate source.
Note that $ is used to denote domestic currency.

YGDP=GDP in current $ billion [SNA]
PGDP=GDP deflator (1980=1.00) [SNA]
I=Private business and government investment in 1980 $ billion [SNA]
IB=Business investment=I−IG−IH
IG=Government investment [SNA Vol. II and OECD87 for smalls]
IH=Housing investment [SNA Vol. II and OECD87 for smalls]
IP=Private investment=I−IG
A=Absorption in 1980 $ billion [SNA]
PA=Absorption deflator (1980=1.00)[SNA]
C=Private consumption in 1980 $ billion [SNA]
G=Govt. expenditures in 1980 $ billion [SNA]
IINV=Change in inventories in 1980 $ billion [SNA]
TI=Indirect taxes less subsidies in current $ billion [SNA]
N=Total employment, millions of persons [OECD86,OECD87]
W=Average annual wage ('000s of $ per employed persons per year)[OECD86,OECD87]
X=Exports of goods and services in 1980 $ billion [SNA]
PX=Price of exports (1980=1.00)[SNA]
RS=Short-term nominal interest rate [Canadian Dept. of Finance and IFS 60]
RL=Average yield of long-term govt. bonds (%)[Canadian Dept. of Finance and IFS 61]
M=Imports of goods and services in 1980 $ billion [SNA]
PM=Price of imports (1980=1.00)[SNA]
NPOP=Total population (millions of persons)[IFS and SNA]
RSCR=Scrapping rate [OECD84 and OECD87 for smalls]
KS=Kickoff value for capital stock in 1980 $ billion [see below]
KINVS=Kickoff value for inventory levels in 1980 $ billion [for G−7 OECD86, for smalls an approximation of .06*K(1960) was used]

$Q=(YGDP-TI)/PGDP$ Real gross output

The wage and employment data for both the G-7 and smalls were derived from INTERLINK supply block data supplied by the OECD.

Capital stock series: For the <u>G-7 countries, total</u> capital stocks were generated from base (1959) kickoff values (KS). For each year, the previous year's stock was added to new investment after allowing for some portion that is scrapped off, i.e., $K(t)=(1-RSCR)K(t-1)+I$. The KS data were taken from the OECD84 tape for the G-7 countries and they are kickoff values for the total gross stock series. In the case of Japan, however, data were available only from 1966; some extrapolation was done to get the 1960 total capital stock as the kickoff value.

For the <u>12 smaller industrial countries, business</u> capital stock data were readily available from the OECD87 supply block tape, with those for Austria, New Zealand, and Switzerland having to be rebased to 1980$.

The OECD87 tape has data on government, business, and housing investments. these data were compared with corresponding data available from OECD SNA, Volume II and updated/revised where necessary. The private investment series was then generated as the sum of business and housing investments, $(IPV=IBV+IHV)$. From this, the 1960s average ratio of private investment to business investment was applied to the stock ratio to derive the kickoff private capital stock in 1960, as in the case with the G-7 countries. The <u>private</u> capital stock series was then generated for each of the 12 smaller industrial countries, using business scrapping rate to approximate the scrapping rate for private capital stock. (The RSCRB data was available from the OECD87 tape. For some countries, however, estimates had to be made for the earlier years, particularly 1960 and 1961.) In the same way, a government capital stock series was generated, which was then added to private capital stock to get the <u>total</u> capital stock series.

The inventory stock series was calculated using the equation $KINV=KINV-1 + IINV$, with KINVS being the base kickoff value.

The 1980 GDP Purchasing Power Parities are obtained from the OECD Annual National Accounts: Main Aggregates computer tape (July 1988). They are available for the full sample of 19 countries examined in this chapter. The values used are: USA 1.00; JAP 258.51; CAN 1.149; FRA 5.941; GER 2.702; ITA 866.974; UKM 0.517; ASL 1.042; OST 16.626; BEL 42.918; DEN 8.517; FIN 5.022; IRE 0.543; NET 2.734; NZL 1.004; NOR 7.334; SPA 70.554; SWE 6.888; SWI 2.449.

The time series Purchasing Power Parities were calculated by taking the 1985 values available from tape and rebasing them to the current year as the following example for Germany shows for 1980: $PPP80=PPP85/(1+PGDPgermany/1+PGDPus)$
The time series PPPs were backcast in a similar manner for each year prior to 1985.

Asia Data Sources

The following data for the eight Asian countries (excluding Japan) were obtained from Summers and Heston (1988):

- population
- real per capita GDP in 1980 U.S. dollars, as adjusted by purchasing power parities
- investment as a fraction of GDP, based on 1980 "international prices"
- consumption as a fraction of GDP, based on 1980 "international prices"
- government spending as a fraction of GDP, based on 1980 "international prices"

– GDP price levels relative to the U.S. (US=100). This is equivalent to the ratio of the PPP to the market exchange rate times 100.

Since capital data are unavailable, we construct a hypothetical capital stock series through combining observed investment rates with assumed initial capital-output ratios and depreciation rates. From the sample of industrial countries, we choose the lowest depreciation rate (1.62%) and initial capital-output ratio (1.88).

Trade data were obtained from IMF International Financial Statistics data t tape. These consist of

– nominal exports million US$ (70..D)
– nominal imports million US$ (71..D)
– export unit price index (US$) 1985=100
– import unit price index (US$) 1985=100

Taiwan trade data were obtained from table 11-4, Foreign Trade, from Taiwan Statistical Data Book (1989).

Employment data for the Asian countries come from several sources, and we have had to use average growth rates for several countries because of the scarcity of reliable data.
Data for Korea, Philippines and Singapore come from
Statistical Yearbook for Asia and the Pacific [various years] (UN)
Statistical Yearbook for Asia and the Far East (UN)
Note that data for Singapore have been smoothed because of the break in reported data. Hong Kong labor-force data reported in "Hong Kong's Economy" by Gavin Peebles are used, with unavailable data computed using average growth rates from ILO Yearbook of Labor Statistics.

The hypothetical employment data for Indonesia, Malaysia, and Thailand have been derived by using the kickoff value .28* population in 1960 (where .28 represents average employment to population in the remaining Asian countries in 1960) and average growth rates from ILO Yearbook of Labor Statistics.

Taiwan employment data are form Taiwan Statistical Data Book (1989) Council for Economic Planning and Development (Republic of China).

Specification and Estimation

Modeling Labor Productivity. The CES two-factor production function that defines normal output q_s is

$$q_s = [\mu(\Pi N)^{(\tau-1)/\tau} + \nu k^{(\tau-1)/\tau}]^{\tau/(\tau-1)}. \tag{A1}$$

The following will first discuss the procedure used to derive expressions for the country-specific parameters ν, μ, and Π. The final values of these parameters depend on the value of τ, the elasticity of substitution between labor and capital, which is determined iteratively. The iteration method used to calculate τ will be examined last.

Equation (A1) can be rewritten by setting $q=q_s$ and by isolating the following expression for Π:

$$\Pi = [(q^{(\tau-1)/\tau} - \nu k^{(\tau-1)/\tau})/(\mu N^{(\tau-1)/\tau}]^{\tau/(\tau-1)}. \tag{A2}$$

Equation (A2) is used to obtain an expression for the parameter ν. First the optimum factor ratio is derived. The partial derivatives of equation (A1) with respect to labor and capital are first calculated and set equal to the prices W and p_k. Assuming the factor ratio is optimal provides the following ratio:

$$\Pi N^*/k^* = (p_k \Pi / w)^\tau (\mu/\nu)^\tau \tag{A3}$$

where the price of capital services is

$$p_k = (<\delta_2> + 0.01 \rho_r) p_a$$

and where $\rho_r = 100 < 1 - (WN + <\delta_2>\bar{k}p_a)/(qp_q)>/<(\bar{k}p_a/(qp_q)>$

so that the ratio of factor costs to revenues is unity, on average (since $<x>$ denotes the sample average of x).

Equation (A2) is substituted into equation (A3). The parameter μ drops out and can be determined empirically when Π is normalized, as shown below. The parameter ν is isolated in the substituted equation, and sample averages are taken to provide the following expression:

$$\nu = <(p_k/W)(q/N)^{(\tau-1)/\tau}>/[<N(N/k)^{1/\tau}> +$$

$$<(p_k/W)(k/N)^{(\tau-1)/\tau}>]. \tag{A4}$$

Note that we normalize so that the sample average of the ratio of the factors raised to the $1/\tau$ power is equal to the average for optimum proportions.

The value of Π, the labor productivity index for Harrod–neutral technical progress, is derived by the following procedure. Output attributable to labor is defined by rewriting equation (A2):

$$\mu \Pi^{(\tau-1)/\tau} = (q^{(\tau-1)/\tau} - \nu K^{(\tau-1)/\tau}/N^{(\tau-1)/\tau}. \tag{A5}$$

In the constant model, the technical progress index is modeled to grow at a constant rate. It is estimated by ordinary least squares by regressing the logarithm of the measured efficiency level, which is the logarithm of the value provided by equation (A5), referred to here as in π_m (note that in the tables that follow, we refer to the logarithm of this productivity measure as ln pimi, for country 'i'), on an annual time index. Given the final value of τ, the fitted values ln $\hat{\pi}$ can be estimated for each year. Using the latter, the value of μ is calculated by setting Π=1.0 in 1980. Given that the value of μ is constant throughout the sample period, the labor efficiency index Π is defined simply as the exponent of ln $\hat{\pi}$ minus 1980 ln $\hat{\pi}$, which ensures it has a value of 1 in 1980.

In the convergence models, the growth of technical progress in the non–U.S. countries is assumed to catch up to either the U.S. rate of growth or to some other growth frontier. For the U.S. frontier, this is modeled by regressing ln π_m on its lagged value and on the lagged measured U.S. value (ln π_{mus-1}), with the coefficients restricted to sum to one. The values of the CES parameters are derived in a similar way to the constant case, using the fitted values of the catch–up case, ln $\hat{\pi}$.

Finally an estimate of τ is needed to derive final values of the above parameters. The iterative procedure uses the expression for the optimum factor ratio, equation (A3). The log of this equation provides the following form, which can be estimated:

$$\ln(\Pi N^*/k)^* = \tau \ln(\mu/\nu) + \tau \ln(p_k \Pi/W).$$ (A6)

τ is the coefficient of the inverse price ratio. An arbitrary value of τ is used to define μ, ν, Π and normal output, q_s. For our final estimates, a variant of equation (A6) was used in which the lagged capital labor ratio was included along with cyclical demand and profitability variables (outlined in Helliwell and Chung, 1990) as right-hand-side variables. The latter were included, since the factor share ratio has, in addition to its responsiveness to relative prices, a cyclical variance caused by the fact that labor adjusts more quickly than the capital stock to changes in desired output. The distributed lag response on the relative price term (which tends to produce a higher estimated equilibrium elasticity of substitution) also provides more reasonable elasticities across countries.

In the pooled estimation, we use an average of the country-specific τ and ν (with value of .99 for τ), thus providing common production function parameters.

Output Equation Specifications. The following provides a brief description of the specification of the output equations used in the nonnested C-tests. We follow the "factor utilization" approach outlined in Helliwell and Chung (1986). The rationale for explicitly modeling factor utilization rates lies in the observation that factors of production are quasi-fixed. That is, it is costly for firms to adjust the levels of inputs in response to short-run changes in demand and cost conditions. Consequently, temporary fluctuations in demand are met by varying the intensity of factor use--working the inputs harder or less hard--or, in other words, by changing the factor utilization rates.

One difficulty with this approach is that factor utilization rates are not directly observable. In particular, we have no idea what constitutes a "normal" factor utilization rate. A simple way around the problem is to define the utilization rate as the ratio of actual to normal output and to form suitable proxies for the demand and cost conditions. When the proxy variables are at their normal values--the sample averages--then we have a normal rate of factor utilization.

The output equation thus has the following specification:

$$\ln q = \ln q_s + beta*\ln sgap + beta1*\ln cq + beta2*\ln igap + e,$$

where sgap is the ratio of sales to normal sales, igap is the ratio of desired to lagged actual inventories and cq is the ratio of current unit cost relative to output price (an inverse measure of profitability). Normal sales are defined as $<s/q_s>*q_s$ and desired inventories are $<kinv-1/q_s>*q_s$, where kinv is inventory stock. The sample averages ensure that the means of sgap, igap, and cq are 1, which ensures "normal" utilization rates on average. For the Asian countries, only sgap was used as an explanatory variable, because of the unavailability of price, wage, and inventory data.

Table 1

Nonnested C-Tests of Output Equations

Industrial Countries:
(1) Constant Case
(2) Catch-up U.S. frontier
(3) Catch-up Regional leader
(4) Catch-up Global frontier
(5) Catch-up U.S. frontier for G-7, U.S., and Europe for European smalls

Model #	Coefficient	T-Ratio	F-Statistic coefficients=.5	F-Test Statistic (significance level in parentheses)
(1)	.193	3.16	25.13* versus	6.63 (1%)
(2)	.807	13.19		3.84 (5%)
(1)	.082	1.02	26.54*	
(3)	.918	11.32		
(1)	.192	2.40	14.73*	
(4)	.808	10.07		
(1)	.129	2.08	35.93*	
(5)	.871	14.07		
(2)	.593	7.17	1.28	
(3)	.407	4.92		
(2)	.777	7.72	7.57*	
(4)	.223	2.22		
(2)	.269	1.91	2.68	
(5)	.731	5.19		
(3)	.641	6.31	1.94	
(4)	.359	3.53		
(3)	.282	3.06	5.61	
(5)	.718	7.79		
(4)	.010	.08	19.61*	
(5)	.990	8.95		

See notes at end of table for C-test method. The F-statistics denoted with an asterisk indicate the pairwise models with coefficients that reject the constraint of equal values of .5. In these cases, the coefficient values are significantly different from each other at the 99% level.

Table 1 (continued)
Nonnested C-Tests of Output Equations

Asian Countries:
(1) Constant Case
(2) Catch-up U.S. frontier
(3) Catch-up Japanese frontier
(4) Catch-up Global frontier
(5) Catch-up U.S. and Japanese frontiers

Model #	Coefficient	T-Ratio	F-Statistic coefficients $=.5$	F-Test Statistic (significance level in parentheses)
(1)	.275	3.18	6.78*	versus 6.63 (1%)
(2)	.725	8.39		3.84 (5%)
(1)	.377	5.22	2.88	
(3)	.623	8.62		
(1)	.395	4.62	1.52	
(4)	.605	7.08		
(1)	.372	5.37	3.43	
(5)	.628.	9.07		
(2)	.596	5.11	0.68	
(3)	.404	3.46		
(2)	1.147	5.28	8.89*	
(4)	-.147	.67		
(2)	.593	4.14	0.42	
(5)	.407	2.84		
(3)	.574	5.66	0.54	
(4)	.426	4.19		
(3)	.394	1.81	0.24	
(5)	.606	2.78		
(4)	.343	2.64	1.46	
(5)	.657	5.05		

Note: Following Davidson and MacKinnon (1981), the C-test involves testing two alternative models:

$$Y_{it} = f_{it}(X_t, Beta) + e_{oit}$$
$$Y_{it} = g_{it}(Z_t, Gamma) + e_{1it}$$

(i $(=1,m)$ indexes country equations and t $(=1,n)$ indexes observations). A single regression is estimated:

$$Y_{it} = alpha * f_{hit} + (1-alpha) * g_{hit}$$

where f_{hit} and g_{hit} are the fitted values of Y_t from the two competing models. If alpha is greater than (1-alpha) and is significant, then f_{it} is the dominating model.

Table 2

Real Exchange Rates, Real GDP per Capita, and
Measured Productivity

Averages for Period:	1962-85	1960s	1970s	1980s
OECD Standard Deviations:				
(1) Real Exchange Rate (logarithm)	.157	.172	.184	.148
(2) Real GDP per Capita (logarithm) (relative to the U.S.)	.212	.255	.202	.195
Correlation between (1) and (2)	.618	.479	.576	.734
(3) Measured Productivity (logarithm) (relative to the U.S.)	.187	.243	.181	.156
Correlation between (1) and (3)	.106	.181	.112	-.056
Asia Standard Deviations:				
(1) Real Exchange Rate (logarithm)	.242	.239	.256	.278
(2) Real GDP per Capita (logarithm) (relative to the U.S.)	.596	.529	.608	.688
Correlation between (1) and (2)	.892	.892	.879	.812
(3) Measured Productivity (logarithm) (relative to the U.S.)	.515	.520	.502	.550
Correlation between (1) and (3)	.882	.913	.861	.754
OECD+Asia Standard Deviations:				
(1) Real Exchange Rate (logarithm)	.354	.339	.388	.346
(2) Real GDP per Capita (logarithm) (relative to the U.S.)	.693	.771	.692	.614
Correlation between (1) and (2)	.936	.914	.922	.907
(3) Measured Productivity (logarithm) (relative to the U.S.)	.469	.510	.464	.441
Correlation between (1) and (3)	.836	.831	.828	.782

Table 3

Regional Evidence of Convergence

	Real Exchange Rate	Real GDP per Capita (relative to the U.S.)	Measured Productivity (relative to the U.S.)
OECD			
1962	76.25	59.81	48.40
1985	83.62	69.21	67.23
Asia			
1962	41.58	13.99	22.42
1985	50.07	31.68	38.95
Asia/OECD			
1962	.55	.23	.46
1985	.60	.46	.58

Note: The OECD numbers are simple unweighted averages of data for the 19 industrial countries, which include Japan. The Asian numbers are simple unweighted averages of data for eight Asian countries, with Japan excluded from the sample. The real exchange rate is defined as the ratio of purchasing power parity to the market exchange rate (defined as national currency per $US) multiplied by 100. Both real GDP per capita (adjusted by PPP) and measured productivity per worker are defined relative to the U.S. (multiplied by 100).

172

Figure 1A

Gross Domestic Product Per Capita for Industrial Countries

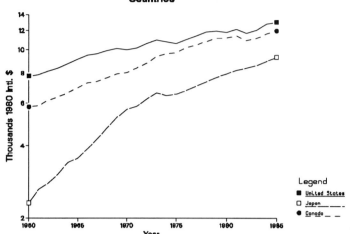

Figure 1B

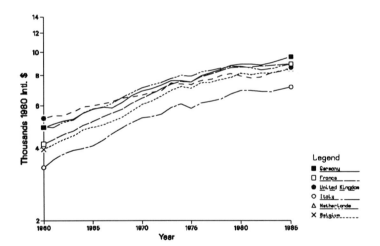

Figure 1C

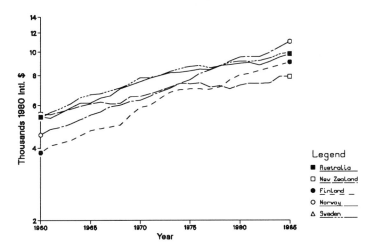

Figure 1D

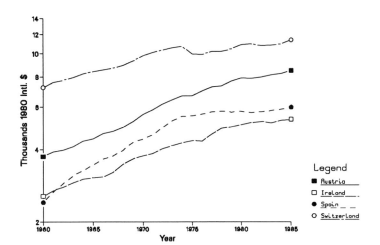

174

Figure 2A

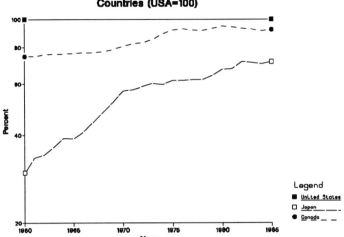

Figure 2A

Gross Domestic Product Per Capita for Industrial Countries (USA=100)

Figure 2B

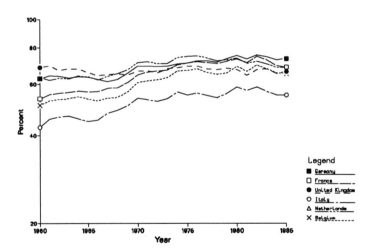

Figure 2C

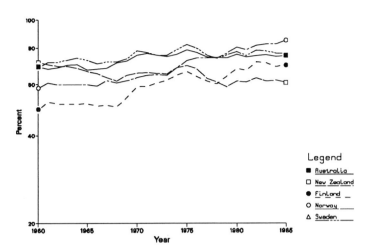

Figure 2D

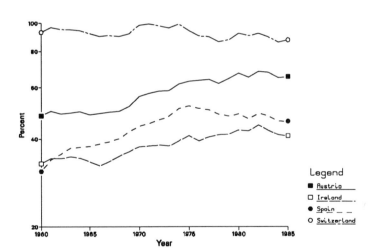

176

Measured Productivity Growth Paths for Industrial Countries

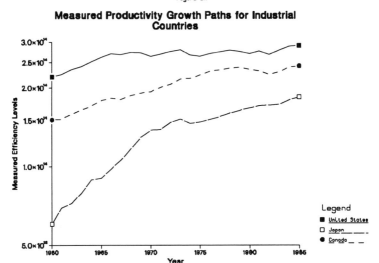

Figure 3B

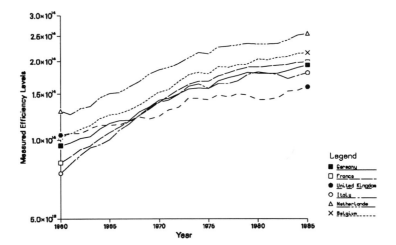

Figure 3C

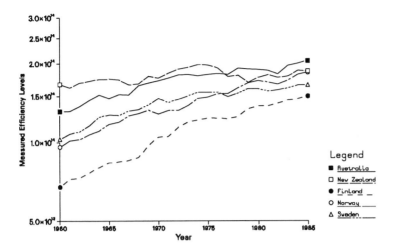

Figure 3D

178

Figure 4A

Measured Productivity Growth Paths for Industrial Countries (USA=100)

Legend
■ United States
□ Japan
● Canada

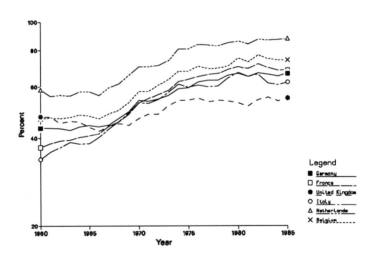

Figure 4B

Legend
■ Germany
□ France
● United Kingdom
○ Italy
△ Netherlands
✕ Belgium

Figure 4C

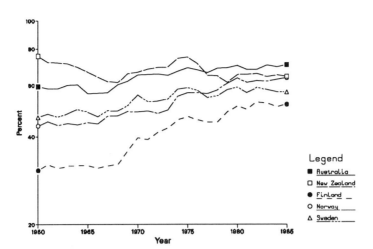

Legend
■ Australia
□ New Zealand
● Finland ___
○ Norway ___
△ Sweden ___

Figure 4D

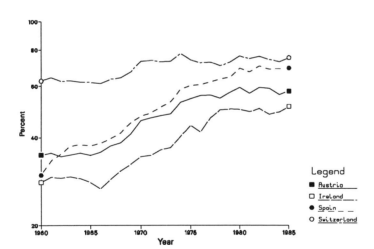

Legend
■ Austria ___
□ Ireland ___
● Spain _ _
○ Switzerland

Figure 5
Gross Domestic Product per Capita for the Asian Countries

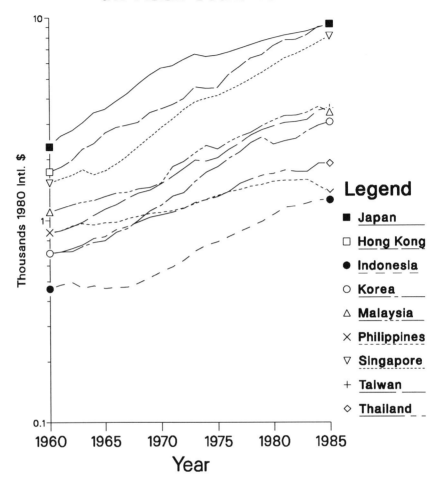

Figure 6
Gross Domestic Product per Capita for
the Asian Countries (USA=100)

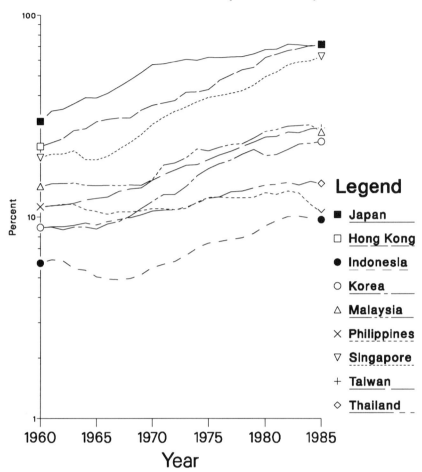

Year

Figure 7
Measured Productivity Growth Paths for
the Asian Countries

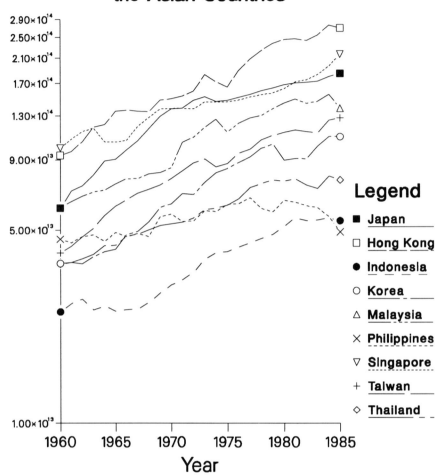

Figure 8
Measured Productivity Growth Paths for the Asian Countries (USA=100)

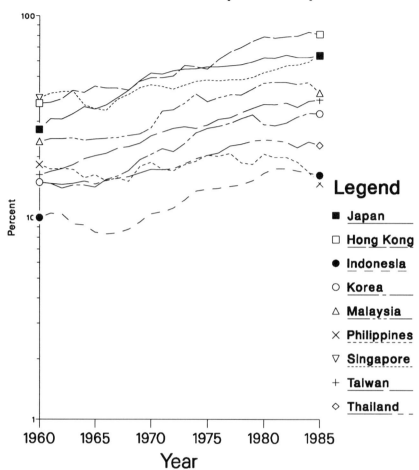

Legend

- ■ Japan
- □ Hong Kong
- ● Indonesia
- ○ Korea
- △ Malaysia
- × Philippines
- ▽ Singapore
- + Taiwan
- ◇ Thailand

Figure 9
International Price Indices and Real GDP per Capita Relative to the US
(Average 1962-85 data).

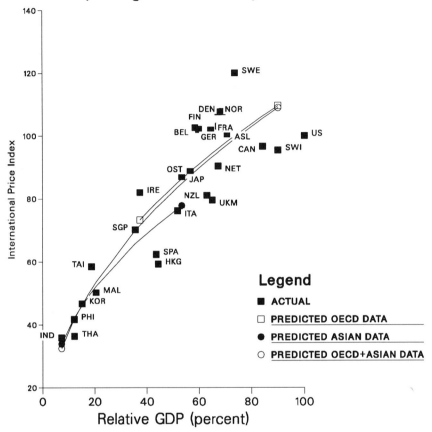

Figure 10
International Price Indices and Real GDP per Capita Relative to the US
(Average 1960s data).

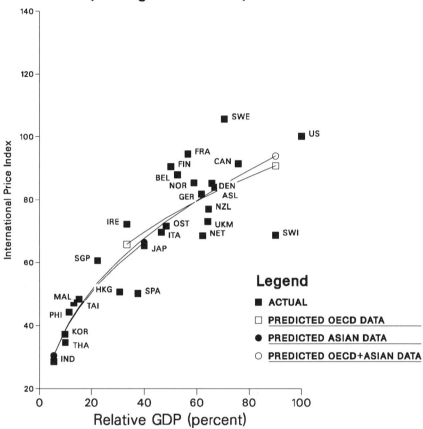

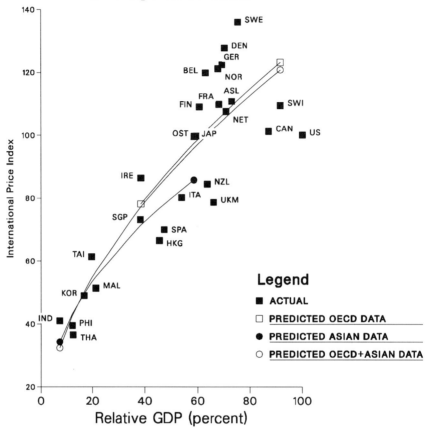

Figure 11
International Price Indices and Real GDP per Capita Relative to the US (Average 1970s data).

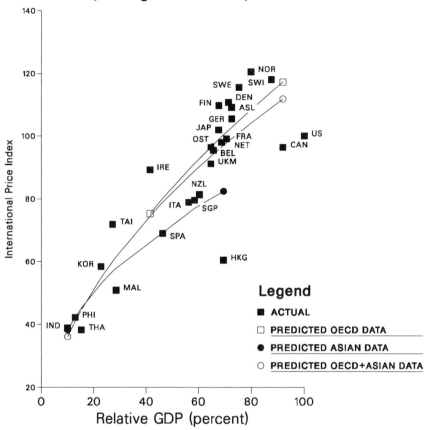

**Figure 12
International Price Indices and Real GDP per
Capita Relative to the US
(Average 1980s data).**

Table A1

(1)

Constant Growth Model of Technical Progress

	RTIME	constant	see	r2	durbin watson
USA	0.0072 (8.63)	32.6900 (412.43)	0.0416	0.6283	0.3379
JAP	0.0406 (14.04)	29.5280 (139.99)	0.1107	0.8835	0.1405
GER	0.0293 (24.26)	30.4760 (345.98)	0.0462	0.9577	0.2306
FRA	0.0371 (20.20)	29.9110 (223.49)	0.0702	0.9401	0.0862
UKM	0.0170 (17.18)	31.2790 (434.72)	0.0378	0.9190	0.4973
ITA	0.0348 (14.39)	30.0270 (170.59)	0.0924	0.8885	0.1335
CAN	0.0193 (16.63)	31.5430 (373.07)	0.0444	0.9141	0.2113
AUS	0.0163 (15.24)	31.5870 (405.06)	0.0409	0.8993	0.4735
OST	0.0338 (20.76)	29.9940 (252.95)	0.0622	0.9431	0.1283
BEL	0.0314 (25.58)	30.4240 (340.04)	0.0469	0.9618	0.2297
DEN	0.0235 (18.13)	30.7910 (326.30)	0.0495	0.9267	0.2911
FIN	0.0325 (26.77)	29.9440 (338.06)	0.0465	0.9850	0.3547
IRE	0.0369 (27.70)	29.5630 (304.78)	0.0509	0.9672	0.5074
NET	0.0294 (22.11)	30.7450 (317.35)	0.0508	0.9495	0.2472
NZL	0.0040 (3.29)	32.5300 (371.39)	0.0460	0.2941	0.5331
NOR	0.0250 (33.18)	30.7450 (559.19)	0.0288	0.9769	0.6701
SPA	0.0422 (23.64)	29.4700 (226.56)	0.0682	0.9556	0.2080
SWE	0.0172 (13.60)	31.3340 (339.94)	0.0484	0.8767	0.3016
SWI	0.0162 (11.39)	31.6750 (305.56)	0.0544	0.8330	0.1841

Note: The dependent variable is ln pimi, logarithm of the measured output attributable to labor. RTIME is a time trend equal to 60 in 1960, 61 in 1961,...and 85 in 1985. Estimation by SUR 1961-1985.

Table **A1** (continued)

(ii)

Output Equations for Industrial Countries
assuming above Model of Convergence

	ln(qs)	ln cq	ln sgap	ln igap	see	r2	dw
USA	1.0000	-0.1732	0.7311	0.0016	0.0085	0.9980	0.7952
	(***)	(13.36)	(24.09)	(0.43)			
JAP	1.0000	-0.1707	0.8528	0.0016	0.0072	0.9997	1.0418
	(***)	(14.18)	(48.63)	(0.43)			
GER	1.0000	-0.3362	0.7883	0.0016	0.0202	0.9901	0.5374
	(***)	(12.76)	(16.21)	(0.43)			
FRA	1.0000	-0.2959	0.8953	0.0016	0.0150	0.9966	0.7355
	(***)	(16.57)	(22.10)	(0.43)			
UKM	1.0000	-0.0721	0.6315	0.0016	0.0255	0.9636	0.2626
	(***)	(3.21)	(8.80)	(0.43)			
ITA	1.0000	-0.0585	1.0441	0.0016	0.0153	0.9958	0.3421
	(***)	(4.17)	(37.68)	(0.43)			
CAN	1.0000	-0.4027	0.6277	0.0016	0.0130	0.9981	0.8345
	(***)	(13.87)	(15.56)	(0.43)			
AUS	1.0000	-0.1136	1.3193	0.0016	0.0125	0.9973	1.3450
	(***)	(9.24)	(14.18)	(0.43)			
OST	1.0000	-0.4904	0.6860	0.0016	0.0205	0.9931	0.5263
	(***)	(12.75)	(18.30)	(0.43)			
BEL	1.0000	-0.2237	0.6236	0.0016	0.0118	0.9974	0.8837
	(***)	(16.87)	(23.37)	(0.43)			
DEN	1.0000	-0.1345	0.6434	0.0016	0.0143	0.9927	0.7636
	(***)	(11.83)	(24.39)	(0.43)			
FIN	1.0000	-0.1138	0.6090	0.0016	0.0177	0.9949	0.4851
	(***)	(7.26)	(13.84)	(0.43)			
IRE	1.0000	-0.1395	0.5688	0.0016	0.0307	0.9889	0.6671
	(***)	(3.97)	(8.87)	(0.43)			
NET	1.0000	-0.2979	0.6348	0.0016	0.0233	0.9887	0.3964
	(***)	(10.78)	(20.51)	(0.43)			
NZL	1.0000	-0.0154	0.7687	0.0016	0.0154	0.9917	1.3657
	(***)	(0.91)	(18.10)	(0.43)			
NOR	1.0000	-0.1932	0.2589	0.0016	0.0153	0.9968	0.9598
	(***)	(5.99)	(5.22)	(0.43)			
SPA	1.0000	-0.1496	0.8192	0.0016	0.0130	0.9978	0.7964
	(***)	(8.82)	(22.38)	(0.43)			
SWE	1.0000	-0.1430	0.5910	0.0016	0.0115	0.9953	1.2770
	(***)	(8.99)	(14.63)	(0.43)			
SWI	1.0000	-0.4749	0.6610	0.0016	0.0276	0.9606	0.4600
	(***)	(8.13)	(9.40)	(0.43)			

Sample 1963-1985. Estimation method by Zellner's SUR estimation technique
with instruments.

Table A2

(i)

Basic Convergence Model US Frontier

	ln(pimi)-1	ln(pimus)-1	constant	see	r2	durbin watson
JAP	0.8554 (46.74)	0.1446 (7.90)	-0.0635 (4.26)	0.0300	0.9896	1.8453
GER	0.9042 (42.01)	0.0958 (4.45)	-0.0310 (2.22)	0.0213	0.9900	1.8747
FRA	0.9130 (91.41)	0.0870 (8.71)	-0.0185 (2.77)	0.0128	0.9977	1.3698
UKM	0.8631 (15.52)	0.1369 (2.46)	-0.0800 (2.01)	0.0269	0.9551	1.9382
ITA	0.8597 (43.93)	0.1403 (7.17)	-0.0591 (4.23)	0.0239	0.9911	1.6989
CAN	0.8939 (28.75)	0.1061 (3.41)	-0.0101 (1.08)	0.0190	0.9821	1.6241
AUS	0.8152 (13.82)	0.1848 (3.13)	-0.0648 (2.40)	0.0274	0.9478	2.2666
OST	0.9203 (55.46)	0.0797 (4.80)	-0.0307 (2.29)	0.0189	0.9942	1.8284
BEL	0.9202 (50.75)	0.0798 (4.40)	-0.0120 (1.17)	0.0207	0.9918	2.2409
DEN	0.8776 (25.49)	0.1224 (3.55)	-0.0626 (2.46)	0.0235	0.9802	2.3930
FIN	0.9238 (39.19)	0.0762 (3.23)	-0.0381 (1.71)	0.0262	0.9876	1.6978
IRE	0.9496 (34.74)	0.0504 (1.84)	-0.0148 (0.53)	0.0359	0.9823	1.8259
NET	0.9222 (37.12)	0.0778 (3.13)	0.0003 (0.03)	0.0243	0.9875	1.8831
NZL	0.8265 (15.10)	0.1735 (3.17)	-0.0637 (2.83)	0.0329	0.6269	1.9402
NOR	0.9411 (29.77)	0.0589 (1.86)	-0.0127 (0.59)	0.0229	0.9836	1.9988
SPA	0.9099 (67.57)	0.0901 (6.69)	-0.0178 (1.73)	0.0214	0.9948	1.6557
SWE	0.7770 (17.12)	0.2230 (4.91)	-0.1223 (4.20)	0.0216	0.9701	2.0550
SWI	0.7898 (18.22)	0.2102 (4.85)	-0.0584 (3.58)	0.0192	0.9752	1.5572

Note: The dependent variable is ln pimi, logarithm of the measured output attributable to labor. pimus is the measured productivity level for the U.S. assuming constant technical progress. Estimation by SUR 1961-1985.

Table A2 (continued)

(ii)

Output Equations for Industrial Countries
assuming above Model of Convergence

	ln(qs)	ln cq	ln sgap	ln igap	see	r2	dw
USA	1.0000 (***)	-0.1717 (11.14)	0.7355 (21.56)	0.0146 (4.22)	0.0084	0.9980	0.7805
JAP	1.0000 (***)	-0.0788 (5.92)	0.8036 (22.75)	0.0146 (4.22)	0.0096	0.9994	0.5659
GER	1.0000 (***)	-0.1561 (8.20)	0.5425 (20.19)	0.0146 (4.22)	0.0080	0.9985	1.8658
FRA	1.0000 (***)	-0.1351 (9.75)	0.7208 (19.75)	0.0146 (4.22)	0.0102	0.9984	0.4589
UKM	1.0000 (***)	-0.0601 (2.76)	0.4359 (6.77)	0.0146 (4.22)	0.0209	0.9756	0.4980
ITA	1.0000 (***)	0.0092 (0.70)	0.7824 (19.07)	0.0146 (4.22)	0.0132	0.9969	0.3604
CAN	1.0000 (***)	-0.3135 (11.20)	0.4823 (9.80)	0.0146 (4.22)	0.0131	0.9980	0.6825
AUS	1.0000 (***)	-0.0886 (5.96)	0.8307 (16.48)	0.0146 (4.22)	0.0114	0.9978	1.2141
OST	1.0000 (***)	-0.1146 (4.74)	0.5101 (24.71)	0.0146 (4.22)	0.0098	0.9984	0.6202
BEL	1.0000 (***)	-0.0680 (4.30)	0.4808 (17.73)	0.0146 (4.22)	0.0118	0.9974	0.6747
DEN	1.0000 (***)	-0.0889 (6.35)	0.3248 (5.99)	0.0146 (4.22)	0.0124	0.9945	0.8014
FIN	1.0000 (***)	-0.0121 (0.90)	0.5438 (12.18)	0.0146 (4.22)	0.0164	0.9957	0.5841
IRE	1.0000 (***)	-0.0921 (2.02)	0.5444 (7.39)	0.0146 (4.22)	0.0296	0.9898	0.7155
NET	1.0000 (***)	-0.0903 (5.09)	0.3967 (17.33)	0.0146 (4.22)	0.0106	0.9977	0.9914
NZL	1.0000 (***)	-0.0423 (2.53)	0.7164 (17.96)	0.0146 (4.22)	0.0143	0.9928	1.5016
NOR	1.0000 (***)	-0.1599 (4.92)	-0.0452 (0.81)	0.0146 (4.22)	0.0191	0.9951	0.7230
SPA	1.0000 (***)	-0.1480 (6.02)	0.9336 (12.44)	0.0146 (4.22)	0.0159	0.9967	0.6105
SWE	1.0000 (***)	-0.0018 (0.10)	0.4053 (6.27)	0.0146 (4.22)	0.0157	0.9913	0.8599
SWI	1.0000 (***)	-0.1322 (4.13)	0.3279 (9.32)	0.0146 (4.22)	0.0144	0.9893	0.6973

Sample 1963-1985. Estimation method by Zellner's SUR estimation technique
with instruments.

Table A3

(i)

Basic Convergence Model with Regional Leaders

	ln(pimi)-1	ln(pimus)-1	ln(pimeur)-1	constant	see	r2	durbin watson
JAP	0.8840 (57.42)	0.1160 (7.53)		-0.0421 (3.26)	0.0290	0.9902	2.0366
GER	0.5894 (6.12)		0.4106 (4.26)	0.0375 (7.79)	0.0215	0.9898	1.5861
FRA	0.7809 (26.43)		0.2191 (7.42)	0.0398 (14.25)	0.0139	0.9973	1.1868
UKM	1.0019 (23.39)		-0.0019 (0.04)	0.0171 (2.78)	0.0271	0.9543	2.0820
ITA	0.6346 (11.69)		0.3654 (6.73)	0.0235 (4.11)	0.0272	0.9885	1.2806
CAN	0.9332 (36.01)	0.0668 (2.58)		0.0007 (0.08)	0.0190	0.9821	1.6186
AUS	0.8683 (18.22)	0.1317 (2.76)		-0.0410 (1.86)	0.0271	0.9491	2.3809
OST	0.6121 (10.17)		0.3879 (6.44)	-0.0217 (2.44)	0.0173	0.9952	1.7915
BEL	0.3102 (5.11)		0.6897 (11.36)	0.1127 (13.88)	0.0176	0.9940	2.3235
DEN	1.0932 (17.48)		-0.0932 (1.49)	0.0343 (4.60)	0.0261	0.9756	2.3593
FIN	0.5645 (9.95)		0.4355 (7.67)	-0.0895 (5.42)	0.0237	0.9898	1.5480
IRE	0.7264 (14.63)		0.2736 (5.51)	-0.0603 (3.26)	0.0332	0.9849	1.6591
NET	0.1033 (1.36)		0.8967 (11.78)	0.2927 (12.77)	0.0206	0.9910	1.3390
NZL	0.8571 (14.81)	0.1429 (2.47)		-0.0516 (2.18)	0.0329	0.6268	1.9817
NOR	0.9809 (21.48)		0.0191 (0.42)	0.0259 (5.29)	0.0240	0.9819	1.9082
SPA	0.7141 (36.73)		0.2859 (14.70)	0.0292 (8.02)	0.0175	0.9965	2.0104
SWE	1.1081 (33.37)		-0.1081 (3.26)	0.0184 (3.59)	0.0256	0.9578	2.1769
SWI	1.0648 (33.37)		-0.0648 (2.03)	0.0007 (0.07)	0.0222	0.9667	1.6394

Note: The dependent variable is ln pimi, logarithm of the measured output attributable to labor. pimus is the measured productivity level for the U.S. assuming constant technical progress. pimeur is the measured European frontier calculated by adding the employment weighted measured productivity levels for the European countries. Estimation by SUR 1961–1985.

Table A3 (continued)

(ii)

Output Equations for Industrial Countries
assuming above Model of Convergence

	ln(qs)	ln cq	ln sgap	ln lgap	see	r2	dw
USA	1.0000 (***)	-0.1581 (11.43)	0.7403 (23.75)	-0.0077 (2.52)	0.0084	0.9980	0.8061
JAP	1.0000 (***)	-0.0956 (9.68)	0.7139 (24.26)	-0.0077 (2.52)	0.0096	0.9994	0.6185
GER	1.0000 (***)	-0.3889 (10.61)	0.3637 (3.11)	-0.0077 (2.52)	0.0171	0.9929	0.9889
FRA	1.0000 (***)	-0.2433 (20.44)	0.6087 (12.27)	-0.0077 (2.52)	0.0120	0.9979	0.6403
UKM	1.0000 (***)	-0.1372 (5.23)	0.5753 (6.44)	-0.0077 (2.52)	0.0263	0.9613	0.2722
ITA	1.0000 (***)	-0.1000 (7.98)	0.7787 (21.59)	-0.0077 (2.52)	0.0144	0.9963	0.3676
CAN	1.0000 (***)	-0.3438 (12.51)	0.4509 (9.62)	-0.0077 (2.52)	0.0114	0.9985	0.9857
AUS	1.0000 (***)	-0.1009 (7.91)	0.7456 (14.56)	-0.0077 (2.52)	0.0110	0.9979	1.3733
OST	1.0000 (***)	-0.2898 (14.13)	0.3624 (16.01)	-0.0077 (2.52)	0.0099	0.9984	0.6107
BEL	1.0000 (***)	-0.0938 (6.14)	0.3109 (9.11)	-0.0077 (2.52)	0.0109	0.9977	1.2689
DEN	1.0000 (***)	-0.1467 (10.85)	0.5565 (14.72)	-0.0077 (2.52)	0.0145	0.9924	0.8127
FIN	1.0000 (***)	-0.0807 (6.18)	0.4400 (9.41)	-0.0077 (2.52)	0.0160	0.9959	0.6659
IRE	1.0000 (***)	-0.0830 (2.92)	0.3692 (6.67)	-0.0077 (2.52)	0.0261	0.9920	0.8072
NET	1.0000 (***)	-0.2594 (12.81)	0.2659 (7.77)	-0.0077 (2.52)	0.0102	0.9978	1.5415
NZL	1.0000 (***)	-0.0640 (4.24)	0.7053 (23.48)	-0.0077 (2.52)	0.0140	0.9932	1.5121
NOR	1.0000 (***)	-0.2835 (9.85)	0.2219 (6.10)	-0.0077 (2.52)	0.0146	0.9971	1.0587
SPA	1.0000 (***)	-0.0343 (1.70)	0.4249 (6.70)	-0.0077 (2.52)	0.0129	0.9978	0.7096
SWE	1.0000 (***)	-0.1175 (7.26)	0.2598 (3.87)	-0.0077 (2.52)	0.0113	0.9955	1.6656
SWI	1.0000 (***)	-0.4139 (10.69)	0.4244 (7.10)	-0.0077 (2.52)	0.0237	0.9710	0.5090

Sample 1963-1985. Estimation method by Zellner's SUR estimation technique
with instruments.

Table A4

(i)

Basic Convergence Model Global Frontier

	ln(pimi)-i	ln(pimglob)-1	constant	see	r2	durbin watson
USA	1.0299	-0.0299	-0.0061	0.0235	0.8374	1.7520
	(34.55)	(1.00)	(0.35)			
JAP	0.8230	0.1770	0.0140	0.0295	0.9899	1.9186
	(32.98)	(7.10)	(1.91)			
GER	0.8514	0.1486	0.0219	0.0197	0.9914	2.1185
	(21.92)	(3.83)	(5.10)			
FRA	0.8515	0.1485	0.0287	0.0124	0.9979	1.4318
	(58.87)	(10.27)	(11.28)			
UKM	0.7426	0.2573	-0.0171	0.0275	0.9531	1.7122
	(9.12)	(3.16)	(1.42)			
ITA	0.7479	0.2521	0.0106	0.0238	0.9912	1.6296
	(22.96)	(7.74)	(1.88)			
CAN	0.8994	0.1005	0.0493	0.0207	0.9789	1.3299
	(12.76)	(1.43)	(2.28)			
AUS	0.8102	0.1898	0.0422	0.0297	0.9387	1.8825
	(9.08)	(2.13)	(3.30)			
OST	0.8682	0.1318	0.0046	0.0179	0.9948	1.9776
	(31.49)	(4.78)	(0.69)			
BEL	0.8439	0.1561	0.0381	0.0195	0.9927	2.4169
	(27.55)	(5.10)	(9.00)			
DEN	0.5306	0.4694	-0.0448	0.0229	0.9812	1.9575
	(5.25)	(4.64)	(2.80)			
FIN	0.8774	0.1226	-0.0103	0.0250	0.9887	1.7969
	(23.79)	(3.32)	(0.75)			
IRE	0.8723	0.1277	-0.0179	0.0355	0.9827	1.7258
	(22.60)	(3.31)	(1.02)			
NET	0.8255	0.1745	0.0674	0.0228	0.9889	1.9449
	(17.11)	(3.62)	(5.61)			
NZL	0.9658	0.0342	0.0109	0.0342	0.5977	1.9872
	(26.29)	(0.93)	(1.14)			
NOR	0.8401	0.1599	0.0125	0.0228	0.9838	1.8365
	(13.07)	(2.49)	(1.75)			
SPA	0.8410	0.1590	0.0257	0.0203	0.9953	1.7457
	(42.79)	(8.09)	(5.50)			
SWE	0.9221	0.0779	0.0145	0.0270	0.9532	1.6508
	(10.61)	(0.90)	(1.95)			
SWI	0.9998	0.0002	0.0186	0.0237	0.9623	1.3637
	(10.46)	(0.00)	(0.90)			

Note: The dependent variable is ln pimi, logarithm of the measured output attributable to labor. pimglob is the measured global productivity level, calculated by adding the sum of employment weighted measured productivity levels for each country in the sample. Estimation by SUR 1961–1985.

Table **A4** (continued)

(ii)

Output Equations for Industrial Countries
assuming above Model of Convergence

	ln(qs)	ln cq	ln sgap	ln igap	see	r2	dw
USA	1.0000 (***)	-0.1962 (10.77)	0.7232 (15.95)	-0.0049 (1.98)	0.0090	0.9977	0.7480
JAP	1.0000 (***)	-0.1300 (10.84)	0.7556 (24.12)	-0.0049 (1.98)	0.0086	0.9995	0.7090
GER	1.0000 (***)	-0.1912 (8.84)	0.3391 (7.63)	-0.0049 (1.98)	0.0110	0.9971	1.3958
FRA	1.0000 (***)	-0.1551 (15.61)	0.5643 (21.06)	-0.0049 (1.98)	0.0096	0.9986	0.5063
UKM	1.0000 (***)	-0.1895 (8.36)	0.1977 (2.07)	-0.0049 (1.98)	0.0228	0.9710	0.5064
ITA	1.0000 (***)	-0.0368 (3.56)	0.7555 (26.57)	-0.0049 (1.98)	0.0140	0.9965	0.3403
CAN	1.0000 (***)	-0.4518 (11.88)	0.5476 (10.35)	-0.0049 (1.98)	0.0129	0.9981	0.9905
AUS	1.0000 (***)	-0.1993 (14.72)	0.5468 (9.14)	-0.0049 (1.98)	0.0096	0.9984	1.4313
OST	1.0000 (***)	-0.2374 (12.09)	0.4711 (22.26)	-0.0049 (1.98)	0.0113	0.9979	0.5015
BEL	1.0000 (***)	-0.0851 (6.04)	0.4021 (13.01)	-0.0049 (1.98)	0.0098	0.9982	1.0530
DEN	1.0000 (***)	-0.1110 (8.65)	0.3844 (8.84)	-0.0049 (1.98)	0.0109	0.9958	1.1496
FIN	1.0000 (***)	-0.0741 (4.53)	0.4721 (8.71)	-0.0049 (1.98)	0.0159	0.9959	0.6631
IRE	1.0000 (***)	-0.0718 (1.59)	0.5450 (8.02)	-0.0049 (1.98)	0.0290	0.9901	0.7429
NET	1.0000 (***)	-0.1401 (9.28)	0.3701 (16.07)	-0.0049 (1.98)	0.0106	0.9977	1.0921
NZL	1.0000 (***)	-0.0337 (2.00)	0.7905 (21.26)	-0.0049 (1.98)	0.0157	0.9914	1.3204
NOR	1.0000 (***)	-0.2010 (6.02)	-0.0585 (1.05)	-0.0049 (1.98)	0.0214	0.9938	0.5916
SPA	1.0000 (***)	-0.1264 (5.58)	0.8316 (12.91)	-0.0049 (1.98)	0.0154	0.9969	0.5720
SWE	1.0000 (***)	-0.2257 (10.94)	0.5285 (11.39)	-0.0049 (1.98)	0.0116	0.9952	1.1877
SWI	1.0000 (***)	-0.6155 (8.64)	0.6298 (6.84)	-0.0049 (1.98)	0.0285	0.9581	0.5503

Sample 1963-1985. Estimation method by Zellner's SUR estimation technique
with instruments.

Table A5

(i)

Basic Convergence Model with US and
Additional Europe Affect for Small European Countries

	ln(pimi)-1	ln(pimus)-1	ln(pimeur)-1	constant	see	r2	durbin watson
JAP	0.8748 (45.38)	0.1252 (6.49)		-0.0490 (3.15)	0.0291	0.9902	2.0004
GER	0.9225 (42.11)	0.0775 (3.54)		-0.0198 (1.39)	0.0206	0.9907	2.0280
FRA	0.9194 (93.88)	0.0806 (8.23)		-0.0146 (2.22)	0.0125	0.9978	1.4367
UKM	0.9016 (16.78)	0.0984 (1.83)		-0.0527 (1.37)	0.0265	0.9566	2.0526
ITA	0.8727 (44.21)	0.1273 (6.45)		-0.0503 (3.57)	0.0234	0.9915	1.8075
CAN	0.9029 (28.55)	0.0971 (3.07)		-0.0076 (0.81)	0.0190	0.9822	1.6349
AUS	0.8425 (14.01)	0.1575 (2.62)		-0.0526 (1.92)	0.0272	0.9488	2.3363
OST	0.7034 (33.29)	0.0225 (1.36)	0.2741 (12.51)	-0.0237 (1.90)	0.0176	0.9950	1.8262
BEL	0.6854 (30.75)	0.0405 (2.27)	0.2741 (12.51)	0.0415 (3.69)	0.0186	0.9934	2.4832
DEN	0.5081 (12.62)	0.2178 (6.65)	0.2741 (12.51)	-0.1555 (6.38)	0.0222	0.9824	1.9976
FIN	0.7074 (27.66)	0.0185 (0.78)	0.2741 (12.51)	-0.0616 (2.92)	0.0240	0.9896	1.6920
IRE	0.7492 (25.49)	-0.0233 (0.89)	0.2741 (12.51)	-0.0375 (1.45)	0.0324	0.9856	1.7820
NET	0.6583 (22.76)	0.0676 (2.98)	0.2741 (12.51)	0.0850 (7.24)	0.0212	0.9904	1.9320
NZL	0.8023 (18.55)	0.1977 (4.57)		-0.0732 (4.01)	0.0330	0.6253	1.9012
NOR	0.5982 (14.69)	0.1277 (4.00)	0.2741 (12.51)	-0.0637 (2.94)	0.0235	0.9827	1.3468
SPA	0.7388 (46.13)	-0.0129 (0.87)	0.2741 (12.51)	0.0388 (3.84)	0.0173	0.9966	2.1282
SWE	0.2527 (4.87)	0.4732 (11.75)	0.2741 (12.51)	-0.2791 (10.84)	0.0182	0.9786	1.9397
SWI	0.2281 (4.03)	0.4978 (10.87)	0.2741 (12.51)	-0.0884 (5.35)	0.0231	0.9640	0.7235

Note: The dependent variable is ln pimi, logarithm of the measured output attributable to labor. pimus is the measured productivity level for the U.S. assuming constant technical progress. pimeur is the measured European frontier calculated by adding the employment weighted measured productivity levels for the European countries. Estimation by SUR 1961-1985.

Table A5 (continued)

(ii)

Output Equations for Industrial Countries
assuming above Model of Convergence

	ln(qs)	ln cq	ln sgap	ln igap	see	r2	dw
USA	1.0000	-0.1784	0.7267	0.0308	0.0084	0.9980	0.7620
	(***)	(11.52)	(20.87)	(8.02)			
JAP	1.0000	-0.0959	0.7857	0.0308	0.0088	0.9995	0.6774
	(***)	(9.32)	(25.00)	(8.02)			
GER	1.0000	-0.1295	0.4946	0.0308	0.0085	0.9983	1.5947
	(***)	(6.67)	(17.02)	(8.02)			
FRA	1.0000	-0.1639	0.8631	0.0308	0.0118	0.9979	0.5269
	(***)	(12.20)	(22.67)	(8.02)			
UKM	1.0000	-0.0499	0.3085	0.0308	0.0207	0.9760	0.5723
	(***)	(2.33)	(3.99)	(8.02)			
ITA	1.0000	0.0314	0.7732	0.0308	0.0131	0.9970	0.3643
	(***)	(2.40)	(16.36)	(8.02)			
CAN	1.0000	-0.3380	0.4151	0.0308	0.0129	0.9981	0.7660
	(***)	(9.57)	(6.83)	(8.02)			
AUS	1.0000	-0.0806	0.7569	0.0308	0.0111	0.9979	1.2220
	(***)	(6.23)	(17.85)	(8.02)			
OST	1.0000	-0.2373	0.4772	0.0308	0.0097	0.9984	0.6708
	(***)	(9.83)	(18.97)	(8.02)			
BEL	1.0000	-0.1114	0.3973	0.0308	0.0099	0.9982	1.0928
	(***)	(8.66)	(13.17)	(8.02)			
DEN	1.0000	-0.0860	0.4092	0.0308	0.0104	0.9961	1.0233
	(***)	(8.16)	(11.65)	(8.02)			
FIN	1.0000	-0.0727	0.4747	0.0308	0.0161	0.9958	0.6109
	(***)	(4.81)	(9.11)	(8.02)			
IRE	1.0000	-0.1072	0.3061	0.0308	0.0250	0.9927	0.8531
	(***)	(2.97)	(4.68)	(8.02)			
NET	1.0000	-0.1603	0.3379	0.0308	0.0100	0.9979	1.1851
	(***)	(8.12)	(12.38)	(8.02)			
NZL	1.0000	-0.0307	0.7038	0.0308	0.0146	0.9925	1.4681
	(***)	(1.88)	(17.67)	(8.02)			
NOR	1.0000	-0.1621	0.0424	0.0308	0.0228	0.9929	0.4618
	(***)	(4.09)	(0.62)	(8.02)			
SPA	1.0000	-0.0349	0.3393	0.0308	0.0121	0.9981	0.8033
	(***)	(1.85)	(4.56)	(8.02)			
SWE	1.0000	-0.0421	0.3394	0.0308	0.0118	0.9951	1.4819
	(***)	(2.52)	(5.30)	(8.02)			
SWI	1.0000	-0.1634	0.3555	0.0308	0.0179	0.9834	0.4388
	(***)	(5.20)	(10.42)	(8.02)			

Sample 1963-1985. Estimation method by Zellner's SUR estimation technique
with instruments.

Table A6

(i)

Asian Countries with Constant Growth
of Technical Progress

	RTIME	constant	see	r2	durbin watson
HKG	0.0417 (29.43)	29.7330 (285.80)	0.0511	0.9719	1.1175
IND	0.0386 (19.21)	28.4350 (193.10)	0.0724	0.9366	0.3542
KOR	0.0475 (20.03)	28.3960 (163.38)	0.0854	0.9414	0.3849
MAL	0.0400 (19.63)	29.3520 (196.26)	0.0735	0.9391	0.6608
PHI	0.0119 (5.35)	30.7630 (188.26)	0.0803	0.5336	0.6240
SGP	0.0261 (17.40)	30.6780 (278.92)	0.0541	0.9237	0.6683
TWN	0.0414 (23.95)	29.0270 (229.04)	0.0623	0.9582	0.3690
THA	0.0311 (23.07)	29.4170 (297.45)	0.0486	0.9551	0.5660

Note: The dependent variable is ln pimi, logarithm of the measured output attributable to labor. RTIME is a time trend equal to 61 in 1961, 62 in 1962,...and 85 in 1985. Estimation by SUR 1961-1985.

(ii)

Output Equations for Asian Countries
assuming above Model of Convergence

	ln(qs)	ln sgap	see	r2	dw
HKG	1.0000 (***)	0.1093 (1.64)	0.0358	0.9962	0.9198
IND	1.0000 (***)	0.1884 (4.08)	0.0413	0.9934	0.3683
KOR	1.0000 (***)	0.2685 (3.51)	0.0636	0.9882	0.2283
MAL	1.0000 (***)	-0.1094 (1.82)	0.0574	0.9884	0.7141
PHI	1.0000 (***)	0.4961 (6.14)	0.0517	0.9787	0.3397
SGP	1.0000 (***)	0.0574 (0.58)	0.0400	0.9955	0.6360
TWN	1.0000 (***)	0.0946 (1.52)	0.0390	0.9949	0.4470
THA	1.0000 (***)	0.8005 (12.33)	0.0194	0.9982	0.4452

Sample 1963-1985. Estimation method by Zellner's SUR estimation technique with instruments.

Table A7

(i)

Asian Countries with Convergence
toward U.S. Levels

	ln(pimi)-1	ln(pimus)-1	constant	see	r2	durbin watson
HKG	0.9509	0.0491	0.0125	0.0528	0.9700	2.0673
	(26.88)	(1.39)	(0.52)			
IND	0.9826	0.0174	-0.0068	0.0425	0.9782	1.4943
	(32.26)	(0.57)	(0.10)			
KOR	0.9490	0.0510	-0.0357	0.0522	0.9781	1.9212
	(28.89)	(1.55)	(0.70)			
MAL	0.9136	0.0864	-0.0625	0.0568	0.9636	1.9920
	(21.98)	(2.08)	(1.32)			
PHI	0.7438	0.2561	-0.4374	0.0597	0.7424	1.7290
	(7.66)	(2.64)	(2.62)			
SGP	0.9966	0.0034	0.0286	0.0450	0.9471	1.3018
	(16.61)	(0.06)	(0.59)			
TWN	0.9310	0.0690	-0.0478	0.0338	0.9877	1.8783
	(39.66)	(2.94)	(1.48)			
THA	0.9253	0.0747	-0.0982	0.0350	0.9768	2.2032
	(26.50)	(2.14)	(1.65)			

Note: The dependent variable is ln pimi, logarithm of the measured output attributable to labor. pimus is the measured productivity level for the U.S. Estimation by SUR 1961-1985.

(ii)

Output Equations for Asian Countries
assuming above Model of Convergence

	ln(qs)	ln sgap	see	r2	dw
HKG	1.0000	0.2683	0.0392	0.9954	0.5170
	(***)	(4.70)			
IND	1.0000	0.3355	0.0399	0.9939	0.4233
	(***)	(9.06)			
KOR	1.0000	0.2747	0.0381	0.9958	0.5498
	(***)	(6.00)			
MAL	1.0000	-0.4662	0.0566	0.9887	1.0606
	(***)	(4.30)			
PHI	1.0000	0.4405	0.0421	0.9859	0.5539
	(***)	(6.00)			
SGP	1.0000	0.1240	0.0452	0.9943	0.4641
	(***)	(1.08)			
TWN	1.0000	-0.0394	0.0283	0.9973	0.9360
	(***)	(0.73)			
THA	1.0000	0.7235	0.0132	0.9992	0.9130
	(***)	(16.79)			

Sample 1963-1985. Estimation method by Zellner's SUR estimation technique with instruments.

Table A8

(i)

Asian Countries with Convergence toward Japanese Levels

	ln(pimi)-1	ln(pimja)-1	constant	see	r2	durbin watson
HKG	0.8591	0.1409	0.0621	0.0536	0.9692	1.8151
	(13.23)	(2.17)	(4.43)			
IND	0.9061	0.0939	-0.0992	0.0384	0.9822	1.7111
	(21.98)	(2.28)	(1.73)			
KOR	0.7096	0.2904	-0.1843	0.0461	0.9829	2.0328
	(12.61)	(5.16)	(4.11)			
MAL	0.6329	0.3671	-0.0985	0.0543	0.9667	1.6123
	(8.48)	(4.92)	(3.41)			
PHI	1.0813	-0.0813	0.0811	0.0647	0.6971	2.0295
	(31.42)	(2.36)	(2.27)			
SGP	1.0213	-0.0213	0.0323	0.0453	0.9465	1.3160
	(19.58)	(0.41)	(3.44)			
TWN	0.7384	0.2618	-0.1109	0.0398	0.9829	1.2341
	(9.73)	(3.45)	(2.41)			
THA	0.9005	0.0995	-0.0655	0.0379	0.9727	1.8901
	(20.39)	(2.25)	(1.55)			

Note: The dependent variable is ln pimi, logarithm of the measured output attributable to labor. pimja is the measured productivity level for Japan. Estimation by SUR 1961-1985.

(ii)

Output Equations for Asian Countries assuming above Model of Convergence

	ln(qs)	ln sgap	see	r2	dw
HKG	1.0000	0.2077	0.0582	0.9899	0.2912
	(***)	(3.24)			
IND	1.0000	0.1730	0.0307	0.9964	0.5109
	(***)	(5.04)			
KOR	1.0000	0.1735	0.0330	0.9968	0.9465
	(***)	(3.47)			
MAL	1.0000	0.0782	0.0440	0.9932	0.8556
	(***)	(1.83)			
PHI	1.0000	0.5740	0.0293	0.9932	0.7169
	(***)	(18.18)			
SGP	1.0000	0.1761	0.0432	0.9948	0.4922
	(***)	(1.96)			
TWN	1.0000	-0.2299	0.0549	0.9898	0.4173
	(***)	(2.50)			
THA	1.0000	1.0400	0.0197	0.9981	0.5375
	(***)	(11.21)			

Sample 1963-1985. Estimation method by Zellner's SUR estimation technique with instruments.

Table A9

(i)

Asian Countries with Convergence
toward Global Frontier

	ln(pimi)-1	ln(pimgl)-1	constant	see	r2	durbin watson
HKG	0.9449 (19.27)	0.0551 (1.12)	0.0482 (4.14)	0.0524	0.9705	2.0922
IND	0.9722 (23.02)	0.0278 (0.66)	-0.0090 (0.15)	0.0418	0.9788	1.5246
KOR	0.8824 (19.34)	0.1176 (2.58)	-0.0536 (1.39)	0.0526	0.9778	1.7786
MAL	0.8033 (13.13)	0.1967 (3.21)	-0.0443 (1.67)	0.0557	0.9651	1.8828
PHI	0.7629 (6.61)	0.2371 (2.05)	-0.2353 (2.02)	0.0638	0.7055	1.5344
SGP	0.9017 (8.00)	0.0983 (0.87)	0.0233 (1.80)	0.0455	0.9460	1.1687
TWN	0.8647 (24.92)	0.1352 (3.90)	-0.0403 (1.76)	0.0339	0.9876	1.7889
THA	0.8275 (13.32)	0.1725 (2.78)	-0.1401 (2.30)	0.0337	0.9784	2.2017

Note: The dependent variable is ln pimi, logarithm of the measured output attributable to labor. pimgl is the measured global productivity level calculated by adding the employment weighted measured efficiency levels for the whole sample of countries. Estimation by SUR 1961–1985.

(ii)

Output Equations for Asian Countries
assuming above Model of Convergence

	ln(qs)	ln sgap	see	r2	dw
HKG	1.0000 (***)	0.2146 (3.62)	0.0393	0.9954	0.5871
IND	1.0000 (***)	0.3248 (8.85)	0.0393	0.9940	0.4238
KOR	1.0000 (***)	0.3088 (7.98)	0.0337	0.9967	0.6397
MAL	1.0000 (***)	-0.4004 (3.87)	0.0570	0.9886	0.9684
PHI	1.0000 (***)	0.4814 (2.93)	0.0574	0.9738	0.2767
SGP	1.0000 (***)	0.2449 (2.19)	0.0513	0.9927	0.4007
TWN	1.0000 (***)	0.0277 (0.57)	0.0298	0.9970	0.7826
THA	1.0000 (***)	0.6754 (13.91)	0.0129	0.9992	0.9905

Sample 1963-1985. Estimation method by Zellner's SUR estimation technique with instruments.

Table A10

(i)

Asian Countries with Convergence
toward U.S. Levels with Additional Regional Japanese Effect

	ln(pimi)-1	ln(pimus)-1	ln(pimja)-1	constant	see	r2	durbin watson
HKG	0.7933 (12.12)	0.0485 (1.18)	0.1581 (2.22)	0.0348 (1.07)	0.0536	0.9692	1.7065
IND	0.8989 (21.00)	-0.0038 (0.12)	0.1048 (2.39)	-0.1062 (1.51)	0.0382	0.9823	1.7127
KOR	0.6468 (9.70)	-0.0254 (0.70)	0.3789 (4.65)	-0.2144 (3.92)	0.0467	0.9824	1.9215
MAL	0.6118 (7.86)	0.0601 (1.48)	0.3281 (4.05)	-0.1511 (3.28)	0.0526	0.9687	1.7020
PHI	0.8972 (9.88)	0.1226 (1.43)	-0.0198 (0.40)	-0.1890 (1.29)	0.0606	0.7349	1.9305
SGP	0.9528 (9.28)	0.0182 (0.28)	0.0290 (0.50)	0.0154 (0.29)	0.0451	0.9470	1.2470
TWN	0.6206 (8.05)	0.0713 (2.44)	0.3082 (3.82)	-0.2346 (4.44)	0.0384	0.9841	1.2454
THA	0.7241 (10.98)	0.1244 (3.48)	0.1515 (3.01)	-0.3243 (3.94)	0.0356	0.9759	1.8711

Note: The dependent variable is ln pimi, logarithm of the measured output attributable to labor. pimus is the measured productivity level for the U.S. pimja is the measured productivity level for Japan. Estimation by SUR 1961-1985.

(ii)

Output Equations for Asian Countries
assuming above Model of Convergence

	ln(qs)	ln sgap	see	r2	dw
HKG	1.0000 (***)	0.3709 (8.48)	0.0500	0.9925	0.2662
IND	1.0000 (***)	0.1399 (4.40)	0.0296	0.9966	0.5356
KOR	1.0000 (***)	0.1660 (3.26)	0.0361	0.9962	0.8361
MAL	1.0000 (***)	-0.0560 (1.08)	0.0484	0.9918	0.8413
PHI	1.0000 (***)	0.5236 (11.19)	0.0399	0.9874	0.5016
SGP	1.0000 (***)	0.1759 (1.78)	0.0507	0.9929	0.3754
TWN	1.0000 (***)	0.1743 (3.17)	0.0424	0.9939	0.3886
THA	1.0000 (***)	0.7189 (19.55)	0.0139	0.9991	0.8646

Sample 1963-1985. Estimation method by Zellner's SUR estimation technique with instruments.

Table A11

Cross Country Evidence of Convergence

(i)

Explanatory Variables	OECD			
	(1)	(2)	(3)	(4)
LRGDP	-2.8345	-2.9140		
	(7.25)	(7.23)		
LGDP		0.0921		0.1446
		(0.89)		(1.47)
ln PIM			-2.6843	-2.8328
			(7.56)	(7.92)
Constant	6.7936	6.5296	89.112	93.298
	(11.47)	(9.80)	(7.79)	(8.17)
RB2	0.7415	0.7382	0.7574	0.7731
SEE	0.5806	0.5641	0.5430	0.5251

Note: The dependent variable is the constant annual percentage growth of the labor productivity index for Harrod-neutral technical progress. The independent variable LRCDP is the logarithm of the initial 1960 level of gross domestic product per capita for each country in thousands of international dollars. The variable ln PIM is the logarithm of measured output attributable to labor in each country in 1960. The sample includes the G-7 and 12 smaller OECD countries. Estimation by ordinary least squares.

A-11 (continued)

(ii)

Explanatory Variables	Asia			
	(1)	(2)	(3)	(4)
LRGDP	0.0597	0.0637		
	(0.07)	(0.07)		
LGDP		0.0910		0.0781
		(0.27)		(0.22)
ln PIM			-0.1750	-0.1022
			(0.20)	(0.10)
Constant	3.5426	3.2887	9.029	6.530
	(9.18)	(3.16)	(0.33)	(0.20)
RB2	-0.1419	-0.3167	-0.1364	-0.3157
SEE	1.1570	1.242	1.1542	1.2419

Note: See notes accompanying (i). The sample includes Japan.

Note: The dependent variable is the constant annual percentage growth of the labor productivity index for Harrod-neutral technical progress. The independent variable LRGDP is the logarithm of the initial 1960 level of gross domestic product per capita for each country in thousands of international dollars. The variable ln PIM is the logarithm of measured output attributable to labor in each country in 1960. The sample includes the G-7 and 12 smaller OECD countries. Estimation by ordinary least squares. The sample includes Japan,

Table A11 (continued)

Cross-Country Evidence of Convergence

(iii)

Explanatory Variables	OECD+Asia			
	(1)	(2)	(3)	(4)
LRGDP	-0.8075	-0.8168		
	(3.42)	(3.00)		
LGDP		0.0114		0.0025
		(0.07)		(0.18)
ln PIM			-1.2982	-0.3005
			(4.26)	(3.84)
Constant	3.6785	3.6464	44.338	44.405
	(12.01)	(6.77)	(4.55)	(4.18)
RB2	0.2923	0.2629	0.3973	0.3722
SEE	0.9805	1.001	0.9049	0.9235

Notes: See notes accompanying (i). The data include those used in (i) and (ii).

Note: The dependent variable is the constant annual percentage growth of the labor productivity index for Harrod—neutral technical progress. The independent variable LRGDP is the logarithm of the initial 1960 level of gross domestic product per capita for each country in thousands of international dollars. The variable ln PIM is the logarithm of measured output attributable to labor in each country in 1960. The sample includes the G—7 and 12 smaller OECD countries. Estimation by ordinary least squares. The data include those used in (i) and (ii).

13. SUMMARY BY PROFESSOR CHIKASHI MORIGUCHI OF SESSION 2: "HARMONIZING GLOBAL REGIONALISM"

The discussion was led by Professor Peter Drysdale, who presented a substantial review of the background to the session, i.e., the role of growing Pacific economic development in the face of rising economic regionalism in the European Community and North America (possibly including Mexico). An abridged version of his commentary is included below.

1. PETER DRYSDALE'S COMMENTS (abridged)

Despite the revolution now taking place in Eastern Europe and the Soviet Union, there is little doubt that East Asian industrialization is bound to be a primary influence on world trade and economic growth in the next quarter century and beyond, just as it was around Japan's emergence as a great industrial power in the last.

The excitement about Europe—the United States of Europe—and the unification of the two Germanies, as Professor Nerb reminded us in his fascinating review of current developments, is fully justified. Eastern Europe adds an economy roughly the size of Italy to European Economic Space. But the reality is that in East Asia, between one quarter and half a billion people are roughly doubling their incomes and trade every decade. And East Asia is, and remains, especially closely tied to North America, across the Pacific. The Asia-Pacific region's contribution to global trade growth is reflected in the data presented earlier in Eaton's chapter. And its implications for the structure of world product growth through the international and regional diffusion of industrial technologies is analyzed in detail in Helliwell's chapter.

Yasuba, in his chapter, details performance and outlook for individual economies within the region and, despite the shocks of 1989 and 1990, comes to the cautious conclusion that East Asia will continue to produce at least more of the same, not a bad result for a group of economies that have been roughly doubling their incomes each decade! Some may think that Yasuba is optimistic about China. I do not; but I shall return to that question later.

I should note that I have just one small quibble with Yasuba's otherwise excellent analysis of developments in the East Asian economy. I refer to his characterization of the Southeast Asian polities as patrimonial states. While it is certainly true that the polities of East and Southeast Asia have in the course of their histories all exhibited powerful elements of the patrimonial state, it also important to observe the huge changes in the political economy of these countries that has been encouraged by the process of economic growth itself. In a recent paper on the Indonesian economy, Hadi Soesastro and I use the concept of oligarchic statism as an initial reference point in describing the Indonesian political process but observe the shift towards constrained pluralism as a powerful process that has been encouraged by Indonesia's successful industrialization in the last decade or so.

The key point to make here is that the countries of East Asia and the Pacific now have to shape their approach to international economic policy in an environment in which their actions have an increasing influence on global outcomes. Japan, of course, has been catapulted into a position of particular influence and responsibility.

Hence, there is interest in the establishment of mechanisms for effective communication of policy interests and priorities, both to exploit the potential for trade growth in a very rapidly changing regional economy, and to project Asia–Pacific interests and define East Asian and Pacific responsibilities in the global arena.

These matters are at the heart of the change in the international economic regime now being cautiously but purposefully put into place by the Asia–Pacific Economic Cooperation (APEC) group of countries, as Higgins' chapter outlines in some detail.

Compared with the elaborate mechanisms for consultation on economic policy matters that have evolved within Europe, or that are enshrined in the OECD, those in the Pacific are as yet quite rudimentary. Nonetheless, they incorporate features uniquely suited to the problem of encouraging policy coordination among Asia–Pacific economies, begun through the PECC in 1980 and, at the political level, through APEC.

There are two issues worth expanding upon. The first is the process of policy progress, to the analysis of which Hamada's chapter makes an important contribution. While the particular two–stage model that Hamada introduced to draw attention to the opportunity for transborder representation of economic policy interests may not be adequate for modeling complex reality, his analysis is certainly pointed in the right direction. Conventional models of political behavior neglect the important opportunities for transnational coalition formation around the representation of common international economic policy interests, and the establishment of mechanisms or processes internationally and regionally to give effect to those opportunities is an important interest and object of policy. The second issue is the structure of diplomatic interests in the Pacific. Simply put, there is no Paris in the Pacific. To attempt to create one would be immensely damaging to regional cooperation interests and would have the effect of ossifying the established structure of economic and political power within a region that is undergoing very rapid economic and political change. This would serve merely to slow the process of change itself and to create political tensions around its management.

As Higgins makes clear in his chapter, there is, in Asia and the Pacific, a close consistency between regional policy objectives and multilateral interna-tional economic policy goals in the structure of economic interaction and interests within the region.

A subtheme in our conversations has been the threat of inward–looking regionalism. Will not the world, post–Uruguay Round, eventually break up into three industrial blocs—in Europe, the Americas, and East Asia? Will the world of the future be a world of economic, and political, tripolar confrontation? Certainly the Asia–Pacific countries have no interest in European–style union or the formation of a discriminatory trading bloc.

I take the evidence that we have been presented and the arguments that we have heard to recommend persistence with the multilateral rule–based framework on the trade front, with GATT or GATT–revised as a steady reference point. However qualified they might be, Eaton's numbers highlight, for example, the importance of trans–Pacific trade and economic interdependence alongside North American integration, and an Asia–Pacific integration that has been market driven but without, as was observed earlier, the framework of discriminatory trading or other arrangements, exclusive of third country interests. My own work on the analysis of international trade flows in International Economic Pluralism supports Eaton's conclusions strongly. Helliwell's global convergence hypothesis implicitly stresses the same interest.

It is important here to take up the question that was raised in earlier discussion of the effect of direct foreign investment on regional economic integration and the conduct of international economic policy. This question was put to Fukao in an earlier session and needs to be addressed here too. The first point to be made is that domestic capital formation is far and away the dominant element in regional capital formation in East Asia, rather than foreign investment, let alone Japanese investment. Foreign investment constitutes a very small percentage of total capital formation in the East Asian economy, though it is, of course, an element of critical importance as a vehicle for the transmission and diffusion of industrial technologies. More specifically, the role of Japanese foreign direct investment in economic and trade integration within East Asia has to be put into proper perspective. There has been a strong link between Japanese investment and trade adjustment, as industrial relocation has proceeded within the East Asian economy. But the bulk of exports, for example, that were generated from East Asia into Japan following the yen appreciation in 1985 derived from independent enterprises, not Japanese affiliated firms. Of the $12 billion worth of additional manufactured goods exports that were lifted out of East Asia into Japan in the few years after the yen appreciation, by far the largest proportion came from independent national firms rather than Japanese affiliated firms.

The whole world has been forced to respond to East Asia's internationally oriented economic growth. The entire framework of international trade has changed in this process and still must find a new stability. Europeans have been motivated to accelerate integration and East Europeans and the Soviet Union to throw off the shackles of closure and command. United States political and intellectual thinking is heavily burdened by ambivalence, in the realization that the very success of postwar American international economic policies and policy commitment has reduced the United States' own relative economic power and weight.

There are three major issues for the future.

The first is the fashioning of a new framework for economic and political security in the post–Cold War era. Interest in the peace dividend is only one element, although an important one, of this interest. The Middle East crisis has forced the articulation of a new international politics for the post–Cold War period. The reassessment by Japan and other countries of their political and security interests in Asia and the Pacific will also profoundly affect stable economic progress in this region and in the world more generally.

The second is the task of protecting multilateral interests against the danger of regionalism that is not open and more generally liberalizing—the danger of confrontational tripolarization. Progress in Europe and the development of an active agenda in Asia and the Pacific for action to extend the freedom of transactions of all kinds, including trade and other economic transactions, in advance of global action is not necessarily inconsistent with open regionalism. But East Asian and Western Pacific economies, for example, need to watch with close interest the nature and progress of the negotiation of any free–trade arrangement between the United States and Mexico, and more generally within the Americas. Such negotiations are not automatically consistent with multilateral interests, unless they are encompassed within (as Higgins points out) a process of general liberalization. It must be stressed, however, that even should there be a less than satisfactory outcome to the

Uruguay Round of trade negotiations, the APEC group of countries should not be diverted from proceeding with most-favored-nation-based trade liberalization.

The third issue is a challenge of a different kind. The challenge for the future of the Asia-Pacific region that is currently most uncertain, as Yasuba pointed out, is the accommodation of China. While any sustained attempt to turn back the clock on reform in China would inevitably lead to a decline in the legitimacy of Communist Party rule and temporarily, at least, to national political disintegration, it will be a huge task to mend the fracture of confidence in the reform process, both inside and outside China. It is particularly important to engage China and all its branches in all the regional endeavors of Asia-Pacific economic consultation. The uncertainty surrounding the immediate future of Chinese reform (and similar events that are bound, from time to time, to disrupt the progress of East Asian industrialization over the long haul) should not divert inevitable involvement and substantial strategic interest in this process.

2. DISCUSSION OF GERNOT NERB'S CHAPTER, "EFFECTS OF GERMAN UNIFICATION ON THE EUROPEAN INTEGRATION PROCESS"

Professor Shibata pointed out that the manner in which the resources in the Eastern part of Germany will be utilized through the shift to a private-ownership system is important for the progress of German unification. He asked Dr. Nerb to clarify further how financial assistance is provided from West Germany to East Germany.

Professor Ono asked about the significance of the Government's protection of Germany's agriculture and the possible similarity between Japan and Germany in this respect.

Professor Levine pointed out that Nerb's chapter underestimated the seriousness of ecological problems in East Germany and in much greater degree in the USSR. He noted that German unification will involve possible disinvestments, e.g., a destruction of five nuclear power plants of East Germany that were built using Soviet technology. This kind of "standardization," he said, will be a serious source of adjustment accompanying German reunification.

Dr. Nerb replied to Shibata, stating that 8000 state companies of East Germany have been taken over by the "Treuhandanstalt," and that they will be sold not only to West German interests, but also to non-German interests. He stressed that there would be no discrimination against foreign companies who wish to participate in the German reunification.

In his response to Ono's question, Dr. Nerb pointed out that Germany is basically in a similar situation with Japan in relation to agricultural policy. He further pointed out that the East German side brings in a large agricultural population, and a further domestic adjustment will be necessary.

3. DISCUSSION OF JOHN HELLIWELL AND ALAN CHUNG'S CHAPTER, "TRIPOLAR GROWTH AND REAL EXCHANGE RATES: HOW MUCH CAN BE EXPLAINED BY CONVERGENCE?"

Hamada raised a question about the meaning of "convergence"; he suggested that convergence of labor productivity through propagation of technology and through structural adjustment is different and should be differentiated. Hamada added that political factors affect the speed of convergence, for instance, through a closed–door policy on technology.

Professor Pauly commented on the problem of identification—that is, the process of convergence of productivity is composed of many different factors: U.S. factors, Japanese factors, and so on. Some factors are taken into consideration by the Helliwell model, but some are not. The actual process of convergence may well be affected by heterogeneous shocks like OPEC 1 and OPEC 2.

Helliwell replied to Hamada that these models are clear and that they allow free estimation of the final path so that internal, societal flexibility could be included just as natural resources are included. He admitted that since there is a whole range of mixed–up factors at the aggregate level, decomposition is simply impossible; he suggested that many studies at a much more micro level aim at disentangling policies from institutions and other factors.

As to the question on openness, Helliwell admitted that opening up more to trade combines some economic factors with some policy factors. He added that he found that those countries that have opened up trade most quickly have had faster rates of convergence.

In reply to Professor Pauly's question, Helliwell agreed that his tests were joint tests of the long–run productivity model and the short–run output model. He suggested that he would get different results if he were to use some other model for short–run output determination within which he would nest the longer–run productivity model. He added that some adjustments for cyclical response have shown that the ranking of the convergence model remains unaffected.

The following chapters from the third session of the conference fit in well with the main problems discussed at the conference and relate nicely to other chapters. Two principal chapters consider the international debt issue, which never really got resolved in an entire decade — called the lost decade of the 1980s, as far as many developing countries were concerned. Two principal areas of debt trouble were Latin America and Asia. Akihiro Amano focused on Latin American debt, while Solita Collas-Monsod dealt mainly with the case of the Philippines — in Asia.

Amano's chapter starts from a model of the debt problem, in terms of the main relationships in a country's international sector, rounded out with some simple relationships for the domestic economy. He simulates regional debt models to examine the Latin American and Asian cases. A feature of his system is that it explicitly deals with capital flight, an often recognized problem, but one that is seldom dealt with at a quantitative level.

Professor Amano effectively treats growth rates among OECD countries, changes in LIBOR, and changes in primary commodity prices (particularly oil prices) to see what their contributions to the total problem are. His perceptive simulation analyses help us look at the problem from this point forward but do not take up the origins of the problem.

Solita Collas-Monsod, however, does analyze the origins of the world debt problem both from the actions or viewpoints of the creditor and debtor countries. As does Amano, she builds an interesting formal structure. She considers a two-gap model based on the growth dynamics of the Harrod-Domar system. She separates public, private, and foreign savings, the last of these representing the external resources gap and the other two the domestic gap. She looks at the foreign exchange constraint facing the developing country and both the need and feasibility of structural adjustment.

Since Mrs. Monsod has actively participated in the debt negotiations of the Philippines as a cabinet minister of the Aquino government, she is in a unique position to give a detailed account in terms of the practical considerations that have been relevant. She points out the inadequacies of the approaches of the governments and international institutions involved. Her arguments are based to a large extent on the ability (or lack thereof) of developing countries to realize net capital inflows.

Giorgio Basevi's chapter complements that of Gernot Nerb on the issue of German unification. Basevi's main concern, however, is with the implications of unification for the extended Common Market and Monetary Union in Europe. He uses international trade and payments theory for studying this problem and also the widening of the EEC to embrace EFTA countries as well as those of Eastern Europe, such as Czechoslovakia, Hungary, and Poland.

He is concerned with the concept of convergence, which was earlier examined by John Helliwell. He too uses growth theory, as did Mrs. Monsod, for studying the widening of the EEC to include EFTA and former WTO countries. Not only does Basevi use carefully reasoned economic theory in his chapter, but also he presents a keen analysis of economic institutions in Europe and the significance of the present business-cycle environment for the way that the present movements towards economic integration work out in practice.

The final chapter from this session was that of Charles Horioka on trends in the Japanese saving rate. This was a highly appropriate subject for this conference for several reasons, not the least of which is the need to evaluate international flows of financial capital that are crucial for appreciating the influence of the two gaps — domestic resources and international capital flows.

The Japanese saving rate, as mentioned also in Chikashi Moriguchi's opening presentation, is a major source of international capital financing. Horioka argues persuasively that the household saving rate and also the total private savings rate are trending downwards, a development that started some time ago. Horioka appreciates the complexity of the savings process and recognizes that many factors affect the Japanese savings rate, but he concentrates on the influence of demographic trends, namely the aging of the Japanese population and the two important <u>dependency</u> ratios — the ratio of elderly people to working-age people and the ratio of children to working-age people. He shows how projected trends in these key ratios might bring down the household savings rate by substantial amounts in the last decade of this century and well into the 21st century.

15. LATIN AMERICAN DEBT: MACROECONOMIC ENVIRONMENT AND ECONOMIC STRUCTURE[1]

Akihiro Amano
Kobe University
School of Business Administration
Rokko, Kobe 657
Japan

ABSTRACT. By using an econometric model of the Latin American region as a whole, the external and domestic factors that have an important bearing on the enduring debt problem in this region have been identified. External factors such as high interest rates, low commodity prices, and sluggish growth of the world economy are found to be important. Capital flight has also been a serious aggravating factor. However, the domestic economic structure characterized by inward-looking development policies and low marginal propensity to save has probably been as important as external factors. Simulation experiments in the projection period suggest that various forms of debt-relief plans cannot be considered to provide final solutions as long as the present economic structure of this region remains unchanged.

1. INTRODUCTION

The problem of removing the severe debt burden from heavily indebted countries still remains as an important aspect in assessing the future prospects of the world economy. Although various efforts by the governments of leading industrial countries, international organizations, and private banks have been partially alleviating the seriousness of the problem, its future development depends on such uncertain factors as the sustainability of strong economic activities in developed countries, maintenance of relatively low world interest rates, strength of oil and nonoil commodity prices, and the pursuit of successful economic restructuring in externally indebted countries.

In section 2 of this chapter, an analytical framework of external debt dynamics will be presented that explains how the interactions of external environment and domestic economic factors can lead to explosive debt accumulation. In section 3, an econometric model of the Latin American region as a whole will be constructed upon this theoretical foundation. As a method of highlighting the structural characteristics of the economies of the Latin American region, a corresponding model has been estimated for the Asian region

[1]The author expresses gratitude to Lawrence Klein for valuable comments on an earlier draft. The present research was financially supported by the Nomura Science Foundation.

as well, and structural parameters have been compared. This enables us to identify some domestic factors that may have an important bearing on the enduring debt problem in the former region.

In section 4, some counterfactual simulations are performed for the period 1975–1988 in order to assess the quantitative importance of external factors, such as world economic activities, interest rates, and the terms of trade, with regard to Latin American and Asian debt problems, respectively. Attention is also given to the finding that capital flight has been a serious, aggravating factor, especially for the Latin American region.

The final section is devoted to the analysis of future prospects of Latin American debt. Will likely developments of the world economy contribute to resolution of the problem in the near future? Will the Brady Initiative and other debt–relief plans be sufficient in scale, or will they be effective as longer–term solutions? What sorts of structural adjustments in this region will be required for supplementing such efforts? These questions will be subject to examination under various scenario simulations for the period 1990–2000.

2. EXTERNAL DEBT DYNAMICS: A THEORETICAL FRAMEWORK

In order to analyze the dynamics of external debt accumulation and to identify internal and external factors contributing to it, we shall consider the following simple model.[2] Assuming that foreign borrowings and capital flight from the debtor country are the only international capital transactions, we can express a net increase in the stock of external debt as

$$\dot{D} = -B + r^*D + f, \tag{1}$$

where D = the stock of external debt, B = noninterest current account balance, r^* = foreign interest rate, f = capital flight, and a dot over a variable denotes the time derivative. In other words, external debt increases by the sum of current account deficit and capital flight. (We neglect interest receipts due to capital flight.)

The noninterest current account balance, B, is assumed to depend upon home export price (p_x), foreign competitors' export price (p^*), home import price (p_m), and home and foreign real GDP (Q, Q^*), as follows:

$$B = p_x X - p_m M \tag{2}$$

$$X = X[-p_x/p^*, +Q^*] \tag{3}$$

$$M = M[-p_m/p_x, +Q] \tag{4}$$

where X and M are quantities of exports and imports of goods and services excluding interest on external debt, and all prices are expressed in terms of a common currency (say, U.S. dollars). A sign before an argument designates the direction of effect of the variable at the margin. We shall assume that p_x, p_m, and p^* are all determined by international prices of primary commodities, fuels,

---

[2]For other "stylized models" of debt dynamics, see, e.g., Cline (1985), Dornbusch and Fischer (1985), and de Pinies (1989).

and manufactured goods.

Totally differentiating equations (2)–(4), and denoting proportionate rates of change by a circumflex over a variable (e.g., $\hat{x} = dx/x$), we can write

$$dB - p_x X(\hat{p}_x + \hat{X}) - p_m M(\hat{p}_m + \hat{M}) \tag{2'}$$

$$\hat{X} = -\eta^*(\hat{p}_x - \hat{p}^*) + \epsilon^* \hat{Q}^* \tag{3'}$$

$$\hat{M} = -\eta(\hat{p}_x - \hat{p}_x) + \epsilon \hat{Q} \tag{4'}$$

where η, η^* = home and foreign price elasticities of import demand, respectively, and ϵ, ϵ^* = home and foreign income elasticities of import demand, respectively. Thus, a change in the noninterest current account balance can be expressed as

$$dB = -p_m M \epsilon \hat{Q} + p_x X \epsilon^* \hat{Q}^* - (p_x X \eta^* + p_m M \eta - p_x X)\hat{p}_x$$
$$+ p_m M(\eta - 1)\hat{p}_m + p_x X \eta^* \hat{p}^*, \tag{5}$$

and from equations (1) and (5) we can express a change in net increase in external debt as

$$d(D) = p_m M \epsilon \hat{Q} - p_x X \epsilon^* \hat{Q}^* + (p_x X \eta^* + p_m M \eta - p_x X)\hat{p}_x$$
$$- p_m M(\eta - 1)\hat{p}_m - p_x X \eta^* \hat{p}^* + r^* dD + D dr^* + df. \tag{6}$$

Equation (6) shows the determinants of changes in external debt. The sign of coefficients of $\hat{p}_x$ and $\hat{p}_m$ depends on the magnitude of price elasticities of import demand. An increase in the home export price will worsen the trade balance and hence tends to enlarge the increase in external debt if the so-called Marshall–Lerner condition (or, more precisely, the Hirschman condition) is satisfied. Or, an increase in home import price tends to discourage debt accumulation provided that the home import demand is price elastic. We shall come back to this question when estimates of these elasticities are obtained. Other factors contributing to an enlargement of external debt flow are an increase in domestic demand, a fall in foreign demand, a fall in foreign export prices, an increase in the existing debt, a rise in foreign interest rates, and an intensification of capital flight.

As for the domestic economy of the debtor country, we assume the following simple structure:

$$C = C[+Y] \tag{7}$$

$$I = I[+Q, -r^*, -K] \tag{8}$$

$$Q = C + I + X - M \tag{9}$$

$$Y = Q - r^*D/p^* \tag{10}$$

$$\dot{K} = I \tag{11}$$

where C = real consumption, I = real capital formation, Y = real GNP, and K = capital stock. Consumption depends positively on real GNP, the latter being the difference between real GDP and real interest payments abroad (since we assume away net factor payments abroad other than interest on external debt in this section). Domestic capital formation is positively related to real GDP and negatively related to foreign interest rates and the level of existing capital stock. Output is demand determined.

Let the marginal propensity to consume be γ and the partial derivatives of real investment with respect to Q, r*, and K be ι, $-\rho$, and $-\kappa$, respectively. Totally differentiating equations (7)–(10) and making use of equations (3') and (4'), we can write

$$dQ = (1/\Delta)[-\gamma(r*/p*)dD - \{\gamma(D/p*) + \rho\}dr* - \kappa dK + X\epsilon\hat{Q}* -$$

$$- (X\eta* + M\eta)\hat{p}_x + M\eta\hat{p}_m + \{X\eta* + \gamma(r*D/p*)\}\hat{p}*], \qquad (12)$$

where $\Delta=1-\gamma-\iota+M\epsilon/Q$. We assume that Δ is positive, because short–run equilibrium would be unstable otherwise. Equation (12) shows that domestic output of the debtor country responds positively to changes in foreign economic activity, home import prices, and foreign competitors' export prices, and negatively to changes in outstanding debt, foreign interest rates, capital stock, and home export prices.

Substituting equation (12) into equation (6), we can express the determinants of net increase in external debt that incorporate their indirect effects through changes in domestic economic activity. Comparison of equations (6) and (12) immediately reveals that for most variables the indirect effects work in opposite directions to the direct effects. In view of the parameters involved in the direct and indirect effects, however, we may safely assume that the former dominates. We shall therefore express the change in external debt over time as

$$\dot{D} = F[+D, -K, +r*, +f, -Q*, \pm p_x, \pm p_m, -p*]. \qquad (13)$$

Finally, with respect to changes in real capital stock, we can derive from equations (8) and (11)

$$d(K) = \iota dQ - \rho dr* - \kappa dK. \qquad (14)$$

Combining this result with equation (12), we can express the determinants of changes in capital stock overtime as

$$\dot{K} = G[-D, -K, -r*, +Q*, -p_x, +p_m, +p*]. \qquad (15)$$

Equations (13) and (15) now form a set of differential equations with respect to two stock variables, D and K. Let $\dot{D} = 0$ and $\dot{K} = 0$ in these equations, and we have

$$D = D[+K, -r*, -f, +Q*, \pm p_x, \pm p_m, +p*] \qquad (16)$$

$$K = K[-D, -r*, +Q*, -p_x, +p_m, +p*]. \qquad (17)$$

Based on these results, the dynamics of external debt and domestic capital formation can be represented as in figure 1. Curves DD and KK represent equations (16) and (17), respectively. It can be seen that DD–curve is upward sloping and that KK–curve is downward sloping. Furthermore, D will rise or fall over time according as whether the point lies above or below the DD–curve. Similarly, K will rise or fall over time according as whether the point lies to the left or to the right of the KK–curve.

Figure 1 shows that the steady state (i.e., the intersection point of the DD and KK curves) is a saddle point. Unless the starting point lies on the stable arm, SS, it will follow a divergent path, approaching the unstable arm UU with the passage of time. This point can be stated more formally as follows: Suppose that all exogenous variables in equations (13) and (15) are kept constant. Taking linear approximations of equations (13) and (15) around the steady-state point, we may write

$$\dot{D} = a_D D - b_D K \tag{13'}$$

$$\dot{K} = -a_K D - b_K K \tag{15'}$$

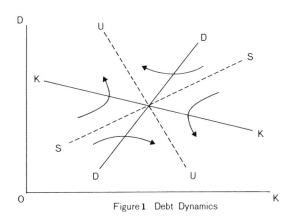

Figure 1   Debt Dynamics

where a_D, b_D, a_K, and b_K are all positive. The characteristic equation of this dynamic system is

$$\lambda^2 - (a_D - b_K)\lambda - (a_D b_K + a_K b_D) = 0. \tag{18}$$

Since the discriminant of equation (18), $(a_D - b_K)^2 + 4(a_D b_K + a_K b_D)$, is positive, eigenvalues are two distinct real numbers (λ_1, λ_2). The third term on the left-hand side of equation (18) represents the product of two roots, which is negative. Hence one root must be positive and the other negative. Suppose λ_1 is the negative root. Then, the corresponding eigenvector may be written as $(b_D, a_K - \lambda_1)$. Therefore, the stable arm SS in figure 1 is upward sloping. In other words, in order to avoid unbounded debt accumulation, the starting point must lie below the stable arm.

Before the debt crisis, developing countries had been able to pursue successful capital formation with external debt, so that the initial point in figure 1 must have been somewhere in the neighborhood of origin. The country would have been moving along a trajectory involving rising external debt and capital stock in the early phase, to be followed by a declining external debt with still rising capital stock. Equations (16) and (17) show, however, that changes in world interest rates and foreign economic activities may shift the DD and KK curves downward. Furthermore, if the stable arm SS suddenly shifts downward to such an extent that it cuts the previous trajectory, then the country will move onto a new trajectory involving an explosive debt accumulation.

Factors that cause a downward shift of the KK-curve are a rise in interest rates, a decline in foreign economic activities, a rise in home export prices, a fall in home import prices, a fall in foreign competitors' export prices, and so on. Those that shift the DD-curve downward include a rise in interest rates, a decline in foreign economic activities, an increase in capital flight, and a fall in foreign competitors' export prices. Much literature attributed the cause of the developing countries' debt crisis to these factors. Our analysis shows that their effects are not a one-time occurrence, but rather, a tendency of transforming a healthy debt-cum-growth process into one of autonomous debt explosion. Of course, the extent of shifts of these curves depends not only on the degree of changes in external environment, but also on structural parameters of the debtor country. Therefore, countries facing the same external environment may not necessarily be driven into an uncontrollable debt explosion.

3. ECONOMIC STRUCTURE: A COMPARISON OF LATIN AMERICAN AND ASIAN REGIONS

In this section, we consider Latin American and Asian regions and construct an econometric model for each region that closely resembles the theoretical model developed in the previous section. This is a necessary step for comparative simulation exercises to be presented in the following section.

The models have been estimated from annual data taken from International Financial Statistics (IMF), World Economic Outlook (IMF), World Debt Tables (World Bank), World Economic Service: Historical Series (the WEFA group), and national account data of the United Nations, Office for Development Research and Policy Analysis.

Each regional model consists of the balance-of-payments block with debt-related variables and the macroeconomic block that determines the activity level in the region. The balance-of-payments block includes the standard export/import functions, export/import price functions, and balance-of-payments identities and quasi-identities for debt-related variables as follows:

Real Merchandise Exports = F[−Relative Export Price,
+Real GDP of Developed Economies] (19)
Real Merchandise Imports = F[−Relative Import Price,
+Real GDP of Home Country] (20)
Export Price = F[+World Commodity Price, +World Oil
Price, +World Export Price of Manufactured Goods] (21)
Import Price = F[+World Commodity Price, +World Oil
Price, +World Export Price of Manufactured Goods] (22)
Trade Balance = Real Merchandise Exports·Export Price
− Real Merchandise Imports·Import Price (23)
Service Balance = F[−Interest Payments on External Debt] (24)
Current Account Balance = Trade Balance + Service
Balance (25)
Interest Payments on External Debt = F[+LIBOR,
+Outstanding Debt$_{t-1}$, −Multilateral Debt Relief
Agreements] (26)

Outstanding Debt = Outstanding Debt$_{t-1}$ − Current
             Account Balance − Other Capital Account Balance
             + Net Increase in Foreign Exchange Reserves   (27)
Amortization Payments = F[+Debt Outstanding$_{t-1}$,
             ±Multilateral Debt Relief Agreements]   (28)
Debt Service = Interest Payments on External Debt
             + Amortization Payments   (29)

Debt/Export Ratio = Debt Outstanding/Value of
             Merchandise Exports·100.   (30)

All trade prices are expressed in U.S. dollar terms. For relative export prices, we use the ratio of export unit value of the region to that of other regions (developed or developing). For relative import prices, the inverse of the terms of trade has been used. External debt outstanding increases by the sum of the current account deficit, other capital account deficit (a large part of which may be some form of capital flight) and net increase in the foreign exchange reserves. In the following model we treat other capital account deficits and net increases in foreign exchange reserves as exogenous. Finally, the variable "Multilateral Debt Relief Agreements" refers to both the value covered under the same heading in World Debt Tables (World Bank) and other financial assistance. This variable is also exogenous.

Next, the macroeconomic block has the following simple structure:

Real Consumption = F[+Real GNP, +Real Consumption$_{t-1}$]   (31)
Real Investment/Capital Stock$_{t-1}$ = F[+Real GDP/Capital
             Stock$_{t-1}$, −Foreign Real Interest Rates]   (32)
Capital Stock = Capital Stock$_{t-1}$ + Real Investment   (33)
Real Exports of Goods and Services = F[+Real
             Merchandise Exports]   (34)
Real Imports of Goods and Services = F[+Real Merchandise
             Imports, +Real GDP]   (35)
Real GDP = Real Consumption + Real Investment + Real
             Exports of Goods and Services − Real Imports of
             Goods and Services   (36)
Real Net Factor Income From Abroad = F[−Interest
             Payments on External Debt/Export Unit Value of
             Developed Region]   (37)
Real GNP = Real GDP + Real Net Factor Income From
             Abroad.   (38)

Data for capital stock in developing regions are hardly available. This is also true for appropriate rates of depreciation of capital stock. We therefore constructed a proxy variable by cumulating real investment since 1950. As can be seen from the above specification, output is demand determined, as in the theoretical model. In the next section, we shall show that even such a simple structure can exhibit fairly good tracking ability in the sample period and reasonable system responses to various exogenous shocks.

Tables 1 and 2 report principal coefficient estimates of the balance-of-payments block and of the macroeconomic block, respectively, of Latin American and Asian regions. Equations have been estimated by the two-stage least-squares method using appropriate instrumental variables. The sample period varies depending on data availability and the length of time lags, but generally speaking it is 1965–1988 for those involving debt–related variables, and 1972–1988 for those involving balance of payments variables. Unless otherwise stated, the parameters in the tables are long–run values. Regional comparisons of these parameters reveal some interesting features.

3.1. Merchandise Trade

Price and income elasticities of exports from the Latin American region are smaller than those of the Asian region. This is especially true for the income elasticity. The price elasticity of Latin American exports is less than unity, whereas the elasticity of Asian exports with respect to its own export price exceeds unity since the equation involves two relative price terms.

On the import side, the income elasticity in the Latin American region exceeds unity. That of the Asian region is less than unity, however, because real merchandise exports are included in the import equation. This reflects the nature of the Asian trade structure in that imports of intermediate and capital goods are strongly related to exports of finished goods. As a consequence, if each region grows at the same rate as other regions, the trade balance in the Latin American region will worsen and that of the Asian region will improve. The price elasticity of imports is less than unity in the Latin American region and is slightly greater than unity in the Asian region. Therefore, the Hirschman con– dition is satisfied in the latter case, but not in the former. A decline in export prices or an increase in import prices thus weakens the growth of external debt in the Asian region but will stimulate a further increase in debt in the Latin American region. With reference to figure 1, a fall of export prices or a rise of import prices will shift the DD–curve upward in the Asian region, thus pushing away the area of figure 1 characterized by explosive debt accumulation. In the Latin American region, on the contrary, the DD–curve will be pushed downward so that the possibility of a debt crisis will be enhanced.

Table 1. Principal Coefficient Estimates of the Balance-of-
Payments Blocks*

Merchandise Exports				
Price Elasticity	LA	-0.31[a]	AS	-0.70[a]
		-0.52[b]		
Income Elasticity	LA	0.48	AS	1.60

Merchandise Imports				
Price Elasticity	LA	-0.26	AS	-1.04
Income Elasticity	LA 1965-81	1.07	AS	0.33
	1982-88	1.04		
Export Elasticity	LA	$--$	AS	0.56

Export Prices				
Commodity Price Elasticity	LA	0.16	AS	0.41
Oil Price Elasticity	LA	0.37	AS	0.19
Manufactured-Goods Price Elasticity	LA	0.34	AS	0.34

Import Prices				
Commodity Price Elasticity	LA	0.13	AS	0.39
Oil Price Elasticity	LA	0.26	AS	0.14
Manufactured-Goods Price Elasticity	LA	0.52	AS	0.44

Interest Payments				
Interest-Rate Coefficient	LA	0.98	AS	0.48
Debt-Outstanding Coefficient	LA	0.107	AS	0.068
MDRA Coefficient[c]	LA	-0.119	AS	$--$

Amortization				
Debt-Outstanding Elasticity	LA	0.80	AS	0.73
MDRA Coefficient	LA	-0.018	AS	2.11

* LA=Latin America, AS=Asia. "Coefficient" is either a coefficient estimate
of a linear regression equation or a converted marginal coefficient of a
regression equation of some other form around sample means. Similarly,
"Elasticity" is either a coefficient estimate of a double log-linear
regression equation or a converted elasticity value obtained from another
equation form using sample means.

a) Relative to developing region export price.
b) Relative to developed region export price.
c) Multilateral Debt Relief Agreements.

Table 2. Principal Coefficient Estimates of the Macroeconomic
Blocks*

Consumption				
Coefficient of Real GNP	LA	0.48	AS	0.37
Coefficient of Lagged Consumption	LA	0.29	AS	0.48

Investment				
Coefficient of Real GNP	LA	0.098	AS	0.099
Real Interest-Rate Semielasticity	LA	-0.18	AS	-0.12

Exports of Goods and Services				
Merchandise Export Elasticity	LA	0.90	AS	0.49
Foreign Activity Elasticity	LA	—	AS	1.49

Imports of Goods and Services				
Merchandise Import Elasticity	LA	0.46	AS	0.68
Real GDP Elasticity	LA	0.86	AS	0.59

Net Factor Income from Abroad				
Coefficient of Foreign Interest Rate	LA	-1.18	AS	-0.78
Coefficient of Foreign Prices	LA	0.096	AS	0.069
MDRA[a] Coefficient	LA	0.078	AS	—
Coefficient of Real GDP	LA	—	AS	0.022
Coefficient of Foreign Activity[b]	LA	—	AS	-0.003

* See note to table 1. "Real Interest-Rate Semielasticity" measures the
percentage changes in real investment when the real interest rate increases by
one percentage point per annum.
a) Multilateral Debt Relief Agreements.
b) With respect to real GDP of the developed region.

3.2. Trade Prices

Export and import prices are assumed to be determined by international market
prices. Coefficient estimates presented in table 1 therefore reflect the
commodity structure of exports or imports in each region. On the export side,
manufactured goods have similar weights in the two regions, but the weight of oil
in Latin America and that of primary commodities in Asia are somewhat higher than
the corresponding figure in the other region. Similar observations apply to the
import side.

3.3. Debt Services

The amount of interest payments on external debt depend on such factors as the
structure of debt (short-term or long-term) and interest rates applied
(concessional or market rates and spreads). For the sake of simplicity, however,
we used six months LIBOR as "the interest rate."

We may assume that the average interest rate on debt outstanding at the end
of the previous period is a function of LIBOR:

$$\text{int}_t = f(r_t) \cdot D_{t-1}$$

where int_t = interest payments in period t, r_t = LIBOR, and D_{t-1} = debt outstanding at the end of previous period. Taking the linear approximation of $f(r_t)$ around the sample means, we can write

$$f(r_t) = f(\bar{r}) + f'(\bar{r})(r_t - \bar{r})$$

and

$$\text{int}_t = \{f(\bar{r}) - f'(\bar{r})\bar{r}\}D_{t-1} + f'(\bar{r})D_{t-1}r_t.$$

If we further approximate $D_{t-1}r_t$ by

$$D_{t-1}r_t = D \cdot \bar{r} + \bar{r} \cdot D_{t-1} + D \cdot \bar{r}_t,$$

then we have

$$\text{int}_t = \text{const.} + f'(\bar{r}) \cdot \bar{D} \cdot r_t + f(\bar{r}) \cdot D_{t-1}.$$

Since this is the form used in estimation, we can approximate the average-interest-rate equation from estimated coefficients and sample means of relevant variables. The results are

$$f(r_t) = 0.0644 + 0.0046 \, r_t \quad \text{(Latin American region)} \quad \text{(39a)}$$
$$f(r_t) = 0.0322 + 0.0038 \, r_t \quad \text{(Asian region)} \quad \text{(39b)}$$

where r_t is expressed in percentage per annum. It can be seen that average interest rates in the Latin American region have both a higher constant term and a higher marginal coefficient. Six months LIBOR rose from 7.6% of the average in 1970–1978 to 14.1% of the average in 1979–1982. Thus, higher world interest rates must have exerted a much stronger impact on Latin American debt dynamics.

The elasticity of amortization with respect to debt outstanding is fairly similar in the two regions. The variable "Multilateral Debt Relief Agreements" has a negative coefficient as expected in the Latin American region, but in the Asian region amortization payments increased sharply in 1983 and 1987 when debt rescheduling occurred in the Philippines.

3.4. Macroeconomic Block

The short-run marginal propensity to consume (MPC) is 0.29 in the Latin American region and 0.48 in the Asian region. However, the long-run MPC is much higher in the former at 0.91 as compared with 0.76 in the latter. Parameters of investment functions are fairly similar, with the marginal coefficient of real GDP being around 0.1 and the semielasticity with respect to real interest rate being $-0.12 \sim -0.18$.

As for exports and imports on the national account basis, items other than merchandise trade appear to have important shares on the export side in the Asian region and on the import side in the Latin American region. Movements of net factor income from abroad in the Latin American region have been dominated by interest payments, but in the Asian region other items are also important.

From the above comparisons, we may observe some characteristic differences in the two regions that are particularly relevant to debt dynamics. In the first place, the trade structure of the Asian region is clearly export oriented, which may be contrasted to the import-oriented bias of the Latin American region. This is a reflection of the history of development strategies in the two regions, but it certainly puts the Latin American region at a disadvantage in that attempts to stimulate expansion can quite easily lead to a worsening trade balance.

Secondly, price elasticities of trade are fairly low in the Latin American region. This means that, when international market prices develop in an unfavorable direction, there is no automatic mechanism for adjusting trade balances. Rather, international price developments will aggravate unfavorable movements of the trade imbalance. We have not dealt with exchange rates explicitly in this chapter. But even if exchange-rate policy can be used to influence trade prices, low price elasticities imply that the orthodox therapy of correcting trade imbalances through price effects would not work effectively.

Thirdly, the structure of external debt in the Latin American region is such that both fixed and floating components of interest rates are much higher than in the Asian region. Since the pattern of amortization is not so different, the burden of debt service is higher in the Latin American region. Higher international interest rates would obviously intensify the burden, and many authors have maintained that extremely high interest rates in the early 1980s were one important cause of the developing-country debt crisis. We shall discuss this problem in more detail later.

Finally, the long-run marginal propensity to consume in the Latin American region is quite high and exceeds the average propensity to consume. This means that the latter tends to rise as the economy develops. This is also an important factor that tends to cause deterioration of the current account balance.

4. SIMULATION ANALYSES: EXTERNAL AND INTERNAL FACTORS

Each regional debt model explained in the previous section is an annual model having 20 endogenous and 12 exogenous variables. Table 3 reports the error measures concerning dynamic, tracking simulations within the sample period (1972–1988). We use the test solution as the standard case and perform various simulations to assess the quantitative importance of external and internal factors that are conceived of having caused or aggravated the debt problems.

Let us first consider what would have happened to Latin American and Asian debts if the following four distinctive events had not occurred in the late 1970s and early 1980s: 1) a slowdown in the rate of growth of developed countries, 2) sharp increases in international interest rates, 3) declines in real commodity prices, and 4) sharp increases in oil prices. Of course, these events were closely related and would not have occurred in isolation. However, separation of their direct effects by counterfactual simulations would help our understanding of their relative importance.

Column 1 of tables 4 and 5 gives actual values of external debt outstanding (including long-term and short-term debt as well as credits from the IMF) in each region, and columns 2–5 report the differences of debt figures from the standard solution. Each simulation is based on the following assumptions, respectively:

Column 2: The average rate of growth of real GDP in the developed region was 3.8% per annum during 1976–1979, but it declined to 1.5% per annum during 1980–1983 (actually, the rate became negative in 1982). After the recovery beginning in 1984, the average rate recorded was 3.6% during 1984–1988. In this simulation, it is assumed that the developed region had maintained 3.6% growth throughout the period 1979–1988.

Column 3: Six-months LIBOR averaged 6.9% in 1975–1978. But in 1979 it rose to 12.1%. After keeping a two-digit level for four consecutive years, it came down to 9.7% in 1983, but in 1984 it again rose to 10.9%. Here, it is assumed that the rate had remained stable at 7% during 1978–1988.

Column 4: The index of nonfuel commodity prices (IMF, International Financial Statistics index with a 1985 base), when deflated by the export unit value index of developed countries, averaged 130.5 during 1966–1970. Except for a temporary but sharp increase during 1973–1974, real commodity prices have shown a trend decline. In this simulation, they are assumed to have remained stable at the 1966–1970 level.

Column 5: Average real oil prices in 1985 dollars (deflated by the export unit value index of developed countries) were $15.63/bbl during 1975–1978. Average real prices after the second oil crisis were $27.37/bbl for the period 1979–1984, but they collapsed in 1986 and the average for the period 1985–1988 was $12.59/bbl. Here, we assume that real oil prices remained constant at $15.63/bbl during 1979–1988.

In other words, these cases attempt to portray a situation in which the effects of an oil-price hike in the second oil crisis and disinflationary policies thereafter had been absent. (Column 8 will be discussed shortly.)

As figures in column 2 show, without a world economic slowdown the total external debt of the Latin American and Asian regions in 1988 would have been smaller by 39.3 and 101.2 billion dollars, respectively. A larger effect in the Asian region is due to the fact that the income elasticity of export demand in this region is three times as large as that of the Latin American region. The average difference of nominal merchandise exports from the standard case is 15.3% in the Asian region against 3.2% in the Latin American region.

The effects of lower interest rates are larger in the Latin American region, as expected (see column 3). However, they are smaller than those to be obtained by simply multiplying changes in interest rates by the amount of existing debt in each period. One reason is that smaller interest payments reduce the amount of debt outstanding in later periods. A more important reason is that lower interest rates tend to raise real GDP by stimulating consumption (through higher real GNP) and investment (through lower real interest rates). These indirect effects lessen the reduction in debt outstanding through an increased non-interest current account deficit. (When we performed the same simulations by dropping the macroeconomic blocks, the resulting reduction of debt outstanding in 1988 was $99.4 billion for the Latin American region and $5.4 billion for the Asian region.) Although lower interest rates do not reduce the nominal magnitude of debt, as simple calculations would show, their effects in raising consumption of indebted countries are fairly large. In the case of the Latin American region, real consumption is larger on average by 2.7% in the simulation period, and a similar tendency is observed for the Asian region as well. Having said all this, however, we must conclude that our simulation results indicate that higher interest rates in the early 1980s were not the prima-facie cause of the developing-country debt problem.

Comparison of column 4 in tables 4 and 5 reveals contrasting effects of changes in primary commodity prices. In the Latin American region, higher export prices lead to higher export value because of inelastic demand for exports, and import prices are not so sensitive to commodity prices.

Table 3. Tracking Simulation Test*

Variables	Latin America	Asia
MAPE (%)		
Value of Merchandise Exports	2.3	1.7
Value of Merchandise Imports	1.8	1.7
Export Prices	3.2	0.9
Import Prices	1.6	0.7
Debt Outstanding	2.6	1.5
Consumption	1.0	0.7
Investment	2.7	1.6
Exports of Goods and Services	3.0	1.1
Imports of Goods and Services	1.7	1.5
Real GDP	1.1	1.0
Real GNP	1.8	1.0
MAE (Bill.$)		
Trade Balance	2.085	1.997
Service Balance	0.713	0.360
Current Account Balance	2.012	0.926
Interest Payments	0.458	0.987
Debt Services	0.802	1.122
Net Factor Income from Abroad	0.823	0.781

* MAPE = mean absolute percentage errors, and MAE = mean absolute errors. Net factor income from abroad is in 1980 prices.

Thus, the trade balance improves. In contrast, the trade balance of the Asian region deteriorates as both export and import prices rise substantially, and the reduction of export value dominates the reduction of import value. Exactly the reverse conclusions apply to the case of no oil—price hike (column 5). External debt would have been higher in the Latin American region and lower in the Asian region. If we combine these two results, it seems that the effects of changes in oil and nonoil real prices tend to cancel each other, leaving only slight effects on the external debt of these regions.

Column 6 gives the total effect of the above four simulations. From them we can derive the hypothetical amount of debt outstanding had there not been the external influences of the second oil crisis (see column 7). The reduction shown in column 6 is smaller than expected in both regions, especially in the Latin American region.[3] But tables 4 and 5 clearly show that international interest

---

[3]The role of the external macroeconomic environment in the developing-country debt problem is often emphasized, a well-known example being Dornbusch. Dornbusch and Fisher maintained, though, that noninterest current account imbalances, rather than higher interest rates per se, are an essential part of the debt problem. Corbo and Melo also arrived at the conclusion that external

rates in the Latin American region and world economic growth in the Asian region are crucial factors in the debt problems of the respective regions. The final column of table 4 and 5 shows the cumulated value of the "other capital account balance" (i.e., net increase in external reserves less current account balance and net increase in debt) since 1972. For both regions the cumulative deficits amount to around $130 billion in 1988, but it is unlikely that these regions are in a position to export capital to such an extent on a regular commercial or official basis. A large part of this stock must therefore be attributable to capital flight.[4] In fact, the years when the "other capital account balance" recorded deficits exceeding $10 billion are 1977, 1980–1983, and 1986–1987 in the Latin American region; and 1977, and 1982 were characterized by severe debt–repayment difficulties.

Column 8 in table 4 and 5 presents our simulation results if the "other capital account balance" had been zero since 1977. A reduction in the deficit of this account would reduce the need for balance–of–payments financing. The resulting reduction of net borrowing would, in turn, reduce debt service payments. These are the factors that curb increases in external debt. On the other hand, reduced interest payments tend to increase imports, since they increase real GNP at a given level of real GDP. Figures in column 8 are net results of these counteracting forces, and the ratio of column 8 to column 11 represents a sort of "multiplier." The region with a high multiplier in this sense tends to translate capital account deficit into a higher external debt. The value of the multiplier in 1988 is 2.4 for the Latin American region and 0.6 for the Asian region. This clearly shows the vulnerability of the former with respect to the balance–of–payments deficit in general.

In either region, figures in column 8 are larger than those in column 6 (i.e., the total effects of external influences). The average ratio of column 8 to 1 is 41% in the Latin American region and 22% in the Asian region. This means that without "capital flight," external debt outstanding would have been about 80% (the Asian region) or 60% (the Latin American region) of the actual level. Column 10 presents other hypothetical levels of outstanding debt if external influences of the second oil crisis and capital flight had been absent (see also figures 2 and 3). Since capital flight is in fact an endogenous variable responding to the expectations of capital losses and exchange control, it does not make much sense if we say that without capital flight there would have been no debt problem. A more appropriate interpretation of figure 2 is that, as far as the Latin American region is concerned, there must be more important factors other than the influences of the external environment.

---

influences were relatively small by means of econometric model simulations.

[4]Many estimates have been published concerning the scale of capital flight from Latin American countries. For instance, Cumby and Levich (1987) estimated the stock of capital flight in 1984 for four Latin American countries (Argentina, Brazil, Mexico, and Venezuela) as $107.2 billion. Cuddington (1987) estimated the cumulative capital flight in seven Latin American countries (the above plus Chile, Peru, and Uruguay) for the period 1974–1984 as $69.3 billion ($93.3 billion if investment income due to flight capital is included). Pastor (1990) gives another estimate of cumulative flows for eight countries (the above plus Colombia) in 1973–1983 as $146.1 billion.

Table 4. External Debt Outstanding in Simulation Cases: Latin America (Bil.$)

Year	Actual	Growth	LIBOR	Com-modity	Oil	Sub-Total	Hypo. Case1 (1+6)	Cap. Flight	Total (6+8)	Hypo. Case2 (1+9)	Cumul. Other Capital
	(1)	(2)	(3)	(4)	(5)	(6)	(7)	(8)	(9)	(10)	(11)
1975	68.9			−0.4		−0.4	68.5		−0.4	68.5	4.6
1976	85.2			−0.3		−0.3	84.8		−0.3	84.8	4.4
1977	130.9			−1.1		−1.1	129.8	−29.4	−30.6	100.3	−25.0
1978	161.5			−2.1		−2.1	159.5	−38.7	−40.8	120.8	−30.5
1979	196.4	−0.2	−2.1	−2.6	1.4	−3.4	193.0	−51.7	−55.1	141.3	−38.7
1980	242.7	−1.0	−7.9	−5.3	5.9	−8.4	234.3	−76.3	−84.7	158.0	−57.2
1981	296.3	−3.1	−16.3	−8.1	10.1	−17.4	278.9	−97.2	−114.5	188.7	−69.2
1982	333.5	−6.9	−28.5	−12.8	18.7	−29.4	304.1	−115.4	−144.8	188.7	−76.1
1983	361.1	−11.4	−37.9	−17.8	31.4	−35.7	325.3	−147.3	−183.0	178.0	−94.5
1984	377.3	−16.2	−44.0	−23.6	46.9	−36.8	340.4	−168.3	−205.1	172.1	−98.4
1985	389.4	−21.2	−52.0	−30.4	62.4	−41.4	348.1	−197.2	−238.5	150.9	−107.9
1986	409.2	−26.4	−58.2	−38.3	69.0	−53.9	355.3	−232.4	−286.3	122.9	−120.6
1987	445.4	−32.5	−62.9	−49.0	78.0	−66.5	378.9	−286.0	−347.1	98.3	−142.7
1988	434.1	−39.3	−68.0	−61.8	83.7	−85.5	348.6	−291.8	−377.3	50.1	−123.5

Table 5. External Debt Outstanding in Simulation Cases: Asia (Bil.$)

Year	Actual	Growth	LIBOR	Com-modity	Oil	Sub-Total	Hypo. Case1 (1+6)	Cap. Flight	Total (6+8)	Hypo. Case2 (1+9)	Cumul. Other Capital
	(1)	(2)	(3)	(4)	(5)	(6)	(7)	(8)	(9)	(10)	(11)
1975	46.3			0.6		0.6	46.9		0.6	46.9	3.8
1976	54.7			0.1		0.1	54.8		0.1	54.8	3.0
1977	75.6			−0.4		−0.4	75.2	−17.8	−18.2	57.4	−42.8
1978	87.9			0.4		0.4	88.3	−20.7	−20.3	67.6	−33.4
1979	100.9	−1.3	−0.1	0.7	−0.4	−1.0	99.9	−20.5	−21.5	79.5	−38.2
1980	126.7	−7.5	−0.3	1.8	−4.2	−10.2	116.5	−28.7	−38.9	87.8	−65.2
1981	146.8	−18.2	−0.7	4.2	−12.9	−27.4	119.4	−27.7	−55.1	91.7	−68.0
1982	173.9	−38.8	−1.3	7.4	−21.5	−54.2	119.8	−39.8	−94.0	80.0	−87.9
1983	194.1	−49.7	−1.8	9.1	−29.2	−71.5	122.6	−40.7	−112.2	81.9	−95.1
1984	204.6	−52.4	−1.9	9.5	−34.4	−79.1	125.5	−41.2	−120.3	84.3	−98.5
1985	236.7	−61.4	−1.9	13.2	−39.6	−89.7	147.1	−48.9	−138.5	98.2	−115.2
1986	265.9	−75.0	−1.9	21.8	−46.6	−101.7	164.1	−56.9	−158.7	107.2	−128.2
1987	298.0	−91.8	−1.7	32.5	−44.8	−105.8	192.3	−74.2	−179.9	118.1	−159.5
1988	301.7	−101.2	−1.4	41.6	−48.3	−109.3	192.4	−84.5	−193.7	107.9	−133.4

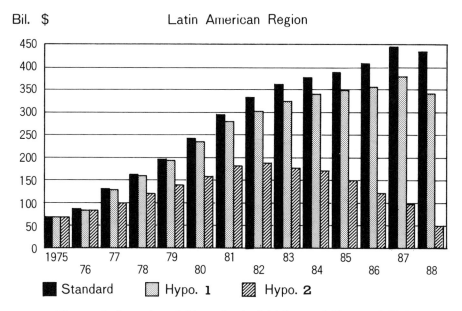

Figure **2** Actual and Hypothetical Values of External Debt

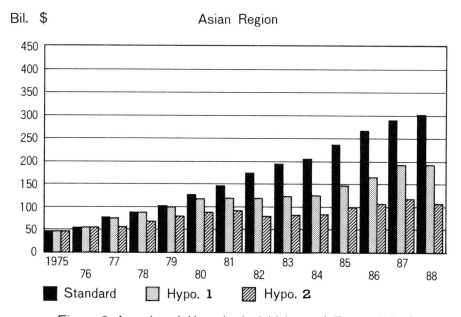

Figure **3** Actual and Hypothetical Values of External Dedt

The above differences in responses of the two regions to favorable changes in the external environment clearly indicate that the different economic structures of these regions examined in section 3 must have some relevance to the seriousness of debt problems. In that section, we pointed out four aspects of structural characteristics of the Latin American region: 1) income elasticities of exports and imports, 2) price elasticities of exports and imports, 3) average interest rates, and 4) long-run marginal propensity to consume. It has already been shown, however, that the quantitative effects of higher interest rates cannot be a principal cause. As to the low price elasticities of exports and imports, this aspect by itself may or may not encourage debt accumulation depending on the direction of international price movements. We shall, therefore, take up only aspects 1 and 4, and consider how situations would change if we modify the parameters in such a way that the Latin American region becomes more like the Asian region in these respects.[5]

For this purpose, we raised the income elasticity of exports from 0.48 to 0.55 and lowered the income elasticity of imports from the level exceeding unity to 0.85 throughout the period. Case 1 in table 6 refers to this case. We also lowered the coefficient of lagged consumption in the consumption function so as to lower the long-run marginal propensity to consume from 0.91 to 0.875 (case 2). Case 3 involves both modifications.

As can be seen from the table, adjustments of income elasticities reduce trade deficits and debt accumulation, which in turn raises real GNP and consumption. On the other hand, a reduction of the long-run marginal propensity to consume also contributes to reducing debt by lowering imports, but it reduces domestic absorption and hence real GDP and consumption. Therefore, in order to transfer resources from domestic and import-competing sectors to the export sector without reducing total output, the two modifications must be combined in an appropriate way. Case 3 gives such an example. External debt outstanding is reduced by $240 billion by 1988 with minor changes in real consumption.

To sum up the foregoing simulation analyses, we may conclude that the Latin American debt problem in the late 1970s and early 1980s can be partly explained by unfavorable developments of external macroeconomic conditions, but that more important causes appear to be attributable to the domestic economic structure of this region involving inward-looking trade structure and a high propensity to consume. If this conclusion is correct, much emphasis must be placed on structural adjustment policies such as tax policies to encourage domestic savings, further transformation of development policies toward export promotions, and industrial deregulations to facilitate smooth transfer of resources from domestic and import-competing sectors to the export sectors.

5. FUTURE PROSPECTS FOR THE LATIN AMERICAN DEBT PROBLEM

Since 1982 when the developing-country debt problem threatened the world financial markets, considerable efforts have been made by international

---

[5]Comparing Brazil and Korea, Abe emphasized that differences in development policies (particularly those in export promotion policies) resulted in contrasting outcome with respect to debt problems. See also Balassa (1989, article 4) regarding the implications of inward- and outward-oriented development policies.

organizations and major governments to avoid the collapse of the international financial system. Private banks with large amount of sovereign loans have also been attempting to reinforce their credit standing by reducing nonperforming loans and strengthening their capital base. Various plans of debt relief have also been proposed, and some of them have been pursued. In spite of these developments, however, the developing-country debt problem is far from being solved and will remain one of the important problem areas of the world economy. In the Latin American region, where most severely indebted countries are concentrated, the standard of living has suffered from austere adjustment policies for several years, and many countries are in serious political situations.[6] In this section we shall concentrate on the Latin American region and consider its future prospects under various scenarios.

Table 6. Hypothetical Structural Change in Latin America and External Debt*

Year	Case 1[a] External Debt (Bil.$)	Case 1[a] Consump- tion (%)	Case 2[b] External Debt (Bil.$)	Case 2[b] Consump- tion (%)	Case 3[c] External Debt (Bil.$)	Case 3[c] Consump- tion (%)
1972	0.0	0.0	0.0	0.0	0.0	0.0
1973	−0.4	0.1	0.0	−0.1	−0.4	0.0
1974	−1.8	0.2	−0.1	−0.5	−4.0	−0.2
1976	−6.8	0.4	−0.6	−0.7	−7.3	−0.3
1977	−11.0	0.7	−2.1	−1.3	−18.5	−0.4
1979	−25.9	1.3	−3.5	−1.6	−28.7	−0.4
1980	−38.8	1.7	−5.6	−2.0	−43.2	−0.3
1981	−54.8	2.2	−8.6	−2.3	−61.6	−0.2
1982	−70.3	2.9	−11.9	−2.8	−79.6	−0.1
1983	−85.5	3.7	−15.5	−3.3	−97.7	0.2
1984	−103.5	4.5	−19.8	−3.5	−119.1	0.7
1985	−123.6	5.4	−24.8	−3.7	−143.2	1.2
1986	−146.0	6.3	−30.4	−3.8	−170.1	1.9
1987	−172.2	7.5	−37.1	−4.1	−201.8	2.7
1988	−202.9	8.8	−45.3	−4.2	−239.2	3.7

* Differences from the standard solution are reported for external debt outstanding, and percentage differences for real consumption.
a) Income elasticities of exports and imports are modified.
b) Long-run marginal propensity to consume is modified.
c) Both.

Before starting our main discussion, it is necessary to point out that the model developed in section 3 has one problem in its application to the projection

_____

[6]Fried and Trezise (1989, pp. 3-4) mentioned two reasons why the attitude of the U.S. administration toward the debt problem has recently changed. One is that the net flow of funds from private banks to heavily indebted countries has turned negative, indicating unsatisfactory achievement of the Baker Initiative. The other is the changing political situation in Latin America.

period. This is its formulation that the net increase in external debt is equal to the balance of payments deficit (or, essentially the current account deficit). (See equation (9) in section 3.) Equation (9) is a balance-of-payments constraint:

Current Account Balance + Net Increase in External
    Debt + Other Capital Account Balance − Net Increase
    in External Reserves = 0.   (9′)

One can determine the net increase in external debt from this equation, given the estimates of other variables. Or, one can separately estimate the net increase in external debt and incorporate some adjustment process that makes the current account balance consistent with equation (9′) (e.g., by increasing or decreasing domestic absorption according to whether the balance of payments is in surplus or in deficit). In the sample period where actual values of net increase in external debt are known, either method can yield reasonable simulation results.

When the model of section 3 is directly applied to the projection period, however, the model projects an ever increasing external debt for this region. For example, let us make the following assumptions as to the future courses of exogenous variables in the projection period 1990–2000.

1. The growth rate of developed countries' real GDP is constant at 3.25% per annum.

2. The rate of increase in the world export price of manufactured goods is constant at 3.5% per annum.

3. The terms of trade of primary commodities and of oil vis-à-vis manufactured goods are constant.

4. Six–months LIBOR is constant at 8.5%.

As shown in case A of table 7, the model predicts that the external debt of this region will come close to $1,000 billion in the year 2000, with the debt/merchandise export ratio exceeding 500%.

This is obviously an unrealistic situation based upon an implicit assumption that the region has unconstrained access to foreign borrowing. In this section, therefore, we incorporate a balance-of-payments adjustment mechanism as mentioned above (i.e., adjustment of domestic absorption), and control the net increase in external debt in each period in the following way: Within the sample period, the net increase in external debt is estimated as

Net Increase in External Debt
   = 10.228 + (0.889 − 0.129 D82C)·Debt Service Payments
           (19.8)   (3.44)
     − 0.973 Other Capital Account Balance
     (21.3)
     − 0.267 Multilateral Debt Relief Agreements
     (14.0)
     + 0.468 Domestic Growth Rate of Investment
     (8.32)
     − 0.381 Debt Service/Merchandise Exports
     (4.22)
     − 4.6 (D75 − D76) − 4.6 (D83 − D84) − 21.8 D85
     (4.15)   (3.94)   (12.4)

$\bar{R}^2$ = 0.992, SE = 1.4, DW = 2.06 (Sample Period=1972–1988)

where a variable Dxx = dummy variable assuming 1 in year 19xx and 0 otherwise, DxxC = dummy variable assuming 1 in and after 19xx and 0 otherwise, and figures in parentheses are t-values.

The above estimation result indicates that debt service payments and "capital flight" are significant factors that caused increased borrowing needs in the sample period, but these variables cannot be used in the projection period. We, therefore, retained only the fourth and fifth explanatory variables in the above equation, and adjusted the constant term so as to make the estimates in 1990 around $25 billion.

Case B of table 7 reports the resulting simulations, which are based on the same set of exogenous assumptions as in case A. We shall take case B as the base case in what follows. It should be noted that both cases in table 7 depict a rather gloomy picture for this region. Even in case A where the region can rely on increasing debt, GDP and real consumption growth rates are quite low. In case B, the debt/merchandise export ratio does decline gradually after 1990, but the average rate of growth of real consumption is only 0.7%.

How will this pessimistic picture be modified if the world economic environment becomes more favorable than assumed in the base case? Conversely, is there any assumption in the base case that is still too optimistic? Will some debt relief program be able to help this region out of the difficulties? And if so, how much extra funding will be required? How does the program of economic restructuring suggested in the previous section compare with these cases?

Table 8 summarizes the results of simulations performed to find the keys to these questions. "Standard" means case B in table 7. Other cases are based on the following scenario assumptions, respectively.

LIBOR: LIBOR is constant at 6%.

Growth: The growth rate of developed countries' real GDP is constant at 4.25%.

Oil Prices: Nominal oil prices rise at a constant rate, reaching $31.5/bbl in 2000.

Commodity Prices: Real commodity prices follow the path projected by the World Bank.[7]

Debt Relief: 10% of existing debt is reduced, as a one-time event, in 1990.

Interest Relief: Interest payments are relieved every year by applying a five-percentage-point lower interest rate than in the base case.

Restructuring: The model parameters are modified as follows: income elasticity of exports = 0.75, income elasticity of imports = 0.85, and long-run marginal propensity to consume = 0.875.

Some explanations may be in order about the oil and commodity price scenarios. After the collapse of oil prices in 1986, there have been some basic changes in the world oil market. That is, oil consumption has been rising more rapidly than in the first half of 1980s, whereas non-OPEC oil supplies have been discouraged. Accordingly, supporters of a view that the world oil market will become tight again sometime in the middle of 1990s have been increasing in number.[8] In the "Oil Prices" scenario, it is assumed that real oil prices (in terms of 1980 dollars) will rise up to $18/bbl in the year 2000. Converting this

---

[7]See World Bank (1989).

[8]See, e.g., IEA (1989).

to current dollars by using world export prices of manufactured goods, we obtain $31.6/bbl with an annual rate of increase at 4.82%.

Table 7. External Debt of Latin American Region: Reference Cases

	1988	1989	1990	1992	1994	1996	1998	2000
Debt Outstanding (Bil.$)								
Case A	428	445	473	544	621	717	834	974
Case B	427	445	469	509	560	602	648	694
Debt/Merchandise Export Ratio (%)								
Case A	420	396	406	426	443	446	493	524
Case B	420	396	416	410	410	400	392	381
Debt Service/Merchandise Export Ratio (%)								
Case A	53.4	51.3	56.5	60.4	63.4	67.2	71.5	76.3
Case B	53.4	51.3	58.0	58.7	59.0	58.4	57.5	56.3

Real GDP Growth Rate (% p.a.)				1991–95 av.	96–2000 av.
Case A	0.8	1.8	1.6	1.9	1.3
Case B	0.8	1.8	−4.5	0.4	1.6

Real Consumption Growth Rate (% p.a.)				1991–95 av.	96–2000 av.
Case A	1.2	1.2	2.5	2.0	1.1
Case B	1.2	1.2	−5.3	0.0	1.5

Real commodity prices, on the other hand, have been on a declining trend since the peak in 1973–1974. In 1984 they recovered somewhat, but the declining trend still continues. The recently published World Bank long–term projections mentioned above are also pessimistic in this respect. Expected rates of increase in real commodity prices are −12.8% in 1990, −1.5% in 1991, −0.8% in 1992, and from then on 0.9% by 1995 and 2.6% by 2000. These projected rates are translated into nominal figures by using world export prices of manufactured goods.

Now, lower interest rates tend to have a modest effect in raising real GDP growth rates but do not lower debt/export ratios exactly because of this expansionary effect. Higher economic growth in developed countries have

Table 8. External Debt and Domestic Growth in Latin America

Debt/Export Ratio (%)				Real GDP Growth Rate (% p.a.)		
	1990	1995	2000		1990	91–95	96–2000
Standard	416	405	381	Standard	−4.5	0.4	1.6
LIBOR	416	408	386	LIBOR	−4.5	0.7	1.5
Oil Prices	414	395	365	Oil Prices	−4.3	0.7	1.7
Commodity				Commodity			
Prices	421	416	387	Prices	−5.4	1.7	1.1
Debt Relief	376	380	366	Debt Relief	−4.5	1.2	1.4
Interest				Interest			
Relief	416	411	388	Relief	0.6	0.2	1.2
Restructuring	412	391	357	Restructuring	−4.6	2.0	3.1

favorable effects on both counts: increases in exports reduce external financing needs and raise domestic output. But continued growth of developed countries at 4.25% is rather hard to expect.

Higher oil prices tend to encourage exports and growth of the region as a whole, since it includes big oil exporters like Mexico and Venezuela. The effect of an assumed rate of increase in real oil prices (1.3% per annum) upon the debt/export ratio matches that of the "Growth" case, and its effect upon domestic growth compares with that of the "LIBOR" case. The effects upon individual countries within the region must, of course, be more divergent, because there are many oil-importing countries as well.

The expected decline in real commodity prices in the early 1990s changes the terms of trade of this region quite unfavorably. This leads to sharp declines in domestic absorption and growth. Our model produces a cyclical response to this shock, and after a few years the growth rates become somewhat higher than those in the base case. The average growth rate for the projection period as a whole is lower, however. This result indicates that the assumption of constant real commodity prices in the base case may involve some optimistic element as far as this region is concerned.

The scale of debt reduction assumed in the "Debt Relief" case amounts to $44.5 billion. Reductions in annual debt service payments are helpful in raising growth rates of this region, the medium-run effects being close to those of raising the developed countries' growth rate by one percentage point. But as the domestic expansion mainly led by consumption growth continues, there will be additional increases in external debt so that the favorable effects gradually fade away. Thus, a one-time debt reduction per se resembles a camphor injection.

Similar observations apply to the "Interest Relief" case, although in this case the impact results in quicker relief. In this simulation, the annual reduction of interest payments amounts to some $5 billion, and the present value of total relief (discounted by LIBOR) in the simulation period is $37.4 billion.

The total amount of available funding contemplated under the Brady Initiative is said to be $20–25 billion over three years with an additional amount from the Japanese government of $4.5 billion again over three years.[9] Since our simulations assume larger injections, and since some doubt exists about their lasting effects, it may be quite probable that similar relief plans will have to be contemplated several years later.

The effects of economic restructuring do not appear immediately, but they are enduring and promising. Traditional IMF conditionality emphasized the orthodox therapy of belt-tightening through financial policies and exchange depreciation, but our simulation exercises ascertained the importance of revising longer-term development policies towards a more outward-oriented direction. It must also be noted that such a strategy is quite complementary to any form of debt-relief arrangements.

Our simulation exercises thus indicate that likely developments in the world economy will not provide a sufficiently favorable environment to resolve the debt problem of the Latin American region in the near future, and that various forms of debt relief-plans cannot be considered as furnishing final solutions as long as the present economic structure of this region remains unchanged.

The Latin American debt problem has highlighted two important dimensions of external debt problems. One is that the development process based on external

---

[9]Fried and Trezise (1989, pp. 7–8).

debt can sometimes become uncontrollable, even if it has started from a sound prospect under given conditions, when world economic conditions slip into a situation with high real interest rates and low economic growth. International financial markets have turned out to be not prudent enough, and major industrial countries thus have the responsibility of preventing such a situation. Another, more obvious dimension is the domestic aspect. When the private sector has a net investment balance to be financed, the generation of an external surplus is politically much easier than suppressing a public-sector deficit. This is where macroeconomic policies must be geared to development policies.

The Latin American debt problem is still far from solved, and yet we are facing the problems of restructuring Poland, Hungary, and a new USSR, as well as some countries even in the Asian region. A more stable world economy is both a precondition for and a consequence of solving these problems.

REFERENCES

Abe, Kiyoshi (1989). "A Comparative Study of the Economic Development and Debt Problem of Asian and American NICs," in H. W. Singer and Soumitra Sharma, eds., Economic Development and World Debt (London: Macmillan), pp. 413-421.

Balassa, Bela (1989). New Directions in the World Economy (London: Macmillan).

Cline, William R. (1985). "International Debt: Analysis, Experience and Prospects," in Carlos Massad, ed., The Debt Problem: Acute and Chronic Aspects, Journal of Development Planning, No. 16, pp. 25-55.

Corbo, Vittorio, and Jaime de Meló (1989). "External Shocks and Policy Reforms in the Southern Cone: A Reassessment," in Guillermo Calvo, et al., eds., Debt, Stabilization and Development (Oxford: Basil Blackwell), pp. 235-258.

Cuddington, John T. (1987). "Macroeconomic Determinants of Capital Flight: An Econometric Investigation," in Donald R. Lessard and John Williamson, eds., Capital Flight and Third World Debt (Washington, D.C.: Institute for International Economics), pp. 85-96.

Cumby, Robert, and Richard Levich (1987). "On the Definition and Magnitude of Recent Capital Flight," in Donald R. Lessard and John Williamson, eds., Capital Flight and Third World Debt (Washington, D.C.: Institute for International Economics), pp. 27-67.

de Piniés, Jaime (1989). "Debt Sustainability and Over-adjustment," World Development, Vol. 17, No. 1 (January), pp. 29-43.

Dornbusch, Rudiger (1989). "Debt Problems and the World Macroeconomy," in Jeffrey D. Sachs, ed., Developing Country Debt and Economic Performance (Chicago: The University of Chicago Press), pp. 331-357.

Dornbusch, Rudiger, and Stanley Fischer (1985). "The World Debt Problem: Origins and Prospects," in Carlos Massad, ed., The Debt Problem: Acute and Chronic Aspects, Journal of Development Planning, No. 16, pp. 57-81.

Fried, Edward R., and Philip H. Trezise (1989). "Overview," in Edward R. Fried and Philip H. Trezise, eds., <u>Third World Debt: The Next Phase</u> (Washington, D.C.: The Brookings Institution), pp. 3-16.

IEA (1989). "World Energy Outlook to 2005," mimeo.

Pastor, Manuel Jr., (1990). "Capital Flight from Latin America," <u>World Development</u>, Vol. 18, No. 1 (January), pp. 1-18.

World Bank (1989). International Commodity Markets Division, "Half-Yearly Revision of Commodity Price Forecasts," (December), mimeo.

16. DEVELOPMENT DILEMMA: THE PHILIPPINE EXPERIENCE

Solita Collas-Monsod
Professor of Economics
School of Economics
University of the Philippines

Abstract. The extensive linkages between the developing countries (the South) and the industrialized nations (the North) are such that world economic stability cannot be attained so long as the economic South is unable to achieve a sustained and satisfactory growth path. A "gap" approach provides the framework within which major construction and economic growth are analyzed. It shows that both structural reforms and foreign savings are necessary to achieve adequate and sustainable rates of growth. The international debt crisis was both a cause and or effect of reduced and even negative transfers of resources to developing countries. The past and present strategy of dealing with the crisis not only has failed to correct the situation but also perhaps has inadvertently sacrificed structural reforms at the altar of debt service. The Philippine experience is used as a case in point.

1. INTRODUCTION

No world economic stability is possible so long as developing nations are unstable. The so-called economic South comprise three fourths of the world's population but account for less than one fifth of its income.

The interdependence between the poor countries of the South and the rich North is too extensive and too complex to admit of any illusions that the latter can ignore or remain unaffected by what is happening in the former. The most common linkages are in trade, investment, and finance—the developing-country debt crisis was also a crisis of the international financial system. But the linkages go farther than that. The two parts of the world share the same physical environment; degradation and pollution cannot be walled in. International migration of labor is a cause of racial tensions in the North. The narcotics problem involves both South and North players.

Environmental degradation, narcotraffic, and labor migration are rooted in poverty. A sustained growth path for developing countries, one that is sufficient to give their people real hope for a better future, is a necessary condition for stability in the South and, therefore, in the world.

Yet the past decade has witnessed retrogressions and even reversals of this growth path. The 1980's has been called the lost decade of development.

The main cause of this phenomenon is the international debt crisis. The manner in which it has been handled—the strategies, past and present—have not only been ineffective, but have also made it harder for developing countries to recover from their collapse and achieve sustained growth at satisfactory levels. Until this is accepted, and unless major changes are made, the prospects for world stability become even dimmer.

This chapter presents a framework within which to analyze the dilemmas faced by debtor countries (section 2) in their quest for development. Within this framework, section 3 further examines the role of structural reforms and foreign savings as well as the impact of the international debt crisis and conventional debt strategy on that quest. Section 4 uses the Philippine experience to illustrate these difficulties concretely. The last section makes specific recommendations on actions needed to increase foreign savings.

2. FRAMEWORK

The dilemmas that face developing countries in debt crises are best understood using the "gap approach" as an analytical framework. Chenery and Bruno (1962) constructed a model showing two major constraints to economic growth—the savings constraint and the foreign exchange constraint. More recently, Bacha (1988) has included government budget limitations as a main source of growth (and inflation) difficulties of highly indebted middle income economies. Lim (1990) applies this to the Philippine case.

2.1. Savings Constraint

We start with the familiar Harrod-Domar growth equation:

$$g = dY/Y = 1/k \ (I/Y)\tag{1}$$

where g is the growth rate, Y is gross domestic product, K is the incremental capital-output ratio I/dY, and I is investment.

The national income identity tells us that any investment is financed by savings:

$$I = S + Z\tag{2}$$

where S is domestic savings and Z is foreign savings. Domestic savings is equal to income minus consumption, and comes from the private sector and the government sector:

$$S = Y - C_p - C_g,\tag{3}$$

$$S = S_p + S_g\tag{4}$$

where C_p is private consumption, C_g is government consumption, and S_p and S_g are private and government savings, respectively.

Government saving is further defined as

$$S_g = T - (G + \theta i^* D_e + i \ D_g)\tag{5}$$

where T is government tax and nontax revenue excluding foreign grants; G is government current expenditure other than interest payments; θ is the proportion of foreign interest payments that are paid by the government; i* is the interest rate on foreign debt; D_e is the external debt stock; i is the interest rate on domestic borrowing; and D_g represents government domestic borrowing.

Government consumption comprises the second term on the right–hand–side of equation (5):

$$C_g \; = \; G + \; \theta i^* D_e + i D_g. \tag{6}$$

We now introduce the familiar balance of payments identity:

$$dR \; = \; X - M - i^* D_e + J + d D_e + dF + E \tag{7}$$

where dR is the change in international reserves; X and M are exports and imports of goods and nonfactor services, respectively; $i^* D_e$ is interest payment on foreign debt; J is foreign grants and transfers; $d D_e$ is the change in the external debt stock; dF is net foreign investment; and E represents other items in the balance of payments, including errors and omissions. The first four items on the right–hand–side of equation (7) compose the Current Account (CA), and the rest compose the Capital Account (CaA) of the balance of payments.

Foreign savings (equation (7)) is defined alternatively as:

$$Z \; = \; M - X + i^* D_e \tag{8}$$

or

$$Z \; = \; J + d D_e + dF + E - dR. \tag{9}$$

It is important to note here that the level of foreign savings available for investment can be maintained in the face of decreasing foreign grants, investments, and foreign loan disbursements if the country's international reserves are drawn down correspondingly.

Dividing equation (2) by Y and substituting for I/Y in equation (1) gives us the <u>savings constraint</u>:

$$g \; = \; (1/k)(s_p + s_g) + (1/k)(z), \tag{10}$$

where $s_p \; = \; S_p/Y$,

$$s_g \; = \; [T - (G + \theta i^* D_e + i D_g)]/Y,$$

$$z \; = \; Z/Y.$$

Equation (10) tells us that given the domestic savings rate, the growth rate is a positive function of the foreign savings rate, with the first term as intercept and $1/k$ as the slope.

2.2. The Foreign Exchange Constraint

The foreign exchange constraint arises because some of the capital goods, raw materials, and intermediate products used by the developing country for domestic production and exports are imported. Breaking down the imports in equation (8):

$$M = M_k + M_r + M_o, \tag{11}$$

where M_k = imports of capital goods,
M_r = imports of raw materials and intermediate products,
M_o = imports of consumer goods and other imports.

We assume that

$$M_k = m_k I \tag{12}$$

and

$$M_r = m_r(C_p + G + I + X). \tag{13}$$

Putting equations (8), (11), (12), and (13) together, dividng by Y, and substituting I/Y in equation (1), we obtain the <u>foreign exchange constraint</u>:

$$g = \frac{1}{k(m_k+m_r)}\left[(1-m_r)\frac{X}{Y} - m_r\frac{C_p+C_g}{Y} - \frac{M_o}{Y} - \frac{i^*D_e}{Y}\right]$$

$$+ \frac{1}{k(m_k + mr)}\, z. \tag{14}$$

Note that the slope of the foreign exchange constraint is steeper than the slope of the savings constraint in the $g - z$ space, since $(m_k + m_r)$ is most likely less than 1.

2.3. The Fiscal Constraint

Start with the government budget equation,

$$T + B_g + \emptyset\, Z = G + \theta i^*D_e + iD_g + I_g + A_g + O \tag{15}$$

where B_g = government domestic borrowing,
$\emptyset$ = proportion of foreign savings that go to the government,
I_g = government investment,
A_g = principal payments on government domestic debt,
O = other items, including changes in cash balance.

The left-hand-side of equation (15) reflects the sources of government funds, while the right-hand-side indicates the uses of funds. The proportion of foreign savings that goes to the government is becoming larger as most of the foreign debt is either government or government- guaranteed, especially since the debt crisis.
Investment is broken down into private and government investment:

$$I = I_p + I_g. \tag{16}$$

Rattso (1988) and Lim (1990) assume that private investment (I_p) is positively related to capacity utilization (u). Moreover, it is also positively related to government investment (I_g), the so-called "crowding in" effect, with the net effect (a_1) of the "crowding in" and the traditional "crowding out" being still positive and less than 1:

$$I_p = a_0 + a_1 I_g + a_2 u. \tag{17}$$

Combining equations (16) and (17),

$$I = a_0 + (1 + a_1) I_g + a_2 u \tag{18}$$

or

$$I_g = (I - (a_0 + a_2 u) / (1 + a_1). \tag{19}$$

Substituting equation (19) into equation (15), and using (1), we obtain the fiscal constraint:

$$g = \frac{(1 + a_i)}{k} \frac{T}{Y} - [\frac{(G + \theta i^* D_e + i D_g)}{Y} + \frac{(B_g - A_g)}{Y} - \frac{0}{Y}$$

$$+ \frac{a_0 + a_2 u}{kY} + \frac{\emptyset (1 + a_1)}{k} z]. \tag{20}$$

The slope of the fiscal constraint is steeper than the slope of the savings constraint in the $g - z$ space. But it is less steep than the foreign exchange constraint, since $0 / (1 + a_1)$ is close to 1, but $(m_k + m_r)$ is assumed to be much less than 1.

2.4. Analysis

Plotting the growth rate against the foreign savings rate $z (= Z/Y)$, would result in a configuration similar to that in figure 1.

The diagram shows the relative steepness of the foreign exchange constraint (EE), the fiscal constraint (TT), and the savings constraint (SS). At low levels of foreign savings as in the area to the left of z', it is the foreign exchange constraint that inhibits growth; at intermediate levels, between z' and z'', it is the fiscal constraint; and at high foreign savings levels, it is the savings constraint.

At a level of foreign savings z' in figure 2, the growth rate of the economy will be g_1. A reduction of foreign savings available to the economy, to z_1, will reduce the growth rate to g_2. It can be retained at g_1 if the intercept of the foreign exchange constraint is raised to $E'E'$, or if the slope is increased, as in $E''E''$.

To achieve a rise in the intercept would require any or all of the following measures: 1) increased exports, 2) decreased private consumption as well as government current operating expenditures other than interest payments, 3) decreased imports of consumer goods and goods other than capital goods or raw materials, and 4) decreased foreign interest payments.

Increasing the slope of the foreign exchange constraint (which would also raise the intercept) would require 1) increasing the efficiency of investment, i.e., decreasing the ICOR or k, or 2) decreasing the proportion m_k of capital goods that are imported, or 3) decreasing the proportion m_r of imported raw materials used in investment, consumption, and exports.

Raising the intercept of the fiscal constraint would require, among other things, raising revenues, lowering total government consumption, raising net domestic borrowing, or lowering other expenditures. Increasing the slope of the fiscal constraint (which would also raise the intercept) requires that the net effect of government investment--the crowding-in less the crowding-out--on private investment becomes larger, and/or the efficiency of investment is improved, (this need not raise the intercept) if foreign inflows are channeled more and more to government.

Finally, the savings constraint could be shifted upward by increasing the private and public savings rate (which will raise the intercept), as well as by increasing the efficiency of investment.

The measures to raise the intercept/increase the slope of the three constraints are what is collectively known as structural adjustment--reform of a country's macroeconomic structural parameters so that these are supportive of its medium-term development efforts (Montes, 1989).

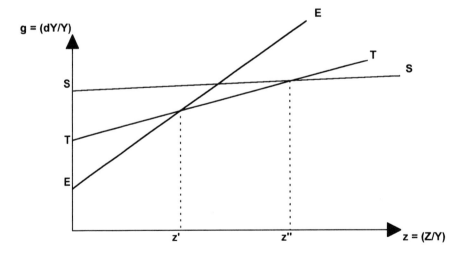

Figure 1. Growth Rate Related to Foreign Savings Rate

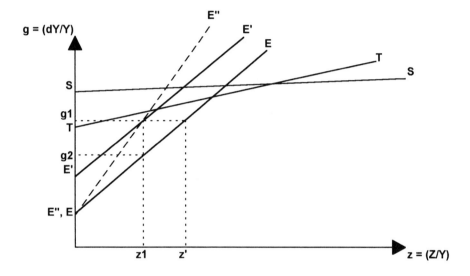

Figure 2. Growth Rate Related to Constraining Foreign Savings Rate and Foreign Exchange

3. STRUCTURAL REFORM AND FOREIGN SAVINGS

The framework described in the preceding section shows that a country's path to sustained growth requires both an appropriate level of foreign savings and internal structural reforms.

3.1. Nature of Structural Reforms

The nature of structural reforms make their implementation difficult. First, they are designed to change the status quo (reduce inefficiency, increase equity). This means a confrontation with vested interests whose political and economic power is derived from the existing structure, and who will exert every effort to maintain the status quo.

Second, structural reforms have a long gestation period; their benefits will be felt in the medium and long term, while their costs are incurred immediately. The sectors that will bear these initial costs, especially if they are the underprivileged sectors of the economy, will need some "safety nets" in the process. Absent these safety nets, the resulting social and political unrest will jeopardize the very environment which the structural reforms are trying to improve.

Third, structural reforms are "lumpy" in character. That is to say, they generally must be undertaken as a package. For example, pursuing trade and tariff reforms without simultaneously correcting an overvalued currency will only make matters worse.

Ironically, a democratic setting, itself a much desired political structural reform, exacerbates the difficulties of implementing macroeconomic reforms. Elective officials are most reluctant to commit themselves to measures whose negative impact in the short run may jeopardize their election or reelection chances. Faced with a set of structural reforms that must be implemented as a package, they may choose some and reject others, or they may suspend implementation in midstream because their political time horizon does not coincide with the economic time horizon of the reforms. Furthermore, the consultations and public debates that can be dispensed with by an authoritarian government delay the decision-making process.

3.2. The Role of Foreign Savings in Structural Reform

Given the long gestation period of structural reforms and the immediate costs that they entail, the role of foreign savings in the process is clear: foreign savings represent the resources needed by the economy to provide the safety nets during the transition. The safety nets facilitate the hard political decisions by blunting the criticism of vested interests and mitigating the adverse effects of the reforms on the more vulnerable sectors of the economy.

Thus, structural reforms and foreign savings are a both-and proposition, rather than an either-or proposition. Actually, it may be possible to use foreign savings in place of structural reforms in achieving satisfactory growth in the medium term. This happened in the Philippines in the 1970s (Dohner and Intal, 1989), a situation of debt-led growth. But the reverse does not hold true, at least in the short and medium term. Structural reforms cannot be substituted for foreign savings.

A concrete example, using the foreign exchange constraint, serves to illustrate the link between structural reforms and foreign savings.

Measures to diversify and increase exports may lead to an increase in m_k and m_r, the proportion of imported capital goods, raw materials, or intermediate product, especially if these require higher degrees of processing and manufacturing. Thus, the attempt to raise the intercept of the foreign exchange constraint may result initially in movements in other parameters which themselves tend to lower both its intercept and its slope.

Moreover, several studies have shown that exports, especially agricultural, respond very slowly to general incentives, e.g., devaluation. Protectionist policies in the industrialized countries make matters worse. Finally, a devaluation has an immediate inflationary impact, which hits hardest the poorer sectors of a developing country.

Clearly, if these structural adjustments are eventually to succeed, their negative impact on current growth rates (and the attendant political repercussions) must be neutralized by higher levels of foreign savings.

The unavailability of foreign resources results in either 1) more reluctance to implement the reform measures in the first place, 2) political pressure to reverse them in midstream because of the perception that they are "ineffective," or 3) greater social and political instability.

3.3. The Impact of the International Debt Crisis

When the international debt crisis erupted with the Mexican moratorium in 1982, the U.S. banking system, and therefore the international financial system, faced the spectre of mass bankruptcy. The exposure of the nine major money-center banks in the U.S. to developing countries was almost three times their capital (Sachs, 1989).

The strategy for dealing with the debt crisis gave precedence to averting the collapse of the banks. Thus, debtor countries were required to service their interest obligations fully as a condition for the rescheduling of their commercial debts. On top of that, much higher premiums over the London Inter-Bank Offered Rate (LIBOR) were imposed raising the real financial cost of indebtedness by over 20% in many cases (ECLAC, 1983).

The tactics used to implement the strategy are the modern version of 19th-century gunboat diplomacy. Official development assistance, both bilateral (Paris Club) and multilateral, was conditioned on restructuring agreements with the commercial banks. Official lending would be suspended until a "successful conclusion of negotiations," or whenever debtor countries go into arrears on their interest payments. In effect, a creditor cartel was formed.

Conventional debt strategy required that debt service (the commercial banks) should take precedence over development (the debtor countries) in what has been called a growth-residual approach (Monsod, 1989). The exception that proved the rule was the Mexican agreement in 1986, in which Mexico received an explicit guarantee that the funds needed to finance its growth target would be forthcoming (ECLAC, 1986). External financing would conform to growth requirements rather than the reverse. The debt-driven growth of the 1970s was replaced by a debt-service-driven collapse of the 1980s.

The impact of the strategy can be seen in terms of the gap framework above. There was a reduction in the level of foreign savings (or a leftward movement in the horizontal axis in the figures) due to the drying up of commercial lending, as well as a drop in net foreign investments (the wait—and—see syndrome). The foreign exchange constraint became binding as the economies of the debtor countries were sacrified at the altar of the international financial system. Their growth rates dropped, many to negative levels. At the same time, the only source of immediate relief from the foreign exchange constraint, i.e., a reduction in foreign interest payments, was not available. On the contrary, as stated earlier, interest payments increased as larger premiums over LIBOR were imposed.

The objective to stave off a collapse of the international financial system was achieved. By the end of 1988, the exposure of the nine major U.S. banks to developing countries had been reduced to 108%, and the head of the U.S. Federal Deposit Insurance Corporation gave them a clean bill of health (Sachs, 1989). The price of success came high, and this was borne by the developing countries in what is now called the "lost decade of development."

Table 1 (at the end of this chapter) shows the growth performance of 17 highly indebted countries (the Baker 17) as well as regions of the South during the period. Table 2 shows the situation of the banks in 1982 and 1988. The deterioration of the debtor countries is in marked contrast to the improvement of the financial situation of the banks.

This state of affairs is explained using table 3, which shows the reversal of the net transfer of resources (loan disbursement minus debt service) to developing countries from positive to negative. The commercial banks, whose net transfers became negative in 1982, are by far the largest beneficiaries of this flow, accounting for $32 billion out of the $37 billion that flowed from South to North in 1988.

What is remarkable is that net transfers of the IMF have been negative from 1985, while those from the World Bank have been negative since 1987. Bilateral net transfers dried up in 1985 and were slightly negative in 1986 and 1987.

4. THE PHILIPPINE EXPERIENCE

The four principal players in a debt crisis are the creditor governments, the debtor governments, the creditor banks, and the multilateral institutions. A combination of wrong policies, weak implementation of the right policies, and greed all contribute to the present crisis. And these remain the causes for its continuation.

4.1. Precrisis Years

A brief account of the Philippine experience serves to highlight the respective roles of the four principal players, although it will focus most on the multilateral institutions (the WB and IMF).

The 1970s for the Philippines was a period of debt—driven growth, with GNP growth rates averaging 5.9% while external debt showed a sevenfold increase. The large amounts of easily available foreign savings were used by the Marcos dictatorship as a substitute for structural reforms, rather than as a cushion for the transitional costs of needed adjustments. During this period, the Philippines entered into several standby agreements with the IMF and structural adjustment loan agreements with the World Bank, all with their accompanying conditionalities. However, the multilaterals were incredibly lax about the implementation of the policy conditionalities, as noted by Montes (1987). At the same time, the World Bank actively encouraged the Philippines to borrow more (Boyce, 1988), and looked the other way as government authorities altered the definitions of such indicators as "debt-service ratio" and "international reserves" to maintain the fiction that statutory debt-service ceilings had not been exceeded, and that international reserves were equal to at least three months worth of imports (de Dios, 1984).

The international economic environment began to deteriorate during the last part of the 1970s. This was followed in the 1980s by a recession in the developed world as oil prices rose and interest rates increased. This necessitated even more borrowing by the country to service its existing debt. Meanwhile, the deterioration of the internal macroeconomic structure continued, as reflected, among other indicators, in the increasing size of the ICOR. Whereas in 1970 it took four units of capital to produce one unit of output, by 1982 almost 10 units of capital were required. Growth decelerated at an increasing pace.

4.2. The Onset of the Crisis

Mexico's moratorium in August 1982 resulted in the drying up of commercial bank credit. The Philippines immediately felt the consequences. Within four months, the international reserves of the Central Bank decreased by over $800 million, representing a decline of more than 30%, as private credits were neither renewed nor increased. The country's financial managers called on their foreign counterparts to persuade the commercial banks of their respective countries not to cut credit so drastically, but they refused to intervene in what they called private-sector decisions.

By March 1983, with reserves decreasing by another $300 million, the Philippine authorities were ready to declare a moratorium. The banks told them to hold off until after the IMF-World Bank meetings in September of that year, since their "plate was full" with negotiations with Latin American countries. The Philippine authorities acquiesced, in an act of faith.

The price of religion came high—another $700 million in reserves was lost in the attempt to maintain the facade of creditworthiness. By the end of September 1983, the Central Bank's reserves were down to $681 million—a loss of $1.9 billion since the Mexican moratorium. This was equivalent to about 23 days of imports of goods and services, down from its former level of roughly three months of imports.

If the Philippine authorities thought that the country would be rewarded for its act of faith by way of more generous terms, they were sadly mistaken. The commercial bank negotiations that followed the moratorium took almost 19 months to finish, while the IMF took one year. The reason given by the creditors for the delay was that the Philippine authorities had been "caught" overstating the reserves of the Central Bank. Finance Minister Cesar Virata categorically denies this. He states that the Philippine authorities themselves discovered the overstatement, and instituted an independent private audit. In any case, it was the most prolonged and probably the most difficult of any negotiations of a developing-country borrower (Dohner and Intal, 1989). By waiting until their reserves were almost exhausted before taking any action (this tendency towards inaction until overtaken by events is a characteristic that continues up to the present), the Philippines had very little leverage during the negotiations. With very few reserves and the turmoil of political events following the Aquino assassination putting pressure on them to reach an agreement with the foreign creditors, the Philippine negotiators found themselves with no option but to accept the terms and conditions of the adjustment program.

The stringency of the terms and conditions imposed on the Philippines are reflected in the growth performance of the economy — a contraction of 7% in 1984 and 4% in 1985. The more strident have blamed the multilateral institutions of maliciously planning the economic collapse of highly indebted countries in order to reduce imports and improve the balance–of–payments situation so that debt payments to creditors can continue. With the picture we have presented, one wonders whether there is possibly an element of truth to these allegations.

4.3. The Aquino Government (1986–1992)

The Aquino government was faced with the task of first recovering from the country's economic collapse, and then achieving a stable growth path, while at the same time undertaking political and social reforms. It was a daunting prospect. And the government was required to do all this while servicing the debt inherited from the previous regime.

Unfortunately, the international acclaim and sympathy for the new democracy was not accompanied by concrete help. No relief from the debt burden was forthcoming. On the contrary, net transfers of resources from creditors, which were declining but still positive up to 1985, turned substantially negative in 1986, a situation that continues to the present time. Tables 4A and 4B show estimates of these net transfers, from two separate sources.

In theory, the conditionalities of the IMF are geared towards easing the foreign exchange constraint, the fiscal constraint, and the savings constraint, all within the context of equity considerations.

In practice, these conditionalities have hampered the process itself, because of the interlinkages previously discussed.

4.3.1. Raising the Foreign Exchange Constraint. The problems inherent in overcoming the foreign exchange constraint have already been discussed. In the Philippines, what happened was that import liberalization was pushed through, without the appropriate changes in the exchange rate. The IMF and the World Bank were adamant about the former but did not insist on the latter, although it was clear (Alburo, 1990) that the Philippine peso had never been competitive with its South East Asian neighbors since the 1970s (table 5). It is no wonder that the country's trade deficit is so large.

The main reasons behind the reluctance of the Philippine government to devalue also explain the IMF's lack of enthusiasm in pursuing the issue.

First, the inflationary impact of a devaluation would not be insignificant. With per capita real incomes still below their 1981 levels, the resulting social turmoil was not manageable without safety nets to cushion the blow on the most vulnerable sectors. These implied increases in government expenditures and a bigger budget deficit, which the IMF was not prepared to accept.

Second, any fall in the value of the peso would immediately be reflected in more increases in the budget deficit, as public foreign debt service denominated in pesos increased. And given the ceilings on budget deficits, as well as on public–sector borrowing, this meant either a cut in other government expenditures or a violation of IMF–imposed ceilings. In either case, the result was more difficult negotiations, possibly more conditionalities, and definitely more uncertainty.

A competitive exchange rate was absolutely necessary to generate a trade surplus. But the IMF could not insist on it while simultaneously requiring that the budget deficit and related ceilings be met. From the Philippine experience, it would seem that the latter are more important to the IMF — the debt tail wagging the economic dog.

But to implement trade liberalization without the accompanying change in the exchange-rate regime was even more myopic. These two measures go together, or not at all. But piecemeal measures help keep up the appearances of action, although they lead nowhere. The net result may have been a higher trade deficit as imports were encouraged through liberalization, but exports were discouraged through an overvalued peso.

It must be noted from the framework that the necessary resources to cushion the impact of a devaluation can be obtained by going into temporary arrears on interest payments to commercial banks, as 48 countries have done. Unfortunately, this option has been ignored so far by the Philippine's economic managers.

4.3.2. **Raising the Fiscal Constraint**. The Philippine attempts to reduce the government budget deficit read like a horror story. They were hampered from the start by an IMF condition that the national government take over the non-performing assets of the two largest government financial institutions, together with other government-controlled corporations. The wonder of it is that the IMF had made no attempt during the previous 14 years to discourage the Marcos dictatorship from the proliferation of these corporations (from 70 to over 300). In any case, the national government takeover increased its outstanding debt by 172.6 billion pesos, to more than double its previous total debt (table 6). The additional debt service amounted to 12.2 billion pesos in interest payments alone (representing more than 10% of the 1987 budget), and 10.9 billion pesos in amortization.

Second, the government budget was already burdened by the huge increases in interest payments, due to the doubling of interest rates in 1984 and 1985 (table 7), which resulted from slavishly following the IMF prescription to "mop up excess liquidity" — the euphemism for tight monetary policy, which has nothing to do with excess liquidity.

Third, the situation was further exacerbated by the fiscal authorities who were helping their monetary counterparts comply with another IMF-imposed ceiling — on money supply. The Central Bank, in 1984 and 1985, issued special bills to choke off domestic demand. And, when those obligations were retired, money was injected into the economy. To remove the effects of this injection, the national government borrowed more than it needed to finance the budget deficit, and promptly deposited its increased cash balances with the Central Bank (table 8). Cash balances increased by 18 billion pesos in 1987 and have increased by large amounts since then.

All these were additional burdens on the budget, caused directly or indirectly by IMF conditions. And they had a cumulative effect on the deficit. The government had to borrow more, which exerted upward pressure on interest rates. Interest expenditures increased because of the increase in total debt as well as in interest rates. This caused the government to borrow even more.... The end result was an ever increasing budget deficit, which can be directly linked to the foreign debt problem.

This is not all. The commitment to remain current on foreign debt service — while the structural reforms to improve the trade account were not implemented, or worse, done piecemeal, combined with a deteriorating capital account— forced the government to draw down its international reserves to finance the shortfall, fuelling speculation against the peso. Having insufficient reserves to defend the peso — the government was in fact a net buyer of foreign exchange (Gochoco, 1990), which increased the money supply — it then used interest rates to keep the exchange rate "stable." Reverse repurchase operations (Central Bank borrowing from the banks) were put into motion. This served two purposes: it made the holding of foreign exchange relatively unattractive, and it brought down the level of money supply (which it caused to increase in the first place) to meet monetary growth targets. The end result was a high-interest regime that exacerbated the government budget deficit and discouraged private investment, thereby negating the goals of high output and employment and low inflation rates. Table 7 shows the movements and large standard deviation of 91-day T-bills, an indication of constrictive and erratic monetary policy (Gochoco, 1990), which is directly related to the attempt to fulfill IMF conditionalities and keep up with the debt service.

Thus, the Philippine government had to deal with an IMF that imposed conditions that increased government expenditures but that at the same time frowned on the resulting large fiscal deficit and the size of its domestic debt service.

This overriding concern about the deficit implies profligacy on the part of the government. Yet comparative data indicate that the national-government budget deficit of the Philippines as a percentage of GNP was lower than the average for several groupings and for the total reporting economies (table 9).

Moreover, although nominal national government expenditures as a percentage of GNP have gone up by five percentage points between 1982 and 1989, the increase can be accounted for by increases in debt service payments by more than seven percentage points, while expenditures on maintenance and capital outlays decreased in their share of GNP (table 10).

In real terms, every item of national government cash expenditures, net of amortization, has decreased from 1982 levels except personal services (teachers and soldiers comprise more than half of government personnel), net lending, and interest payments, the latter being almost five times the base year figure (table 11). Note that large decreases have been suffered by infrastructure and maintenance expenditures. These decreases will have a future dampening effect on private investments, especially in the countryside. But this is ignored.

There is, in fact, very little "fat" in the budget. Recommendations to remove personnel are facile. Given civil service regulations, due process is required before personnel can be removed. An "early retirement" program has been tried—it resulted in the resignation of the more competent government personnel, who found immediate employment in the private sector. And the program was costly. The third suggested alternative has been to freeze government pay levels and force the government personnel out. Considering that one of the biggest problems in government is graft and corruption due to low government wages, this suggestion is not to be considered.

There remains one avenue left to reduce the budget deficit—and that is by increasing tax revenues. Unfortunately, the present tax structure is already heavily regressive, and the most convenient tax measures are indirect taxes. The legislature will not hear of this, and rightly so. They prefer a more efficient administration of the tax system — which, unfortunately, will take time to accomplish.

The attempts by the government to increase tax revenues or reduce expenditures are meeting with more and more opposition, with a very potent argument: why should we be asked to sacrifice for the benefit of creditors who lent to the corrupt Marcos dictatorship with full knowledge and consent?

What must be mentioned is that any attempt at a reform of the fiscal structure that will involve a net loss of revenue or an increase in expenditures, especially in the short run, is immediately rejected by the IMF, and often with tragic results. In 1986, a move to realign the duties on crude oil and taxes on petroleum products with the reformed tax structure was resisted successfully—it would have meant a reduction in easily collectible revenues. A move to increase the pay of the military to subsistence levels was deferred.

When oil prices increased in the next year, and were rightly passed on but without reducing the (ad valorem) tax rates, the result was the first nation-wide transport strike—which in turn was exploited by rightist elements in the military to stage a coup attempt, hoping to ride on the dissatisfaction of the social sectors over the slow pace of reforms and of the military on the low level of pay and benefits (Fact-Finding Commission, October 1990).

Only then did the government decrease crude oil duties and increase military pay. But the wrong signals had been given, and the resulting instability cost the economy more than would the loss in tax revenues and the increased military expenditures.

Given that the exigencies of the international debt strategy and the conditionalities of the IMF are inimical to structural reform, what explains the growth of the Philippine economy in the period 1986 to 1989?

Using again the gap framework, we can see several reasons.

The first is that increased transparency and accountability, combined with large unutilized capacity as a result of the collapse, contributed to an increase in investment efficiency—the ICOR decreased, allowing more growth per unit of incremental investment. The latter was temporary. With capacity utilization at very high levels, it has become more difficult to increase output with relatively the same increases in capital.

The second reason is that the euphoria over the regained democracy caused many Filipino citizens abroad, as well as foreign citizens of Filipino origin, to transfer funds to the Philippines (it is inaccurate to call it a return of flight capital). There was a remarkable increase in international reserves—over $1.5 billion—between February and December of 1986, bringing reserve levels up to 3.6 months worth of imports (table 12). This was used to boost the foreign exchange available to the economy in the succeeding periods. Present reserve levels are down to 1 1/2 months worth of imports.

Finally, there were external circumstances such as lower interest rates, lower oil prices, and higher prices of agricultural exports. But these have since been reversed.

Thus, real GNP growth rates increased up to 1988 (1.86% in 1986, 5.81% in 1987, 6.75% in 1988), declined in 1989 (5.67%), and as of the first semester of 1990 was down to 3.4%.

The much-touted Brady Plan has been a deep disappointment. After all was said and done, Philippine negotiations under this plan achieved a 2.5% net reduction in its debt stock, net interest savings of $85 million annually (compared to a total interest bill of $2.4 billion), and "new money" of $700 million (when the country needed, by IMF estimates, $1.4 billion to achieve its targets for 1990). So much for that plan.

Given the exogenous shocks in the second half of this year of a major earthquake and the Middle East Crisis, the Philippines is almost back to square one, i.e., the 1983 collapse. And the country is considered to be one of the best performers of the Baker 17!

5. INCREASING FOREIGN SAVINGS

Unquestionably, if any progress is to be made towards world economic stability, highest priority should be given to increasing the level of foreign savings available to developing countries in order to allow meaningful (as opposed to piecemeal or token) structural adjustments to take place. Concretely, this means action to stop the net transfer of resources from the South to the North, which is the first point of a six-point program recommended by the South Commission (1990). And it will involve all major players in the international debt crisis.

5.1. Creditor Governments

The most obvious step that can be taken by the bilaterals is to meet the global target of 0.7% of GNP for official development assistance adopted by the United Nations over 22 years ago. Denmark, the Netherlands, Norway, and Sweden have already exceeded this target, and so have Kuwait and Saudi Arabia—all without impairing their own economic performance and without losing public support. The biggest laggards in this regard are the United States, the Federal Republic of Germany, and the United Kingdom, whose aid-to-GNP ratios have in fact fallen between 1980–1984 and 1988, with Japan not far ahead (World Bank, 1990). Ironically, the reasons cited by these countries to justify their failure to meet the targets are economic and political difficulties.

Alternatives to increasing flows to the South also exist. For one, the quality of assistance can certainly be improved. Johnson's (1967) observations in this regard, made 24 years ago, are still valid today. Capital assistance more often than not involves inappropriate forms of technology, overspecification, overvaluation, tied assistance on onerous terms, etc. To use an analogy: the developing countries need motorcycles, and they are sent compact cars valued at luxury prices. The effect on ICORs, not to mention the increased maintenance costs, are disastrous. If the bilaterals were to judge their performance in this regard the way they judge aid recipients, the performance of the latter might outshine theirs.

The bilaterals can also practice what they have been preaching to the commercial banks as part of the Brady Plan—debt reduction through lower principal and interest payments. The Paris Club practice is still to restructure both principal and interest.

It is unfortunate that the bilaterals have forgotten the formula they used in the case of Indonesia during its debt crisis in the mid-1960s: significant debt reduction and new money flows, which allowed Indonesia to institute its structural reforms and maintain a sustained growth path.

5.2. The Multilateral Institutions

There can be no excuse on the part of the multilaterals for the negative net resource transfers to the developing countries in recent years. Structural changes in the manner of lending should be made. Bloated bureaucracies and overcentralized decision making, criticisms which the multilaterals level against client countries, are also applicable to themselves. A much higher proportion of program over project loans than is presently the case is indicated. Megaprojects with long gestation periods are the preference of multilaterals—then they turn around and accuse the debtor countries of poor absorptive capacity, because of the disparity between loan commitments and loan availabilities.

The tendency to ignore the time dimensions, whether in projects or in structural reform programs, must be overcome. Likewise, a reassessment of priorities between the exigencies of debt service and the necessary conditions for structural reform must be made.

5.3. The Commercial Banks

It will be recalled that the debt strategy adopted at the outset was tailored to ensure that the commercial banks would not collapse. The net transfer problem arose because of this. Debtor countries were required to service their debt fully in the face of smaller "new loney loans" (or none at all) because the banks were too weak and had to be strengthened. At present, debtors are told to expect even fewer new money loans and/or "concessions" for the opposite reason: banks are on their backs and refuse to take the risk of lending to financially weak countries.

It seems that the creditor cartel still exists. The Brady Plan calls on commercial banks for a combination of debt reduction and new money. But this is all voluntary—in the interest of free play of market forces—on the part of the banks. The asymmetric treatment of the banks today and the debtor countries at the beginning of the crisis is painfully clear: the latter were given no choice.

If any real progress is to be made in reducing the net transfer of resources to the banks, the cartel must be broken. The debtor countries and the banks must be left to their negotiations without third- and fourth-party interference, as was the case during previous international debt crises (Lindert and Morton, 1989). The Brady Plan and the IMF pronouncements about allowing lending into arrears—that is, official lending to continue to countries who have not reached agreements with the commercial banks—is still practically the exception rather than the rule.

5.4. The Debtor Countries

The debtor countries have borne the brunt of the costs of the debt crisis. But their helplessness is partly their own doing—or perhaps their lack of doing. They have wrung their hands about their lack of negotiating strength, but have not acted to change the situation. In many instances, they have also failed to display the political will to change the status quo of great disparities of wealth and power in their societies.

At the same time, the failures experienced in spite of "following a structural adjustment program" have reduced the credibility of the multilaterals and bilaterals. The disparity between what is practiced and what is preached has increased cynicism and resentment.

This, too, must be overcome. After all, during the halcyon days of easily available foreign finance, they took the path of least resistance, the soft option, as it were, and used these resources to substitute for structural reforms. At this point, what is important is not to postpone the necessary structural reforms any longer. And the necessary resources that go hand in hand with these reforms must be obtained—unilaterally if need be.

REFERENCES

Aburo, Florian (1991). "Towards a More Open Philippines: Monetary and Exchange Rate Policy." University of the Philippines School of Economics DP 9106, July.

Bacha, Edmar (1989). "A Three-gap Model of Foreign Transfers and the GDP Growth Rate in Developing Countries." Preliminary Paper. Catholic University of Rio de Janeiro, Brazil, February.

Chenery, Hollis and Michael Bruno (1962). "Development Alternatives in an Open Economy: The Case of Israel." Economic Journal, 72, pp. 29–103.

de Dios, Emmanuel S. (ed.) (1984). An Analysis of the Philippine Economic Crisis. Diliman: University of the Philippines Press.

Dohner, R. and P. Intal, Jr. (1989). "The Marcos Legacy: Economic Policy and Foreign Debt in the Philippines," in Jeffrey Sachs and Susan M. Collins, eds., Developing Country Debt and Economic Performance Vol. III. Chicago: University of Chicago Press, pp. 371–614.

Economic Commission for Latin American and the Caribbean. (1983–1989).

"Economic Survey of Latin America and the Caribbean," annual reports, 1983.

Gochoco, Ma. Socorro (1990). "The Conduct of Monetary Policy in the Philippines and its Effects on Money, Interest Rates, and Exchange Rates." Draft for NEDA report.

Johnson, Harry G. (1967). "Economic Policies Toward Less Developed Countries." New York, Frederick A. Praeger, Inc.

Lim, Joseph Y. (1990). "An Application of Bacha's Three-gap Model: The Case of the Philippines." Philippine Review of Economics and Business, Vol. XXVII No. 1, June, pp. 63–84.

Lindert, P. and P. Morton (1989). "How Sovereign Debt Has Worked" in Jeffrey Sachs, (ed.), Developing Country Debt and the World Economy. Chicago: University of Chicago Press, pp. 225–235.

Montes, Manuel F. (1987). The Philippines: Stabilization and Adjustment

Policies and Programmes." Country Paper. Helsinki: WIDER Publications, March.

Montes, Manuel F. (1989). "Philippine Structural Adjustment, 1970–1987." Philippine Macroeconomic Prespective: Development and Policies. Tokyo: Institute of Developing Economies, pp. 45–90.

Rattso, Jan (1988). "Restrictions to Economic Growth: Growth Programming for Zimbabwe." Draft, Institute of Economics, University of Trondheim, Norway, December.

Sachs, Jeffrey D. (1989). "Making the Brady Plan Work." Foreign Affairs, 89, pp. 87–103.

South Commission (1990). The Challenge to the South. (Oxford: Oxford University Press).

World Bank (1989–90). World Development Report.

World Bank (1989). World Debt Tables.

TABLE 1A.   Average growth rates of 17 highly
indebted countries

Year	Average annual growth of GNP per capita (percent)	Average annual growth of GDP (percent)
1965-73	4.2	6.6
1973-80	2.6	5.2
1980-85	-2.6	0.2
1986	1.7	3.5
1987	0.5	1.7
1988[a]	-1.0	1.5

[a]Preliminary

Source: World Bank, World Development Report,
        1990.

TABLE 1B.   Total and per capita GDP growth rates, 1960 - 1988

Region	Total GDP			Per capita GDP		
	60-70	70-80	80-88	60-70	70-80	80-88
Africa	5.9	4.1	1.1	3.2	1.1	-1.9
Asia	6.1	6.0	5.0	3.6	3.8	3.2
Latin America	5.3	5.4	1.4	2.5	2.8	-0.8

Source: South Commission, "The Challenge to the South,"
          An Overview and Summary of the South Commission
          Report 1990.

TABLE 2. Exposure of U.S. banks in the debtor countries

	End-1982	End-1986	End-1988
Nine major U.S. banks – percentage of bank capital in:			
Developing countries	287.7%	153.9%	108.9%
Latin America	176.5	110.2	83.6
All other U.S. banks – percentage of bank capital in:			
Developing countries	116.0 %	55.0 %	32.2 %
Latin America	78.6	39.7	21.8
Total bank capital (in billion of dollars)			
Nine major banks	$29.0	$46.7	$55.8
All other U.S. banks	41.6	69.4	79.8

Source: Federal Financial Institutions Examination Council: "Country Exposure Leading Survey," 1983, 1987 and 1989.

From: Sachs, 1989.

TABLE 3. Net resource transfers, all countries, 1980-1988

	1980	1982	1983	1984	1985	1986	1987	1988
Net transfers*	30,480	20,025	4,409	-9,934	-20,195	-23,577	-33,884	-36,978
Public and publicly guaranteed	27,205	25,142	12,877	1,410	-10,251	-14,234	-24,143	-27,572
Official creditors	14,280	16,464	13,741	12,959	7,283	6,013	3,951	1,255
Multilaterals	5,291	8,758	7,316	8,169	7,244	6,418	4,106	1,198
Concessional	2,221	3,320	3,112	3,187	3,515	4,175	4,737	4,914
IDA	1,476	2,399	2,169	2,312	2,574	2,821	3,488	3,372
Nonconcessional	3,070	5,438	4,204	4,982	3,729	2,244	-630	-3,716
IBRD	1,751	2,729	3,054	2,954	1,779	432	-1,439	-4,034
Bilateral	8,989	7,706	6,424	4,790	39	-406	-156	57
Concessional	5,601	5,400	3,861	4,225	3,554	3,012	5,302	4,664
Private creditors	12,925	8,677	-863	-11,549	-17,534	-20,247	-28,094	-28,827
Bonds	-378	3,487	-342	-1,125	4,116	603	-1,526	-1,745
Commercial banks	7,325	1,857	-2,355	-9,950	-20,834	-20,421	-22,104	-22,762
Other private	5,978	3,333	1,833	-474	-817	-429	-4,464	-4,320
Private nonguaranteed	3,275	-5,117	-8,468	-11,343	-9,944	-9,343	-9,740	-9,406
Memo: total commercial banks	10,600	-3,260	-10,823	-21,293	-30,778	-29,764	-31,845	-32,168
IMF	3,365	5,179	9,214	1,805	-2,074	-5,478	-8,472	-11,874

*Does not include IMF.

Source: World Debt Tables 1989-90. Volume 1. World Bank, 1989, p. 80.

TABLE 4A. Philippine Net Resource Transfers, 1980-1985

	1980	1981	1982	1983	1984	1985	1986	1987	1988
NET TRANSFERS[a]	744	674	592	811	70	77	-736	-1,502	-1,586
Public and Publicly Guaranteed	796	752	890	1,114	306	81	-521	-1,342	-1,363
Official creditors	228	612	267	761	432	34	-253	241	332
Multilateral	176	401	150	523	146	0	-188	-241	-306
Concessional	6	9	7	27	7	4	28	30	26
IDA	1	7	7	12	9	12	7	7	2
Nonconcessional	170	392	143	496	139	-4	-216	-271	-332
IBRD	123	315	77	395	29	-23	-217	-231	-313
Bilateral	52	211	117	238	287	34	-65	481	639
Concessional	59	232	109	104	124	168	172	586	702
Private creditors	568	139	623	353	-126	47	-268	-1,582	-1,695
Bonds	44	-60	-29	-27	-123	-185	-120	-219	-226
Commercial banks	452	184	653	228	-174	14	-74	-1,290	-1,472
Other private	72	16	-1	152	171	218	-74	-73	3
Private Nonguaranteed	-52	-78	-298	-303	-236	-5	-215	-160	-223
Memo: total commercial banks	400	106	355	-75	-410	10	-289	-1,451	-1,695
IMF	259	124	-158	69	-232	65	-112	-276	-176

[a]Total excludes IMF.

Source: World Debt Tables, 1989-90, Volume 2. World Bank, 1989, p. 312.

TABLE 4B. Philippine net resource transfer (NRT),
In million U.S. dollars, 1986-1992

	1986	1987	1988	1989
Net resource transfer[a]	-1,341	-1,836	-1,956	-1,391
Banks and FIs	-826	-1,222	-1,112	-1,456
Multilateral	-248	-476	-542	-44
Bilateral	93	263	91	233
Others	-360	-401	-393	-124

[a]Negative entry means net outward flow of resources.

TABLE 5. Real effective exchange rate index, Philippine
Peso, Malaysian Ringgit, Thai Baht, and Indonesian
Rupiah, May 1970 = 100

	Philippines	Malaysia	Thailand	Indonesia
1970	105.5	100.0	100.0	100.0
1971	110.0	97.8	93.8	88.0
1972	103.9	98.5	84.1	79.4
1973	103.3	101.1	80.4	84.1
1974	123.5	103.7	89.6	104.5
1975	108.4	97.6	83.8	101.0
1976	111.4	89.6	83.8	111.6
1977	110.2	85.2	78.7	110.7
1978	100.7	77.7	67.9	95.3
1979	110.0	79.1	71.1	79.0
1980	116.2	78.3	78.0	84.9
1981	118.4	77.3	80.1	85.9
1982	120.4	82.5	84.5	99.0
1983	103.5	70.3	84.2	74.0
1984	103.1	85.3	77.6	71.9
1985	108.3	78.7	67.0	74.5
1986	74.1	62.4	57.1	55.1
1987	69.6	58.1	53.4	35.8
1988	68.5	53.2	54.2	34.5
1989	72.3	52.9	56.4	35.7

Source: Central Bank of the Philippines.

TABLE 6. Outstanding debt of the national government, 1980–1989, in million pesos

Particulars	1980	1981	1982	1983	1984	1985	1986	1987	1988	1989
DOMESTIC	26,290	33,779	44,106	52,800	73,529	88,368	189,779	234,212	269,333	285,667
Regular	26,290	33,779	44,106	52,800	73,529	88,368	113,513	161,970	203,251	228,564
Assumed	0	0	0	0	0	0	76,266	72,242	66,082	57,104
FOREIGN	41,262	50,295	73,565	146,355	205,020	61,469	132,759	206,122	216,794	233,959
Regular	41,262	50,295	73,565	146,355	205,020	61,469	36,417	94,989	107,474	129,700
Assumed	0	0	0	0	0	0	96,343	111,132	109,320	104,259
Total	67,552	84,074	117,671	199,155	278,549	149,837	322,538	440,334	486,127	519,626

TABLE 7. Treasury bill rates (91-day), 1980–1989

Period	1980	1981	1982	1983	1984	1985	1986	1987	1988	1989
January	13.181	12.265	13.036	14.403	15.500	35.230	16.660	9.067	13.516	16.996
February	11.953	12.366	13.376	14.047	16.400	31.036	23.431	7.706	11.575	16.625
March	11.949	12.910	13.579	14.043	16.500	33.312	29.566	11.756	13.875	15.497
April	11.944	12.370	13.691	14.034	16.600	34.000	19.650	11.797	14.941	15.697
May	11.943	12.410	13.980	13.966	18.400	33.365	15.784	11.651	15.088	16.536
June	11.961	12.449	14.014	13.561	25.400	30.584	14.667	11.200	14.363	17.106
July	12.126	13.080	14.188	13.704	31.600	25.012	14.590	10.913	14.737	17.556
August	12.342	12.696	13.705	14.061	33.500	19.850	13.000	11.671	14.550	19.197
September	12.293	12.529	13.922	14.299	37.800	17.888	12.750	12.599	14.667	22.683
October	12.303	12.552	13.935	14.577	42.000	17.042	12.563	12.586	15.565	28.156
November	12.330	12.842	14.004	15.038	43.000	16.625	11.319	19.183	16.958	23.249
December	12.309	12.797	14.027	15.382	42.200	16.450	9.547	13.599	16.740	20.452
Yearly Average	12.141	12.606	13.811	14.173	28.240	27.048	14.432	11.390	19.406	19.333

TABLE 8.   Changes in national government cash
deposits, 1980-1989

```
--------------------------------------------------
Year        Change in Cash Deposit/Withdrawal (-)
--------------------------------------------------
1980                       1,143
1981                       3,382
1982                       1,281
1983                       2,638
1984                       8,207
1985                       1,771
1986                      (2,500)
1987                      19,800
1988                      18,058
1989                      13,200
--------------------------------------------------
```

TABLE 9.   Central government surplus/deficit as a
percentage of GNP, selected countries, selected years

	1972	1987	1988
Lower Middle Income Countries	-4.6	-6.4	-3.7
Middle Income Countries	-3.2	-7.7	-3.9
Upper Middle Income Countries	-1.8	-8.7	
High Income Countries	-1.9	-4.3	-3.3
Highly Indebted Countries	-2.7	-9.2	-3.8
Philippines	-2.0	-5.0	-2.8
Total Reporting Countries	-2.1	-4.8	-3.6

Source: World Bank, World Development Report, 1989, 1990.

TABLE 10. Expenditure program of the national government by expense class, 1980–1989 (Percent of GNP)

	1980	1981	1982	1983	1984	1985	1986	1987	1988	1989
Current operating expenditures	8.9	9.1	9.7	9.1	8.1	9.2	11.6	13.4	14.4	14.8
Personal services	3.7	4.3	4.1	3.8	3.5	3.7	4.6	4.5	5.3	5.4
Maintenance and other operating expenses	3.4	3.2	3.7	3.1	2.0	2.3	2.5	2.8	2.7	2.9
Interest payments	0.9	0.8	1.1	1.3	2.0	2.5	3.5	5.2	5.6	5.7
Assistance to local government units	0.5	0.6	0.7	0.7	0.5	0.6	0.6	0.5	0.5	0.3
Subsidy to corporations	0.5	0.2	0.2	0.2	0.2	0.2	0.3	0.2	0.3	0.4
Tax expenditures	0.0	0.0	0.0	0.0	0.0	0.0	0.0	0.2	0.1	0.0
Capital outlays	4.7	6.3	4.4	4.1	3.2	2.6	3.6	2.9	2.2	2.8
Infrastructure	1.8	2.0	1.7	1.6	0.9	1.0	0.9	1.0	1.0	1.0
Corporate equity	2.2	3.5	2.2	1.5	1.7	0.8	2.0	0.7	0.3	0.3
Other capital outlays	0.7	0.7	0.5	1.0	0.6	0.6	0.6	1.3	0.9	1.5
Net lending	0.3	0.3	0.7	0.6	0.8	2.1	2.5	1.1	0.6	0.2
Principal amortization	0.5	0.5	0.4	0.9	0.9	0.7	1.0	4.7	3.1	2.9
GRAND TOTAL	14.4	16.2	15.2	14.7	13.0	14.6	18.6	22.0	20.3	20.7

Source: Department of Budget and Management.

TABLE 11. National government cash disbursements as a percentage of 1982 real levels, 1980-1987

	1980	1981	1982	1983	1984	1985	1986	1987
Current Operating Expenditures	92.9	90.2	100.0	97.4	80.7	88.0	104.8	139.5
Personnel Services	105.5	108.3	100.0	116.7	94.6	108.7	116.7	141.7
Maintenance and Other Operating Expenses	98.0	92.7	100.0	81.1	56.2	50.6	56.7	66.4
Assistance to Local Government Units	77.4	70.5	100.0	98.0	69.8	74.9	74.8	84.0
Interest Payments	77.6	74.0	100.0	125.6	174.8	208.1	301.9	480.8
Subsidies	37.8	28.7	100.0	49.9	13.0	25.8	43.2	43.0
Capital Outlays	83.4	120.8	100.0	77.5	62.9	62.8	75.8	43.1
Infrastructure	130.5	159.7	100.0	91.8	55.3	41.1	57.5	50.3
Corporate Equity	58.1	93.6	100.0	54.8	62.8	77.5	65.5	21.9
Other Capital Outlays	50.9	117.1	100.0	123.7	84.1	66.4	76.5	103.2
Net Lending	36.6	45.4	100.0	96.6	119.2	38.2	339.6	148.0
Total Disbursements	87.2	99.1	100.0	90.3	76.0	77.0	104.4	105.7

TABLE 12. Gross international reserves of the Central Bank,
1980–1990, in million U.S. dollars

End of Period	Q_1	Q_2	Q_3	Q_4	Months of Imports (End of Period)
1980	2,530.54	2,712.43	2,726.17	3,155.37	(3.6)
1981	2,865.10	2,596.50	2,548.78	2,573.96	(2.8)
1982	2,498.77	2,585.19	2,448.53	1,711.38	(1.8)
1983	1,368.14	1,134.43	681.65	864.70	(0.9)
1984	869.07	631.78	471.26	886.06	(1.1)
1985	587.96	1,036.91	1,436.57	1,061.14	(1.5)
1986	1,243.56	1,601.79	1,710.35	2,458.98	(3.6)
1987	2,484.29	2,359.57	2,111.83	1,958.68	(2.3)
1988	1,807.48	1,725.10	1,628.87	2,059.00	(2.1)
1989	1,799.25	1,564.00	1,537.00	2,324.00	(1.9)
1990	1,751.03	1,974.00			(1.5)

17. SOME IMPLICATIONS OF THE DEVELOPMENTS IN EASTERN EUROPE FOR THE EUROPEAN ECONOMIC AND MONETARY UNION

Giorgio Basevi[1]
University of Bologna
Italy

ABSTRACT. This chapter will consider what could be some important consequences of recent developments in Eastern Europe for the present fabric of the European Community (EC) and its evolution into a European Economic and Monetary Union (EEMU).

The main issue discussed will be the possibility that the recent developments in Eastern Europe could make it more attractive for the countries at the core of the EC to widen the geographical scope of the Community as a common market for goods, while at the same time making it less attractive to proceed further towards integration of the old Community within a full monetary union. Thus, the issue is whether the attempt to enlarge the EC in order to help reshape the economies of Eastern Europe may widen the "economic" side of the EEMU (let us call it the EEU)) at the cost of shrinking its "monetary" side (let us call it the EMU). The first side of this issue—widening the EC—is mainly discussed in section 1; the second side—deepening the EC—is mainly discussed in section 2. Interrelations between the two sides are intrinsic to the issue, and so such programmatic separation is somewhat artificial. Thus, in section 3, an attempt will be made to pull together the two arguments and attempt some conclusion.

The analysis of this issue will be limited to economic reasoning, even though because of this limitation, the conclusions may very well be different from those that would follow if political elements were also considered. In fact the very distinction between economic and political points of view is artificial in the context of structural changes such as those that have affected Europe in the last few years.

1. WIDENING THE EUROPEAN COMMUNITY

1.1. The Economic Dimensions of a Wider EC.

Because the political geography of Europe could experience additional changes — following those that, for the time being, have culminated in the reunification of the two Germanies— it may be useful to start with some basic statistical data

---

[1]I am grateful to Casper de Vries for the useful discussions we had on the implications of his work for the problems discussed in this chapter. I also benefitted from a debate with Francesco Giavazzi at a forecasting meeting of Prometeia, Bologna. Giorgio Poli has helped with his usual kind assistance.

on the dimensions of the European countries and their possible new aggregations, relative to the U.S. and Japan. This is done in table 1.

The successive enlargements of the EC considered in the aggregations of table 1 are hypothetical (except for the first one, which has already taken place with the political unification of Germany). Their character frames the analysis of this chapter within a long run point of view, since it is difficult to expect that the necessary political developments-- assuming that they will take place-- would proceed as fast as in the case of Germany.

These hypothetical widenings of the EC are based on 1) the inclusion of East Germany, already realized; 2) the additional enlargement to the EFTA countries; 3) the additional enlargement to the three countries of Eastern Europe that seem more likely to meet the criteria for admission in the EC at some future date, namely Czechoslovakia, Hungary, and Poland.[2]

Comparing the situation before German unification with the one that would result if 1988 population data were to apply to the largest new EC here considered (i.e., the NNEC), the EC would move up from being (before German unification) 1.3 times the U.S. and 2.6 times Japan, to becoming 1.8 times the U.S. and 3.5 times Japan. In terms of GDP, the EC would move from being about equal to the U.S. and 1.7 times Japan, to becoming 1.3 times the U.S. and 3.5 times Japan.

By enlarging its domain, the EC would also be larger in terms of its export trade. Regarding the net of intra-area trade, the EC would increase its export trade from being 1.3 times that of the U.S. and 1.6 times that of Japan, to becoming, in its wider hypothetical enlargement, 1.6 times that of the U.S. and twice that of Japan.

However, its impressively larger economic size will clearly not give to the EC a comparable political weight until the process of economic and political integration of the Community is completed.

1.2. Advantages and Problems from Widening the EC

Because much trade is already taking place between the present EC and the EFTA countries, and, even more importantly, because more trade could develop from enlarging the EC to the East European countries (including the already realized enlargement to East Germany), it is arguable that--particularly for the core countries of Europe, with Germany at the center--the new challenges and opportunities offered by economic restructuring of Eastern Europe will overshadow the momentum already triggered by the incoming enactment of the integrated "internal" market at the end of 1992.

In fact, it is probable that the economic (and political) center of the EC will drift eastward, possibly at the expense of the EC Mediterranean members. This may explain, quite aside from political reasons, the different and partly new attitudes that are developing in Germany and her closest neighbors, on one side, and in France, Italy, Spain and their minor neighbors, on the other side, also with respect to transforming the EC into a full EEMU--with the United

---

[2]For the chances of such admission, see "The makings of a new constella-tion," in The Economist, August 4, 1990, pp. 17-18. For a useful survey of the prospect of expanding the Community as a result of the East European events see "A survey of the European Community," The Economist, July 7, 1990.

Kingdom being able, for once, to present its originally odd position as a compromise rather than as a dilatory one.

While these different attitudes will be interpreted in section 2 as reflections of other elements, they can also be justified by the preferential position in which the central countries of Europe are placed, relative to the peripheral ones, with respect to their capacity to exploit the new opportunities for trade with the East and with the EFTA countries, if these were all to join the EC. Table 2 shows (columnwise) that, while export trade directed towards EFTA and towards the Eastern countries (East Germany, Czechoslovakia, Hungary, and Poland) by the EC group composed of West Germany, Benelux, and Denmark, is larger than similar export trade by the two other EC groups, one composed of France, Italy, Spain, and the rest of the EC, and the other composed of the U.K. only, yet it is relatively much larger towards the Eastern European group than towards EFTA (72.89/64.69 is the highest of the three ratios). On the other hand, considering the total in table 2 across rows, while all three EC groups are more interested by EFTA, the U.K. is comparatively more interested, while the comparative importance of the Eastern countries is larger for the EC group centered around West Germany (11.96/88.04 is the largest of the three ratios, and 7.81/92.19 is the smallest).

The preferential position of the central countries of Europe with respect to the prospective East European members may also result from the larger financial exposure that the latter have vis-à-vis the central European countries than vis-à-vis the peripheral ones. It seems natural to assume that, on the one hand, such larger exposure will continue to generate larger concentration of East European imports from their main European creditor countries, and, on the other hand, that the European creditor companies, in order to reduce such exposure, will try to redirect their imports from their traditional suppliers to their main debtors in Eastern Europe.

Another set of challenges from widening the EC concerns the consequences for the European Common Agricultural Policy (CAP). These consequences may result in a a net advantage for the Community; however, the distribution of advantages and disadvantages is ambiguous. The current, although gradual, application of CAP to the whole of Germany, and prospectively to other members from the East or from EFTA, provides a healthy opportunity for reconsidering it radically. Its reconsideration may, however, take both positive and negative tracks. On the positive side:

1. the greater industrial development that will result, at least in central Europe, from integration with the Eastern markets should, for given specialization, reduce the economic and political importance of the agricultural sector in the core countries of the EC, and thus make it easier for the EC to reduce its protection, which weighs heavily on the industrial sector (not dissimilarly from the situation of Britain at the time of the Corn Laws);

2. the need to search for a liberalized structure of comparative advantage vis-à-vis the EFTA countries, with whom trade is mainly of the intra-industry type, and the different agricultural policies of these countries, should in any case require redesigning CAP, possibly in a more rational way; and

3. the need to reestablish a more traditional basis of comparative advantage, mainly characterized by interindustry (rather than intra-industry) trade, with the East European countries, should also require leaving to them a larger share of agricultural production, where they will probably enjoy in the long run a sounder comparative advantage than the artificial one created in the EC by CAP.

On the negative side, those members of the EC that will reap smaller benefits from the new industrial development of an enlarged EC may object to reconsidering that part of CAP that protects their agricultural products. However, positive forces could play against this negative effect, e.g., the need to help in a different way (i.e., with more trade, rather than with aid) the African countries that are associated with the EC and that will suffer from the eastward redirection of EC investments and general economic interest. This would mean reducing protection of Mediterranean agricultural products—which is requested by the Southern members of the EC—and compensating them with a larger share of the gain that the whole EC economy would get from a less protectionist CAP and higher industrial growth.

The eastward drift of the economic center of the EC and the new opportunities for trade that this will involve cast some shadows on the relative importance of the new "internal" market to be enacted at the beginning of 1993. In preparation for that event—which implies a full European economic union, EEU —some estimates have been provided of its economic importance.[3] Similarly, a study is currently under way at the Commission to measure the advantages that would result from extending the EEU to full economic and monetary union (EEMU). While aspects of EMU will be mainly discussed in section 2, it could be argued that the economic advantages of 1993 (EEU) may be either overestimated or made uncertain as a consequence of the new developments in Eastern Europe.

These advantages may be overestimated because the new challenges and opportunities of enlarging the EC eastward may reduce the economic interest of the core EC countries in further integration with their traditional EC partners. Instead they may redirect their investment of resources—human and capital— towards the newly opening markets and the huge needs of their reconstruction.

The advantages of EEU may be made uncertain because the widening of the Community's scope eastward—and in particular the monetary unification of Germany—already seem to have started slowing down the process of completing EEU with EMU (and thus moving to full EEMU). Witness the recent difficulties in setting a date for the beginning of phase 2 that was programmed in the Delors Report, or for determining its length before the final inception of phase 3. This slowing down—even though denied politically or attributed to prexisting economic factors or failures by some EC members, such as Italy, Spain, or the U.K.—is an already observable fact, and contains the risks that even the old structure that interconnects the present members of the EC may suffer some dangerous cleavages.

2. DEEPENING THE EUROPEAN COMMUNITY

2.1. Widening the EC at the Expense of its Deepening.

Section 2 suggests that the developments in Eastern Europe have released economic forces that may lead to a widening of the EC (beyond the already achieved reunification of Germany), through inclusion of some or all of the EFTA countries and some of the East European countries. A concern has been raised that such widening may be gained at the cost of less deepening of the economic integration of the traditional EC. This danger is further analyzed in this section, particularly with respect to integrating the EC as a market both for goods and for factors of production (thus moving towards the EEU component of EEMU), and

---

[3]See "Cecchini Report" (1988) and Baldwin (1989).

with respect to the process leading to European monetary unification (thus also moving towards the EMU component of EEMU). In this respect, rather than the developments in the rest of Eastern Europe, the triggering element has been the monetary and now also political unification of Germany, which is fast proceeding to its full economic integration. This has raised a number of questions.

The first set of questions asks whether German unification will slow down or accelerate the progress towards EEMU. Usually the answer is based on political arguments; it is suggested that unification would strengthen the desire of Germany's partners to unify Western Europe, in order to check within it the overwhelming power of the new Germany. A subsidiary form of these questions is whether the fast monetary unification of the two Germanies revitalizes the "two speeds approach" to integration of the remaining EC countries. Another subsidiary question is whether German unification will further delay or anticipate Britain's entrance into the exchange rate mechanism (ERM) of the European Monetary System (EMS) and its eventual transformation into EMU. This first set of questions is dealt with in section 2.2.

The second set of questions asks whether German unification will change the outcome of the EEMU process, and in particular the monetary and fiscal policies and institutions that shall eventually characterize it. This set of questions is dealt with in section 2.3.

Both sets of questions may also be raised from a slightly different view-point: Why has German monetary unification (GMU) been accomplished in one step rather than gradually, by choosing as the common currency and central bank those of one of the two countries? In the case of EMU, the process designed by the Commission is gradual, and the resultant currency and institutions should be new ones. The relation between this point of view (which is discussed in Willms, 1990) and the two sets of questions analyzed in this section 2 is clear. In fact, this chapter analyzes whether German unification will change the process and the final outcome of EEMU; Willms (1990), on the other hand, wonders what is specific to the case of Germany that makes the process and the outcome of GMU different from that of EMU. Knowledge of such specificity may throw light on the question of whether the process and the outcome of EEMU may or should be changed as a consequence of GMU.

2.2. The Progress Towards EEMU.

Clearly, German unification could either accelerate or slow down the process of integration of Western Europe. Less clearly, it could disintegrate the set of countries involved in that process by making some of them keen to accelerate it and others more inclined to slow it down. Thus it could revive the so-called "two speeds approach" to European integration.

While the economic side of the process and the outcome of EEMU is already well specified and on track at least until 1993, so that the danger of slowing or disintegrating it is less likely, its monetary side—designed last year in the Delors Report (1989)—has been the subject this year of renewed debate, initially and more openly from the British side, but more recently also from the Spanish and, most notably, the German side.[4]

2.2.1. Convergence of Monetary and Fiscal Policies. The view of the Commission, in brief, is that the plan and the schedule drafted in the Delors Report should be made more precise and accelerated in reply to the challenge of German unification and Eastern European developments. Recent declarations by the Deutsche Bundesbank have thrown cold water on this view.

The position of the German monetary authorities is now openly opposed to proceed further or faster until greater convergence of fundamental monetary and fiscal variables is achieved among the members of the EC that really want to embark into EMU, and not just be part of EEU. Whether or not this change in attitude is really determined by the reasons officially presented will be considered later; however, it is at least clear that, in relation to this new German stand, the British position recently reshaped in the form of a proposal for a parallel currency, called the "hard ECU," that would never be depreciated vis-à-vis the national EC currencies is less than in the past exposed to the criticism of being inspired by ideological or political obstructionism. For once, the British may even play a mediatory role, between tough German leadership and Brussels cooperative federalism.[5]

If, we concentrate on the German position for both its political weight and simplicity, we may summarize it by stating that convergence should come before and not after monetary integration or unification.[6] On the basis of this position, it is far from clear that all countries that are supposed to move towards full monetary unification during phase 2 of the Delors plan, have already achieved the degree of convergence that is necessary for giving up realignments

---

[4]The relative positions of the various countries with respect to this debate are well presented in "Rethinking Europe's EMU" and "Not so fast, Jacques," The Economist, September 15, 1990.

[5]For the British position, as presented in June by Mr. John Major, Chancellor of the Exchequer, see Financial Times, June 22, 1990. The "new" position of the Bundesbank has been presented in a press communique in September 1990.

[6]This is no new argument, since it has often reappeared in the history of European unification. It was particularly developed during the projects leading to the aborted Werner plan for monetary unification at the end of the 1960s and in the early 1970s. The two positions were at that time identified as a "monetarist" one (whereby monetary unification, by coming first, could bring with it deeper economic integration) and an "economist" one (supporting a reversed procedure; monetary unification could not succeed unless preceded by economic convergence and integration). More recently, at least in academic circles, the "monetarist" position has apparently gained ground by being newly based on a mix of political and economic arguments that emphasize the importance of the Central Bank's reputation and the credibility of its precommitments, or the superiority of monetary rules over discretionary policies. On this, see, among others, Giavazzi and Pagano (1988) and Giavazzi and Giovanini (1989).

of exchange rates during that phase. Moreover, such incomplete convergence does not bode well for the the independence of the new European Central Bank, or for a currency such as the traditional ECU, that should at least initially be a weighted average of the individual currencies of the present 12 members of the EC, managed by separate Central Banks, although cooperatively.

Since the reservations of the Deutsche Bundesbank concern the ability of a cooperative European monetary policy to be aimed only at price stability, independently of fiscal or other political considerations, the empirical basis of the Bundesbank's distrust must be based on variables measuring that ability for the various countries that should be part of EEMU. Price inflation is certainly one such variable. More than by the statutes of central banks, political independence is usually represented by the danger that large Government debts or reckless fiscal policies may eventually bend monetary policy to fiscal purposes rather than to price stability—in other words, that the need to finance current Government expenditures or to reduce the accumulation of past Government deficits may be resolved through the inflation tax. Thus, in addition to actual price inflation, the danger of future inflationary policies is measured by the importance of current Government deficits or by the weight of Government debt.

Figure 1 shows the average price inflation rates during the period 1970–1989 for a partition of the EC countries and for EFTA. West Germany, the group of Benelux plus Denmark, and EFTA present the best performance (with Germany clearly in the lead); France and the U.K. occupy the middle positions; Italy, Spain, and the rest of the EC come gradually last. However, figure 2A shows that the dispersion of inflation rates (measured by the coefficient of variation across each individual country belonging either to the EC or to EFTA), after having reached a peak in 1986, has been falling since. Because the German criticism is directly addressed to the countries belonging to the EMS, figure 2B presents the corresponding graph for them only. Notice that, relative to the larger group of EC and EFTA countries, the EMS group has had a lower dispersion of inflation rates throughout the period. Notice also how dispersion has been falling since 1986: that year marks, with the last effective realignment of EMS parities at the beginning of 1987, the end of a regime of adjustable parities in the EMS and its "de facto" transformation into a regime of fixed parities, with stronger discipline on monetary policies in the more inflationary–prone countries of the EC. In fact, at the end of the period, the degree of dispersion of inflation rates has almost reached the same low level that it had at the beginning when exchange rates were still fixed according to the Bretton Woods system.

Figure 3 graphs the difference between the inflation rates of the main EC countries and of the Benelux plus Denmark, relative to West Germany, during the same period. The graph shows that, although all inflation differentials have been progressively reduced since about 1980 —with the exception of the Spanish datum for 1986— the EC remains divided into two groups: France and the Benelux (plus Denmark) on one side, with an inflation rate which has already been lowered to the German one; and the U.K., Italy, and Spain, on the other side, with a still significantly higher inflation.

Figure 4 depicts the behavior of Government deficits (measured as the difference between consumption expenditures of the Government net of taxation) as ratios to GDP. Here the odd country is reduced to one, namely Italy, while the others have more or less converged to the West German level by 1989. Noting this, enables us to examine the grounds for the argument that some fiscal policies are persistently out of line in the EC, without implying that their convergence should be advocated, regardless of the economic cycle in different countries. In any case, since the worries about the inflationary potential of fiscal deficits are based on the needs to finance the whole of Government expenditure requirements, a better measure is provided by comparing the different countries' Public-Sector Borrowing Requirement (PSBR). This is done in figure 5, which shows the same odd situation for Italy, and somewhat less convergence to the German level for the other countries (but here the "best" recent performance is by the U.K.).

Both the data on inflation rates and on Government deficits (or PSBRs) show the current evolution of monetary and fiscal policies. However, the worries referred to above are based even more on the inflationary potential accumulated through past deficits and their influence on future behavior of monetary policy. This is described more directly by the accumulated Government debt, whose burden may become unbearable and thus may make it impossible to maintain a monetary policy independent from fiscal needs. Figure 6A presents, again for the main countries of the EC, the Government debt ratios with respect to GDP in 1989. Again Italy appears to be the odd country, and the U.K. the best one. West Germany takes the lead when considering net Government debt (figure 6B), while Italy remains in last position. However, if we were also to consider the smaller EC countries, Italy would not be the worst of the group.

Thus, on the basis of the admittedly simple evidence presented in these graphs, it seems that there are empirical grounds for considering the EC as being composed of countries with systematically different attitudes towards inflation, and with different fiscal and debt heritages hanging on the future of their monetary policies. On the first point, there appears to be a low-inflation group, made up of both Germany and France, plus Denmark and the Benelux countries, and a high inflation group, made up of the U.K., Italy, and Spain. On the second point, there seems to be only one country (namely, Italy) on the odd side—at least if we consider only the main ones.

Thus, the German stand for a program of monetary unification that is either delayed for all countries, or, if it cannot be delayed, should only apply to a subset of the EMS countries, does not seem to be unreasonable. However, one curious element should make us suspicious about accepting this as the only justification for the German stand. After all, the odd position of some EC countries with respect to inflation and fiscal policy has been known for a long time. It is strange that, just at this time, the Deutsche Bundesbank has come out so bluntly to restate that its convergence to the average (or, rather, to the German) level is a prerequisite for proceeding further towards EEMU or for admitting those countries into the new club.

We should therefore search for new elements that may justify why the German position, although not really new, has certainly been expressed with a new tone and at a well-chosen time, i.e., just before the incoming political conferences to determine the new schedule and shape of EEMU. One naturally thinks of the new developments in Eastern Europe, and more particularly German monetary unification. Rather than looking for justification only in the monetary and fiscal policies of the EC countries, we should also consider structural economic elements, old and new. These may refer not only to Germany's partners, but also to Germany itself and to its relations with the economic structures of East Germany and the East European countries. It will be shown in the next sections that a more complete and convincing picture appears when we add these structural elements to the traditional arguments about the inadequate convergence of monetary and fiscal policies.

2.2.2. **Convergence of Economic Structures.** The arguments and data presented above refer to variables of primary interest to those monetary authorities who, like the German ones, give high priority to price stability and independence. But perhaps, on the grounds of economic variables different from purely monetary or fiscal ones, the EC countries should not all proceed at the same speed or in one step towards full economic integration. The question then becomes less one of debating a "monetarist" versus an "economist" school, and more one of knowing whether it is possible or advisable that all countries proceed at the same speed toward both monetary and economic integration.

The theoretical framework for analyzing the process of structural economic integration depends upon the objective of the analysis. This could be finding the sustainable sequences among the many that are possible, or identifying the optimal sequence among the set of sustainable sequences in the process of economic integration.

In a recent paper, Dellas and De Vries (1990) distinguish two strands of thought in previous economic literature in this field, and propose a third one. The first two strands rely on "second-best" arguments for a gradual process towards integration, whereas the third one relies on "first-best" arguments. A fourth strand takes the direction of traditional trade theory, which can be used to examine how the integration of East European countries (and in particular of East Germany) within the framework of market economies may require changing the terms of trade or the real exchange rates among the EC countries. This would strain their monetary relations, possibly endangering the fabric of the EMS and even the completion of the EEMU, unless room is left in that fabric either for entering it at different stages or for some intermediate flexibility. This fourth strand of analysis has something to say both on the process and on the final outcome of EEMU.

The first two strands of thought identify market frictions or market failures as the basis for moving toward unification in a gradual way; thus they are second-best arguments relative to a first-best economic situation, where no frictions or failures exist so that no such argument could apply.

According to the first strand, these frictions are due to costs of adjustment or costs of delay, so that countries may want to move faster or slower depending on their particular cost functions. Similarly, according to the second strand, frictions could be different for different markets, with some markets finding their equilibrium faster than others, thus requiring countries to integrate first the markets that adjust less rapidly towards equilibrium (such as the product and labor markets), and only later the fast-adjusting markets.

Notice that the argument of this second strand of the literature refers different speeds of integration to different markets, rather than to different countries. However, insofar as different markets may find their equilibrium more or less efficiently in different countries, this argument may also suggest internationally different speeds of integration. Thus labor markets may be more or less regulated in some countries, and their variables (wages and salaries, or employment) may be more or less sensitive to market disequilibria. Countries with more efficient labor markets could presumably integrate at lower costs than countries with less efficient ones.

Notice also that, according to this line of thought, it seems difficult to understand why labor markets in the Community have been integrated less or later than product markets. Insofar as they are less efficient than product markets, they should have been integrated first. Also, if they are less efficient, trade theory could not be invoked to argue that integrating product markets will produce the same equilibrium that would result from integrating factor markets. Hence the very rationale of the 1993 "internal" market program is that free trade of products throughout the EC is not enough. Unless other factor markets—both capital and labor—are also fully integrated, and unless nontradable sectors are opened to indirect competition from other member countries through freedom of establishment, full economic integration of the EC will not be achieved.

However, let us disentangle positive from normative analysis. On the positive side, it could be argued that more efficient markets are easier to integrate, at least economically: thus capital markets should come first, product markets second, labor markets last. On the normative side, because of the costs of adjustment, it could be argued that countries should first integrate the slow-adjusting markets, in order to avoid a backlash from efficient markets on the less efficient ones, with the overshooting effect so familiar from the exchange-rate literature.

In any case, the relationship between the cost of integration and its speed must be clearly specified; in the end, it should involve both the sequence of costs and benefits, and the social versus the political rates for discounting that sequence. Only an analysis based on the discounted value of social and political objective functions could deal with a normative evaluation of the results.

If, with much simplification, we summarize the process of integration already followed or still planned in the EC, it would appear that a compromise has been struck between positive and normative points of view, since tradable product markets have been integrated first, general labor markets second, money and financial markets third, and the nontradables or other artificially protected markets coming last. A question that arises with respect to the new challenges coming from Eastern Europe ––and in particular with the migration of labor already experienced from those countries and at least temporarily diminished from East Germany–– is whether the same sequence will also be adopted with respect to the eastward enlargement of the EC.

The third strand of analysis, proposed by Dellas and De Vries (1990), is cast in terms of a neoclassical growth–theoretic model.[7] Their reference is to positive theory (identifying the sustainable sequences in the integrating process), but they can hardly avoid normative implications (identifying the optimal sequence). Also, the sequential difference that they discuss is one between an international liberalization of factor markets that immediately leads to an integrated endowment of factors (one–stroke or "precipituous" integration), and a liberalization that must be preceded or accompanied by steps aimed at making the eventual merging of factor endowments sustainable (gradual or "piecemeal" integration).

As already mentioned, this analysis does not rely on market frictions or failures, but on the possible existence of multiple equilibria, in order to justify a gradual process towards international economic integration. Thus the approach, although grounded on theoretical characteristics that may be difficult to test, has the advantage of being a "first–best" argument for gradualism; as such it is complementary to, rather than a substitute for, "second–best" arguments for gradualism, as discussed by Willms (1990) on the basis of the theory of "optimum currency areas."

---

[7]For the model used by Dellas and De Vries, see Blanchard and Fischer (1989), ch. 3.

The gist of the argument is captured by figure 7, where the function g is the capital accumulation function that, on the basis of the production capacity and savings behavior of a country, relates current--to previous-period capital/labor ratios. Even with a well-behaved neoclassical production function, more than one equilibrium point could exist. In figure 7 three positively valued equilibria exist, with the low and the high K/L ones being stable and the intermediate one being unstable. This can be checked by projecting successive K/L ratios through the diagonal: if a country's K/L ratio is to the left of point B, it will progressively step down to point A; if it is to the right of B, it will progressively step up to C.

A worrying possibility is that two countries that find themselves in equilibria separated by an unstable one (as at points A and C in figure 7), may --by deciding to integrate their capital and/or labor markets, i.e., to merge their separate K/L ratios into a common weighted one-- end up in one stroke to the left of the unstable equilibrium point B, and thus converge together to A, the lower of the two stable equilibrium points. In this case the low-capital/labor-ratio country (i.e., the one with the $(K/L)_L$ ratio) attracts the high one (i.e., the one with the $(K/L)_H$ ratio) into its low original position. This position is considered less efficient than that for the high capital/labor, since with given labor endowments in the two countries or given equal rates of growth, it corresponds to smaller production possibility sets.

In this case it can be shown that, while a precipitous (i.e., one-stroke) integration of the two countries' capital and labor markets may lead to the low equilibrium point, there may also exist a preliminary transfer of capital from the high to the low K/L ratio country (or a contrary transfer of labor from the low to the high K/L country), followed by an integration of their factor markets, such that the two merged countries would land to the right of the unstable equilibrium point, and therefore jointly converge from there to the highest K/L equilibrium point.

Notice an interesting implication of this case. Other things being given, precipitous factor market integration is more likely to be efficient the larger is the capital-abundant country relative to the labor-abundant country--where size is measured by the ratio of a country's labor force to the total of the two countries' labor force. This suggests that countries of similar size should be more careful in integrating their factor markets in a precipitous way, whereas countries of smaller size could, with a higher probability of success, proceed to one-stroke integration of their factor markets with larger countries.

Although obtained from a simple but elegant theoretical model, in which many empirical economic and political elements are missing, such a result suggests why smaller countries that are clustered around a larger one--such as the Benelux countries, Denmark, or even Austria and Switzerland, not to speak of East Germany--may find it easier than larger countries to integrate their economies with that of the largest country (e.g., West Germany). Notice that this result is in line (although for different theoretical reasons) with an element of the theory of optimum currency areas, i.e., the one based on the degree of trade openess of a country vis-à-vis its prospective main partner.

According to this model, it could be against the interest of a large country (e.g., Germany) to integrate with countries of not much smaller size (such as France and Italy), since these could be large enough to attract it into their lower equilibrium point. The large country may instead be indifferent, and thus possibly willing, to integrate with much smaller countries (such as, again, the Benelux and other small countries neighboring Germany). On their side, the smaller countries would be indifferent between precipitous or gradual integration —-indeed between integrating or not with the large country-- if integration were to attract the larger country into the smaller-country equilibrium. The smaller countries would be interested only if integration, gradual or otherwise, were leading them to the higher position of equilibrium. Thus the large country would be interested in integration --whether with small or large countries-- only if it could eventually obtain from its partners a compensation for bringing them up to its higher position.

These results partly fit the actual experience of the EC. Until recently, the EC's larger members, such as France and Italy, found difficulties in moving to fast integration of their capital markets with that of Germany, while smaller members were more inclined to move fast. Also in line with these results is the greater willingness of Germany to integrate itself closely with smaller than with about equal-sized countries. Even though political elements were clearly dominant, the model could also be stretched to explain the desire of East Germany to integrate quickly with West Germany, and some initial attempts by the latter to slow down that process. In fact the German case seems to fit the "transfer cum integration" approach and the likelihood that, in the long run, the larger country (West Germany) will be "compensated" for the transfers that it has to grant initially in order to implement a successful integration with East Germany.

Clearly, other elements must be introduced in the model in order to capture the complexities of the German case. A possibility, that would link this analysis to the traditional trade-theoretic model discussed below (section 2.3.1.) is that German unification, by making the capital stock of East Germany suddenly obsolete and thus to be partly scrapped, would land East Germany to the left of a lower and unstable equilibrium. From here East Germany would move to an even lower one (see the movement from point $(K/L)_M$ to point $(K/L)_L$ in figure 8), possibly attracting West Germany (initially located at $(K/L)_H$) down to that equilibrium point as well unless the latter were to assist it with transfers high enough to take the joint K/L ratio to the right of the unstable point D.

Another possibility is that, rather than requiring capital stock to be scrapped, transformation of the East German economy into a market economy would require changing its production function to a more efficient one (from g_e to g_w in figure 9). In this case, the new higher capital accumulation function would, for the same K/L ratio, correspond to a point to the left of a new unstable equilibrium, and thus make East Germany fall to a lower K/L ratio (from $(K/L)_L$ to $(K/L)_{LL}$). Again, adequate assistance in the form of a capital transfer from West Germany might be necessary prior to integrating at a point to the right of C so that both could proceed to point D.

As already pointed out with respect to "second-best" arguments for gradualism in economic integration, it is not easy to distinguish between gradualism with reference to different markets and with reference to different countries. This can be easily done within the "first-best" model just discussed, since in its simpler formulation there is just one homogenous product, and the two factor markets (labor and capital) play a symmetric role in the process of integration. Indeed, this model provides a simple but elegant theoretical basis for arguing in favor of the so-called "two speeds approach" to European economic integration. This approach, particularly discussed in relation to integrating capital markets among the EMS countries and moving ahead towards narrower bands for exchange-rate fluctuations in the ERM, is now again on the foreground of debate concerning the fate of the Delors plan.

In order to analyze meaningfully the "two speeds approach," we need to consider in our model at least three countries and three stable equilibrium points. An example is shown in figure 10, where, with four stable equilibrium points, three correspond to the K/L ratios of three different countries before integration of their factor markets.

Apparently, with three countries, there are five possibilities: 1) precipitous integration of all three countries, 2) gradual integration among all three countries, 3) precipituous integration between countries 1 and 2, followed by their gradual integration with country 3, 4) precipitous integration between countries 1 and 3, followed by country 2, and 5) precipitous integration between countries 2 and 3, followed by country 1. Clearly, for the "two speeds approach," only possibilities 3 to 5 are of interest. Upon closer consideration, however, a larger set of possibilities can be identified. The two countries to be selected for merging their factor markets before integration with the third country, may themselves move to such merging with or without a preliminary transfer (i.e., by piecemeal or by precipitous integration), and then successively integrate in a precipitous or piecemeal way with the third country. Conceptually, therefore, each one of the three pairings of countries gives rise to four possibilities. Thus, there are in total 12 possibilities in which a "two-stage" (rather than a "two speeds") approach could be applied to a community composed of three groups of countries. The first stage is when a pair of countries (or of groups of countries) integrates first (whether precipitously or gradually); the second stage is when that pair of countries, having completed integration of their factor markets, decides to integrate (in a precipituous or piecemeal fashion) with the third one. In any case, whether the two-speed approach with three countries should encompass either 3 or 12 different possibilities only the three different pairings of countries will now be considered, without further specifying whether integration among them (and subsequently with the remaining country) is one-stroke or gradual.

It is clear from the enumeration of all possible cases that the number grows rapidly with the number of countries involved. Rather than casting doubts on the usefulness of such theoretical analysis, this should induce us to be cautious before jumping to conclusions about what seems to be (even on pure economic grounds) the best or most likely reaggregation of countries within the existing or within a larger EC, for the process of gradual and differential movement towards EEMU.

Returning to the three-country example, which of the three countries (groups of countries) should integrate first depends upon 1) the shape of the capital accumulation function g, and in particular the distance between the stable equilibrium points from which the countries start considering integration, and 2) the countries' relative economic size. However, the choice cannot be based only on such positive elements; in the dynamic setting of the model, the choice must also involve the present value of the countries' social welfare or policy objective functions with appropriate weights.

Some interesting questions arise in this context, two of them strictly interconnected. The first is whether two countries with capital/labor ratios at opposite extremes (ratios $(K/L)_H$ and $(K/L)_L$ in figure 10) may find it advantageous to integrate their economies at a stable equilibrium point lower than the point from which the highly placed country starts, so that they can integrate subsequently and gradually with a third country that was placed at an intermediate ratio (ratio $(K/L)_M$ in figure 10). This might be possible if there are more than three stable equilibrium points, if the midcountry starting point is below the one to which the two fast-integrating countries decide to step (e.g., point $(K/L)^*$ in figure 10), and if the lowest-placed country is sufficiently small relative to the highest-placed one. This point, although lower than the starting one for the highest-placed country, would be more efficient for the three countries as a whole, if the highest-placed equilibrium cannot be reached by any combination of one-stroke and gradual integration of all three countries' factor markets.

A second and analogous question is whether a country may efficiently proceed to gradual integration with the other two only if these two are allowed to move to their integration first and in one stroke.

The analysis of these two cases could be applied to the German unification process. It may be generally advantageous that West Germany (possibly the highest K/L country in the EC) is integrating its economy first and/or faster with East Germany (possibly the lowest K/L country, as compared with the rest of the EC), in order to make it subsequently viable for the united Germany to integrate with the rest of the EC. The West German "sacrifice" would be necessary in order to make it possible for the rest of the EC to integrate with the united Germany.

Perhaps more suggestive with reference to the other prospective members of the EC—such as Czechoslovakia, Hungary, and Poland—is to apply the analysis and argue that stricter integration of their markets with only some of the present members of the EC is a prerequisite to making it subsequently possible also for the other present members to integrate with them.

A third question is whether, out of the multiple pairings of countries (or groups of them, when there are more than three) as candidates for faster integration, more than one pairing leads to the same stable equilibrium. If so, the choice among alternative country pairings should, as mentioned above, be based on the higher present value of the sequence of steps leading to the steady state. In other words, and again applying the analysis to the German unification, a precipitous integration of East and West Germany and their alternative integration at the same pace as with the rest of the EC could have eventually landed all EC countries in the same steady-state position. However, the paths leading to that position would have been different under the two alternatives; presumably the present value of the integration path, which has led to German unification first, is (at least when discounted at the German political discount rate) higher than the present value of the alternative path.

In any case, in order to see how the model may throw some light on our empirical problems, it should be useful to examine the capital/labor ratios of the countries (or groups of countries) in the EC. Figure 11 shows them for the year 1988. Unfortunately, data for East Germany are too unreliable to be used; moreover, as already suggested above, East Germany's actual capital stock may need to be scrapped when faced with the efficiency standards of a market economy. Thus we cannot see how close East Germany is with respect to its other newly acquired EC partners. We cannot therefore judge whether the hints, suggested above at a purely theoretical level with respect to German precipitous integration, have some more empirical basis. Even so, figure 11 shows that the EC countries may be clustered in two groups, according to the K/L criterion. The first one, made up of West Germany, the U.K., France, and the Benelux plus Denmark group, is actually close to the more capital-rich EFTA group. The second one, although less homogeneous, is made up of Italy, Spain, and the rest of the EC.

Thus we may argue that, unless there is a political willingness on the part of the higher K/L group to assist, with transfers, a gradual integration with the lower group, fast integration of the EC factor markets is more likely to take place among the first group of countries, possibly even with EFTA, rather than with the second group. Clearly, this argument assumes that there might be unstable points of equilibrium that separate the two groups of countries, and that knowledge of the danger of falling into a trap may partially explain the reluctance to move towards EEMU integration of all EC members at the same speed.

The argument is based on structural rather than economic policy differences across countries. More empirical research is clearly in order before accepting the argument as a relevant additional explanation of the difficulties currently experienced in the process of forming EEMU. However, before rejecting it as just theoretical or simply artificial, we may want to consider how relevant it could be in order to explain history. For example, some economic historians argue that the precipitous integration of North and South Italy in the 19th century, accompanied by an immediate monetary unification, did not so lift the South up to Central European standards of development, but rather pulled the North down to a lower level than it could have reached with a different choice of partners for political integration, or with a transitory monetary arrangement short of full monetary union with the South.

The fourth strand of literature used to analyze the consequences of East European developments on the process (but also on the final outcome) of creating EEMU is based on traditional trade theory. In particular, two models have been applied to analyze the effects of these developments on the terms of trade of the main countries in the EC, particularly those of Germany. Depending on the model, the terms of trade (sometimes identified with the real exchange rate) are defined as the relative price of tradable vs. nontradable goods, or as the relative price of exports vs. imports. The first concept is used by Gros and Steinherr (1990), and the second one by Fitoussi and Phelps (1990).

According to these models it could be argued that, either because of the higher demand for German products that will result from restructuring the Eastern economies, or because of the higher net demand for German exports that would follow from the transfer of purchasing power as an aid to the ailing Eastern European countries, the real exchange rate of the DM, or the terms of trade of Germany, should improve.[8]

This result, if empirically true, will have important implications for the evolution of the EC and the EMS towards a full EEMU, both in terms of process and outcome. In fact, in order to change the relative price of German products in the direction required by the argument, the EEMU should allow in the next few years either a nominal appreciation of the DM or a higher relative rate of inflation in Germany, or both. Clearly the Deutsche Bundesbank is less ready now than before to allow a higher price inflation; after having had to bow to political decisions during the preparation of German monetary unification, it now has to prove to the outside world that this historical compromise was inevitable and wholly exceptional, one that will certainly not be repeated on the occasion of European monetary unification. Hence the improvement in Germany's terms of trade, if necessary, shall come about through nominal appreciation of the DM. Since this would be made difficult by moving now and fast into phase two of the Delors plan, and would definitely be excluded by accomplishing phase two and moving to phase

---

[8]Actually, Gros and Steinherr (1990), after having theoretically presented such arguments, counteract on various grounds that the real exchange rate of the DM need not appreciate significantly or at all.

three, the reserved attitude of the Deutsche Bundesbank toward moving ahead with the Delors plan is more convincingly explained by this theory than by the lack of other countries' convergence.

2.3. The Outcome of EEMU

In the preceding section I have presented arguments based either on lack of convergence in economic policy (section 2.2.1) or on differences in economic structure (section 2.2.2). These arguments may help in analyzing the implications of developments in Eastern Europe and, more specifically, of German unification, for the choice between different time processes that lead to European economic integration. In addition, the current cooling of the German attitude vis-à-vis EEMU has acquired a new and possibly clearer meaning.

The present section considers the final outcome of this process, as described both by market equilibrium and by the economic institutions and policies that will characterize it. Admittedly, a clear-cut separation of outcomes and processes that lead to them is not always possible. Moreover, as already pointed out above, a normative choice among different final outcomes cannot ignore the present value of the preceding stages, and therefore of the different processes. Yet, for classification purposes, this section will analyze only the final outcomes.

2.3.1. The Static Trade Model. The first analyses of the problems raised by German unification have often utilized the theoretical framework of neoclassical theory of trade, i.e., the Heckscher–Ohlin–Samuelson model (e.g., Fitoussi and Phelps, (1990); Siebert, (1990)).

A simple application of that model to the German case is to consider the relative K/L endowments of the two Germanys, and how merging them would affect equilibrium after trade as compared to equilibrium before trade. Assuming that East Germany is relatively labor abundant (West Germany relatively capital abundant), that the merged country will still be capital abundant relative to the rest of the world, and that East Germany was not previously trading on the basis of comparative advantage, the model suggests that merging the two countries at given relative prices will reduce the unified country's output of its export good (the capital–intensive product) and increase that of its import good (the labor–intensive product). In order to restore equilibrium, the terms of trade of the unified Germany (i.e., the price of its exports relative to the price of its imports) should increase. This result could imply tensions in the process and the final outcome of the EEMU, and it may help to explain ––together with the similar result that follows from the transfer model analyzed at the end of section 2.2.2.––the current coolness of the Deutsche Bundesbank towards the Delors plan. In fact, this explanation may be better than the traditional German request for policy convergence to low inflation and fiscal prudence.

Other applications of the same model point to the temporary consequences of the need to set relative prices (in East Germany or in other Eastern European countries) closer to competitive world market prices. This may imply scrapping at least part of the existing stock of plant and machinery, as already briefly discussed in section 2.2 (figure 8) with reference to the multiple equilibria model. In the framework of the neoclassical trade model referred to here, and without considering the accumulation of new capital to a higher steady state, this obsolescence effect—by implying that East Germany will have an even lower effective K/L ratio—further reinforces the terms of trade effect pointed out above, as well as its consequences for Germany's exchange rates and/or relative rates of inflation vis-à-vis its EMS and EC partners.

This model can also be used to analyze the search for a new equilibrium, one that may involve not just merging the capital and labor endowments of the two Germanys—or integrating those of some East European countries with the rest of the EC—but also moving factors of production in either direction, with capital going east or labor west, or both. Under appropriate conditions, trade (movement of products) is a perfect substitute for movement of factors; however, we can assume that this may not be the case in the actual German and European application. Clearly, free trade between the EC and East Germany is going to reduce the inducement for East German labor to migrate—an inducement that has already been reduced by other, mainly political, factors. Insofar as some inducement may remain, however, is it immaterial which of the factor movements (labor westward or capital eastward) is going to prevail? In the standard neoclassical trade model referred to above, and in absence of market imperfections, this is indeed immaterial. Thus we must make the model more complex in order to enable it to provide meaningful answers to the question. It seems that a minimum complexity to add is economic growth.

2.3.2. The Growth Model. Growth is based on investment, which clearly requires savings. It is less obvious that, once we consider savings, the basis for trade in products need no longer be comparative advantage: it is enough to have countries with different propensities to save (or different tastes between present vs. future consumption). This is theoretically convenient, since it allows the use of even one-product models and a simple description of countries that are open to trade. Indeed, this has already been done with the multiple equilibria growth model in section 2.2. That model was used to analyze the implications of German unification for the process of European integration. Here it is mentioned again, in order to analyze alternative steady states, i.e., final outcomes, independent of the process that leads to them.

In the model of section 2.2, countries had the same production and savings functions, and they differed only for their K/L ratios. In reality, countries also differ in their savings propensities, as is often discussed with reference to Japan or Italy as opposed to the U.S. In the German case it is likely that, aside from a temporary adjustment of a long-repressed propensity to spend, the savings ratio will be higher in East than in West Germany and the other EC partners, at least for a number of years during the necessary catching up period. A higher savings rate, other things equal, makes for a higher g function, and thus a higher steady-state K/L equilibrium for a united Germany than for its EC partners. The merging of the two Germanies may therefore lead to a joint steady-state situation that is above the one that could previously be reached by West Germany alone. While beneficial to Germany, this could have opposite effects on the inducement to complete EC integration. On the one hand, it should also enable Germany's partners in the EC to reach, in due time, a higher steady state by successfully merging with the new Germany. On the other hand, the greater distance that would separate the unified Germany's steady state from her partners' could give rise to the possible existence of points of unstable equilibrium that would (in absence of transfers) make it no longer interesting for the new Germany to integrate with the other EC partners.

However, East Germans are not the only people that may help West Germans to move to higher equilibria of steady growth. Figure 12 presents the total savings ratios (private plus Government) in the countries or groups of countries analyzed in this chapter, again for the year 1988. Now Spain has moved up the ladder, while the U.K. has fallen to last positon. It is still true that West Germany should have a strong incentive to integrate with the EFTA countries, but now the differences with respect to all other countries or groups of them in the EC are no longer so wide, except perhaps vis-à-vis the U.K.

3. CONCLUSIONS

Rather than a summary of a chapter that is already long, the main conclusions of the analysis are stated below.

1. A hypothetical enlargement of the EC eastwards and in the direction of the EFTA countries is of different interest for the existing members of the EC. Widening the Community eastward is mainly of interest to Germany and its smaller surrounding countries; enlarging it to include the EFTA countries is mainly of interest to the U.K. The two interests are not opposed, and they may be complementary in surmounting possible oppositions by the other countries and by the Commission in Brussels.

2. However, widening the EC, in particular its already realized enlargement to East Germany, endangers the pursuit of deepening its integration and transforming it into a truly unified market for products and factors of production. The dangers for moving ahead with the present plans of monetary unification are even greater.

3. While this gives a unique opportunity to the U.K. for changing its traditional dilatory position into one of compromise, it has also brought to the surface—particularly after German monetary unification—the issue that the German position vis-à-vis European monetary unification is no longer as clear as before, at least in terms of its motivations. Germany was traditionally in favor, provided that prospective members would first reach convergence of their policies towards low inflation and fiscal restraint; however, Germany now appears to be less interested in the project, or less timid to let it be understood that the only interesting unification would be under the leadership of the Deutsche Bundesbank and with a currency as good as the DM, rather than under a European Central Bank, with national currencies linked by fixed exchange rates, eventually replaced by a soft ECU as the common new currency.

4. This change in attitude is not justifiable only by the lack of convergence; divergence has been reduced, and what is left has been there for a long time. In this chapter, the changed German attitude—or perhaps, the open expression of an attitude that has always been in the background—is justified on the basis of more fundamental structural differences, whose importance has suddenly and dramatically surfaced as a consequence of German unification. If this interpretation is correct, we have to wait for this unification to overcome its difficulties, before the process of converting the EC into a more integrated European Economic and Monetary Union may be resumed. In the meantime, the other European countries should better adapt themselves to the two-speed approach, and enjoy the overall advantages that will anyway derive from the enlargement of the Community eastward, and possibly also towards the EFTA countries.

REFERENCES

Baldwin R. (1989), "The Growth Effects of 1992", <u>Economic Policy</u>, vol.4, n.2, pp.247–282.

Blanchard O.J., S. Fischer (1989), <u>Lectures on Macroeconomics</u>, (Cambridge, The MIT Press).

"Cecchini Report" (1988), "The Economics of 1992. An Assessment of the Potential Economic Effects of Completing the Internal Market of the European Community", <u>European Economy</u>, n.35, March 1988.

Dellas H., C. G. de Vries (1990), "Piecemeal Versus Precipitous Factor Market Integration", <u>mimeo</u>, May.

"Delors Report" (1989), Committee for the study of economic and monetary union, <u>Report on Economic and Monetary Union in the European Community</u>, April 12.

Fitoussi J.P., E. Phelps (1990), "Global Effects of Eastern European Rebuilding and the Adequacy of Western Saving: An Issue for the 1990s", paper presented at the 2nd Villa Mondragone Conference, Rome, <u>mimeo</u>, July.

Giavazzi F., M. Pagano (1988), "The Advantage of Tying One's Hand: EMS Discipline and Central Bank Credibility", <u>European Economic Review</u>, vol.32, pp.1055–1075.

Giavazzi F., A. Giovannini (1989), <u>Limiting Exchange Rate Flexibility. The European Monetary System</u>, (Cambridge, The MIT Press).

Gros D., A. Steinherr (1990), "Macroeconomic Management in the New Germany: Its Implications for the EMS and EMU," paper presented at the CEPS Conference on "German Unification in European Perspective," Brussels, September 14–15, 1990, <u>mimeo</u>.

Siebert H. (1990), "The Economic Integration of Germany," Kiel, <u>Discussion Paper</u> n.160.

Willms M. (1990), "German Monetary Unification and European Monetary Union: Theoretical Issues and Strategic Policy Problems," paper presented at the Conference on "European Monetary Integration. From German Dominance to an EC Central Bank?," American Institute for Contemporary German Studies, The Johns Hopkins University, Washington, D.C., <u>mimeo</u>, July.

```
=======================================================================
```
Table 1. - Population, product, and export trade (in 1988)
        of alternative wider European Communities relative
        to the United States and Japan
```
-----------------------------------------------------------------------
```

	Population (in mln)	GDP (in $bln)	Exports (in $mln)
EC	325	4831	427395
NEC	341	5038	434386
NECFTA	373	5743	503990
NNEC	437	6265	522063
USA	246	4818	320386
Japan	123	2843	264943

```
-----------------------------------------------------------------------
```

Notes:
EC = European Community of 12, with intra-EC trade excluded
    but intra-German trade included
NEC = EC + East Germany; trade between East Germany and EC excluded
NECFTA = NEC + EFTA; intra-area trade excluded
NNEC = NECFTA + Czechoslovachia, Hungary, Poland
    (trade among the four E.European countries included)
Sources: OECD data
```
=======================================================================
```

```
================================================================================
```

Table 2. - Relative importance of EFTA and East European prospective
          members (E.Germany, Czechoslovakia, Hungary, Poland)
          for exports by three groups of EC members ($mln in 1988)

```
--------------------------------------------------------------------------------
```

	EFTA	EGe+CZ+HU+PO	totals
WGe+BNLDK	73216.32	9948.735	83165.06
Fr+It+Sp+REC	28348.08	2716.959	31065.04
UK	11607.6	983.401	12591
totals	113172	13649.1	126821.1

Shares:	EFTA	EGe+CZ+HU+PO
WGe+BNLDK	64.69	72.89
Fr+It+Sp+REC	25.05	19.91
UK	10.26	7.20
totals	100	100

Shares:	EFTA	EGe+CZ+HU+PO	totals
WGe+BNLDK	88.04	11.96	100
Fr+It+Sp+REC	91.25	8.75	100
UK	92.19	7.81	100

```
--------------------------------------------------------------------------------
```

Notes: BNLDK = Benelux + Denmark
        REC = Rest of the EC

```
================================================================================
```

Fig.1: Average price inflation
consumer price index (1970–89)

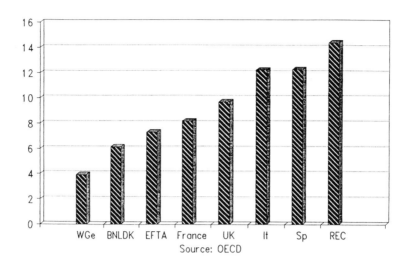

Source: OECD

Fig.2a: Dispersion of inflation rates
EC and EFTA countries

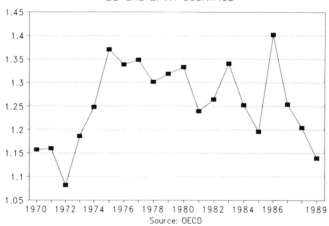

Source: OECD

Fig.2b: Dispersion of inflation rates
EMS countries

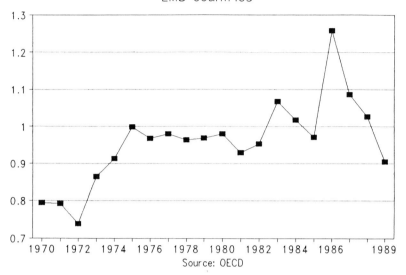

Source: OECD

Fig.3: Differential inflations
relative to W.Germany (1970−89)

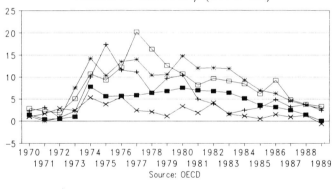

Source: OECD

Fig.4: Govt. deficit relative to GDP
(1970–89)

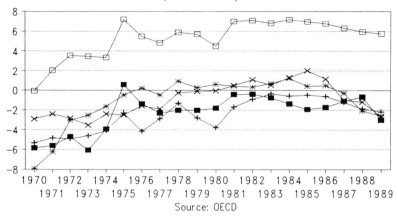

Source: OECD

Fig. 5: PSBRs relative to GDP
(1970–89)

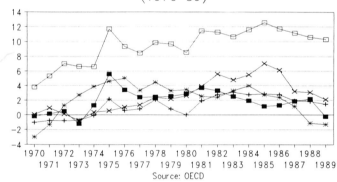

Source: OECD

Fig.6a: Govt. debt relative to GDP
(1989)

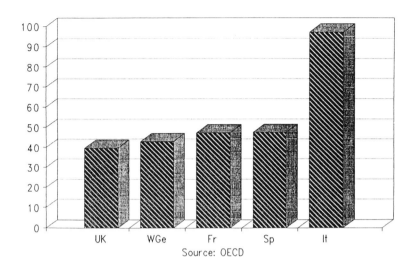

Source: OECD

Fig.6b: Govt. net debt relative to GDP
(1989)

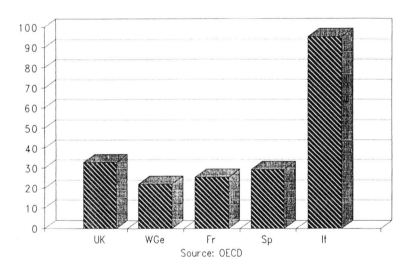

Source: OECD

296

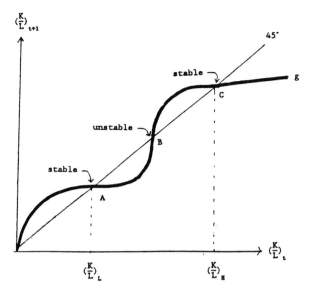

Figure 7. Capital Accumulation Function.

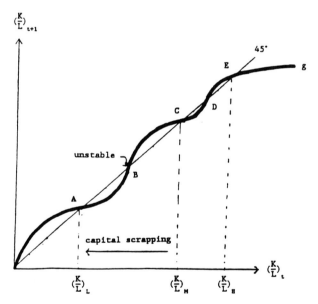

Figure 8. Capital Accumulation Function – German Case.

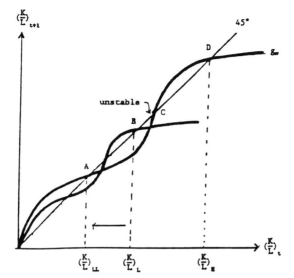

Figure 9. Capital Accumulation Function — Production
Efficiency in East Germany.

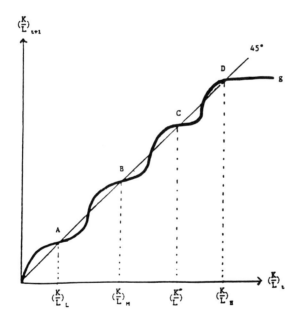

Figure 10. Capital Accumulation Function — Three Country Case.

Fig.11: Capital/labour ratios
(1988)

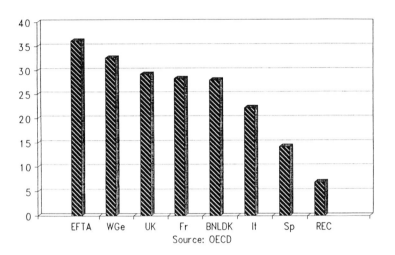

Source: OECD

Fig.12: Total saving relative to GDP
(1988)

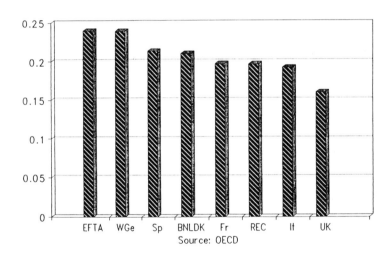

Source: OECD

18. FUTURE TRENDS IN JAPAN'S SAVING RATE AND THE IMPLICATIONS THEREOF FOR JAPAN'S EXTERNAL IMBALANCE *

Charles Y. Horioka
Institute of Social and Economic Research
Osaka University
6-1, Mihogaoka
Ibaraki, Osaka 567
Japan

ABSTRACT. This chapter first presents data on Japan's saving rate and discusses the reasons for its high level and its determinants of trends over time. The chapter then surveys recent attempts to project future trends in Japan's saving rate and their impact on Japan's current account surplus. The various studies agree that Japan's saving rate will decline sharply in the coming years due to the rapid aging of the country's population and other factors, and that it will fall to close to zero or even become negative by 2015-2030. As a result, Japan's current account surplus is also projected to decline and to go into deficit sometime during the early part of the next century.

1. INTRODUCTION

Japan's saving rate is one of the highest in the world. It has played a valuable role throughout the postwar period, providing the funds needed to finance corporate investment in plant and equipment during the high-growth era of the 1950s, 1960s, and early 1970s, and helping to finance the central government's deficits and to meet capital shortages abroad during the post-1973 era of stable growth. However, there are many who blame Japan's high saving rate for her massive current account surpluses, claiming that the excess of domestic saving over domestic investment has led to capital exports (capital account deficits) that must be offset by current account surpluses of corresponding magnitude. Thus, there is agreement that Japan's high saving rate has had important consequences for the domestic and world economies, but there is disagreement about whether those consequences have been favorable or unfavorable.

   Similarly, there is widespread agreement that Japan's saving rate will decline in the future due to the rapid aging of her population and other factors, but there is less agreement about what the consequences of that decline will be for the domestic and world economies. Emmott (1989) predicts that the decline in Japan's saving rate will cause her capital exports to decline and that this will, in turn, cause her international influence to wane. Hamada and Iwata (1989) find that Japan will come to own a much smaller fraction of the net capital stock of the United States if Japan's saving rate falls (they find that

Japan will come to own 38.7% of the U.S. net capital stock by 2015 if her saving rate remains at its present level but only 22% if her saving rate falls by ten percentage points). Auerbach et al. (1989) and Noguchi (1989) predict that the decline in Japan's saving rate will not have an appreciable effect on her capital exports or current account surplus for at least a quarter century because her investment rate will also decline sharply.

The objective of this chapter is to survey recent attempts to project future trends in Japan's saving rate and their impact on Japan's current account surplus. Before doing so, however, some data pertaining to Japan's saving rate are presented, and the reasons for the high level thereof and the determinants of trends over time therein are discussed.

2. DATA ON JAPAN'S SAVING RATE

In this section, data pertaining to Japan's saving rate will be presented. Here as well as throughout this chapter, three saving rate concepts are utilized (all of which are net of depreciation):

1. the household saving rate, defined as the ratio of household saving (the sum of the saving of households, private unincorporated nonfinancial enterprises, and private nonprofit institutions serving households) to household disposable income (the sum of the final consumption expenditure and saving of households, private unincorporated nonfinancial enterprises, and private nonprofit institutions serving households);

2. the private saving rate, defined as the ratio of private saving (the sum of household saving and corporate savings) to private national income (the sum of household disposable income and corporate savings); and

3. the national saving rate, defined as the ratio of national saving (the sum of household, corporate, and government saving) to national income (the sum of private national income, government consumption, and government saving).

Looking first at trends over time in each of the three saving–rate concepts, all three saving concepts have shown a hump–shaped pattern over time, with the household saving rate peaking in 1976 and the private and national saving rates peaking in 1970 (see table 1 and figure 1). (The only major exceptions are that the private and national saving rates showed downward trends during the 1961–1965 period and that the national saving rate has shown a slight upturn since 1983.) The household, private, and national saving rates were respectively 21%–23%, 27%–28%, and 30%–31% at their peak, which is high by any standard.

With reference to an international comparison of saving rates, table 2 shows data on the household saving rate for the member countries of the Organiza- tion for Economic Cooperation and Development (OECD) for which data are avail- able. As this table shows, Japan's household saving rate averaged a full 18.4% during the 1975–1987 period and was second only to that of Italy among the OECD countries for which data are available. In fact, Japan's household saving rate was more than twice as high as those of at least six OECD countries (Sweden, Norway, Finland, the United Kingdom, the United States, and Spain).

It should be noted, however, that a number of OECD countries for which household saving–rate data are not available (such as Greece and Luxembourg) show higher overall saving rates than Japan and that a number of non–OECD countries (such as Singapore, South Korea, and Taiwan) also show higher saving rates than Japan. Thus, Japan's saving rate is one of the highest in the world but not the highest. Moreover, it has shown a downward trend since the 1970s, as noted earlier.

3. THE CAUSES OF THE HIGH LEVEL OF JAPAN'S SAVING RATE

This section will briefly discuss the causes of the high level of Japan's saving rate. A large number of factors have been suggested as possible explanations of Japan's high saving rate, among them:
1. culture/tradition (for example, the influence of Confucianism)
2. the age structure of the population
3. the high proportion of the self-employed
4. the bonus system
5. the unavailability of consumer credit
6. the intensity of competition among banks and other financial institutions for deposits
7. the existence of the postal savings system
8. the availability of tax breaks for saving
9. the lack of tax breaks for debt
10. the government's saving-promotion activities
11. the low level of social security benefits
12. the rapid rate of economic growth
13. the low level of assets as a result of wartime destruction and the postwar hyperinflation
14. the greater prevalence of earthquakes, volcanic eruptions, typhoons, and other natural disasters
15. conceptual differences[1]

There are not many studies that have tried to quantify the importance of each of these factors, but a few examples exist. For example, Modigliani and Sterling (1983) conducted such an analysis using 1960-1970 data for 21 OECD countries, while Horioka (1989) conducted such an analysis using 1975-1984 data for virtually the same countries as those used by Modigliani and Sterling (the only difference being that Portugal was dropped while Iceland was added).

Modigliani and Sterling (1983) found that, during the 1960-1970 period, Japan's much higher rate of growth of real per capita disposable income was the major explanation of the high level of Japan's private saving rate relative to both the U.S. level and the sample mean. The much lower ratio of the retired population to the population aged 20 and over (or to the male labor force) was the second most important explanation. Horioka (1989) found that, during the 1975-1984 period, the much lower ratio of the aged population to the working-age population in Japan was the major explanation of the high level of Japan's private saving rate relative to both the U.S. level and the sample mean.

Furthermore, both studies found that the relatively low proportion of children also contributed toward the high level of Japan's private saving rate: Modigliani and Sterling (1983) found that the low level of the ratio of the young to the population aged 20 and over (or to the male labor force) contributed toward the high level of Japan's private saving rate relative to the U.S. level (but not relative to the sample mean), while Horioka (1989) found that the low

---

[1]More comprehensive surveys can be found in Hayashi (1986), Horioka (1990a), and Sato (1987).

ratio of the young to the working-age population contributed toward the high level of Japan's private saving rate relative to both the U.S. level and the sample mean.

Ishikawa and Ueda (1984), using time series data for Japan instead of cross-country data, found that the bonus system (whereby 11% to 25% of employee compensation is paid in the form of semiannual bonuses) raised Japan's household saving rate by up to three percentage points during the 1958-1978 period (with the effect being even larger during the late 1960s and 1970s).

Thus, the reasons for the high level of Japan's saving rate have varied over time. The rapid rate of income growth was the dominant explanation during the high-growth era of the 1960s and early 1970s, but its importance has waned since 1973 due to the sharp decline in growth rates associated with the first oil crisis. The age structure of the population (especially the low proportion of the aged) and the bonus system have contributed toward the high level of Japan's saving rate throughout the postwar period but were especially important in the 1970s and (in the case of the former) the 1980s. In other words, Japan's saving rate has remained high because, as some of the factors behind its high level have decreased in importance, other factors have increased in importance.

Turning finally to why the age structure of Japan's population has contributed to the high level of her saving rate, it is because the age structure of her population has shown the somewhat unusual pattern of having relatively few children as well as relatively few aged individuals due to the large number of wartime casualties, the swelling of the ranks of the working-age population (after 1967) as the first postwar baby boom generation (born in 1947-1949) attained the age of majority, and other factors. Table 3 shows an international comparison of the age structure of the population, and as this table shows, the levels of both AGE (the ratio of the population aged 65 and over to the population aged 20 to 64) and DEP (the ratio of the population aged 19 and under to the population aged 20 to 64) have been relatively low in Japan. The level of AGE in 1986 was only 0.17, putting Japan in 22nd place among the 25 OECD countries, well behind such countries as Sweden (0.31), Norway (0.28), the United Kingdom, and Denmark (both 0.26), and Austria, Germany, and Switzerland (all 0.24), and somewhat behind the United States (0.21). Only three countries — Australia (0.17), Yugoslavia (0.14), and Turkey (0.11) — had lower levels of AGE than Japan. Similarly, the level of DEP in 1986 was only 0.47, putting Japan in 15th place among the 25 member countries of the OECD, well behind such countries as Turkey (1.12), Ireland (0.76), Iceland (0.65), New Zealand (0.60), Australia (0.57), and Portugal (0.56) and somewhat behind even the United States (0.50).

And since (according to the life-cycle hypothesis) the aged finance their living expenses by drawing down their previously accumulated savings and since children contribute to consumption without contributing to income, the proportion of both groups exerts downward pressure on the saving rate and the low proportion of both groups contributed to the high level of Japan's saving rate.

4. THE DETERMINANTS OF TRENDS OVER TIME IN JAPAN'S SAVING RATE

As noted in section 2, all three saving concepts have shown a hump-shaped pattern in the case of Japan, with the peak occurring in 1976 in the case of the household saving rate and in 1970 in the case of the private and national saving rates. This pattern needs to be explained.

Horioka (1991) conducted a regression analysis using time series data for Japan for the 1956–1987 period and found that trends over time in the age structure of the population –– in particular, trends over time in AGE and DEP –– can by themselves explain this pattern.

As table 4 and figure 2 show, AGE increased throughout the period of analysis, due primarily to increases in life expectancy, while DEP decreased throughout, due primarily to the decline in the birth rate. Moreover, Horioka (1991) found by means of regression analysis that, as expected, both AGE and DEP have a negative and significant effect on the three saving–rate concepts defined in section 2. Thus, the increase in AGE caused Japan's saving rate to decline throughout the period of analysis, while the decline in DEP caused it to increase throughout. In other words, AGE and DEP worked in opposite directions, and hence the direction of change of Japan's saving rate cannot be determined without knowing the relative magnitudes of the impact of AGE and that of DEP.

Until the early 1970s, the rate of decline of DEP was relatively rapid compared to the rate of increase of AGE, and as a result the impact of DEP exceeded that of AGE, causing the saving rate to show an upward trend. After the early 1970s, however, the rate of increase of AGE was relatively rapid compared to the rate of decline of DEP, and as a result, the impact of AGE came to exceed that of DEP, causing the saving rate to begin declining.

Numerous other factors have been suggested as determinants of trends over time in Japan's saving rate; many of them have been shown to be significant, and a few of them (such as the ratio of bonus income to employee compensation) have been shown to be capable of explaining the hump–shaped pattern in Japan's saving rate (see Ishikawa and Ueda, 1984). Thus, there is no consensus that the age structure of the population is the dominant determinant of trends over time in Japan's saving rate, but it is noteworthy that it is one of the few factors that can, by itself, explain the observed pattern in Japan's saving rate.

5. FUTURE TRENDS IN JAPAN'S SAVING RATE: THE IMPACT OF THE AGE STRUCTURE OF THE POPULATION

The two previous sections have shown that the age structure of the population is a major (if not the dominant) determinant of not only the high level of Japan's saving rate but also of trends over time therein. This suggests that the age structure of the population will be a major (if not the dominant) determinant of future trends in Japan's saving rate as well, and thus it seems appropriate to obtain initial estimates of future trends in Japan's saving rate by focusing exclusively on the impact of the age structure of the population.

There are a number of possible ways of estimating the impact of demographic trends on future trends in the saving rate, and each of these will be discussed in turn.

5.1. Projections based on Regression Analysis

One way is to estimate the impact of the age structure of the population on the saving rate by means of regression analysis and to use the estimated regression coefficients in conjunction with estimates of future population by age group to project future trends in the saving rate. This method was used by both Horioka (1989) and Horioka (1991). As noted in section 3, Horioka (1989) estimated the impact of AGE and DEP on the private saving rate using cross–country data for 21 OECD countries, while as noted in section 4, Horioka (1991) estimated the impact of AGE and DEP on the household, private, and national saving rates using time series data for Japan.

Representative results from both studies are shown in table 5, and as this table shows, the coefficients of AGE and DEP are, as expected, negative and at least marginally significant, and the magnitudes of the coefficients are stable as well as reasonable except that the coefficient of AGE is implausibly large in the time series regression using the national saving rate as the dependent variable. If this regression is disregarded, the results imply that a one–percentage–point increase in AGE causes the saving rate to decline by 1.0 to 1.1 percentage points and that a one–percentage–point increase in DEP causes the saving rate to decline by 0.3 to 0.4 percentage points.

Horioka (1989) and Horioka (1991) used the coefficients shown in table 5 in conjunction with estimates of future values of AGE and DEP (see table 4 and figure 2) in order to project future trends in Japan's saving rate. The results for the case of the household and private saving rates are shown in table 6 and figure 3 (the results for the national saving rate are not shown because the coefficient of AGE is implausibly large in the regression using the national saving rate as the dependent variable). As this table shows, Japan's household and private saving rates are projected to show a long–term decline until at least 2018–2019. The primary reason for this is, of course, the long–term increase in AGE that is projected to occur.[2]

The rate of decline of the saving rate is projected to be relatively moderate until around the turn of the century (0.5 percentage points per year or less until 1994 and less than 1.0 percentage point per year until 1999), partly because the increase in AGE will be relatively moderate at first and partly because DEP will decline until 1997 as the second postwar baby–boom generation (born in 1967–1974)[3] reaches the age of majority. (The decline in DEP will put upward pressure on the saving rate and will thus partly offset the downward pressure thereon due to the increase in AGE, as it did during the 1956–1987 period.)

After around the turn of the century, however, the rate of increase of AGE will accelerate as the first postwar baby–boom generation reaches retirement age, and DEP will show an upturn as the second postwar baby–boom generation marries and starts having children. Both of these factors will cause the rate of decline of the saving rate to accelerate. The saving rate is projected to decline by a full percentage point or more in most years during the 2000–2016 period and to become negative by 2005–2013.[4]

---

[2]A similar increase in AGE is occurring in most countries, but it is expected to occur at a much faster pace in Japan and to cause Japan's population to become virtually the most aged in the world by 2025.

[3]The second postwar baby–boom generation is, of course, the children of the first postwar baby–boom generation (born in 1947–1949).

[4]Future values of the private saving rate based on time series data differ from those based on cross–country data largely because the time series data were taken from Japanese Government sources and are based on replacement cost depreciation, whereas the cross–country data were taken from OECD sources and are

After 2015, however, DEP will begin declining again as the third postwar baby-boom generation reaches the age of majority, and after 2020, AGE will also begin declining as the first postwar baby-boom generation passes away. Both of these factors will cause the saving rate to bottom out in 2018-2019 and to begin increasing anew. However, the saving rate is projected to increase only moderately, and as a result, it is projected to remain negative until well into the latter half of the 21st century. It should be noted, though, that these projections, which are based on a very crude methodology, are meant to be merely suggestive and that the exact figures (especially the large negative values) should not be given much weight.

5.2. Projections based on Other Methods

There are at least two other ways of estimating the impact of demographic changes on future trends in the saving rate. One is to use data on the saving rate of each age group in conjunction with estimates of future population by age group, and the other is to use simulation techniques in conjunction with estimates of future population by age group. Fukao and Doi (1985), Keizai Kikaku-chō (Economic Planning Agency) (1985), Maki et al. (1990), and Noguchi (1989) used the first method, while Auerbach et al. (1989), Masson and Tryon (1990), and Noguchi (1986, 1987) used the second method. Of those using the second method, Auerbach et al. (1989) and Noguchi (1986, 1987) used an overlapping generations general equilibrium model that considers Japan in isolation rather than as part of a closed world system, while Masson and Tryon (1990) used a multicountry macroeconometric model.

The findings of the various studies are summarized below. Studies that project future trends in Japan's household saving rate are discussed first, followed by studies that project future trends in Japan's private and national saving rates.

1. Fukao and Doi (1985) and Keizai Kikaku-chō (Economic Planning Agency)(1985) projected that Japan's household saving rate will fall to 6.9% to 12.6% by 2016-2030, depending on whether the pensionable age for public old-age pensions is kept at 60 or raised to 65 and on whether the propensity to save remains high or falls. Note, however, that these figures are based on the saving concept used in the Family Income and Expenditure Survey (Kakei Chōsa), which is

---

based on historical cost depreciation. The two can be made roughly comparable by reducing the figures based on time series data by 3.5 percentage points (the amount by which the private saving rate based on replacement cost depreciation exceeded that based on historical cost depreciation in 1987) or by increasing the figures based on cross-country data by the same amount. If the latter adjustment is done, future values of the private saving rate based on cross-country data become negative in 2009, only two years later than future values of the private saving rate based on time series data. Similarly, future values of the household saving rate based on time series data can be converted to an historical cost basis by reducing them by 1.9 percentage points (the amount by which the household saving rate based on replacement cost depreciation exceeded that based on historical cost depreciation in 1987). (The results of the various adjustments are shown in table 7 for the case of the initial trough value of the saving rate.)

conducted by the Statistics Bureau of the Management and Coordination Agency (Sōmu-chō, Tōkei-kyoku), formerly the Statistics Bureau of the Prime Minister's Office (Sōri-fu, Tōkei-kyoku). This saving concept differs substantially from the national income accounts concept (for example, it is gross of depreciation and is calculated from a consumption concept that excludes the imputed rent on owner-occupied housing); because of these differences, the household saving rate based on the saving concept used in the Family Income and Expenditure Survey is consistently higher than that based on the national income accounts concept. For example, the former was 20.9% in 1983 (the benchmark year in Fukao and Doi's and the Economic Planning Agency's projections), while the latter was only 16.3% (14.1%) in the same year if depreciation is valued at historical cost (replacement cost). Thus, there was a full 4.6 (6.8) percentage-point difference between the two in 1983 if depreciation is valued at historical cost (replacement cost). If this same difference is assumed to persist in the future as well, the aforementioned projections imply that the household saving rate based on the national income accounts concept of saving will fall to 2.3% to 8.0% if depreciation is valued at historical cost and to 0.1% to 5.8% if depreciation is valued at replacement cost.

2. Maki et al. (1990) projected that Japan's household saving rate will fall to −9.8% to 8.7% by 2020-2025, depending on whether the pensionable age for public old-age pensions is kept at 60 or raised to 65, on whether or not the contribution rate for medical insurance is raised, and on what assumption is made concerning the consumption behavior of the aged. However, as in the case of Fukao and Doi (1985) and Keizai Kikaku-chō (Economic Planning Agency) (1985), Maki et al. (1990) used a household savings rate that is based on the Family Income and Expenditure Survey concept of saving, which is consistently higher than the household saving rate based on the national income accounts concept of saving due to conceptual differences. For example, the former was 22.5% in 1985 (the benchmark year for Maki et al.'s analysis), while the latter was only 15.9% (13.8%) in the same year if depreciation is valued at historical cost (replacement cost). Thus, there was a full 6.6 (8.7) percentage-point difference between the two in 1985 if depreciation is valued at historical cost (replacement cost), and if this same difference is assumed to persist in the future as well, the aforementioned projections imply that the household savings rate based on the national income accounts concept of saving will fall to −16.4% to 2.1% if depreciation is valued at historical cost and to −18.5% to 0.0% if depreciation is valued at replacement cost.

3. Noguchi (1986) projected that Japan's household saving rate will decline to −2.6% to −1.3% by 2015, depending on whether the economy is assumed to be closed or open and on whether or not the effects of social security are considered. Note, however, that the simulation results track the actual household saving rate only imperfectly. For example, the household saving rate for 1985 is 7.8% to 9.6% according to the simulation results, whereas the actual household saving rate based on national income accounts data was 15.9% (13.8%) in the same year if depreciation is valued at historical cost (replacement cost). Thus, the figures based on Noguchi's simulation analysis are 6.3 to 8.1 (4.2 to 6.0) percentage points lower than the actual figures based on national income accounts data if depreciation is valued at historical cost (replacement cost). If this same difference is assumed to persist in the future as well, Noguchi's results imply that the household saving rate based on national income accounts data will decline to 3.7% to 6.8% if depreciation is valued at historical cost and to 1.6% to 4.7% if depreciation is valued at replacement cost.

4. Noguchi (1987) projected that Japan's household saving rate will decline to −7.0% to −3.0% by 2020, depending on whether the government finances increased social security expenditures by means of a tax on labor income or by means of a consumption tax. However, in the case of this analysis as well, the simulation results track the actual household saving rate only imperfectly. For example, the household saving rate for 1985 is 6.6% to 6.7% according to the simulation results, which is 9.2 to 9.3 (7.1 to 7.2) percentage points lower than the actual household savings rate based on national income accounts data if depreciation is valued at historical cost (replacement cost). If this same difference is assumed to persist in the future as well, Noguchi's results imply that the household saving rate based on national income accounts data will decline to 2.3% to 6.2% if depreciation is valued at historical cost and to 0.2% to 4.1% if depreciation is valued at replacement cost.

5. Noguchi (1989) projected that Japan's household saving rate will decline to −8.5% to 0.2% by 2020, depending on what assumption is made about the rate of dissaving of the aged. However, the simulation results track the actual household saving rate only imperfectly, partly because Noguchi used before−tax income rather than disposable income in the denominator and partly because he used net financial saving rather than total saving. For example, the household saving rate for 1985 is 6.8% according to Noguchi's simulation results, which is 9.1 (7.0) percentage points lower than the actual household saving rate based on national income accounts data if depreciation is valued at historical cost (replacement cost). If this same difference is assumed to persist in the future as well, Noguchi's results imply that the household saving rate based on national income accounts data will decline to 0.6% to 9.3% if depreciation is valued at historical cost and to −1.5% to 7.2% if depreciation is valued at replacement cost.

6. Masson and Tryon (1990) projected that Japan's private saving rate (defined as the ratio of net private saving to gross national product) will decline by 4.3 percentage points over the 1995−2025 period. Since private national income was 70.1% (67.2%) of gross national product in 1987 if depreciation is valued at historical cost (replacement cost), 4.3 percentage points of gross national product corresponds to 6.1 (6.4) percentage points of private national income. And since the private saving rate (with private national income in the denominator) is projected to be 14.4% (10.9%) in 1995 if depreciation is valued at historical cost (replacement cost) and the computations are done using the regression results based on time series data (see section 5.1), Masson and Tryon's results imply that Japan's private saving rate (with private national income in the denominator) will decline to 8.3% (4.5%) by 2025 if depreciation is valued at historical cost (replacement cost).

7. Auerbach et al. (1989) projected that Japan's net national saving rate (defined as the ratio of net national saving to net domestic product) will decline from 20.1% to 20.8% in 1985 to 1.8% to 3.7% in 2030, depending on whether or not government outlays remain constant per member of the total population, on whether or not the pensionable age for public old−age pensions is raised by two years, on whether or not there is a uniform 20% cut in public old−age pension benefits, and on whether the economy is assumed to be a closed one or a small open one.[5] These figures are based on a historical cost valuation of deprecia−tion, and in 1985, the net national saving rate was 5.2 percentage points lower

---

[5]The results were also reported in Kotlikoff (1989).

when depreciation was valued at replacement cost than when it was valued at historical cost. If this same difference is assumed to persist in the future as well, Auerbach et al.'s results imply that the net national saving rate based on a replacement cost valuation of depreciation will fall to −2.7% to −1.0% in 2030.

As table 7 shows, the various studies surveyed obtain remarkably similar results—namely, that Japan's saving rate (household, private, and national) will decline to close to zero or even become negative by 2015–2030 as a result of the rapid aging of her population, at least if the saving rate is measured on a national income accounts basis and depreciation is valued at replacement cost. The fact that there is such close agreement among the various studies despite differences in methodology and in the saving rate concept used gives us confidence that the prediction of a sharp decline in Japan's saving rate is correct.

Moreover, a number of casual observations lend even further credence to this prediction:

1. The Japanese government is predicting that the rate of population growth will become negative after 2013 and remain negative until at least 2085 (Kōsei-shō (Ministry of Welfare), 1987), and the life cycle hypothesis predicts that an economy in which the rate of population growth is negative will show a negative saving rate.

2. The household saving rate has already become negative in a number of countries in which the aging of the population has proceeded farther than in the case of Japan. For example, Norway has shown a negative household saving rate since 1985, Sweden since 1987, and Finland since 1988.

6. FUTURE TRENDS IN JAPAN'S SAVING RATE: THE IMPACT OF OTHER FACTORS

We have thus far focused exclusively on the impact of demographic changes on future trends in Japan's saving rate, but there are many other factors that may also influence these trends. For example, the following factors could conceivably contribute toward the decline in Japan's saving rate:

1. the decline in the rate of economic growth since the first oil crisis of 1973–1974
2. the improvement in the benefit levels of public pensions since 1973
3. the increase in the availability of credit cards and consumer credit
4. the strengthening of property income taxation, including:
    (a) the abolition of the tax exemption of interest on small–lot savings (the maruyg system) and most other tax breaks on saving on April 1, 1988
    (b) the strengthening of taxation of capital gains on equities effective April 1, 1989
    (c) the strengthening of land taxation, including the introduction of a new land tax on April 1, 1992
5. the increase in household asset holdings as a result of the high household saving rate and the run–up in land and stock (equity) prices
6. the reduction in working hours as a result of the diffusion of the five–day work week and the increase in vacation time
7. the increase in the retirement age (it has been increased from 55 to 60 and will probably eventually be increased further to 65)

8. the weakening of traditional values such as diligence and frugality and the emergence of spendthrift pleasure-seekers (see, for example, Emmott, 1989)

At the same time, the following factors could conceivably exert upward pressure on Japan's saving rate or cause it to maintain its current level:

1.   the decline in the labor force participation rate of the aged (this refers to the decline in the labor force participation rate of those aged 65 and over who are past the age of formal retirement; thus, this factor is not related to, and not inconsistent with, the increase in the retirement age mentioned earlier)

2.   the introduction of a large-scale consumption tax on April 1, 1989

3.   financial deregulation and the introduction of new investment alternatives

4.   continued increases in life expectancy

5.   the recent collapse of stock prices

6.   increased uncertainty about the future caused by increased trade and investment friction with other countries, increased political instability abroad, etc.

7.   the fear of cutbacks in social security either through an increase in the pensionable age from 60 to 65[6] and/or a cut in benefit levels[7]

8.   the persistence of the bonus system of compensation

Thus, there are factors working in both directions, but the factors exerting downward pressure on Japan's saving rate seem to be far more powerful than the factors exerting upward pressure on it or causing it to maintain its current level. Thus, a sharp decline in Japan's saving rate seems inevitable barring any unforeseen circumstances.

7. FUTURE TRENDS IN JAPAN'S CURRENT ACCOUNT

As we saw in the previous two sections, all signs point toward a precipitous decline in Japan's saving rate. However, this does not necessarily imply that Japan's current account surplus will decline. The reason is that the current account surplus is a function not of the saving rate but of the excess of domestic saving relative to domestic investment (the IS balance). The current account surplus will not decline, no matter how much the saving rate declines, if investment declines by as much as saving does.

Thus, we need to project future trends in both saving and investment in order to be able to predict future trends in the current account surplus. Fortunately, Noguchi (1989) conducted just such an analysis using simulation techniques, and according to his results, the ratio of investment to GNP will decline until 2015 (with the sharpest decline occurring between 1995 and 2000) and increase thereafter. (The primary reason for the decline is, of course, the

---

[6]Auerbach et al. (1989), Fukao and Doi (1985), Keizai Kikaku-chō (Economic Planning Agency) (1985), Maki et al. (1990), Nihon Keizai Kenkyū Senā (Japan Economic Research Center) (1990), and Sakamoto (1990) estimated the impact of the increase in the pensionable age on the saving rate.

[7]Auerbach et al. (1989) estimated the impact of a reduction in public old-age pension benefits on the saving rate.

decline in the working–age population and the resultant decline in the labor force.)

Noguchi's results further indicate that the decline in the saving ratio will exceed that in the investment ratio between 1985 and 1995 and after 2015 but that the decline in the investment ratio will exceed that in the saving ratio between 1995 and 2015. Thus, his results imply that Japan's current account surplus will narrow between 1985 and 2000 and after about 2015 but that it will widen between 2000 and about 2015 despite the fact that the saving rate will continue its decline. However, Noguchi's results indicate that Japan's current account surplus will narrow rapidly after 2015 –– to zero just after 2020 and to –1% of GNP in 2025.

Moreover, Noguchi's earlier studies obtained broadly consistent results. For example, Noguchi (1986) found that the current account balance will go into deficit after about 2015 if the effect of social security is neglected and that it will go into deficit between about 1990 and 2005 and after about 2015 if the effect of social security is taken into account, while Noguchi (1987) found that the current account balance will go into deficit after about 2010 (2015) if the government finances increased social security expenditures by means of a tax on labor income (a consumption tax).

Auerbach et al. (1989) conducted their own analysis using similar simulation methods and obtain somewhat different results.[8] They found that Japan's current account surplus will widen until 1990, when it reaches an all–time high of 5.6% of GNP, narrow between 1990 and 2030, becoming negative by 2030, and widen anew after 2030, eventually reaching its long–run level of 2.3% of GNP.

Finally, Masson and Tryon (1990) conducted a multicountry simulation analysis and obtained the following results for the case of Japan: during the 1995–2025 period, Japan's private saving rate (as a percent of GNP) will decline by 4.3 percentage points, but her rate of gross private investment will also decline (by 1.8 percentage points), as a result of which her private sector IS balance will deteriorate by only 2.5 percentage points. During this same period, the general government financial balance will deteriorate by 1.6 percentage points, meaning that Japan's overall IS balance and thus her current account balance will decline by 4.0 percentage points. As a result, Japan's current account balance will be negative by 2000 and will decline further until at least 2015.

Thus, the various studies agree that Japan's current account surplus will not decline as sharply as her saving rate will because her investment rate will also decline, but that it will go into deficit sooner or later. However, they differ with respect to the projected time path of the current account balance, with Auerbach et al. (1989) and Noguchi (1986, 1987, 1989) predicting that it will go into deficit sometime during the 2010–2030 period and Masson and Tryon (1990) predicting that it will go into deficit by 2000. Since the Masson–Tryon study is the only one based on a multicountry model that takes into account the developments in other countries, its results may be more reliable. It thus appears that Japan's current account surplus and capital exports will disappear sooner rather than later.

---

[8]The results were also reported in Kotlikoff (1989).

8. CONCLUSION

It seems clear that both saving and investment will decline in Japan during the coming decades due to the aging of her population and other factors, but it is much more difficult to predict future trends in the current account surplus, which equals the difference between domestic saving and domestic investment. In order to do so with any degree of accuracy, we need to obtain more precise estimates of future trends in both saving and investment, preferably in a multicountry framework. However, it seems safe to conclude that Japan's current account surplus will eventually go into deficit and that this could occur even before the turn of the century.

REFERENCES

Auerbach, Alan J., and Kotlikoff, Laurence J. (1989), "Demographics, Fiscal Policy, and U.S. Saving in the 1980s and Beyond," National Bureau of Economic Research Working Paper No. 3150 (October).

Auerbach, Alan J.; Kotlikoff, Laurence J.; Hagemann, Robert; and Nicoletti, Giuseppe (1989), "The Dynamics of an Aging Population: The Case of Four OECD Countries," National Bureau of Economic Research Working Paper No. 2797 (February).

Emmott, Bill (1989), The Sun Also Sets: Why Japan Will Not Be Number One (London, England: Simon and Schuster Ltd.).

Fukao, Mitsuhiro, and Doi, Kazuaki (1985), "Jinkō Kōrei-ka to Chochiku-ritsu" (The Aging of the Population and the Saving Rate), Keizai Seminā, no. 369 (October), pp. 63-69 (in Japanese).

Hamada, Koichi, and Iwata, Kazumasa (1989), "On the International Capital Ownership Pattern at the Turn of the Twenty-first Century," European Economic Review, vol. 33, no. 5 (May), pp. 1055-1085.

Hayashi, Fumio (1986), "Why Is Japan's Saving Rate So Apparently High?" in Stanley Fischer, ed., NBER Macroeconomics Annual 1986, vol. 1 (Cambridge, Massachusetts: MIT Press), pp. 147-210.

Hayashi, Fumio (1989a), "Is Japan's Saving Rate High?" Federal Reserve Bank of Minneapolis Quarterly Review, vol. 13, no. 2 (Spring), pp. 3-9.

Hayashi, Fumio (1989b), "Japan's Saving Rate: New Data and Reflections," National Bureau of Economic Research Working Paper No. 3205 (December).

Heller, Peter (1989), "Aging, Savings, and Pensions in the Group of Seven Countries: 1980-2025," Journal of Public Policy, vol. 9, no. 2 (April/June), pp. 127-153.

Horioka, Charles Yuji (1989), "Why Is Japan's Private Saving Rate So High?" in Ryuzo Sato and Takashi Negishi, eds., Developments in Japanese Economics (Tokyo: Academic Press/Harcourt Brace Jovanovich Japan, Inc.), pp. 145-178.

Horioka, Charles Yuji (1990a), "Why Is Japan's Household Saving Rate So High? A Literature Survey," Journal of the Japanese and International Economies, vol. 4, no. 1 (March), pp. 49-92.

Horioka, Charles Yuji (1990b), "Nihonjin no Seikatsu wa Hontō ni Yutaka ka?" (Do the Japanese Really Lead Affluent Lives?), Nihon Keizai Kenkyū (JCER Economic Journal) (Nihon Keizai Kenkyū Sentā/Japan Economic Research Center, ed.), no. 20 (May), pp. 45-55 (in Japanese).

Horioka, Charles Yuji (1991), "The Determinants of Japan's Saving Rate: The Impact of the Age Structure of the Population and Other Factors," _Economic Studies Quarterly_, vol. 42, no. 3 (September), pp. 237–253.

Horne, Jocelyn; Kremers, Jeroen; and Masson, Paul (1989), "Net Foreign Assets and International Adjustment in the United States, Japan, and the Federal Republic of Germany," Working Paper WP/89/22, International Monetary Fund, Washington, D.C. (March).

Ishikawa, Tsuneo, and Ueda, Kazuo (1984), "The Bonus Payment System and Japanese Personal Savings," in Masahiko Aoki, ed., _The Economic Analysis of the Japanese Firm_ (Amsterdam: North–Holland/Elsevier Science Publishers B. V.), pp. 133–192.

Iwamoto, Yasushi (1989), "Comment on 'Some Macroeconomic Implications of Aging Populations,' by Laurence J. Kotlikoff," unpublished (Faculty of Economics, Osaka University, Osaka, Japan).

Keizai Kikaku–chō (Economic Planning Agency) (1985), _Keizai Hakusho_ (Economic White Paper), 1985 edition (Tokyo: Dkura–shō Insatsu–kyoku/Ministry of Finance Printing Bureau) (in Japanese).

Keizai Kikaku–chō (Economic Planning Agency) (1989), _Keizai Hakusho_ (Economic White Paper), 1989 edition (Tokyo: Dkura–shō Insatsu–kyoku/Ministry of Finance Printing Bureau) (in Japanese).

Kōsei–shō, Jinkō Mondai Kenkyū–sho (Institute of Population Problems, Ministry of Health and Welfare) (1987), ed., _Nihon no Shōrai Suikei Jinkō: Shōwa 61–nen 12–gatsu Suikei_ (Population Projections for Japan: 1985–2085) (Tokyo: Zaidan Hōjin Kōsei Tōkei Kyōkai/Health and Welfare Statistics Association) (in Japanese).

Kotlikoff, Laurence J. (1989), "Some Macroeconomic Implications of Aging Populations," paper presented at the Conference on the Economics of Aging jointly sponsored by the Nihon Keizai Kenkyū Sentū (Japan Economic Research Center) and the National Bureau of Economic Research, held on September 8–9, 1989, in Tokyo, Japan.

Maki, Atsushi; Furukawa, Akira; Watanabe, Shin'ichi; and Tamura, Hiroyuki (1990), "Jinkō Kōreika ni yoru Kakei Chochiku–ritsu no Henka ni kansuru Kenkyū Chōsa: Kōhōto Bunseki ni yoru Kakei Chochiku–ritsu no Shōrai Suikei" (Research on Changes in the Household Saving Rate due to the Aging of the Population: Estimates of Future Trends in the Household Saving Rate based on Cohort Analysis), Discussion Paper No. 1990–01 (September 20), Ygsei Kenkyg–sho (Institute for Posts and Telecommunications Policy), Tokyo, Japan (in Japanese).

Masson, Paul R., and Tryon, Ralph W. (1990), "Macroeconomic Effects of Projected Population Aging in Industrial Countries," _International Monetary Fund Staff Papers_, vol. 37, no. 3 (September), pp. 453–485.

Modigliani, Franco, and Sterling, Arlie (1983), "Determinants of Private Saving with Special Reference to the Role of Social Security —— Cross–country Tests," in Franco Modigliani and Richard Hemming, eds., _The Determinants of National Saving and Wealth_ (London: The Macmillan Press Ltd.), pp. 24–55.

Nihon Keizai Kenkyū Sentā (Japan Economic Research Center) (1990), Dai 17–kai 5–ka–nen Keizai Yosoku Chgkan Hōkoku: Kōzō–men kara Mita 90–nen–dai no Nihon Keizai (Interim Report on the 17th 5–year Economic Forecast: The Structure of the Japanese Economy of the 1990s) (Tokyo: Nihon Keizai Kenkyū Sentā/Japan Economic Research Center, August) (in Japanese).

Noguchi, Yukio (1986), "Demographic Conditions, Social Security, and Capital Accumulation: A Simulation Analysis," Discussion Paper No. 9 (September), Institute of Fiscal and Monetary Policy, Ministry of Finance, Tokyo, Japan.

Noguchi, Yukio (1987), "Kōteki Nenkin no Shōrai to Nihon Keizai no Taigai Pafōmansu" (The Future of Public Pensions and the External Performance of the Japanese Economy), Finansharu Rebyū (Financial Review) (Ōkura-shō, Zaisei Kin'yū Kenkyū-sho/Institute of Fiscal and Monetary Policy, Ministry of Finance, ed.), no. 5 (June), pp. 8–19 (in Japanese).

Noguchi, Yukio (1989), "Macroeconomic Implications of Population Aging," paper presented at the Conference on the Economics of Aging jointly sponsored by the Nihon Keizai Kenkyū Sentā (Japan Economic Research Center) and the National Bureau of Economic Research, held on September 8–9, 1989, in Tokyo, Japan.

Noguchi, Yukio (1990), "Jinkō Kōzō to Chochiku/Tōshi: Kakkoku Hikaku ni yoru Bunseki," (The Age Structure of the Population and Saving/Investment: An Analysis based on Cross-Country Comparisons), Finansharu Rebyū (Financial Review) (Ōkura-shō, Zaisei Kin'yū Kenkyū-sho/Institute of Fiscal and Monetary Policy, Ministry of Finance, ed.), no. 17 (August), pp. 39–50 (in Japanese).

Sakamoto, Yasuhiro (1990), "Nenkin Kaikaku: Shōhi Seikō, Dhaba ni Teika" (Pension Reform: The Propensity to Consume Will Decline Sharply), Nihon Keizai Shinbun (Japan Economic Journal), September 6, p. 27 (in Japanese)

Sato, Kazuo (1987), "Saving and Investment," in Kozo Yamamura and Yasukichi Yasuba, eds., The Political Economy of Japan, vol. 1: The Domestic Transformation (Stanford, California: Stanford University Press), pp. 137–185.

Notes

* The author is grateful to Hidekazu Eguchi, Kyōji Fukao, Kōichi Hamada, Toshihiko Hayashi, Kazuhiro Igawa, Toshihiro Ihori, Kazumasa Iwata, Carl Kester, Tetsuya Kishimoto, Lawrence Klein, Masahiro Kuroda, Ygsuke Onitsuka, Noriyuki Takayama, an anonymous referee, and participants of the "U.S.-Japan Conference on Investment and Trade Friction," which was co-sponsored by the Center for Japan-U. S. Business and Economic Studies, Leonard N. Stern School of Business, New York University; The Council for Better Corporate Citizenship; and Keizai Kōhō Center (Japan Institute for Social and Economic Affairs) and held in Tokyo, Japan, on November 15–16, 1989, and of the International Symposium on "A Quest for a More Stable World Economic System," which was sponsored by the Kokusai Kōtō Kenkyū-sho (International Institute for Advanced Studies) and held in Osaka, Japan, on October 22–25, 1990, for valuable comments and discussions. Any errors and omissions that remain are the responsibility of the author alone, and any opinions expressed are those of the author and should not be attributed to any institution or organization. This chapter was originally published in Japan and the World Economy, vol. 3, no. 4 (1992). The author is grateful to the publisher, Elsevier Science Publishers B. V., for permission to reprint it here.

Table 1. Trends over Time in Japan's Saving Rate

Calendar Year	Household Saving Rate Unadjusted	Adjusted	Private Saving Rate Unadjusted	Adjusted	National Saving Rate Unadjusted	Adjusted
1955	12.2		13.6		15.2	
1956	13.1		14.6		17.4	
1957	12.7		17.0		20.3	
1958	12.7		15.7		18.1	
1959	14.0		17.7		20.4	
1960	14.6		21.7		24.8	
1961	15.9		23.1		26.9	
1962	15.5		20.9		24.8	
1963	14.8		20.0		23.6	
1964	15.3		20.3		23.7	
1965	15.6		19.2		22.3	
1966	14.8		20.6		23.2	
1967	13.9		22.7		25.6	
1968	16.6		25.2		27.9	
1969	16.8		26.4		29.2	
1970	17.6	16.8	27.9	27.6	31.1	29.8
1971	17.8	16.9	24.8	24.0	28.5	26.9
1972	18.2	17.3	25.4	25.3	28.2	27.2
1973	20.5	18.7	26.0	24.5	29.3	26.7
1974	23.2	20.8	23.6	18.2	26.7	20.8
1975	22.9	21.1	22.2	17.4	22.4	16.9
1976	23.2	21.3	24.0	18.9	23.0	17.0
1977	21.8	19.9	23.1	18.1	22.5	16.5
1978	21.0	19.2	24.4	20.0	22.9	17.4
1979	18.3	16.0	22.1	16.9	21.8	15.5
1980	18.0	15.3	21.1	15.3	21.1	13.9
1981	18.4	16.0	20.3	15.2	20.8	14.5
1982	16.6	14.4	19.4	14.4	19.8	13.5
1983	16.3	14.1	18.7	14.1	18.7	12.7
1984	16.0	13.9	18.9	14.2	19.8	13.8
1985	15.9	13.8	18.9	14.9	20.9	15.7
1986	16.3	14.6	19.3	15.3	21.0	15.9
1987	15.0	13.2	17.5	14.1	21.3	16.7
1988	14.7		17.0		22.4	

Notes: Refer to the text for variable definitions. The "unadjusted" figures are based on historical cost depreciation, while the "adjusted" figures are based on replacement cost depreciation. The adjustment was made using the same method as that used by Hayashi (1986).

(continued)

Table 1 (continued)

Sources:
(for 1955-1969 data)   Keizai Kikaku-chō Keizai Kenkyū-sho (Economic
Planning Agency, Economic Research Institute), ed., *Kokumin Keizai
Keisan Hōkoku (Chōki Sokyū Suikei)* (Report on National Accounts from
1955 to 1969) (Tokyo, Japan: Ūkura-shō Insatsu-kyoku, 1988).

(for certain 1970-1974 data)   Keizai Kikaku-chō, Keizai Kenkyū-sho
(Economic Planning Agency, Economic Research Institute), ed., *Shōwa
55-nen Kijun Kaitei Kokumin Keizai Keisan Hōkoku* (Report on Revised
National Accounts on the Basis of 1980), volume 1 (Tokyo, Japan:
Ūkura-shō Insatsu-kyoku, 1986).

(for 1970-1988 data) Keizai Kikaku-chō, Keizai Kenkyū-sho (Economic
Planning Agency, Economic Research Institute), ed., *Kokumin Keizai
Keisan Nenpō* (Annual Report on National Accounts), 1990 edition
(Tokyo, Japan: Ūkura-shō Insatsu-kyoku, 1990).

Table 2. An International Comparison of Household Saving Rates

Country	1975-79	1980-84	1985-87	1975-87
Australia[1]	11.6 (8)	8.4(11)	7.3(11)	9.4(10)
Austria	10.2(10)	9.1 (9)	10.6 (8)	9.8 (9)
Belgium	16.8 (3)	15.1 (4)	12.1 (5)	15.1 (3)
Canada	12.5 (7)	15.4 (3)	11.6 (7)	13.4 (4)
Denmark	--	--	--	--
Finland	4.5(14)	5.1(14)	2.6(14)	4.3(14)
France	13.8 (4)	11.5 (8)	9.6[3](9)	12.3[4](7)
Germany, W.[2]	13.0 (6)	12.2 (6)	12.0 (6)	12.5 (6)
Greece	--	--	--	--
Iceland	--	--	--	--
Ireland	--	--	--	--
Italy	22.6 (1)	20.3 (1)	15.9 (1)	20.1 (1)
Japan	21.4 (2)	17.1 (2)	15.8 (2)	18.5 (2)
Luxembourg	--	--	--	--
Netherlands[2]	13.2 (5)	13.6 (5)	13.5 (4)	13.4 (4)
New Zealand	--	--	--	--
Norway	5.6(13)	4.2(15)	-4.3(16)	2.8(15)
Portugal	--	--	--	--
Spain	--	8.3(12)	8.4[5](10)	8.4[6](11)
Sweden	4.0(15)	2.5(16)	-0.9 (15)	2.3 (16)
Switzerland	11.3 (9)	11.8 (7)	13.8 (3)	12.0 (8)
Turkey	--	--	--	--
U.K.[1]	7.7(12)	8.2(13)	5.3[5](13)	7.5[7](13)
U.S.	9.3(11)	8.6(10)	6.1 (12)	8.3 (12)
Yugoslavia	--	--	--	--

Notes:
The figures represent the saving rate (in percent) of households, private unincorporated enterprises, and private nonprofit institutions serving households (except where noted) and were calculated as the sum of the net saving of the three entities divided by the sum of the net saving and final consumption expenditure of the three entities.

(continued)

Table 2   (continued)

The figures are based on calendar year data denominated in current units of the currency of each country except that the figures for Australia and New Zealand are on a fiscal year basis (July 1 - June 30 in the case of Australia and April 1 - March 31 in the case of New Zealand).

The figures in parentheses represent the rank of each country.

1. Excludes private nonprofit institutions serving households. However, in the case of Australia, a portion of the final consumption expenditure of private nonprofit institutions serving households is included in the final consumption expenditure of the household sector.

2. Excludes private unincorporated enterprises.

3. Represents the figure for 1985.

4. Represents the average for 1975-1985.

5. Represents the average for 1985-1986.

6. Represents the average for 1980-1986.

7. Represents the average for 1975-1986.

8. "--" denotes "not available"

Sources: Organization for Economic Cooperation and Development, Department of Economics and Statistics, *National Accounts*, Volume II: *Detailed Tables*, *1975-1987* (1989 edition) (Paris: OECD, 1989). However, data for France were taken from the 1987 edition of the same source, and data for Italy were taken from the 1985 and 1990 editions of the same source.

318

Table 3. An International Comparison of the Age Structure of the Population

Country	AGE	DEP	Year
Australia	0.174(23)	0.571 (5)	1983
Austria	0.243 (5)	0.434(19)	1986
Belgium	0.229(10)	0.447(18)	1984
Canada	0.176(21)	0.478(14)	1986
Denmark	0.258 (4)	0.431(20)	1986
Finland	0.208(17)	0.430(21)	1986
France	0.229 (9)	0.490(12)	1987
Germany, W.	0.241 (6)	0.360(25)	1986
Greece	0.231 (8)	0.505 (9)	1984
Iceland	0.185(20)	0.651 (3)	1984
Ireland	0.212(15)	0.765 (2)	1985
Italy	0.216(13)	0.478(13)	1984
Japan	0.174(22)	0.473(15)	1986
Luxembourg	0.212(14)	0.394(24)	1985
Netherlands	0.203(18)	0.454(17)	1986
New Zealand	0.187(19)	0.596 (4)	1986
Norway	0.283 (2)	0.490(11)	1986
Portugal	0.217(11)	0.557 (6)	1986
Spain	0.217(12)	0.535 (7)	1987
Sweden	0.315 (1)	0.413(22)	1987
Switzerland	0.240 (7)	0.390(23)	1986
Turkey	0.105(25)	1.117 (1)	1980
U.K.	0.265 (3)	0.466(16)	1986
U.S.	0.209(16)	0.497(10)	1987
Yugoslavia	0.142(24)	0.528 (8)	1985

Notes: AGE = the ratio of the population aged 65 and over to the population aged 20 to 64.

DEP = the ratio of the population aged 19 and under to the population aged 20 to 64.

The figures in parentheses indicate the rank of each country.

Source: United Nations, *Demographic Yearbook* (1987 edition) (New York: United Nations, 1989).

Table 4. Trends over Time in AGE and DEP

Year	AGE	DEP	AGE+DEP
1955	0.103	0.838	0.941
1956	0.102	0.819	0.922
1957	0.102	0.798	0.900
1958	0.103	0.775	0.878
1959	0.104	0.759	0.863
1960	0.105	0.743	0.848
1961	0.106	0.721	0.826
1962	0.106	0.698	0.804
1963	0.108	0.677	0.785
1964	0.109	0.657	0.766
1965	0.110	0.646	0.756
1966	0.112	0.637	0.750
1967	0.114	0.617	0.732
1968	0.115	0.593	0.708
1969	0.116	0.568	0.684
1970	0.117	0.551	0.668
1971	0.118	0.538	0.657
1972	0.120	0.531	0.651
1973	0.123	0.526	0.649
1974	0.126	0.524	0.650
1975	0.129	0.520	0.649
1976	0.133	0.518	0.651
1977	0.137	0.517	0.654
1978	0.141	0.515	0.656
1979	0.146	0.511	0.657
1980	0.150	0.508	0.658
1981	0.154	0.504	0.658
1982	0.157	0.499	0.656
1983	0.160	0.493	0.654
1984	0.163	0.487	0.650
1985	0.168	0.478	0.646
1986	0.173	0.474	0.647
1987	0.178	0.465	0.642
1988	0.182	0.454	0.636
1989	0.187	0.446	0.633
1990	0.193	0.437	0.630
1991	0.200	0.428	0.628
1992	0.206	0.419	0.625
1993	0.213	0.409	0.622
1994	0.220	0.401	0.621
1995	0.227	0.394	0.622
1996	0.235	0.391	0.626
1997	0.243	0.389	0.632
1998	0.252	0.389	0.641
1999	0.260	0.390	0.650
2000	0.268	0.393	0.661
2001	0.278	0.397	0.675
2002	0.287	0.401	0.688
2003	0.295	0.405	0.700

(continued)

Table 4 (continued)

Year	AGE	DEP	AGE+DEP
2004	0.301	0.409	0.710
2005	0.309	0.414	0.723
2006	0.319	0.420	0.739
2007	0.331	0.426	0.756
2008	0.341	0.430	0.771
2009	0.351	0.435	0.786
2010	0.357	0.437	0.794
2011	0.360	0.437	0.797
2012	0.372	0.440	0.812
2013	0.388	0.443	0.832
2014	0.405	0.446	0.851
2015	0.418	0.447	0.865
2016	0.428	0.446	0.873
2017	0.434	0.443	0.877
2018	0.438	0.439	0.878
2019	0.440	0.435	0.875
2020	0.440	0.430	0.870
2021	0.440	0.425	0.865
2022	0.437	0.420	0.857
2023	0.435	0.416	0.851
2024	0.433	0.413	0.845
2025	0.431	0.410	0.841
2026	0.428	0.409	0.837
2027	0.426	0.409	0.834
2028	0.424	0.409	0.834
2029	0.424	0.411	0.835
2030	0.425	0.414	0.839
2031	0.422	0.417	0.839
2032	0.424	0.421	0.844
2033	0.426	0.425	0.852
2034	0.430	0.430	0.860
2035	0.434	0.436	0.870
2036	0.439	0.441	0.880
2037	0.445	0.446	0.891
2038	0.452	0.451	0.903
2039	0.458	0.456	0.914
2040	0.463	0.459	0.922
2041	0.466	0.461	0.927
2042	0.467	0.462	0.929
2043	0.467	0.462	0.929
2044	0.466	0.460	0.926
2045	0.464	0.458	0.922
2046	0.461	0.455	0.916
2047	0.457	0.452	0.909
2048	0.454	0.448	0.901
2049	0.449	0.444	0.893
2050	0.444	0.440	0.885

Table 4   (continued)

Notes: AGE = the ratio of the population aged 65 and over to the population
          aged 20 to 64.

          DEP = the ratio of the population aged 19 and under to the
               population aged 20 to 64.

          The figures shown are as of July 1 and were converted from an October
          1 basis to a July 1 basis by interpolating linearly.

Sources: The figures for 1955-1988 were calculated from data presented in
          Sōmu-chō, Tōkei-kyoku (Statistics Bureau, Management and Coordination
          Agency), *Jinkō Suikei Shiryō* (Estimates of Population), except that
          the figures for years ending in 0 or 5 were calculated from d a t a
          presented in Sōmu-chō, Tokei-kyoku Statistics Bureau, Management and
          Coordination Agency), *Kokusei Chōsa* (Census of Population).

          The figures for 1989-2050 were calculated from the medium estimates
          (chūi suikei) of population by age group presented in Tables 2-1,
          2-2, and 2-3 (pp. 46-51) of Kōsei-shō, Jinkō Mondai Kenkyū-sho
          (Institute for Population Problems, Ministry of Health and Welfare)
          (1987).

Table 5. Coefficients of AGE and DEP

Dependent variable	Coefficient of AGE (T-stat.)	Coefficient of DEP (T-stat.)	Other variables included
Cross-country regression, 21 OECD countries			
Private saving rate	-1.0947 (-2.377)	-0.4350 (-1.729)	Growth rate of income, reciprocal of income, labor force partici- pation rate of the aged
Time series regressions, 1956-87, Japan			
Household saving rate	-1.1279 (-3.7112)	-0.3020 (-5.0948)	Growth rate of income, inflation rate, corporate saving
Private saving rate	-1.0374 (-1.8006)	-0.2904 (-2.8992)	Growth rate of income, unemploy- ment rate
National saving rate	-2.4978 (-3.2906)	-0.4751 (-2.9203)	Growth rate of income

Sources: Horioka (1989) for the cross-country regression and Horioka (1991) for the time series regressions.

Table 6. Future Trends in Japan's Saving Rate

Year	(1) Household saving rate	(2) Private saving rate	(3) Private saving rate
1975-84	--	--	21.4*
1985	13.8*	14.9*	20.7
1986	14.6*	15.3*	20.3
1987	13.2*	14.1*	20.2
1988	13.0	13.9	20.2
1989	12.7	13.6	20.0
1990	12.3	13.3	19.7
1991	11.8	12.8	19.4
1992	11.4	12.4	19.1
1993	10.9	12.0	18.8
1994	10.4	11.5	18.4
1995	9.7	10.9	17.8
1996	9.0	10.2	17.2
1997	8.1	9.4	16.3
1998	7.1	8.6	15.4
1999	6.2	7.7	14.4
2000	5.1	6.7	13.4
2001	4.0	5.6	12.2
2002	2.8	4.6	11.0
2003	1.8	3.6	10.0
2004	1.0	2.9	9.1
2005	-0.1	1.9	8.0
2006	-1.4	0.6	6.6
2007	-2.9	-0.7	5.2
2008	-4.2	-1.9	3.8
2009	-5.5	-3.1	2.5
2010	-6.2	-3.8	1.8
2011	-6.5	-4.1	1.5
2012	-8.0	-5.4	0.0
2013	-9.9	-7.2	-1.9
2014	-11.8	-9.0	-3.8
2015	-13.4	-10.4	-5.3
2016	-14.4	-11.3	-6.3
2017	-15.1	-11.9	-6.9
2018	-15.4	-12.3	-7.2
2019	-15.5	-12.3	-7.2
2020	-15.4	-12.2	-7.0
2021	-15.1	-12.0	-6.7
2022	-14.7	-11.6	-6.2
2023	-14.3	-11.2	-5.8
2024	-14.0	-10.9	-5.5
2025	-13.7	-10.6	-5.1
2026	-13.4	-10.3	-4.8
2027	-13.1	-10.1	-4.5
2028	-13.0	-9.9	-4.4
2029	-12.9	-9.9	-4.4

(continued)

Table 6   (continued)

Year	(1) Household saving rate	(2) Private saving rate	(3) Private saving rate
2030	-13.2	-10.2	-4.7
2031	-13.0	-10.0	-4.5
2032	-13.2	-10.2	-4.8
2033	-13.7	-10.6	-5.3
2034	-14.2	-11.1	-5.9
2035	-14.8	-11.7	-6.6
2036	-15.6	-12.4	-7.4
2037	-16.4	-13.2	-8.3
2038	-17.3	-14.0	-9.2
2039	-18.2	-14.8	-10.1
2040	-18.8	-15.4	-10.7
2041	-19.2	-15.7	-11.2
2042	-19.3	-15.9	-11.3
2043	-19.4	-15.9	-11.3
2044	-19.2	-15.8	-11.2
2045	-18.9	-15.5	-10.9
2046	-18.5	-15.1	-10.4
2047	-18.0	-14.6	-9.8
2048	-17.4	-14.1	-9.3
2049	-16.8	-13.6	-8.6
2050	-16.1	-12.9	-7.9

Notes: The figures in columns (1) and (2) were computed using the regression
results based on time series data, while the figures in column (3)
were computed using regression results based on cross-country data.   T h e
regression coefficients used for the projections are those shown   in Table 5,
while the AGE and DEP data used are those shown in Table   4.

The figures in columns (1) and (2) are based on replacement cost
depreciation, while those in column (3) are based on historical cost
depreciation.

* Actual value.

Table 7. Summary of Projections of Future Trends
in Japan's Saving Rate

Source	Saving rate concept	Year	Saving rate		
			Unadjusted	National income accounts basis	
				Depreciation valued at historical cost	Depreciation valued at replacement cost
Section 5.1 of this chapter	Household	2019	-15.5	-13.6	-15.5
Fukao and Doi (1985) and Keizai Kikaku- chō (Economic Planning Agency) (1985)	Household	2016-2030	6.9 to 12.6	2.3 to 8.0	0.1 to 5.8
Maki et al. (1990)	Household	2020-2025	-9.8 to 8.7	-16.4 to 2.1	-18.5 to 0.0
Noguchi(1986)	Household	2015	-2.6 to -1.3	3.7 to 6.8	1.6 to 4.7
Noguchi(1987)	Household	2020	-7.0 to -3.0	2.3 to 6.2	0.2 to 4.1
Noguchi(1989)	Household	2020	-8.5 to 0.2	0.6 to 9.3	-1.5 to 7.2
Section 5.1 of this chapter (re- sults based on time series data)	Private	2018-2019	-12.3	-8.8	-12.3
Section 5.1 of this chapter (results based on cross- country data)	Private	2018-2019	-7.2	-7.2	-10.7
Masson and Tryon (1990)	Private	2025	--	8.3	4.5
Auerbach et al. (1989)	National	2030	1.8 to 3.7	1.8 to 3.7	-2.7 to -1.0

Note: Refer to the text for details.

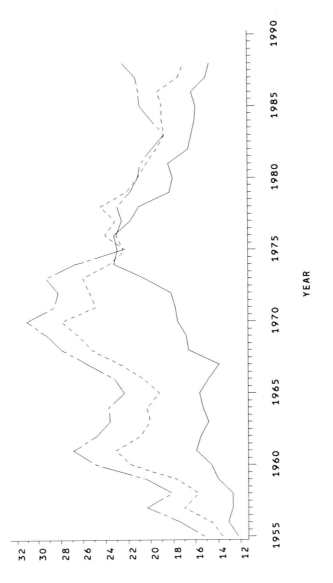

Figure 1: Trends over Time in Japan's Saving Rate

———— Household saving rate
------- Private saving rate
-·--·-· National saving rate

Note: Based on historical cost depreciation.

Source: Table 1.

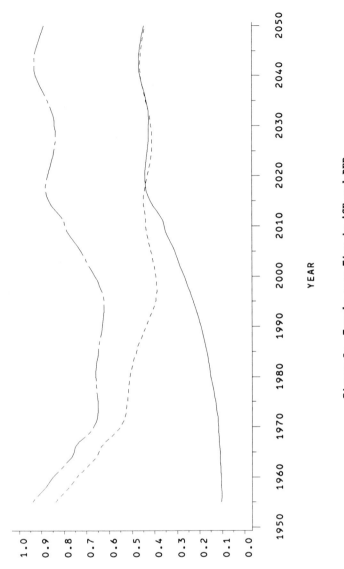

Figure 2: Trends over Time in AGE and DEP

AGE ——
DEP ------
AGE + DEP -·--·--·

Source: Table 4.

328

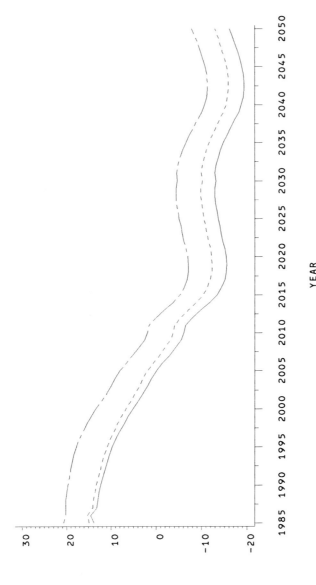

YEAR

Figure 3: Future Trends in Japan's Saving Rate

——— Household saving rate (based on time series regression results)
------- Private saving rate (based on time series regression results)
· · · · · Private saving rate (based on cross-country regression results)

Source: Table 6.

19. SUMMARY BY DR. CHRISTOPHER HIGGINS OF SESSION 3: "THE DEBT PROBLEM AND INTERNATIONAL FINANCIAL MARKETS"

1. DISCUSSION OF AKIHIRO AMANO'S CHAPTER, "LATIN AMERICAN DEBT: MACROECONOMIC ENVIRONMENT AND ECONOMIC STRUCTURE"

Professor Onitsuka supported Amano's main conclusion that structural adjustment is the only solution to the external debt problem--that relief measures such as debt and interest forgiveness would not produce significant effects in the Latin American situation. He was concerned, however, that the model being used to address structural adjustment issues was basically of the demand-determined type. He felt that it should be supplemented by an investment-saving balance approach and by distinction between importables, exportables, and nontraded goods, with their relative prices playing an important role. Neglect of the supply side meant that an adjustment program could not be made explicit and had to be left as a "black box," only being specified in terms of import and export elasticities.

Professor Igawa conjectured that the differences between Latin American and Asian economies might be so great as to preclude the use of a common model of the type Amano employed. He had in mind financial systems and inflation-proneness. He suggested that a real balance effect in a monetary growth setting would be a suitable alternative mechanism for generating the desirable saddle-point characteristic. Professor Kawai was troubled by the inherent instability in the model and would prefer a specification that removed it since, in his view, economies were not characterized by permanent instability. Professor Hamada noted that instability was not all that infrequent. Professor Amano noted that every model has its advantages and disadvantages. This instability property was necessary to generate the observed debt explosion within a relatively short period.

Professor Kawai also pointed out that the debt variable might preferably be net external liabilities rather than gross debt to account, inter alia, for capital flight. Professor Eaton noted that such funds were typically not available to the public authorities, having basically been "stolen" and being outside the domestic tax base. Professor Kawai felt it was an important omission not to have explicitly modeled the government sector, given that notions of macroeconomic populism seem to be important in understanding the Latin American situation.

Referring to Prebisch's arguments about relative elasticities, Professor Klein asked Amano if he was confident that in some instances Asian income elasticities of exports were higher than those of Latin America. Similarly, price elasticities of exports for Asia were not much above those of Latin America. Had Amano carefully examined lag structures? Professor Amano said he had, but being restricted to total trade variables probably shortened the average lag.

In conclusion, Professor Amano underlined that his model illustrated the possibility, on the one hand, of largely explaining the Asian experience by reference to external factors, whereas, on the other hand, internal as well as external factors were necessary to explain the Latin American case. This was important, he felt, as a counterweight to the stress that some (such as Rudiger Dornbusch) placed on external factors in the Latin American case. He accepted Professor Onitsuka's "black box" point, but noted that the major policy implication—namely, that the resolution of the Latin American problem necessarily required domestic action—was clear.

2. DISCUSSION OF SOLITA COLLAS-MONSOD'S CHAPTER, "DEVELOPING COUNTRY DEBY: QUO VADIS?"

Professor Onitsuka accepted the model that Professor Monsod had used, but was not prepared to endorse what he took to be the basic message: that foreign financing should come first and structural adjustment later, or maybe at the same time. Professor Eaton similarly observed that it seemed to him that those countries in which there had been more structural adjustment — such as Indonesia and South Korea — were the ones making the larger transfers to creditors. Something similar was perhaps now occurring in Mexico and Brazil. He felt certain, in any event, that in Latin America there had been little structural adjustment when the resource flows were going the other way. Professor Helliwell noted that in cross-section analysis there was an inverse relationship between reliance on foreign savings and growth performance in the 1960s and 1970s.

Professor Monsod said her main message was that foreign savings and structural reforms are a "both/and" proposition, whereas, unfortunately, the current debt strategy is "either/or." She argued that South Korea and Indonesia did much of their structural adjustment in the 1970s as recipients of foreign savings, placing them in a better position when the debt crisis erupted in the 1980s. The Philippines and most Latin American countries had used foreign savings as a substitute for structural adjustment. This was relevant to Helliwell's observation.

Professor Igawa wondered why the slope of the saving constraint was less steep than that of the fiscal constraint — if they were reversed there would be strong policy implications. Professor Monsod pointed out that provided government investment has a net positive effect on private investment — which she felt was realistic — then the slope relativities held. Professor Eaton took issue with the basic "fixed rigidity" features of the n-gap models. Changes in policies can often remove these rigidities, he argued, so that these models have contributed to misleading policy implications. On this point Professor Monsod wryly observed that the parameters one wanted to be flexible were often rigid, and vice versa. For example, import protection fosters poor-quality production, and so when it is removed, even with high tariffs, producers are willing to pay more for quality, leading to a sharp lift in imports. Exports, unfortunately, do not respond so fast.

Professor Eaton observed in relation to Monsod's point that some structural adjustment is very harsh on the poor—that in many developing countries policies that hurt the poor seem easy to undertake, but when policies threaten the rich they seem very difficult.

Concerning what Professor Monsod referred to as the "creditor cartel," Professor Igawa noted that this kind of "free riding" was rational behavior for the banks. He felt that to solve the problem, incentive-compatible market mechanisms were required and the multilateral institutions had a role to play in designing those. Professor Monsod observed that breaking the "creditor cartel" would be market-conforming. Professor Eaton felt that Monsod's chapter had done a nice job in exposing the net transfer going on from multilateral institutions to the commercial banks, rewarding them for their incompetent lending practices of the 1970s. Professor Onitsuka argued that the world would have been in a much worse situation if a number of commercial banks had been allowed to fail. Moreover, he said, we cannot blame private agents for acting in their own interest, including to avoid bankruptcy. Professor Klein observed that it was not easy to assign culpability in all this — it was probably in the original approach to the recycling of the petro-surplus, in which the multilateral institutions and the banks were both involved, that the mistakes were made. Professor Monsod said her view was that all parties were culpable, yet all the burden is on the debtor countries. She argued that by the end of 1988 the major U.S. commercial banks had been given a clean bill of health; the time had come to shift from "favored bank treatment to favored nation treatment."

3. DISCUSSION OF GIORGIO BASEVI'S CHAPTER: "SOME IMPLICATIONS OF THE DEVELOP-MENTS IN EASTERN EUROPE FOR THE EUROPEAN ECONOMIC AND MONETARY UNION"

Professor Onitsuka saw a great deal of heuristic power in Basevi's model, particularly in motivating a two-speed approach to European unification. He worried, however, that these results were obtained in a closed economy setting.

Onitsuka was also concerned that the analysis was comparative dynamics whereas the shift of production functions involved in integration should itself be modeled. Professor Basevi acknowledged this.

Professor Igawa commented on three of Basevi's four strands of adjustment. With respect to the second — markets with slow adjustment being integrated first — he referred to trade theory results that if commodity markets are first integrated, then large costs of factor movement will be avoided. Did this not suggest the opposite order of integration? Basevi pointed out, however, that it was important to distinguish between differences internationally in speeds of adjustment and differences by markets. The overshooting literature shows us that the problem being faced in integration arises from different speeds of adjustment between markets, not countries. In that circumstance, which he referred to as a "second-best" situation, the trade theory result does not carry through (as discussed in his chapter).

On the second — the multiple equilibria rationale — Igawa asked whether the fact that scale economies are large for small economies and not large for large countries might be an alternative explanation. Basevi thought this might be the case and generalized the point in relation to German integration. Thus, scale economies plus differentiated products, etc. (cf. new trade theory à la Krugman-Helpman) may help to explain why Germany is more interested in integrating with the East than it has been in the past with some countries in the West.

On the fourth strand, Igawa questioned whether postintegration concern with inflation in Germany might not be overstated in the event that Germany's terms of trade do improve. Professor Niwa argued that there was some excess capacity in Europe, so that moderate expansion in the money supply should be accepted. Professor Basevi disputed this, particularly with respect to products in which the additional demand would be concentrated — capital goods and sophisticated consumer goods. He went on to argue for immigration from the East or elsewhere and reduction in EC protection vis-à-vis the rest of the world, particularly in agriculture.

Professor Pauly admired the model, but suspected it illuminated little of the present behavior of the German monetary authorities. He felt they were anxious to avoid (the next time around, as it were) what they felt were mistakes into which they were forced with German monetary union—namely, they had moved too quickly at incorrect exchange rates. He also asked why budgetary coordination in a monetary union is necessary. Why not let the market assign risk premiums to individual countries and enforce discipline on the budgetary side through market forces? Professor Kawai asked a related question: were intra–EMS fiscal transfers a serious problem for European Monetary Union? Basevi agreed with Pauly, but argued that the Bundesbank's basic concern was not with fiscal coordination per se, but rather was to avoid monetizing the past debt accumulated by, say, Italy, Spain, Greece, or Belgium. In the same vein, intra–EMS fiscal transfers were not a weighty consideration.

Basevi added that while the overlapping generations model does not perhaps explain the whole story, it does provide an insight into the "structural" reservations about rapid integration. Second-best arguments have normally been advanced to argue why integration has to be postponed (e.g., remove labor–market rigidity first). These ended up being not very compelling: whatever amount of liberalizing has been achieved, it is said to be not enough. He had therefore looked for deeper rationalizations for a two-speed approach.

4. DISCUSSION OF CHARLES Y. HORIOKA'S CHAPTER, "FUTURE TRENDS IN JAPAN'S SAVING RATE"

Professor Onitsuka was very skeptical of long-run projections driven solely by age-structure. He advocated inclusion of income, wealth, financial assets, etc. Professor Igawa concurred, and Professor Horioka accepted this line of criticism.

Professor Hamada observed that microeconomic studies do not support the underlying model, which assumes that older generations decumulate to expected zero assets at the time of expected death. Horioka agreed it was hard to reconcile the micro and macro results.

Professor Igawa pointed out that the national saving rate includes government saving. Professor Horioka accepted that it was necessary to take the government balance into account short of full Ricardian equivalence. He noted that, on the one hand, the government may choose to offset the projected decline in private saving but, on the other, as the population ages the budget will be faced with growing age-related expenditures.

Professor Niwa argued that a gradual decline in Japan's saving rate does not necessarily mean a decline in the growth rate. He gave as an example the experience of the 1930s with Keynesian fiscal policy. Horioka responded that in his view, while this may be possible for a short period, it would not be viable in the long run in the absence of reliance on foreign capital.

In the keynote chapters and the more highly focused chapters by Gernot Nerb and Giorgio Basevi, great attention is paid to the structural shifts taking place in the formerly socialist economies of Eastern Europe and the Soviet Union. The concluding session of the conference dealt entirely with this problem — how to go from a planned to a market economy, the capital transfers involved (together with their international consequences) the reductions in military spending, and the conversion of production facilities from military to civilian objectives. These topics are of great importance, yet they are not well understood. It was therefore fitting to have an entire session devoted to these issues, even though they appeared in previous presentations and permeated the entire conference discussion.

Herbert Levine's chapter provides an excellent analysis of how things stood in October 1990, but events overtook the plans that were being discussed then. For example, the Shatalin (500–day) Plan was much discussed then, but was not implemented. Professor Levine's chapter provides an analysis of how the Soviet economic predicament developed and rationalized the joint political and economic forces that were at work. Professor Levine rejects radical reform, fearful of the chaos that would result, and shows, in a positive sense, what is needed from the workings of the market system. His chapter addresses the central issue of how to move from plan to market but does not lay out the step–by–step process of moving from one system to the other. This is probably an impossible task.

Haruki Niwa's chapter also deals with the swift passage of events. He considers the economic reform problem in an environment in which the Soviet Union remains as a superpower. After the conference, the country became a split and transformed entity.

Niwa fully anticipated the inflation that has ensued — in excess of 100% annually, one year later—and the continuing process of financing budget deficits by printing paper money. He recognizes that a successful transition will have to reduce public deficits substantially and eliminate the ruble overhang.

In addition to treating the Soviet and East European situation, Professor Niwa studies the economic abilities of Japan and the Asian NIEs. He looks for continuing good economic performance, but 1991 was not so favorable for some of the countries involved, especially Japan and South Korea.

Two gloomy issues were pointed out by Professor Niwa: an oil crisis and trade friction. Energy problems remained, but not in crisis form in the oil market. Trade friction, however, persists. He perceives good prospects for Japan in dealing with these two issues in the years to come.

Finally, he comments on PAX RUSSO–AMERICANA. This may not be a relevant subject one year later, but Professor Niwa points out that the USSR would have to restructure its economy and cut military expenditures in order to continue in peaceful coexistence and maintain a calm world situation.

Peter Pauly uses the models of Project LINK to analyze the effects of resource transfers from Western industrial countries to Eastern Europe and the Soviet Union. He considers a program of assistance that is roughly two–thirds the size of the Marshall Plan after the second World War, and estimates the effects on both creditor and debtor countries (West and East, respectively) of resource transfers made under three scenarios:

1. Best case—no interest-rate response to the transfer
2. Worst case—interest rates up by 100 basis points, world-wide
3. Neutral case—accommodating monetary policies calibrated to hold rate increases to 20–50 basis points.

In the best case, both East and West would realize gains. Large changes would occur in Eastern Europe and the Soviet Union; after five years, their GNP values would be up by about 3%. Relative to the gains that were realized under the Marshall Plan, these appear to be small. The feedback affects on Western donor nations would occur, but the effects would be much more modest in percentage terms.

In the worst case, Eastern Europe and the Soviet Union would gain, as before, but there would be no gains in the West because interest-rate increases would hurt capital formation and offset any feedback gains from higher exports to Eastern countries.

In the neutral case, the East gains as before, but there would be virtually no change in Western levels of activity, except for the United States, where there would be a small decline in economic activity.

The sole conference participant from the USSR, Vladimir Faltsman, took up conversion and reform in the USSR. By conversion he meant changing production flows from military to civilian uses by altering the composition of production at the plant level. He provided a very knowledgeable analysis of the potential magnitude of conversion for certain lines of production, how conversion could be financed (mainly self-financed), how it could be managed, and how its efficiency could be improved. All in all, Dr. Faltsman gave a realistic but moderately encouraging analysis of what gains might be realized for the civilian economy by reducing the claims on the economy's resources by the military.

21. SOVIET ECONOMIC REFORM: THE TRANSITION ISSUE

Herbert S. Levine
University of Pennsylvania

ABSTRACT.   In the first part of this chapter, the problems inherent in the transition from central planning to a market system are discussed.   Essentially they stem from the interrelated nature of an economic system that requires that a bundle of changes have to be made simultaneously for any meaningful reform to get started.   This creates a dilemma in that a large bundle of simultaneous changes in the old system will lead to a danger of significant economic, social, and political destabilization.   In the second part of the chapter, Soviet reform measures from 1987 through 1990 are described and analyzed.

1.   THE BASIC DIFFICULTY FACING THE SOVIET ECONOMY

The fundamental issue facing Soviet economic reform today is the problem of transition from a centralized to a decentralized economic system.   Even if the design for a new economic mechanism were perfect, the dominant problem would still be how to get there from here.   This chapter will focus on the issue of transition — its meaning and its consequences for the progress of Soviet economic reform.

It is important to note from the start that while there is abundant Western theory to help Soviet economists design a market system, there is no available theory of transition from a centralized arrangement of economic institutions to a decentralized one.   Western economists have not been concerned with this issue, since the development of decentralized economic mechanisms in the West took place slowly over long periods of time spanning more than a century.   And Soviet economists themselves have only recently begun to work on the issue.   Previously it was not a subject of concern, since radical market-type reform itself was not openly discussed.   Hence there are no theoretical guides, either Western or Soviet, that Soviet leaders and economists can draw upon as they attempt to deal with the problems of transition.

At the basis of the transition problem is the interrelated nature of an economic system.   One element of the system cannot be changed without changing other elements if true change in economic behavior is to be achieved.   Thus, in order to give Soviet managers decision-making power over what they are to produce, they must also be given the power to decide what inputs they will use: materials, labor, and machinery.

First, if managers are to have the power to decide what materials they will use, the centralized system of material supply, introduced in the 1930s, has to be abolished, and a system of wholesale trade put in its place.   But given the widespread nature of material shortages in Soviet industry, there is a fear that the removal of the centralized materials-rationing system will exacerbate these shortages and cause massive disequilibria in the economy.   Supporters of reform, however, argue that the rationing system itself contributes to the appearance of shortages, because managers, operating within the administrative centralized supply system, order an excessive amount of inputs to protect themselves against the inefficiencies and uncertainties of the command system.

Second, Soviet managers have to be given increased power over the hiring and firing of workers. If managers are to be encouraged to seek out and adopt advanced technology in the pursuit of the reform's goal of economic moderniza- tion, they have to have the right to adjust their labor force to the quantity and quality levels appropriate to the new technology. This means giving managers the right to fire not only workers who are malingering, but also those who are working hard but who are made redundant by the new technology. Thus the extensive job security enjoyed by Soviet workers, especially during the Brezhnev period, will be diminished. But as many Soviet economists argue, the Soviet guarantee of full employment should guarantee the Soviet worker a job, not guarantee his job. Institutional arrangements will have to be expanded for handling unemployment and for the retraining and redistribution of labor.

Third, managers have to have the power to acquire the capital equipment that they decide they need. This again involves the abolition of the centralized system of materials and equipment supply and its replacement with a market system of wholesale trade. It also, however, involves the question of investment and credit. If managers are to have the power to acquire capital equipment on their own, then they have to have access to the financial means to acquire this equipment. Moreover, to maintain the goal of decentralization, the banking institutions that decide on the allocation of investment credit must also be decentralized and should make their decisions upon the commercial creditworthi- ness of loan applicants rather than on any centralized investment plan.

If this freedom for Soviet managers to acquire the inputs they decide they need is not to lead to rampant inflation, their demands must be constrained. With the removal of centralized control over supplies and labor, the constraint that must be instituted is a hard budget constraint. That is, managers must be required to cover the cost of their inputs out of the revenues they earn. If they fail to do so, the process of bankruptcy must be enforced. Without the vulnerability to bankruptcy, the freeing-up of managerial decision making will not work.

Furthermore, if managers are to make their own output and input decisions, independent of central planners, they will need meaningful signals with regard to economic costs and benefits so that the pursuit of profit will lead to the efficient use of resources. Otherwise, decentralized decision making will lead to substantial inefficiency and waste. This means that the Soviet price system will have to undergo radical reform. Not only will subsidies have to be removed, but also the system for setting prices will have to be changed. Buyers and sellers must be given the right to negotiate their own prices in a free and flexible way so that prices adequately reflect the conditions of supply and demand in the economy.

The reform of the Soviet economy is, in essence, a monetization of economic transactions and decision making. The target planning of the command system is to be replaced by producer and user decision making involving magnitudes calibrated in monetary terms. Therefore, monetary stability becomes critical. Issues of macroeconomic policy and control — the size of the money supply and of the government deficit — become of great importance. If the required monetary control is not exercised and if reasonable monetary stability is not achieved and maintained before and along with the introduction of the reforms, then the resulting surge of inflation will seriously weaken or destroy the effectiveness of the reform.

Finally, the reforms described so far may not work in the absence of one further element, namely competition. Without the introduction of competition, without buyers being given a choice among competing suppliers, decentralization will not lead to the meeting of customer's demands, efficiency, and technological dynamism, but to monopoly and the danger of continued technological stagnation and price inflation. Therefore, an additional element of the required set of reforms may be the introduction of a Soviet antitrust policy.

What all this means is that due to the interrelatedness of an economic system, a number of reforms must be introduced more or less simultaneously in order for economic reform to begin to have any effect. In other words, to get the rocket of economic reform off the launching pad, an initial bundle of simultaneous reforms is required. One of the aims of an economic theory and policy of transition should be the pursuit of "minimum simultaneity," i.e., the development of a minimum bundle of simultaneous reforms required to launch the economic reform. For if everything has to be done at once, then the introduction of a decentralizing reform will face overwhelming obstacles. Especially under conditions of extensive market disequilibria, an abrupt shift from a centralized system to a full price-profit-market-money system would produce chaos.

In the elaboration of a theory of transition, it is necessary that the destabilization produced by the introduction of institutional changes be constrained to a level that allows the economy to continue to function. Certainly this is a policy constraint demanded by political leaders. Officials at GOSPLAN and the economic ministries are criticized for continuing to operate in the old ways. But at the same time, they are held responsible for the performance of the economy. The only way these officials know how to carry out this responsibility is by means of the old planning and control methods.

The key problem here is that the leaders want reform, but they want to bring it about without acutely destabilizing the economy. The maintenance of some of the old forms of planning and control is necessary to prevent destabilization. Thus, the transition process initially involves the introduction of new forms alongside the old forms, rather than immediately in place of them, with the idea that the new forms are to grow and in time replace the old forms. This growth and replacement process is, however, not well understood. To what extent does the maintenance of old forms inhibit, or even prevent, the development and growth of new forms, and what is the nature of the replacement process if it does take place?

There is, in addition, another underlying tension in the politics-economics relationship. An effective economic mechanism is one that produces rapid adjustment to changing conditions, to changes in technology and changes in people's desires. But adjustment involves the pain of dislocation. It reduces people's security. It affects rewards and penalties and the distribution of income. A socialist system politicizes the allocation of pain. A capitalist market system tends to depoliticize it. Though people in all countries look to their governments for protection against pain, in socialist countries this feeling is particularly strong. Thus there is the danger that the political pressure for government protection and intervention will prevent the economy from adequately adjusting to change, thus inhibiting the progress of economic reform or limiting its effectiveness.

2. THE RECORD OF REFORM

When Gorbachev came to power in March 1985, his initial economic program was focused on the reinvigoration rather than the reform of the economy. He called for growth acceleration and economic modernization based upon sharp increases in investment directed toward machine building and energy, plus extensive changes in administrative and management personnel. It was not until June 1987, that discussion of serious economic reform began. At a meeting of the Central Committee of the Soviet Communist Party, a resolution calling for the radical restructuring of the Soviet economy was adopted. The resolution recognized that the interrelatedness of an economic system required a bundle of changes to be made for any real change in the functioning of the economy to result. It did not, however, appear to recognize the difficulties of transition that would be involved.

The June 1987 resolution was accompanied by a new law on state enterprise. Together they formed a program that promised a substantial move toward economic decentralization. The program called for the virtual abolition of the annual state plan and its obligatory targets, significant independence of enterprise managers from control by the center and the industrial ministries, enterprise incentives based on the pursuit of profit and financial responsibility, flexibility in the payment and allocation of labor, and reform of prices and the system of price formation. The new system was to be in place by the beginning of the 1990s. Until then, some aspects of centralization were to be retained, e.g., the so-called "state production orders" that were obligatory for the enterprises to fulfill.

A year later, in June 1988, Gorbachev launched a radical political reform affecting both central and local governments. An elected congress of people's deputies was created, which in turn elected a president and a legislative parliament (Supreme Soviet). And local councils (soviets) were to be directly elected by the people. Gorbachev appears to have concluded that political reform is a necessary precondition for economic reform. In order for economic reform to succeed, decision makers must have the information they need to make decisions and they must be free of arbitrary government intervention in carrying out their decisions. Leaders in government and in the economy must be accountable for the results of the actions they take. They must have credibility in the eyes of the people. Thus, glasnost and democratization are prerequisites for successful economic reform.

What can be said about the accomplishments of radical economic reform so far since its launching at the June 1987 meeting of the Central Committee of the Soviet Communist Party? Clearly, little progress has been made. The reform is barely off the launching pad. And there are a number of highly serious and troublesome developments, in particular the growth of inflationary forces, the spreading shortages of consumer goods, and the recent decreasing levels of output. Indeed, a thick cloud of crisis hangs over the economy, and the people's expectations for the future are bleak.

Among the major causes of the present situation, it can be argued, is first of all an initial lack of sufficient understanding and appreciation by Soviet economists and leaders of the macroeconomic factors involved in the transition to a decentralized economic mechanism. Wage inflation (and through it, price inflation) has been a direct function of money creation resulting from 1) the government deficit, which has been substantial (even when account is taken of the fact that in the Soviet Union most of the investment in the economy is on the government budget), and 2) enterprise managers' pressure to increase money wages far beyond increases in productivity, given the flexibility of the incentive wage system accompanying the reform. Much of the current problem of empty shelves and consumer-goods shortages is demand related, that is, a consequence of the sizable increases in money wages, which would not have been possible except for the action of the printing presses bloating the supply of money and the growth of the monetary overhang in the economy.

There has also, however, been a slowdown in the growth of output. This has been a result of the fact that while some of the glue of the old administrative-command methods of management that held the economy together has been removed, new economic methods of management have not developed fast enough to replace it. The first part of the economic mechanism to be affected has been that of inter-enterprise flows of materials. The coordination mechanism in the economy has been seriously weakened, leading to a slowing down of growth and this year an actual decrease in output.

A further critical flaw has been the failure to introduce price reform. The maintenance of below-market-clearing prices, often through the payment of subsidies, contributes to the government deficit and to the prevalence of goods shortages. And the maintenance of the centralized system of price setting means that prices are not flexible signals of the relationship between supply and demand.

Thus the simultaneity problem in the transition to a decentralized economic system has proved to be a formidable barrier to the progress of Soviet economic reform.

In light of the failure of economic reform to get started and the growing sense of crisis in the country, several important developments have occurred with regard both to increased understanding of the economic issues and the working out of proposed programs for economic reform, particularly for the handling of the issue of transition.

First there has been a growing understanding among Soviet economists of the principles and importance of macroeconomic policies. Fiscal and monetary policies are discussed in a clear and straightforward manner, with the stress placed on the role they will play in the reformed Soviet market economy, particularly their role in managing inflation. Much attention in the public discussion of economic reform has been given to the monetary overhang and to ways of stopping its growth and of decreasing it: taxing excessive increase in money wages, and sale of shares, bonds, apartments to the public.

Another important development in economic discussions over the past year has been the increasing focus on property rights and the creation of new, diverse nonstate property relations. "Destatization" has become a rallying cry. What is of great importance here is the growing perception that a profit incentive is not enough to give an enterprise manager the needed sense of responsibility for the economic assets under his control. An ownership relationship is also necessary. Ownership brings with it not only an interest in an increase in the flow of profit (income) but also an interest in an increase in the value of the property (wealth), which leads to the protection and nurturing of society's assets.

In addition to the progress in understanding of economic issues, there have been two or three major programs for economic reform that have been put forth in the last year, each with a strong focus on the transition issue.

First there was a report issued in October 1989 by the State Commission on Economic Reform headed by the economist Abalkin, a Deputy Prime Minister in the

Ryzhkov government. The report outlines a design for a future Soviet market economy and discusses in some detail the measures that have to be taken to move the Soviet economy through the transition from a centralized structure to a future decentralized market structure.

The vision of a reformed Soviet economy spelled out in the report goes far beyond that proposed in the resolution of June 1987. While that resolution was ambiguous about the extent to which the new system would be a market economy, the Abalkin report unambiguously envisions a market economy. It states that on the basis of Soviet experience, it is clear that there is no reliable alternative to a market mechanism as a means of coordinating the action and interests of economic units. It goes on to state that the market is also the most democratic form of regulating economic activity. The Abalkin report makes clear that a market system contains an array of markets. In addition to goods markets (for both consumers' goods and producers' goods), it includes financial markets (markets for securities and a stock market) and labor markets.

The report stresses that in the reformed economy there will be many forms of property ownership: leasing and cooperatives, farmer and peasant property, joint-stock companies, corporations, joint-ventures, and private property (though private individual property will not be permitted to lead to the "exploitation of man by man"). The report also declares that the state should transfer the administration of the economic property that it retains to the workers' collectives on the basis of lease contracts.

According to the report, the financial sector—fiscal and monetary and banking institutions—should be thoroughly developed. And the state should exercise its influence on the economy through a wide assortment of economic means—fiscal and monetary policies—rather than administrative controls.

Finally, extensive attention is paid in the design of the reformed economy (and elsewhere in the report) to social guarantees for all members of society, including those with low skills.

A major part of the report is devoted to the issue of transition. Three possible approaches are discussed. What are termed the conservative and radical approaches are dismissed, the first because it will never produce any progress in reform, and the second because it will lead to chaos. What is called the "radical-moderate" approach is the one preferred. In essence it is a step-by-step approach of preparing and then introducing a bundle of simultaneous reforms that include a well-developed set of government fiscal and monetary controls. These will be used to manage the inflation, which is inevitable with the introduction of markets in an environment of shortages. Again, extensive attention in the report is paid to the protection of the people in light of the painful adjustments that are required. This protection will help people adapt to a market system. Included here are the indexation of incomes and pensions. It is clearly aimed at reviving popular support for the economic reform and the movement to the market.

The report also sketches out a schedule for the transition to the reformed economic system. Four stages are described covering the periods 1990, 1991–1992, 1993–1995, and 1996–2000, by the end of which a new economic system will be established.

The report was discussed at a large conference of economists in November where it was criticized from both the right and the left. Conservatives attacked the conversion of the Soviet economy to a market economy. And the radicals attacked what they considered to be the excessive protection of workers from economic adjustments that they argued were necessary for the success of economic reform, i.e., the creation of a flexible, efficient, responsive economic mechanism.

In December, Prime Minister Ryzhkov stated that he supported the Abalkin program, but called for a two-year delay in its introduction during which heavy centralized priority would be put on increasing the production of consumer goods to eradicate consumer shortages. This echo of the administrative-command approach was not well received. It was followed in May 1990 by a formal government plan put forth by Ryzhkov that was similar in many ways to the Abalkin program, but that called for beginning the transition to a market economy with an immediate (July 1990) doubling of basic food prices, coupled with indexing of wages and pensions. This was rejected by the Soviet parliament, and Ryzhkov and Abalkin were instructed to return in September with a revised program.

In the interim, dramatic changes were taking place in the Soviet political scene. Power was shifting from the Communist Party to the elected government bodies and from the center to the republics. In April 1990, Yeltsin was elected president of the Russian republic. He immediately made clear his intentions to assert Russian republic sovereignty over the economy of the Russian republic, and his intention to move the republic quickly -- in 500 days -- to a market economy. In July at the end of the Soviet Communist Party Congress, Yeltsin left the party, removing himself from its discipline.

Gorbachev thus faced a serious political challenge, particularly sharp in the economic sector. He responded with a compromising approach. A joint Gorbachev-Yeltsin working group was set up at the end of July, under the direction of the respected economist Shatalin, a member of Gorbachev's Presidential Council, with the task of drawing up a program for the transition to a market economy. The working group met during the month of August, and at the beginning of September submitted a lengthy report, including drafts of over 20 laws, which comprised a program for the transition to a market economy in 500 days.

The essence of the Shatalin transition program was quite different from that of Ryzhkov and Abalkin. The heart of the program lay in the rapidity of the transition process in the dominant role it gave to privatization and stabilization, and in its recognition of the sovereignty of the republics as the foundation for the creation of an economic union.

The rapidity of the transition process was symbolized by the phrase "500 days." This time frame was not to be taken literally, but it represented a commitment to move ahead resolutely with a tightly sequenced bundle of reforms, recognizing the simultaneity problem. Such a commitment was critical in establishing the credibility of the reform program, which in turn was so important for the program's success. Furthermore, the members of the Shatalin group made clear that they were talking about the transition to a market system, not the full development of such a system. The latter, it was generally acknowledged, would take several decades.

Second, the transition to the market was to be built on the basis of privatization rather than on the decentralization of state enterprise management. Privatization was to proceed from the top (turning state enterprises into joint-stock companies) and from the bottom (helping private people to set up small and medium-sized firms, with credit and access to space and materials). Financial institutions necessary for privatization (stock markets, commodity exchanges, etc.) were to be set up.

Third, stabilization policies were to be introduced immediately. Investment financed through the state budget was to be cut sharply, as were the defense and KGB budgets. Tight monetary policy was to be initiated. Monetary reform through confiscation was to be avoided. Rather, the monetary overhang was to be absorbed through the increased supply of consumer goods (production and imports) and sales to the public of apartments and a range of state assets. The prices of up to 150 basic consumer goods were to remain fixed for the entire period of 1 1/2 years. Reform of other prices was to begin as soon as the stabilization program began to take hold.

The aim of the stabilization program was to make the ruble the accepted, totally fungible, legal tender throughout the Soviet Union—as some members of the Shatalin group put it, to make the ruble "real money."

The fourth key element in the approach of the Shatalin program was that it started with the recognition of the sovereignty of the republics and tried to create institutional arrangements that would encourage the republics to give up some of their sovereignty in order to share in the benefits of these arrangements. A good example of such an institution was the proposed central bank, which was designed along the lines of the American Federal Reserve System. The Board of Governors of the bank consisted of a chairman and representatives from each of the republics. Thus each republic that joined the system would have a voice in the setting of monetary policy for the entire economic union.

The battleground is now in the political sector. Since the old economic, social, and political structures are being destroyed, and new structures are slow in developing, instability is increasing. To deal with the situation, it is necessary for political leaders, primarily Gorbachev and Yelstin, to reach certain agreements. First, they must agree on the nature of the new Soviet political union and the level of sovereignty of the republics. Without this, the political power to implement economic reform is lost. And second, they must agree on a program of economic reform, one that addresses the major problems of transition — "minimum simultaneity," property rights, and macroeconomic balance. Two different approaches have already been proposed, and more are possible. If they come to an agreement soon, then there is a chance that by the turn of the century the Soviet economy will look substantially different from what it was and is today, and will begin to show signs of becoming a market economy with economic, financial, and legal institutions resembling those of the advanced industrial economies.

If, on the other hand, there is great delay in the political acceptance and introduction of significant reform measures, then the disequilibria and instability in the economy will intensify and the reimposition of economic controls will be likely. Where this path leads is not clear. It can be argued, however, since recentralization will not solve the problems facing the Soviet economy, that in five to ten years another cycle of economic reform will be initiated. In perestroika-II, Soviet leaders and the Soviet people, with the experience they have gained, may be more successful in dealing with economic reform and its transition problems, and a Soviet market economy may begin to take shape toward the end of the first decade of the 21st century.

22. THE WORLD ECONOMY IN THE POST–COLD WAR ERA AND THE ROLE OF JAPAN

Haruki Niwa
Kyoto Sangyo University
Kyoto, Japan

ABSTRACT.   Problems of public finance and money supply complicate Russia's economic transition.   Japan and Asian partners can provide assistance, and present economic sluggishness should not deflect attention from long run gains in relationships with Russia.   Attention must be paid the internationalization of the former Soviet military complex.
This chapter was originally written in September, 1990.[1] From autumn, 1990 to the end of 1991, vast changes occurred in the Soviet Union. The author has added a brief supplementary analysis about these changes.

1. ON THE SOVIET TRANSITION PROGRAM

The "transition program to market economy" for the Soviet Union (or Russia) has important worldwide significance. If the "transition program" attains its goal the economic system of the Soviet Union will be virtually transformed into a Western–type "capitalist" economy. This would probably lessen the Cold–War–style confrontations between "East" and "West," making a great contribution to world peace.

However, actual present–day developments in the Soviet economy are in a severe crisis, and the carrying out of the transition program is extremely difficult.

The most dangerous source of difficulty seems to be demand–pull–type inflationary pressure coming from the accumlated cash holdings of Soviet consumers. The estimated value of these holdings was around 500 billion rubles in 1989, or 76% of national income.[2] According to a statement by the Soviet Minister of Finance, Mr. Pavlov, the ratio of volume of high–powered currency to available consumers' goods in the Soviet economy increased eightfold from 1960 to 1989.[3] Such excessive cash holdings in the Soviet economy are due to the continued deficit in the state budget (see table 1), a large part of which has

---

[1] See Haruki Niwa, "The World Economic System in the Post–Cold–War Era and the Role of Japan: A General View," The Annual of Japan Economic Policy Association (1991), No. 39, pp. iv – xii.

[2] N. Shmelev, "Obekstrennykh merakh po predotvrashcheniu razvala sovetskoi ekonomiki," Voprosy ekonomiki, 1990, No. 1, pp. 19–20.

[3] See Embassy of the USSR in Tokyo, Kon Nicki no So Ren Pou (Soviet Union Today), No. 18, September 15, 1989, p. 63.

been financed by newly issued paper money accompanied by a very insufficient supply of commodities. In this regard, it should be remembered that the initial and formidable increase of the deficit under Mr. Gorbachev's administration was primarily due to the ambitious budgetary allotments for investment (especially in the machine-building and munition-producing industries) and military buildup, with very little caution to the sources of revenue, at the starting point of the 12th FYP.[4]

In the original state budget for 1990, the deficit had been proposed to be reduced to 60 billion rubles from 92 billion roubles (provisional official figure) in 1989.[5] Despite the rather small value of the deficit during the January–May period in 1990 (which was reported by the Soviet State Committee of Statistics), President Gorbachev strongly emphasized the critical seriousness of the budget–deficit problem in his speech of May 27, 1990.[6] A large increase in the world market prices of oil since August 1990 would be a favorable development for the Soviet state budget. However, owing to the decreases in profits of state enterprises (due to declining tendencies in industrial production) and increases in excessive wage payments, the fulfillment of the deficit–curtailment program for the state budget in 1990 will be a very hard task. Or—which is virtually the same thing—"Gosbank" would be compelled to do her financing in a very irresponsible way (as the switching from state–budget expenditures), depending on the intensive use of printing machines. We must consider that the accumulated excessive cash holdings and the inflationary pressures in the Soviet economy continued to increase in 1990. According to an official announcement, in the Soviet economy in 1990, the year–end volume of the high–powered currency increased 1.5 times from the previous year's end.[7]

Frankly speaking, the Soviets should nullify a large part of the excessive cash holdings through some sort of currency reform, as soon as possible.[8] In

---

[4]As for the investment and military buildup in the original plan of the Soviet 12th FYP, see the excellent analysis in Plan Econ Report, Vol. 11, January 1986, pp. 1–8. See also an econometric simulation analysis that was worked out by the author, Haruki Niwa, "An Econometric Forecast of Military Expenditures in the Soviet 12th FYP" (in Japanese), in The Annual of Japan Economic Policy Association, Vol. 36, 1988, pp. 127–137.

Recently, through his speech of April 27, 1990, Mr. Gorbachev leaked the original planned figure for the increase in Soviet military expenditures in the 12th FYP. It was a very ambitious one, i.e., a 45% increase in five years. See Pravda, April 29, 1990, p. 1.

[5]See Pravda, November 11, 1989, p. 2. See also Pravda, September 26, 1989, p. 3.

[6]See Economika i zhizn', No. 32, August 1990, p. 15. See also Pravda, May 29, 1990, p. 2.

[7]See Economika i zhizn', No. 5, January 1991, p. 9.

[8]In the latter half of the 1940s, immediately after World War II, some countries carried out "currency reform" in order to eliminate the inflationary excess purchasing power that had been generated and accumulated during wartime. In the Soviet Union, such a currency reform had been carried out on December 16,

the present-day Soviet Union, a comprehensive reduction of the budget deficit is an urgent prerequisite that should be implemented at all costs for successful transition to a market economy. In this respect, a drastic reduction of military expenditures is a vital requirement for the Soviet economy.[9]

Necessary steps for the successful completion of the Soviet or Russian current transition program are as follows:

1. the freezing or reducing of the accumulated excessive cash holdings,
2. a restriction of the budget deficit, mainly through drastic reductions of military expenditures, and
3. provision of large-scale economic aid and cooperation from Western countries, especially from Japan and Asian NIES. (A prerequisite for this would be the establishment of the convertibility of the Soviet or Russian currency.)

If these steps are not taken, the inflationary pressure will burst very soon. The result might be either a runaway hyperinflation or, to make matters worse, a rapid spreading of repressed inflation, i.e., price controls and rationing over all the sectors and aspects of the economy. The latter would be nothing other than the decisive failure of the Soviet "transition program" and of her "perestroika" policy, at least for the time being. (It should be

---

1947, under Stalin's administration. According to the estimate by BIS, the Soviet Government eliminated 480 billion old-rubles from the total value of the accumulated purchasing power, i.e., 580 billion old-rubles. See BIS, The 18th Annual Report, Basel, 1948, p. 140. In Japan, the same sort of currency reform had been carried out in 1946 by the government of Baron Shidehara. On January 23, 1991, the Soviet government partially executed a similar currency reform by halves, though it was extremely insufficient.

[9]Soviet Prime Minister Ryzhkov leaked the total "real" military expenditures in 1989 as 77.3 billion rubles; in addition to this, the yearly average war expense in Afghanistan was cited as around 5 billion rubles. See Ekonomicheskaya gazeta, No. 24, June 1989, pp. 4–5. It would be worth around 13% of the "national income by use." For 1990, the Soviet official planned budget for "real" military expenditures was reported as 70.9 billion rubles, or 14.5% of the total state budgetary expenditures. See Pravda, September 26, 1989, p. 3 and November 11, 1989, p. 2. The official budgetary planned figure for the Soviet military expenditures in 1991 was reported as 96 billion rubles, or 35% increase from the previous year. See Pravda, January 12, 1991, p. 2.

However, through his statement of July 3, 1990, at the Party Congress, the Soviet Minister for Foreign Affairs, Mr. Shevardnadze, said that the Soviet military expenditures would be one-fourth of the total state budget expenditures (see Pravda, July 5, 1990, p. 5). President Gorbachev also leaked, through his speech of April 27, 1990, the fact that the Soviet military expenditures would be 18% of the national income (see Pravda, April 29, p. 2). From these statements of both Soviet leaders we can derive a figure of the Soviet total "real" military expenditures in 1990 as around 120 billion rubles.

As for the author's estimates and analyses of the Soviet "real" military expenditures from the 1930s to 1985, see the author's book: Haruki Niwa, Soren Gunji Shishutsu no Suikei (The Analytical Estimates of the Soviet Military Expenditures), Hara Syobo, Tokyo 1989.

remembered that, in the present-day Soviet Union, the widespread use of repressed-inflation-type direct controls is the actual state of affairs.)

In the very long run, however, the Soviet (or Russian) economy will complete her transition process to a market economy. This will happen because there is little hope for efficiency improvements through use of the institutional reforms of the old-fashioned Soviet-type command economy.

2. ON THE ECONOMIC ABILITIES AND POWERS OF JAPAN AND ASIAN NIES

An important factor in the economic capabilities and powers of Japan and Asian NIES is the effect and meaning of the recovery of business activity since the latter half of 1987 in Japan.

During the very long period from 1974 to 1986, Japan had been suffering from a stagnant economic situation. In this period, compared with the high-growth-rate period of the 1960s (10.7 % growth per annum on average for real-term GNP), real growth in the Japanese economy decreased to a low figure of approximately 3.7% per annum on the average.[10] The stagnant trends in Japan in that period were due to the anti-Keynesian-type retrenchment-oriented fiscal policy of the Japanese Ministry of Finance. During this period in Japan, owing to an insufficient domestic total demand, a strong export drive was induced. It was virtually a time of "beggar-my-neighbor" policy by Japan, and a great deal of trade frictions arose from it.[11]

From the autumn of 1985 to 1987, the exchange rate for the yen jumped from ¥ 245 = $1 in the summer of 1985 to ¥ 123 = $1 at the end of 1987. During the years up to the first half of 1987, the large increase in the value of the yen in the international money market constitutes a sudden heavy burden for export industries in Japan. It resulted in a gloomy climate for the business world of Japan. From the standpoint of the Asian NIES, the rocketing up of the value of Japanese yen was a great gift for them. It made their industries competitive.

In the post-1985 period, however, had the Japanese economy fallen into a severe depression as a result of a slump in her export industries, the economic activity of the NIES would have also lost its vigor. Japan has been a great customer, a very important investor, and a high-technology supplier for the economy of Asian NIES. Fortunately, since the autumn of 1987, Japan entered a process of recovery in her trade cycle. This was primarily due to the low domestic interest rate in Japan at the time, which resulted from her big export

---

[10]These figures on the growth rates of the Japanese economy are derived from the official figures published by the government of Japan. See Research and Statistics Department of the Bank of Japan, Comparative Economic and Financial Statistics, Japan and Other Major Countries, Vol. 25, Tokyo 1988, p. 30. See also The Economic Planning Agency of the Japanese Government, Keizai Youran (1988). (The Economic Statistical Handbook), Tokyo 1988, p. 222.

[11]For detailed explanations about this judgment by the author, see the author's book: Haruki Niwa, Keinzusyugi no Fukken (The Revival of the Keynesian Policy Thought), Bijinesu Sya, Tokyo 1987, pp. 121-135.

surplus.[12] The economic recovery in Japan, however, was promoted at least in part by a revival of Keynesian–type fiscal policy.

To our surprise, in the post–1985 period, a large part of the export industries in Japan did not lose their competitiveness. It has been established that the level of technology in the up–to–date "high–tech industries" in Japan is extremely good. These industries have succeeded in remaining competitive even in the post–1985 period, while Japanese consumers enjoyed a rapid increase in supplies of cheap imported manufactured goods from foreign countries (especially from Asian NIES).

This situation was beneficial for the Asian countries.[13] They enjoyed many benefits from the rapid growth of their exports to the large market in Japan. In the case of the NIES, they have succeeded in a remarkable development of the "horizontal trade" with Japan. In terms of dollar value, the ability of Japan to invest in foreign countries grew markedly in the post–1985 period, because of the exceedingly high value of the yen in the international money market. Nowadays, Asian countries receive a large capital inflow and technology transfer from Japan.

Since the latter half of 1989, there has been a large increase in the domestic rate of interest in Japan. In the short run, there are some fears about the ending of the economic boom. Even in Korea, there is a sluggish tendency, in economic activity. In the long run, however, the mechanism of mutually sustained growth in East Asia will be continued for several decades.

This means that the growing economic power of Japan and the East Asian NIES could afford to provide considerable support to the "transition program" of Soviet Russia and Eastern Europe. In case the Soviets (or Russians) do decide to return the Japanese "Northern Territories" (which have been occupied by the Soviet Troops since September 1945) and at the same time to carry out the drastic reductions of their military expenditures, they could be in good position to obtain large–scale support and cooperation from Japan.

3. ON THE PROSPECTS FOR OVERCOMING THE "OIL CRISIS"

This section and the next will consider two gloomy problems: the oil crisis and trade friction.

At the present time, in the autumun of 1990, the world economy is suffering from "the third oil shock," which has come from the Iraqi invasion of Kuwait. From the point of view of a Japanese economist, the long–run forecast might be rather optimistic in this matter.

---

[12]For detailed discussions by the author about the process of economic recovery in the Japanese economy since the latter half of 1987, see the author's paper, "Nichi Tai Kan Tou-hoku Ajia Jiyuu Keizai-ken no Yakushin to Kongo no Sekai Jousei" (The Great Progress in the Free Economy Area in North East Asia and the Coming Word Situations), which was presented at the 1988 Fukuoka Symposium, in Higashi Ajiya ni okeru Seiji no Minshuka to Keizai Kyouryoku (The Political Democratization and Economic Cooperation in East Asia), edited and published by The Association for the Japan-ROC Cultural Exchange (Fukuoka), Fukuoka 1988, pp. 54-64.

[13]See the author's paper cited in footnote 11.

These days, the economic journals and papers published in Tokyo or Kyoto/Osaka are filled with tidal waves of news reporting successes in research and development for energy-saving technologies in Japan. It seems that breakthroughs for high technologies are concentrated in R & D with regard to new systems of electricity, i.e., superconductivity, solar cells, condenserlike super secondary batteries, etc.

In the coming decades, human beings will surely solve the energy problem by using these new technologies. In the 1990s and in the first 10 years of the 21st century, Japan will be an important supplier of the necessary new technologies in this area.

4. ON THE TRADE FRICTIONS

The Japan–U.S. trade friction is another gloomy problem. In the post–Cold–War period in the 1990s, there is a possibility that a few shortsighted American opinion leaders would be eager to regard Japan (instead of the USSR) as the "adversary" of the U.S. This would inevitably accelerate the appearance of protectionist trade policies in the U.S. In the worst case, it is conceivable that Japan–U.S. trade will be severely restricted through direct bureaucratic controls of the U.S. government. This would create considerable damage for world trade.

In view of the very modest attitude of Japanese policy makers, it is unthinkable that Japan would dare to undertake retaliatory actions against the U.S. protectionist trade restrictions. Under such conditions, Japan will continue her free-trade-oriented policy to the best of her ability.[14] Even in the worst case, in which the U.S. armors her whole domestic economy with a great number of direct protectionist restrictions like a strong fortress, Japan will be able to continue her economic prosperity if she has succeeded in keeping close free-market-oriented relationships with the Asian, Oceanian, and European nations, inclusive of the new market economies of the Soviet (or Russia) and East European countries. It would be a very good remedy for the world economy, which might be suffering from the burden of the protectionist fortress in America.

An indispensable requirement for Japanese policy is to keep a Keynesian-type growth-sustaining and "enriching-my-neighbor" attitude in fiscal and

---

[14]The author considers that Japan is a rather good open market for foreign suppliers of manufactured industrial goods. The import of foreign-made machines by Japan had been increased 2.6 times from $12.4 billion in 1985 to $32.4 billion in 1989. Even in the stagnant period from 1985 to 1987, it increased 1.55 times. See The Economic Planning Agency of the Japanese Government, Japanese Economic Indicators, No. 11, November 1986, p. 110 and Japanese Economic Indicators Quarterly, No. 1, July 1990, p. 114.

This extremely rapid increase in machinery imports by Japan was due mainly to the "price effect," which came from the rocketing up of the value of the yen in the international money market. This in itself would be very good evidence indicating that the door of the domestic market of Japan has been sufficiently opened for foreign-made manufactured commodities.

monetary choices.[15]   It must oppose anti–Keynesian and "beggar–my–neighbor" policies.

In 1989–1990, the Japanese economy had nearly realized full employment. The export surplus of Japan is rapidly decreasing. In other words, today, the economy of Japan is approaching a well–balanced equilibrium. Japan in 1990 is already not the problem case in the world economy. The government of Japan must implement some policies to keep this good position. It must not go back to the policies that brought imbalances before 1987.

5. ON THE NEW SYSTEM OF THE "INTERNATIONAL PUBLIC GOODS"

In the coming decades, in spite of prospective agreements for arms reduction or arms control, both the United States and the Soviet Union (or Russia) will keep their global positions as the military super powers. For world peace and the national security of every nation, the global system of the "Pax Russo–Americana" should be indispensable in the coming post–Cold–War era.

As well known, the "Pax Russo–Americana" in the 1960s and 1970s was based upon the mutual deterrence system of the Cold–War regime. The strategic posture of the Cold–War regime came from the hostile confrontation between the capitalist market economic system and communist–socialist system of command economy.

In the 1990s, the coming system of the new "Pax Russo–Americana" will be and must be based upon friendly relationships between both military super–powers. For the smooth functioning of the new regime, the Soviet (or Russian) "transition program" to a market economy must be carried out successfully. And for the successful execution of the transition program, in turn, some drastic reductions in Soviet/Russian military expenditures are a vitally necessary prerequisite, as stated above.

After the completion of the Soviet/Russian transition program, Soviet or Russian military forces will become "international public goods," the same as their counterparts in the U.S. In the 1990s, in view of the prospects for very rapid economic growth, the East Asian countries, especially Japan, must make some contributions to the maintenance and working of the "international public goods."

---

[15]The author has confirmed the effective feasibility of Keynesian–type policies in the Japanese economy in the surroundings of the contemporary open international economic systems by the use of both theoretical analyses and econometric simulations. See Haruki Niwa and Katsuhiro Miyamoto, "Trade balance in the Floating Exchange–rate System and IS–LM Framework: A Theoretical Analysis of the US–Japan Imbalance and the Recommended Policy–mix," The Asian Economic Journal, Vol. 5, Number 2, September 1991, forthcoming. See also Taichi Katsuki, Hiroshi Kato, Haruki Niwa, Katsuhiro Miyasmoto and Bungo Ishizaki, "Nihon Keizai ni tsuiteno Keiryouteki Seisaku Shimyureishon" (An Econometric Policy–Simulation of the Japanese Economy), Working Paper, No. 1, The Modern Economic Research Center (Tokyo) and Kobe Art and Technological University Foundation (Kobe), September 1986.

SUPPLEMENT: ON THE DOWNFALL OF THE UNION GOVERNMENT IN THE USSR

Owing to severe commodity shortages in the Soviet Union, a struggle for natural resources, various capital assets, and manufactured goods among member republics has come about since the autumn of 1990. The situation has pushed forward nationalist aspirations toward "real" independence in these member republics. The trend was damaging for the Union Government.

In 1991, it became clear that the Union Government of the USSR had lost her tax collection system, because control over state enterprises was transferred to member republics. The member republics were unmindful of their duty to pay their tax revenue to the Central Union treasury.

In the first half of 1991, the budget revenue of the Union Government of the USSR stayed at a very low level — around one third of the planned figure — even though the core part of Mr. Gorbachev's administration was controlled by the conservative/hawk group of the Soviet Communist Party. In the latter half of that year, especially after the unsuccessful coup d'etat by the conservatives, the union budgetary revenue became virtually nil.

This led to serious increases in the vast deficit of the Union Government's budget, which had to be financed with newly issued paper money. Inflationary pressure was aggravated all the more.

The Soviets (Union Government) executed a partial currency reform in January 1991 (see footnote 6). This reform, however, was insufficient. In April of that year, they increased retail prices (in state retail stores). This increase was necessary to reduce inflationary pressure (which came from the accumulated excessive cash holdings); it was, however, ineffective because of the induced large increase in wages. Along with the overall declining tendency of production and productivity in the Soviet economy, such a wage increase brought about huge operating deficits in most state enterprises. The deficits had to be covered with loans from Gosbank. Such financing also accelerated the increases in supplies of paper money.

As far as the budgetary situation was concerned, the downfall of the Union Government of the USSR was inevitable. It actually occurred at the end of 1991.

It seems that the prospective successor of the USSR would be the Russian Federated Republic. The new Russia would take a role as the engine for the CIS, which is a loose organization of former member republics.

At the very beginning of 1992, Russia carried out the liberalization of retail prices. The measures, however, have been taken without any currency reform to reduce the inflationary pressure that comes from excessive cash holdings. A burst of hyperinflation with very large increases in prices will be unavoidable.

For the takeoff of the market mechanism and economic recovery in Russia, a marked reduction of deficits in the government budget and the reestablishment of a reliable currency system are indispensable preconditions. It seems that a drastic cutback of military expenditures in the Russian government budget will be necessary for this. A cessation of irresponsible deficit financing from the central bank to state enterprises is also urgently needed.

In view of the potential human power and natural resources in Russia, the Russian economy should start to grow in a few years, although her economic situations in 1992 will be poor.

If this growth occurs, as is likely, Russia alone (not the Soviet Union) would still be a military giant. Her military power should be included in some system of "international public goods," as the author suggested in the text.

Table 1. The Soviet Government Budget, 1983 – 1990*

	Expenditure	Revenue	Deficit	Budget Deficit as Share of National Incom (NMP by use) %
	– in billion current roubles –			
1983	354.3	338.4	15.9	3.0
1984	371.2	356.3	14.9	2.7
1985	386.5	372.6	13.9	2.4
1986	417.1	371.6	45.5	7.9
1987	430.9	378.4	52.5	9.0
1988	459.5	378.9	80.6	13.0
1989				
planned	495	395	100	15
forecast				
(Maslyukov/	...	...	120	18
Gosplan)			−121	
provisional	...	...	92	14
actual	482.6	401.9	80.7	12
1990				
planned	489.9	429.9	60	9
actual	510.1	452	58.1	9

* .... Including the budgets of local governments.

Sources:
  Total expenditures and revenues

    1983–1987   Plan Econ Report, Vol.5, Numbers 34–35, September 1, 1989,
                 p. 31 and Vol.6, Numbers 7–8, February 21, 1990, p. 13.
    1988   Pravda, November 11, 1989, p. 2 and Narodnoe khoziaystvo
                 SSSR v 1989 g., pp. 611 – 612.
    1989
     (Planned)   Pravda, October 28, 1988, pp. 4–5 and October 29, p. 2.
     (Forecast and provisional)
                 Pravda, August 5, 1989, p. 1 and Ekonomika i zhizn', No.6,
                 February 1990, p. 15.
     (actual)   Narodnoe khoziaystvo SSSR v 1989 g., pp. 611 – 612.
    1990
     (Planned)   Pravda, November 11, 1989, p. 2.
     (actual)   Ekonomika i zhizn', No. 5, January 1991, p. 9.
  National income ('NMP by use'in current roubles)
    1983–1988   Narodnoe khoziaystvo SSSR v 1985 g., p. 411, c za 70 let,
                 p. 430 and c v 1988 g., p. 16.
    1989   Narodnoe khoziaystvo SSSR v 1989 g., p. 15.
    1990   The author assumed that the rough estimate of national
                 income by use in 1990 would be 675 billion roubles.

23. GLOBAL ECONOMIC IMPLICATIONS OF RESTRUCTURING IN EASTERN EUROPE AND THE SOVIET UNION

Peter Pauly
Institute for Policy Analysis
University of Toronto
140 St. George Street
Toronto, Ont. M5S 1A1
Canada

ABSTRACT. This chapter is concerned with a theoretical and empirical evaluation of the potential effects on world financial markets, international trade flows, and on global macroeconomic activity of incremental claims on world financial resources for the purpose of aiding the restructuring process in Eastern Europe and the Soviet Union. Within the context of a global macroeconometric model, we simulate the international economic implications of a transfer package under a variety of accompanying macropolicies. The results suggest that feasible strategies for Western aid policies exist, which are at the same time neutral with respect to world economic activity.

1. INTRODUCTION

During the past year the world economy has been subjected to several fundamental changes. Arguably, none of these will end up being of more significance in the medium to long term for international economic relations and the structure of the world economy than the ongoing restructuring of economies in Eastern Europe and the Soviet Union. The fundamental changes taking place in these countries, together with the economic and political unification of Germany, will have profound impacts on economic relations within Europe, as well as between Europe and the rest of the world. While the progress of economic reform has not been uniform across countries, it is probably fair to say that Poland and Hungary are well on their way to becoming market-based economies. The USSR and Czechoslovakia are moving at a much slower pace, but are ultimately expected to implement more radical reform programs as well, while the economies of Bulgaria and Romania are, at present, still characterized primarily by a structure of comprehensive central planning. The German unification as of this October has de facto and de jure eliminated the GDR, but for the purposes of this analysis we shall focus on the German adjustments as well.

    Above and beyond the fundamental structural changes expected to be implemented in all these countries, for the process of transition to a market-oriented economic organization it is generally recognized that to be successful, substantial technical assistance, conceptual advice, and financial support from Western developed market economies will be required. The analogy with the European Economic Recovery Program, designed just after the Second World War to rebuild the economies of Western Europe, comes to mind immediately. Just as the

Marshall Plan provided seed investments during that period, a concerted Western financial aid program at the present time might be a necessary component of a successful transition strategy. Western assistance programs will , of course, be only one piece in the puzzle. Within the Eastern economies, the institutional, monetary, and currency systems have to be adjusted; marketization and privatization efforts must be continued; and the integration of these countries into the institutions of the Western international economic community have to be intensified.

One of the many issues that are of concern to economists in the context of an analysis of economic restructuring in Eastern Europe and the Soviet Union is that of the global economic repercussions of this process. At least two dimensions of the problem warrant further exploration:

1.   If the economies of the region—through a process of marketization, privatization, and reallocation of resources—indeed manage to attain higher productivity and growth levels, how is that going to affect activity levels and trade relations globally? In addition, how is the rest of the world affected by the adjustment process?

2.   To the extent that the adjustment process requires financial support from other countries, how are the flows financed and what are the likely impacts of the incremental claims on world financial resources on international capital markets?

In this chapter, we shall attempt to provide a preliminary assessment of the implications of such assistance programs for the global economy. In particular, it is the purpose of this chapter to present some empirical estimates of the orders of magnitude of the macroeconomic effects on world economic activity, trade flows, world prices, and international financial markets. The results are based on various simulation exercises performed with the world econometric model system of Project LINK. The model is singularly well suited for such an exercise, since it represents explicitly all the economies of Eastern Europe and the Soviet Union, as part of a system covering more than 130 countries of the world, represented by 79 econometric models. The international effects are captured by a multifaceted approach, modeling merchandise and service trade flows, international price linkages, capital flows, and exchange rates, among other international transmission mechanisms, so as to generate a consistent picture of the global economy.

It is important to emphasize that our analysis is very much macroeconomic in nature; the perspective is that of an international economist. In particular, we will have little to say about the specific microimplications of the adjustment processes in Eastern Europe, apart from pointing out that all results are generated under the implicit assumption of a gradual successful continuation of the process of marketization. We are, of course, quite aware of the substantial uncertainties associated with an assessment of future developments in Eastern Europe and the Soviet Union and of the effects of such policies on these countries. The speed with which the formation of markets will proceed, or the effects of marketization on economic activities, can hardly be analyzed fully within a traditional macroeconometric framework. The subsequent empirical results, therefore, incorporate extraneous adjustments at various levels representing the best assumptions available to this group at the present time.

While motivated primarily by current events, the issues addressed in this chapter are, of course, far from being new. The determinants of real interest rates on a worldwide scale have been explored recently by Barro and Sala-i-Martin (1990), building on earlier work by Blanchard and Summers (1984), among others;

in the political domain, the issue has been examined repeatedly as well (European Economy, 1989, 1990). There is also a rather extensive literature on fiscal policy effects in open economies, most prominently represented by the work of Frenkel and Razin (1985,1987). Our empirical analysis within the framework of a complete dynamic global econometric model should provide a better assessment of the general equilibrium effects of such transfers, as well as a rich characterization of the short- and medium-term adjustment paths.

This chapter is organized as follows. In sections 2, 3, and 4 we shall outline heuristically a prototypical adjustment path for Eastern European economies, the corresponding responses in Western developed-market economies, and a simple theoretical framework for the analysis of expected global effects. Subsequently, in sections 5 and 6 we present a set of simulation results based on alternative adjustment scenarios and accompanying policy settings in the West. A summary evaluation is provided in section 7.

2. THE MACROECONOMICS OF RESTRUCTURING: THE IDEAL PATH

The complex process that we refer to as economic restructuring has a number of elements, ranging (among others) from changes in the industrial organization and new designs of the monetary system to a new system of ownership and property rights. It will be helpful to first characterize a prototype course of events as it might be described in terms of a few key macroeconomic concepts.

For the purposes of this study, it is probably easiest to represent the expected future economic processes as responses to an increase in the expected rate of return on capital. The basic notion underlying this argument is that the return on capital, particularly on human capital and infrastructures, has been compressed by an ineffective system of incentives and resource-allocation mechanisms. The current economic reforms consist of replacing this framework, at different speeds and with important nuances in the actual implementation, by a more efficient organization. As a result, system productivity is expected to increase, and with it the rate of return on capital.

The increase in the expected rate of return on capital raises investment and therefore domestic demand. In the short to medium term, this effect of increased demand dominates the effects of increased supply resulting from productivity gains; consequently, the countries will generate current account deficits and continue to build up net external debt. In the long run, the supply effects are expected to dominate the demand effects. Indeed, it is the defining characteristic of the "long run" that increased productivity generates sufficient supplies to satisfy the demands initialized by higher investments. At this stage, the countries will increase their net exports and, simultaneously, decrease their prices. This allows them to begin debt repayments to the West and to resume a steady growth path, with initial levels of per capita incomes close to the current levels of Western European economies at the lower end of the income scale.

The crucial role of outside investment in this process is clearly evident. Where will these funds come from? Some corporations will be, and have already been, attracted to the new market potential in Eastern Europe.   But these investments will be only modestly helpful, particularly since they can be expected to be moderate in size during the early adjustment period. Political uncertainty during the transition to a decentralized economy will continue to deter large investments. Corporate funds cannot overcome the burden of a weak infrastructure and a decaying industrial plant, and can hardly generate international competitiveness. Questions about ownership rights, the possibilities of profit repatriation, and currency convertibility remain, and the scope of barter trade will always be rather limited. Indeed, recent experiences with large international commercial or institutional lending have been quite disappointing; besides, the current high level of global interest rates makes it virtually impossible for the countries in question to gain access to private funds. The only viable alternative, then, is for a consortium of major industrial countries, through institutions such as the European Development Bank, to provide grants, aid, and soft loans to the East. This chapter examines the effects of such policies.

This focus of our analysis on the role of public monies over the relevant short-run horizon is crucial to an analysis of the process. In the short run, initial investments are likely to be financed by foreign (and international) public monies, while in the medium term the current account deficits will be financed through private net capital inflows as the increased prospects of positive returns attract private capital to exploit profit opportunities. With the exception of the German case, we thus feel compelled to focus specifically on the catalytic nature of initial public flows. Incidentally, these are also the only ones that, at least potentially, carry the conditionalities that may be required to secure additional funds for already heavily indebted countries.

In most respects, the transitional problems for the ex-GDR in a unified German economy are no different from those of the other countries. The major differences are two: the sources of financial transfers into the ex-GDR are almost entirely German funds; and in addition, increased demand resulting from Eastern restructuring will, for the most part, be satisfied by German production. Other countries will, for the most part, benefit indirectly.

3. THE MACROECONOMICS OF ADJUSTMENT: THE WESTERN PERSPECTIVE

To some extent, the expected course of events in the West is, of course, the mirror image of what goes on in the East. The initial seed support for Eastern development will generate an incremental deficit for the public sector, and possibly exert upward pressures on interest rates. In the medium term, increased Eastern demands for Western products will, through standard trade multipliers, lead to an increase in net exports. The positive demand stimulus should generate further upward pressures on interest rates and cause exchange rates to appreciate.

The effects on interest rates and exchange rates could, of course, be mitigated by an expansionary monetary policy. Accommodating the increased demand resulting from an increase in net exports would further fuel inflationary tendencies. In addition, on the budget side, the problem is to what degree the increase in net exports will be allowed to crowd out net budgetary expenditures; in that case, the resulting increase in interest rates may crowd out interest-sensitive components of demand. It is assumed subsequently that all additional transfers are indeed entirely bond financed and that no fiscal policy adjustments are made.

The literature on fiscal policies in open economies (Frenkel and Razin, 1987) suggests that one should expect the feedback effects of a transfer to depend critically upon whether the donor country exhibits a net current account surplus or a net deficit. In the latter case, the net effects of financial transfers are more likely to be negative, since the upward pressure on world real interest rates will tend to lead to a further current account deterioration.[1] That distinction will be made explicit in our theoretical discussion in the following section. Similarly, a crucial aspect in examining the global effects is their distribution across developed market economies. The increase of demand from the East will probably be distributed unevenly. To a first approximation, the present shares of East–West trade in total trade of various countries will be indicative of these distributional imbalances. Thus, Europe will be more exposed to a positive demand shock than the U.S. and Japan; Germany, and to a lesser extent Italy and France, will benefit most from this windfall of demand.

For industrial countries outside Europe and for developing countries, the main concern in the context of these adjustment processes should be related to the nature of the trade effects and the extent to which national money markets are affected. As for the latter, while a certain part of the adjustment in financial markets will no doubt be contained within Europe, the nature of integration of global capital markets will make interest–rate and exchange–rate effects elsewhere unavoidable. This will potentially have negative effects on investment behavior in these countries, and debtor countries may experience slightly higher debt service burdens.

On the trade side, the initial stimulus of an increase in world trade will be positive for all regions in the world. However, it is often believed that with an improved level of competitiveness in Eastern Europe, at least some amount of trade diversion is likely to occur. This concern is most vocally expressed by the group of developing countries, and by some of the NIEs and semi–NIEs, which will expect to face competition from Eastern Europe on global markets. A detailed analysis of these adjustments is beyond the scope of this chapter, since it is believed that most of these issues will not be central in the short to medium term.[2]

4. GLOBAL EFFECTS: SOME BASIC THEORY

The global macroeconomics of financial transfers can best be illustrated within the context of a simple multiregion AD–AS framework.[3] For purposes of our

---

[1]This may be one of the reasons for the present differences in the degree of support for the Eastern European process of transformation between Western European and North American policy makers.

[2]A detailed study of the export composition of the countries in question reveals that they are, in terms of the product mix of their exports, most similar to each other. For example, on the EC market, for only a small number of product groups will there be significant competition between former CMEA countries and present NIEs and developing countries. On the other hand, this also indicates that it will be difficult for Eastern European countries to gain world market shares with their current product mix.

[3]For a more detailed theoretical discussion of these issues in the context of a multiregion intertemporal Ramsey growth model, see Avesani, Gallo, and Pauly

analysis, we define three regions : a (current account) surplus region, a deficit region, and the recipient region. The latter is to be understood as either being in the (European) East or in the South. For simplicity, we shall assume that all funds are provided by those industrial countries that are in surplus; the deficit region then contains all third countries.[4] In figure 1, we analyze regional price and activity reactions. A conditionalized transfer into the recipient region provides a stimulus to demand; in the medium term, through increases in the capital stock and improvements in total factor productivity, the supply side effects a shift as well. Equilibrium income is raised to Y', and prices adjust to p'. At the same time, both the original donor region and third countries benefit from trade creation as a result of improved activity in recipient countries. The demand shock shifts aggregate demand to D', respectively, and will tend to increase prices and real activity. In the donor region (and potentially in all other regions), this outward shift in aggregate demand is counteracted by the crowding-out effect of higher real interest rates (see below). The ultimate effect on inflation and activity remains ambiguous and depends upon the relative size of trade effects vis-à-vis the crowding-out effect of real interest-rate changes.

In a world of (nearly) integrated capital markets, the real interest rate will adjust so as to equilibrate regional saving-investment imbalances on a global scale : the current account constraint determines the interest rate. In figure 2, saving and investment functions for the three regions are graphed. At the initial interest rate r, the current account surplus in the surplus region just offsets the corresponding deficit elsewhere; the current account in the recipient region is assumed to be in equilibrium initially. The incremental investment projects in the recipient region ceteris paribus generate an excess demand for funds that would raise interest rates to a new level at r', at which rate the ensuing current account deficit in the recipient region is facilitated by an increased surplus (reduced deficit) in both other regions. Obviously, the outcome depends critically on saving and investment behavior in the original surplus and deficit regions. Any autonomous increase in private- or public-sector saving or any reduction in investment in either of these regions would allow world interest rates to remain at the original level or increase to a level below r'. The global real interest rate effects thus depend as much on the interest elasticity of saving and investment as on behavioral reactions in the private and public sectors.

5. SCENARIO DESIGN

The Spring 1990 baseline forecast of Project LINK already incorporates the assumption of rapidly rising deficits for the countries of Eastern Europe and the USSR, amounting to about $7 billion in 1990 and $18 billion in 1991, increasing to about $24 billion by 1994. Except for the ex-GDR, this does not reflect private capital inflows but rather some amounts of international official aid

---

(1991).

[4]The analysis could easily be extended to allow for part of the transfers to originate in industrial countries with current account deficits; the present simplification is adopted for purposes of illustration only.

(for Poland) and significant gold sales and receipts on the repayments of ruble debt on the part of the Soviet Union. Low expected rates of return, limited barter possibilities, and ownership uncertainties are assumed to limit private inflows in our baseline.

There is, of course, not only uncertainty about the future institutional conditions in recipient countries. Obviously, considerable uncertainty is also attached to any estimate of the size of financial transfers that are likely to be mobilized in international capital markets and through official channels in support of restructuring efforts. In our subsequent analysis, we take a rather agnostic stance in this regard, and try to provide a realistic estimate of the amount of funds that is likely to be available under present conditions.[5] It is assumed that additional (public) support would amount to about $5 billion in 1990 and gradually increase to $40 billion in 1994. The total size of the package over a period of five years is approximately $100 billion, which corresponds to about two thirds of the Marshall Plan in today's prices. About three quarters of these transfers are accounted for by intra-German transfers, i.e., the support for the former GDR amounts to about $75 billion over this period. The remaining $25 billion are split as follows: Bulgaria, $2.3 billion; Czechoslovakia, $3.0 billion; Hungary, $4.3 billion; Poland, $14.6 billion; Romania, $1.7 billion; and the Soviet Union, $1.8 billion. One way to interpret the size of these transfers is to note that the total is about twice the current allocation of the EBRD. It is assumed that World Bank and IMF loans to Hungary and Poland account for the remainder of the total sum; the distribution corresponds to current EBRD allocations. The inflows into the former GDR are assumed to be generated entirely within Germany, in equal parts in the private and public sectors.

Obviously, current reality has already exceeded the assumptions made in this scenario. For example, in the German case the public transfers over this period are likely to be more than twice as large as assumed here, and also appear to be much more front-loaded. Also, for the USSR we know now that even initial transfers are likely to be higher, not the least as a result of the German unification agreement. Nonetheless, the subsequent results may be indicative of the effects to be expected from larger transfers as envisaged at the present time.

It was outlined above how crucially dependent the effects of these policies on the West are upon the ensuing pressure on interest rates. Yet, in the absence of a consistent world flow-of-funds system, it is extremely difficult to gauge the financial market effects of these additional transfers. The order of magnitude of the additional resources generated within Western public sectors is relatively small, so it is quite conceivable that very little upward pressure on interest rates would result from additional government deficits caused by such a package. At the same time, expectations in financial markets, in particular inflationary expectations, can well produce significant increases at the high end of the term structure. Furthermore, national monetary policy responses are hardly predictable.

---

[5]An alternative (normative) approach would be to derive net capital inflow requirements from a specific development target. In general, the results of such exercises tend to suggest substantially larger transfers.

In this situation, we have performed our transfer scenarios under three alternative assumptions regarding the response of monetary authorities in the West:

1. the first set of results ("interest rate target") is based on the assumption that monetary authorities monetize the ensuing public deficits and stabilize interest rates at baseline levels;

2. in our second scenario ("inflation target"), at the opposite end of the spectrum of possible responses, we have implemented a monetary policy aimed at stabilizing inflation, thus allowing for a significant increase in interest rates worldwide, in response to the additional withdrawal of financial resources from Western capital markets; the resulting interest rate increase amounts to about 100 basis points in Europe and about 50 basis points elsewhere, thus reflecting less than fully integrated capital markets; and

3. in the third alternative ("money supply target"), we have assumed that central banks in the West will follow monetary policies aimed at stabilizing the paths of some appropriate monetary aggregates around baseline values. This results in interest-rate increases between 20 and 50 basis points in the major industrial economies.

Note that in all cases it is assumed that the responses are the result of coordinated policy actions; they do not, however, constitute "optimal" policy responses in terms of a well-defined joint criterion function.

In addition, the following major supplementary assumptions are made.

1. Fiscal policies in all industrial countries remain at baseline settings; particularly, no tax increases are implemented to finance the intra-German flows.

2. No allowance is made for a rescheduling of interest or principal payments for Eastern hard currency debts or any debt forgiveness.

3. The additional financial resources in Eastern Europe and the Soviet Union are used entirely to facilitate spending on fixed investment.[6]

4. Except for the case of the former GDR, incremental imports are allocated completely to non-CPE exporters according to the pre-shock trade shares.

5. For the former GDR, three quarters of the incremental imports are allocated to the former FRG; the remainder is allocated according to preshock non-FRG shares.

6. No adjustments are being made to third-country exports into recipient countries' export markets.

6. EMPIRICAL RESULTS

The results for these three alternatives are summarized in figures 3 to 5, 6 to 8, and 9 to 11, respectively. In all cases, we report deviations from the Spring 1990 LINK baseline projection for the world economy.[7]

---

[6]This may not be fully appropriate for the former GDR, where some of the transfers are made for public consumption purposes.

[7]All indications are that the results are sufficiently linear that the basic features of our scenarios will not be sensitive to the choice of a particular baseline path.

In the absence of noticeable interest–rate effects, financial transfers into Eastern Europe and the Soviet Union generate unambiguously favorable effects for all regions in the world, thus reflecting simply the positive transfer. Increased purchasing power in the East leads to an export demand stimulus for developed market economies in the West. By 1994, world trade is seen to be about 1.5% higher than without the transfers, while world activity has increased by 0.7%. Unemployment rates are slightly lower, while the inflationary impact amounts to about 0.1% annually. The GNP gains are, of course, concentrated in Western Europe, mostly in Germany, but the trade multipliers generate positive spillovers everywhere.

The GNP effects for the recipient countries reach 3% after five years. This seems small relative to the effects of the Marshall Plan, even when proper adjustments for the size of the stimulus are made. However, the economic environment in which the aid can be effective is very different in the present case. The postwar economies had state–of–the–art technologies, convertible currencies, free–enterprise systems in place, and a reservoir of entrepreneurial-ly inclined individuals, as well as a broad base of well–qualified skilled workers. Many of these components are still not in place in Eastern Europe.

Furthermore, a large fraction of the transfer does not immediately lead to domestic production activity, but leaks into imports. While the shock as implemented corresponds to a classic supply–side policy by restricting the use of funds to investment purposes, the capacity effects of such investments are relatively slow to materialize. The trade balance effects are indicative of this: recipient countries accumulate an incremental net foreign debt of close to $90 billion, almost the equivalent of the initial transfer. While some trade–balance benefits accrue to developing countries, most of the counterpart to the Eastern deficit appears in the OECD, and most significantly in the EEC.

The results are, of course, likely to be quite different if one were to experience a sharp rise in world interest rates as a result of activist monetary policies in the face of additional claims on world financial resources. The growth effect in the East would be virtually the same, but the stimulus on Western economic activity would be completely negated. The negative effects of interest–rate increases would dominate, and the OECD economies would experience a net loss in economic activity. Despite the larger trade multiplier, this is the case even for the EEC, since for the European region the interest–rate effect is at the same time larger than elsewhere. The trade effects are not significantly different from the earlier scenario. Obviously, then, if the risk of imposing additional strains on world financial markets really are deemed nontrivial or if a tight monetary policy response is considered likely, a policy of providing substantial financial aid to Eastern Europe may indeed entail the possibility of real losses for the OECD countries.

In our assessment, however, such a response is unlikely and would only be realistic if there were excessive speculative effects. A much more likely adjustment path would involve a prudent monetary policy such as that assumed under the third scenario. Such a policy would accommodate some of the demand stimulus and thereby allow for only a moderate increase in interest rates. The implied monetary tightening would, for the OECD as a whole, generate no GNP losses. The distribution of the Western activity effects remains, however, uneven. In North America the monetary tightening would not be accompanied by sufficiently large trade effects to avoid some GNP losses. For the other areas, the slightly higher interest rates would almost exactly offset the positive trade stimulus and keep levels of economic activity just about at baseline levels.

Such a scenario would, therefore, trade off desired increases in economic activity in Eastern Europe and the Soviet Union against a trade balance shift in favor of the OECD. In other words, it would involve classical external debt financing of initial development in the region, without noticeable negative effects on activity elsewhere.

7. SUMMARY

We conclude our analysis by observing that, based on this limited set of simulations, it appears that sufficiently conditionalized Western public support in the form of loans, combined with some grants, can play an important role in Eastern restructuring efforts without necessarily straining the Western financial system. Provided the institutional environment in the recipient countries continues to improve as assumed here, Western transfers can jump-start the process of increasing Eastern productivity while at the same time generating positive feedbacks elsewhere, which could only be negated if the (avoidable) interest-rate effects of these transfer policies were really substantial.

The results are, of course, model dependent. However, they appear to be broadly in line with those obtained in related work that is based on other international models (e.g., Alexander and Gagnon, 1990; Masson and Meredith, 1990). Many analysts would claim that computations such as the ones presented here even underestimate the positive effects of the initial stimuli by underestimating the efficiency gains through marketization and privatization. While some allowance for a systematically higher contribution of the Solow-residual on total factor productivity in the recipient countries has been made in this study, the extent of such effects cannot but remain highly speculative. While it is hoped that these effects would indeed turn out ultimately to be more important than the replacement and expansion of the capital stock, there is some doubt as to whether these efficiency gains would indeed materialize over the five-year horizon considered here.

On the contrary, all indications are that even under favorable assumptions about the extent of technical and organizational improvements, in order to achieve per capita incomes comparable to middle-level Western European industrial countries by, say, early next century, investments on a much larger scale than considered here are going to be required. Whether, in the unfortunate case that these savings cannot be generated within recipient countries, the effects of additional transfers will turn out to be linear in the size of the shock remains to be examined.

REFERENCES

Alexander, L.S. and J.E. Gagnon (1990), "The Global Economic Implications of German Unification," Board of Governors of the Federal Reserve System International Finance Discussion Papers, No. 379, Washington, D.C., April.

Avesani, R.G., G. Gallo and P. Pauly (1991), "Regional Saving-Investment Imbalances and the World Real Interest Rate," paper presented at the NBER International Seminar on Macroeconomics, Madrid, June.

Barro, R.J. and X. Sala-i-Martin (1990), "World Real Interest Rates," NBER Macroeconomics Annual, 15-69.

Blanchard, O.J. and L.H. Summers (1984), "Perspectives on High World Real Interest Rates" Brookings Papers on Economic Activity, No. 2, 273-324.

European Economy (1989), "Saving, Investment, and International Financial Markets: an Overview," No. 42, Nov., 163-177.

European Economy (1990), "Saving, Investment, and Real Interest Rates," No. 46 Dec., 201-216.

Frenkel, J.A. and A. Razin (1985), "Fiscal Expenditures and International Economic Interdependence," in: W.H. Buiter and R.C. Marston (eds.), International Economic Policy Coordination, (Cambridge: Cambridge University Press), 37-73.

Frenkel, J.A. and A. Razin (1987), Fiscal Policies and the World Economy, (Cambridge: MIT Press).

Masson, P.R. and G. Meredith (1990), "Domestic and International Macroeconomic Consequences of German Unification," in: L. Lipschitz and D. McDonald (eds.), German Unification : Economic Issues, IMF Occasional Paper # 75 Washington, D.C., December, 93-114.

Pauly, P. (1990), "Economic Restructuring in Eastern Europe and the Soviet Union: Implications for the World Economy," in: D. Purvis (ed.) Economic Developments in the Soviet Union and Eastern Europe, (Kingston: John Deutsch Institute), 91-103.

Pauly, P. (1991), "Global Investment and Saving Flows: Some Macroeconomic Scenarios" in: L. Waverman (ed.) Developments in Eastern Europe: Saving, Investment, and Spillovers to North America and LDCs (Norwell: Kluwer Academic Publ.), forthcoming.

Figure 1: Global Financial Transfers
Quantity and Price Effects

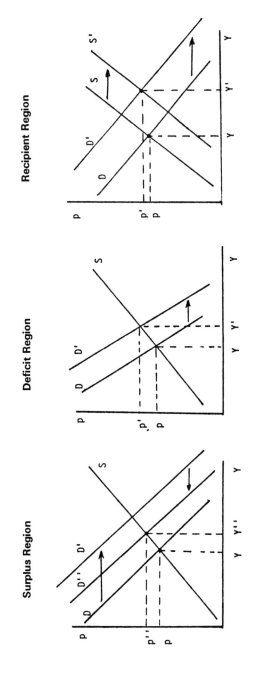

Figure 2: Regional S-I Imbalances and the World Real Interest Rate

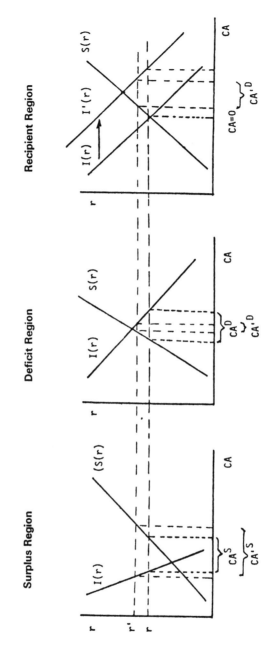

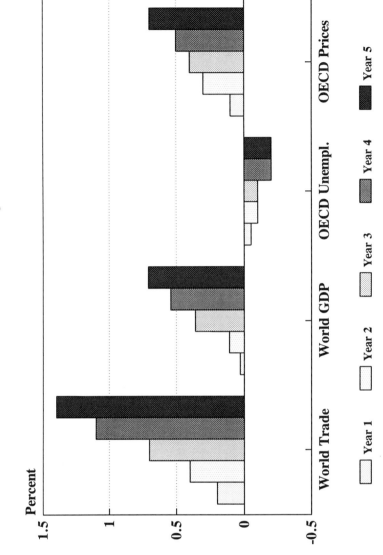

Figure 3: Global Effects, CPE Transfers
Interest Rate Target

Percent

Source : Project LINK

367

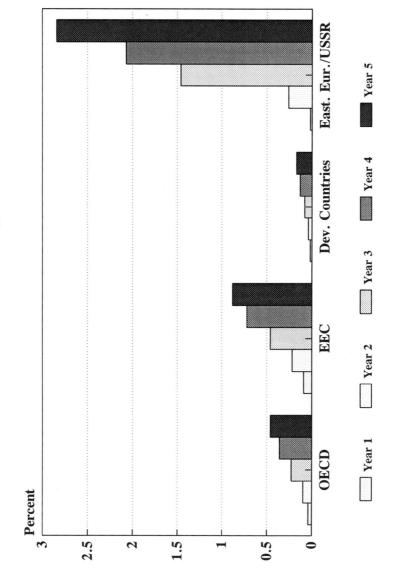

Figure 4: Regional Effects, CPE Transfers
Interest Rate Target

Source : Project LINK

Figure 5: Trade Balance Effects, CPE Transfers
Interest Rate Target

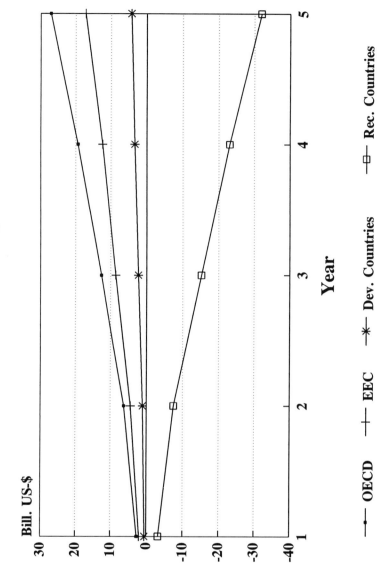

Bill. US-$

Year

—•— OECD   —+— EEC   —*— Dev. Countries   —□— Rec. Countries

Source : Project LINK

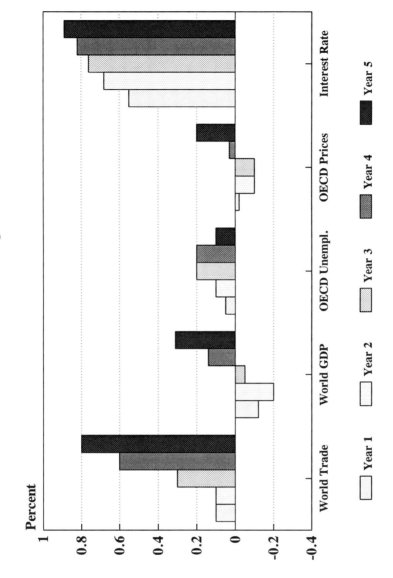

Figure 6: Global Effects, CPE Transfers
Inflation Target

Source : Project LINK

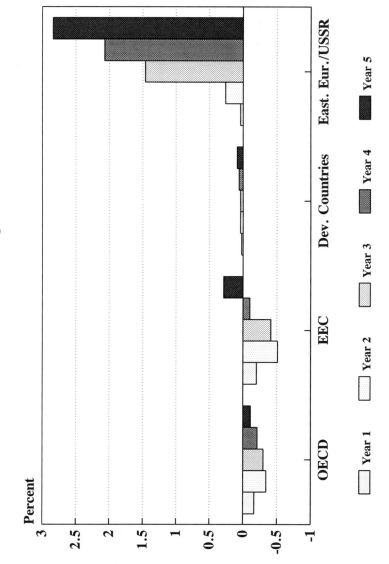

Figure 7: Regional Effects, CPE Transfers

Inflation Target

Source : Project LINK

Figure 8: Trade Balance Effects, CPE Transfers
Inflation Target

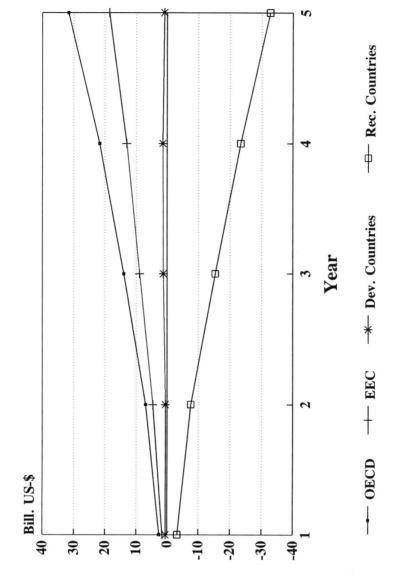

Bill. US-$

Year

—•— OECD   —+— EEC   —✳— Dev. Countries   —☐— Rec. Countries

Source : Project LINK

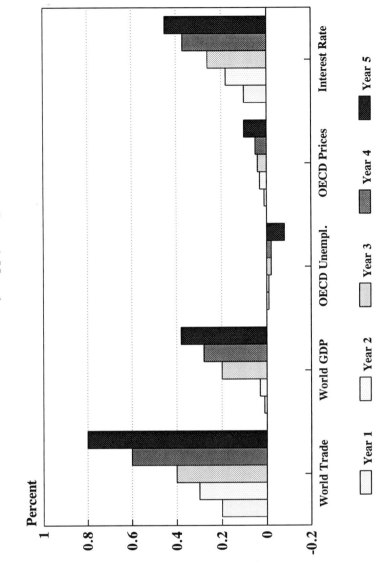

Figure 9: Global Effects, CPE Transfers
Money Supply Target

Source : Project LINK

Figure 10: Regional Effects, CPE Transfers
Money Supply Target

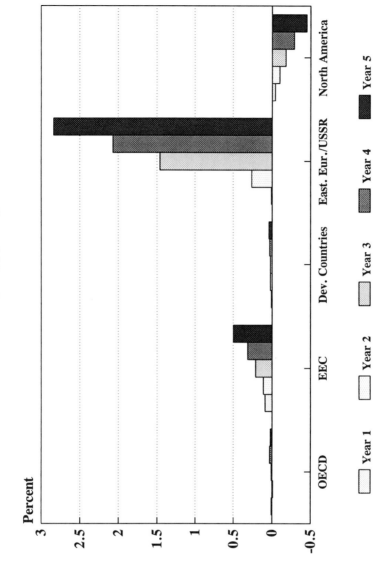

Source : Project LINK

Figure 11: Trade Balance Effects, CPE Transfers
Money Supply Target

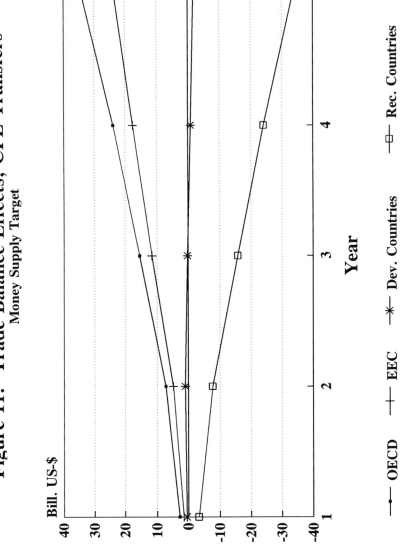

Source : Project LINK

24. CONVERSION AND ECONOMIC REFORM

V. K. Faltsman
Academy of Sciences of the USSR
Institute of Economics
Moscow
USSR

ABSTRACT. This chapter discusses the Soviet program for the conversion of military industry to civilian production in the period 1991–1995. It begins with an analysis of the effect the program might have on the Soviet economy and on the standard of living of the Soviet people. It then tries to evaluate the program with regard to its practicability, completeness, and comparison with foreign experience. It ends with some suggestions about how the efficiency of the conversion program might be increased.

During 1989, conversion became one of the most popular elements of the current economic reform. It is mentioned in the political programs of many Soviet parliament members. Nevertheless, it is not merely a political campaign, but also an objective economic process. There are at a minimum eight reasons, which demonstrate the inevitability of Soviet economic demilitarization, combining cuts in military expenditure, and the conversion of the Soviet defense complex.

1. _Social_. The society can no longer tolerate one-sided defense priorities at the expense of other social programs: consumer, health, and environmental. The majority of the population, including the nonnomenclature strata of the military industry and the Armed Forces, suffer from the outdated consumer sector and services.

2. _Financial–economic_. Its roots are in the budget deficit. The country cannot afford both huge military expenditures and a high budget deficit.

3. _Military–economic_. The extremely high priority of the defense sector cannot ensure the quality of military hardware while other sectors lag behind.[1]

4. _Military reform_. Its aims are effective defense with minimal costs, good composition of the Armed Forces, and high arms quality. As the Soviet President claims, general state programs are required for large-scale reduction in the armed forces, weapons, and military spending.[2]

---

[1] In the view of American specialists, Soviet military power used to make the West take Soviet interests into consideration. But in the 1970s the power of the military complex started to undermine the position of the USSR. The excessive rate of militarization caused a weakening of Soviet security. (P. Grenier, E. Stubbs, _A Farewell to Arms:_ Council on Economic Priorities, April 1989)

[2] _Pravda_, 05.09.1990.

5. _Foreign trade_. The raw material sector can no longer yield enough foreign currency for the import of consumer goods and technological equipment. Conversion allows for a reduction in these imports and, perhaps in the future, the substitution of raw material exports by the export of manufactured goods.

6. _Political_. Demilitarization is a precondition for democratization and the dismantling of the command and administrative system. This system is a characteristic feature of military management in any country.

7. _Decrease in international demand for armaments_. According to the Stockholm Institute for Peace Research, Soviet exports amount to one third of the world total foreign purchases of conventional arms. The share of arms in overall Soviet exports is 17.5%.

8. _Worsening of interethnic relations in the USSR_. From one side, this requires the strengthening of the militia (police) and interior troops. From the other side, increasing emigration and republican self-determination will lead to a reduction in military spending, the size of the Army, and the defense industry.

Therefore, there is no alternative to military expenditure cuts and conversion. That means that they will be implemented under any version of economic reform. However, the course and socioeconomic consequences of conversion depend on the reform's success.

In its turn, conversion can either facilitate or hinder economic reform. An effective conversion program is a support for economic reform, facilitating social trust in it. At the same time, unsuccessful conversion would be an additional source of social tension and would discredit an important part of the reform. So, a thoroughly elaborated conversion program is needed.

"The State Program of Military-Industry Conversion for the Period to 1995" has been prepared."[3]

In the light of this, the purpose of this chapter is, first, to analyze the program from the national economic viewpoint. Second (and most important), the program is to be evaluated for its practicability, completeness, and conformity to foreign experience. Third, some ways to increase its efficiency should be noted.

A number of conceptual issues of conversion are omitted in this chapter. They include such matters as conversion's national economic consequences, importance, principles and limits in the short and long run, timing, specific features in the planned and market economies, and general characterization of the defense sector of an economy. These issues were presented to the government in "The Proposals for the Economic Concept of Conversion" and were included in a published paper.[4]

1. THE ROLE OF CONVERSION IN THE SOLUTION OF MAJOR SOCIAL PROBLEMS

The normative concept assumes that the social consequences of conversion are positive and significant to the population. To avoid mistakes and disappoint-

---

[3]I.V. Smyslov, _Izvestia_, February 28, 1990; I.S. Belonogov, _Pravda_, August 28, 1989.

[4]V. Faltsman, "The Economic Concept of Conversion," _Voprosy ekonomiki_, 9, 1989.

ments, this concept requires a thorough consideration. To this end, let us evaluate the impact of conversion on social problems.

The contribution of conversion to the production of consumer durables is considered to be decisive. For example, during the seven years of planned conversion (1989–1995), there is to be an increase in the output (measured in physical units) of tape recorders by 40%, refrigerators, TV, and radio sets by 50%–60%, vacuum cleaners by 100%, sewing machines by 130%, and VCRs by 3200%. The military industry produces practically the entire amount of these items. Conversion can eliminate "tension" in these markets within the next 2 to 3 years.

The population will certainly notice the balance between supply and demand in the market for traditional consumer goods. But how will the increase in production affect the life of the average citizen? To answer this question, we calculated the output of consumer durables per 1000 population (see table 1). Two levels of the indicator were calculated for the year 1995. The first corresponds to the conversion program; the second is the extrapolation of the 1981–1988 trend. One can evaluate the impact of conversion on the output of consumer durables by comparing these two levels.

The table shows that the output of three out of eight goods in question is lower under conversion than according to the extrapolation of the 1981–1988 trend. These three are color TV sets, tape recorders, and washing machines. Only half of Soviet families have a tape recorder, one third have a color TV set (one fifth in rural areas), and two thirds have a washing machine.

Table 1.　Production (Units per 1000 of population)

	1970	1980	1988	1989	1990	1995	1995
				(program)		(program)	(trend)
1. Radio sets	32	32	28	30	37	42	25
2. TV sets	28	28	34	34	38	49	40
3. Including							
color	0.2	8.5	19.9	22	25	39	42
4. Tape recorders	4.9	11.5	19.4	19.7	25.6	25.2	30
5. Refrigerators	17.1	22.4	21.7	22.4	22.4	31	21
6. Washing machines	21.7	14.5	21.3	23.1	21.7	22.8	30
7. Vacuum cleaners	6.2	12.2	16.7	17.6	23.4	30.5	22
8. Sewing machines	5.8	5.0	5.4	5.4	6.5	11.4	5.8

The per capita output of the other five goods is higher under conversion. For example, the radio set output per 1000 heads was 32 in 1980, reducing to 28 in 1988. Preserving this negative trend, the 1995 output will approximate 25. However, the conversion program plans an increase up to 42 in 1995.

The significance of the radio–set output increase can be viewed by considering the stock of radio sets per capita. The number of radio sets per 1000 people was 289 in 1988. The per–1000–person output increase of 17 (42–25=17) is equivalent to a 6% increase of the stock. Every Soviet family has a radio set now. (In the U.S. in 1972, there were 1700 radio sets per 1000 heads.) To double the radio–set stock per capita, 12 years will be required with 6%

yearly increase of the per capita output and even more if replacement is taken into account.

The yearly increase of the stock of other consumer durables is as follows: 3% for TV sets, 4% for refrigerators, 6% for vacuum cleaners, and 3% for sewing machines.

So, in spite of the overall positive impact of conversion on the supply of consumer goods, we cannot anticipate an economic miracle during the next 5 to 6 years.

In addition to its impact on the quantity of consumer goods, conversion will probably increase the quality of consumer goods. However, we were unable to provide a measure of such an increase.

Aside from addressing the shortage of consumer durables, conversion should have a positive impact on the problems of food supply, infrastructure, and health. We have indirectly measured this impact via the output dynamics of certain types of equipment. Table 2 presents the planned growth rates under conversion compared with the past period.

The data presented show that the conversion program is supposed to increase sharply the output of equipment for storage, processing, and consumption of food. Besides this, conversion provides the basis for an increase in the quantity and quality of air and water transportation and communications services. The procurement of new types of medical equipment can also be anticipated.

However, taking into consideration the extremely difficult situation in the above sectors, the conversion program will be only a minor step on the way to economic improvement. For example, the program aims at the provision of 45–50 telephones per 100 families in 1995 (30 in 1990). This cannot bridge the huge gap between the USSR and many foreign countries and ensure the modest normative level proposed in this country in the early 1970s (one telephone per family).

Table 2. Planned growth rates under conversion compared with past period

Social Problem	Technological Equipment	Average annual output growth rates, %	
		1981–1988	1989–1995
Food	For the Agra-rian and Industrial Complex (processing sectors)	4.4	12.2
	For trade and public catering	5.1	8.9
Infra-structure	Civil aircraft	NA	18.6
	Civil vessels	NA	5.3*
	Communication	NA	9.8*
Health	Medical	7.8	14.6

* 1991–1995.

The conversion program calls for high growth rates of civilian aircraft production and delivery and satisfaction of the demand for such aircraft in the immediate future. But the problems of civilian aviation are not solved with that. New airport construction and extra fuel supplies are necessary to satisfy the demand for air transportation. Judging from the Chinese conversion experience, it might be helpful to transfer military airfields and fuel resources to the civilian sector.

We should evaluate the chances of fulfilling the conversion program. The year 1989 showed that the defense ministries failed to meet the orders for many types of processing equipment for the agro-industrial complex.[5] The main reason for that was the incompetence of military designers in the sphere of their new activity. So the technological models, even if copied from foreign examples, appear to be unfit for our conditions, or they are so expensive that the customers reject them.

Under conditions of economic shortage, the success of the conversion program to a great extent depends on the supply of parts, metals, and other material resources. A part of these resources can be obtained by reducing the output of military equipment. The reduction is planned to approximate 20% in 1991–1995. At the same time, the output of civilian goods in the defense sector is planned to increase by 80%. The share of civilian output in the defense complex, almost 50% in 1990, will rise to 60% in 1995.

Though metal usage in civilian output is probably less than in military output, an extra demand for material resources in the defense sector is inevitable. According to some calculations, the defense-sector demand for ferrous metals, aluminum, and copper for civilian production will increase by 70%–100%. So it is necessary either to expand capacity or to import the necessary materials. Neither way is realistic.

The necessary resources for conversion include much more than just metals. Thus, successful conversion requires coordination of many sectors, which is difficult to organize through the firms' own efforts. For example, the Chelyabinsk tractor plant decided to use capacities freed by conversion to produce mini-tractors, which are in great demand in this country. However, the 1990 plan to produce 1 million tractors will fail, since the suppliers of the engine and other parts have not accepted the orders of the Chelyabinsk Plant.

The conversion program projects a number of positive shifts in the production of many consumer goods, as well as the manufacture of technological equipment for the agro-industrial complex, infrastructure, and medicine. However, conversion can offer only some intermediate solutions to social problems, preserving the Soviet lag behind the developed countries. Even these modest plans are likely to fail due to poor resource support.

2. SELF-FINANCING OF THE CONVERSION PROGRAM

Given that a large number of programs are not supported by financial resources, the reality of a new program is related to its self-financing capabilities. Thus, a necessary (but not sufficient) condition for the conversion program's feasibility is a reduction in military spending that exceeds both the budget revenue cuts due to the decline in military production and the increases in budgetary expenditures. The latter include the capital investments necessary to increase civilian production, expenditures for social protection of individuals

---

[5]Trud, February 2, 1990.

hurt by the conversion program, and for the environment, the cost of demolishing military equipment and of the shift of resources.

Without self-financing, the program will depend on the allocation of additional resources, including the redistribution of capital investments from other sectors. Given the overall reduction in capital investment resources and high investment demand, the possibilities of increasing capital investments in civilian production within the military sector are very unlikely.

The self-financing condition for the conversion program certainly does not mean that it should be applicable for any individual firm. On the contrary, as the experience shows, the state must make the major part of investments in social welfare, environmental protection, and major civilian research projects. However, 'in the current financial situation, the employed resources cannot exceed the reduction in military spending.

To evaluate the available financial resources, it is necessary to define the scope of military spending cuts. The USSR has stated its intentions to reduce the share of military expenditures in the national income by 33%-50% by 1995. Table 3 presents the dynamics of the military spending on the basis of this.

Table 3. Dynamics of military spending

	1989	1990	1995*
The share of military expenditures in national income, %	12.0	11.8	6-8
Military expenditures, billion rubles			
Total	77.3**	70.9	45.4-60.6
Including:			
Armament procurement	32.6	31.0	NA
R&D	15.3	13.1	NA
Maintenance of the Army and Navy	20.2	19.3	NA
Military construction	4.6	3.7	NA
Pensions	2.3	2.5	NA
Other	2.3	1.3	NA

* The conversion program assumes a military-spending reduction of more than one third in 1995. That corresponds to the upper limit of the interval.
** According to some foreign estimates, Soviet military expenditures amount to 115-125 billion rubles.

The data show that military spending in 1990 is supposed to decrease by 6.4 billion rubles, which amounts to 8.3% and is significant. At the same time, it is only 5% of the budget deficit, an insignificant amount.

The absolute reduction in military spending will be 10–25 billion rubles (1995 in comparison with 1990).[6] Under an assumption of a 1% population growth rate, the per capita reduction will amount to 7–17 rubles per year. With the current per capita annual income of 1836 rubles, this reduction, even if spent completely on consumption, will raise income only by 0.4%–0.9%.

The conversion impact on the elimination of the 160 billion rubles monetary overhang will not exceed 7%–8% of it.

Thus, even very dramatic military spending cuts will not have a decisive impact on the budget deficit and consumer market. Under these conditions, other steps are necessary for financial recovery, e.g., the reforms of prices, taxation, monetary circulation in general, and the creation of security markets.

Conversion is both a consequence of military spending cuts and a cause for a significant civilian expenditure increase. First of all, conversion requires extra capital investment in civilian production. In 1990, such investment is to exceed 4–4.5 billion rubles. This is less than the military expenditure cuts (6.4 billion rubles). The 1991–1995 maximum estimate of military spending reduction is twice as large as the required investment in civil production in the defense sector. But the minimum estimate amounts to only 80% of this investment. In the latter case, conversion self–financing is unattainable. The conversion program should take into consideration the extra expenditure for social benefits for the former defense–sector employees. Let us proceed on the assumption that conversion will not require new workplaces. (This assumption is likely to be rejected in the near future.) Even with this assumption there is a need for extra investment in reeducation, unemployment benefits, and housing construction. Thus, a part of the defense cuts should be reallocated to education, social welfare, and housing.

Obviously, the conversion program takes into account only a small part of these expenditures. Proceeding from the 1991–1995 projections for capital investment in the Ministry of Defense, capital investment in the social programs of the Army and the Navy are to increase by 67%. This is only the first step towards improving the poor social welfare of the military. It will aid the popularity of the conversion program among them.

We can determine what are the necessary expenditures for social welfare in light of the experience of the U.S. Department of Veterans Affairs. The annual budget of the Department exceeds $28 billion,[7] 95% of which goes to direct allowances, services, pensions, housing loans, life insurance, medical service, etc., including the maintenance of 112 national cemeteries and free tombstones. The annual per head expenditures average $400. From the previous estimates, assume that conversion will affect 4 million military, employees and dependents. Let us assume that one fourth of them will need economic support. Proceeding from the fact that social welfare in the socialist society cannot lag behind that in the capitalist society, the per head expenditures cannot be less than 2500 rubles, or 2.5 billion rubles per 1 million people.

---

[6]This amount is calculated under the assumption of 3% annual growth of national income in 1991–1995. If the growth rate is higher, the reduction will be lower (under the assumption of constant share of the military expenditures). If the growth rate is lower, the reduction will be higher. With zero growth, the reduction will amount to 19–32 billion rubles in 1995.

[7]Facts and Figures, Department of Veterans Affairs. VA Pamphlet, 1989.

These calculations are purely illustrative. Nevertheless, they show that these extra 2.5 billion rubles plus 4–4.5 billion rubles of investment in civilian production in the defense sector will exceed the planned defense-spending cuts, i.e., 6.4 billion rubles. Thus, the conversion program will not be self-financed.

These are not all the conversion expenditures. A part of the defense budget cuts must be invested in the destruction of military equipment. The necessary technologies either exist or are still in the process of development. The authors of the conversion program correctly believe that conversion may yield savings in the use of different materials in several branches of production.

The program lacks calculations of the costs of demolishing military equipment. Large expenditures are required to demolish special military structures and building. According to foreign experience, the costs of weapon destruction may exceed the revenue from recycling. According to Hungarian estimates, $4,000–$12,000 is required to dismantle a tank.[8] The planned liquidation of 5000 Soviet tanks will require $120 to $360 million, i.e., about 1 to 2 billion rubles.

It is difficult to estimate the expenditures for minireprocessing plants to extract usable chemicals from chemical weapons at the place where they are stored.

The defense sector is one of the most ecologically dangerous. Let us consider the hazardous effects of production, tests, and storage of nuclear and chemical weapons. Conversion will require large environmental expenditures. For example, according to American specialists, U.S. nuclear plants have been negatively affecting the health and security of their employees and neighboring residents for decades. In light of this, a question about shutting down a number of reactors, nuclear plants, and research centers has been raised.

Conversion of the projects dealing with radioactive materials requires a long and expensive deactivation. According to the U.S. Department of Energy, it is necessary to spend $66 to $100 billion during the next 50 years to reduce the contamination of 16 major nuclear plants to the level that meets the Environmental Law standards.[9]

Extra capital investments are required even under passive conversion, i.e., the mere redistribution of resources from the military to the civilian sector. For example, the costs of civilian production will increase if a sector uses special materials from the aerospace sector. Even intersectoral redistribution of petroleum products will probably require investments in the transportation network and oil-refinery capacity.

A special calculation should be made to evaluate the probable budget revenue losses due to military output reductions and simultaneous budget revenue increase due to civilian output increase. If net losses emerge, they must be compensated by defense spending cuts.

The conversion program proceeds from the decrease in the budget revenue from the military sector. We believe that conversion is unlikely to inflict

---

[8]T. Palankai, Conversion: The Hungarian Case, Prospects and Problems in the Late 1980s and Early 1990s.

[9]G. Bischak, "Economic Conversion and Diversification Strategies for the Nuclear Weapons Complex," The New Economy, vol. 1, No. 1, Aug.–Sept. 1989.

considerable losses on budget revenue. The civilian output of the military sector is supposed to grow faster than the military output decreases. A 1% increase of the share of consumer goods in total industrial output yields three times as much financial resources (profit and turnover tax) as does the respective increase of producer goods.[10] But conversion will probably require state subsidies for some firms, since the cost of a man-hour in military production is 2 to 6 times higher than in civilian production.

The conversion program projects constant average wages in the military sector during the period of worker retraining. In spite of the decrease in profits, the enterprises' social development funds have been planned to remain at constant levels. The financial resources for that will be acquired by introducing higher normative coefficients for the funds formation. This will lead to losses in budget revenue. Our financial analysis of the conversion program has shown that the projected expenditures for social support, environment, and arms destruction are underestimated. Thus, conversion self-financing is far from obvious. In the case of minimum reduction in military spending, self-financing is unattainable.

The conversion program needs further work to achieve reality. We probably have to reduce either the projected military spending or the expenditures for civilian production. Taking into consideration the current economic situation, we will probably postpone some conversion expenditures. Hence, the effect will also be postponed. This is better, though, than to disperse the available small resources and to fail to achieve even the most modest plans.

It is possible to cut military output without the restructuring or demolition of plants. Such a conversion can be called passive or "lazy."

We should search, however, for ways of active conversion, which implies new construction and renovation in the military sector. And after all, the investments in social programs should not be cut. The best way to achieve self-financing is to raise the efficiency of conversion.

3. WAYS TO RAISE THE EFFICIENCY OF CONVERSION

We consider the possibilities of increasing conversion efficiency from three standpoints: 1) the efficiency of capital investment and construction; 2) the rational use of the high intellectual and innovative potential of military R&D; and 3) the system of management, which would provide the stimuli for high-quality civilian production.

The projected efficiency of capital investment in the military sector for civilian production purposes is rather high. The actual increase in total industrial output per ruble of capital investment was 0.45 rubles in 1981-1985, and 0.81 rubles in machine-building.[11] The anticipated 1991-1995 level of this indicator for the military sector is 1.52-1.56 rubles. Hence, the anticipated effect of capital investment in the military sector is approximately three times higher than in industry as a whole and two times higher than in machine-building.

---

[10] Voprosy Ekonomiki, 1, 1990, p. 6.

[11] The latter indicator was based on the volume of investment minus increase in unfinished construction.

We can put forward a number of hypotheses for such a high efficiency. The first deals with the high prices of civilian output in the military sector. The output of many traditional consumer goods is projected to increase by 50%–60% if measured in physical units during the next five years and by 80% if measured in rubles. If this higher ruble increase is not accompanied by quality improvements, that means that the outward appearance of high investment returns is actually caused by statistically underestimated inflation.

The second possible reason deals with the use of military fixed assets for civilian production. According to some estimates,[12] 20% of military capacities used for civilian production are equivalent to 17 billion rubles worth of new fixed assets. According to later data, conversion will allow the shift of fixed assets to civilian production equal to 3%–4% of total fixed assets in industry, or 26–35 billion rubles.[13] This amount is equivalent to the state civilian-purpose capital investment in the military sector in the previous five–year–plan period.

If the high efficiency of capital investment in the military sector is determined by switching fixed assets to civilian production, then this fact must be supported by a high share of reconstruction and technical renovation. However, 80% of capital investment in 1991–1995 is planned to be spent on new construction.

Renovation usually requires less investment in structures and more investment in equipment than does new construction. That leads to a higher increase in output. In 1991–1995, the share of investment in structures will be 23% under renovation and 35% under new construction. This, incidentally, averages to 32% of total capital investment, which is significantly below what is planned for the national economy as a whole (38%).

A high share of investment in equipment with a small share of investment in renovation is probably the cause of high investment efficiency in the military sector; i.e., the converted fixed assets include a high proportion of buildings and structures. There are also, perhaps, some other reasons for high investment efficiency and the small proportion of investments in structures, e.g., use of the cheap labor force of military construction personnel.

It is highly probable that the actual return on capital investment in the military sector (measured as the ratio of the increase in production over the level of investment) will be less than planned, because all the projects and programs usually underestimate the level of investment.

The overestimation of the projected level of investment efficiency sometimes takes place abroad as well.

Let us take as an example the conversion of five military shipyards in France in the 1960s, after the Algerian war. Only one shipyard went smoothly through conversion. State investment in the other four considerably exceeded the planned level. Large extra investment was required, for instance, in the sales network.

The productivity of the retrained workers also appeared to be less than projected. The composition of the workplace in the converted shipyards differed greatly from that in the normal unconverted shipyards. As a result, it turned out that the costs of the resulting civilian output would be less if the

---

[12]Voprosy ekonomiki, 6, 1989, p. 52.

[13]Literaturnaya gazeta, May 9, 1990, p. 15.

investment were made in the existing civilian shipyards. The state had to subsidize heavily the converted shipyards since they were nonprofitable.[14]

Since the high R&D potential is the main advantage of the defense sector, success of conversion greatly depends on its use. From this standpoint, defense cuts should be made at the expense of mainly military output, not R&D. For example, the Americans keep a constant share of R&D, at 13%, in the projected (1991–1994) reduced military budget.[15]

According to table 4, Soviet military R&D expenditures decline faster than other defense expenditures, and so the R&D share in defense budget decreases.

In 1991, military expenditures on R&D are planned to be 14% lower than their 1988 level.

Space research deserves a special analysis. According to published data, space expenditures amount to 6.9 billion rubles a year, including 3.9 billion rubles.

Table 4. The Defense Budget (Percentage of Total)

	1989	1990
R&D	19.8	18.5
Procurement of equipment	42.2	43.7
Maintenance of the Army	26.1	27.2

(or 56%) for military space. According to published data, the economic effect of the space program has already reached 12 billion rubles. The space sector is projected to become profitable by 1995. These assertions certainly need to be verified. Even if they appear to be wrong, we should be very cautious in cutting space expenditures in order to keep intact the sector's high innovative potential.

The conversion program plans increases in civilian R&D in the defense sector that exceed the reduction in military R&D. Civilian R&D will soar by 31% in 1991 and by another 21% in 1995. Budget subsidies will support 75% of these expenditures. Under these conditions, the intellectual and innovative potential of the military sector appears to grow. But there are severe difficulties in switching R&D to new fields.

The program envisions the development of new technology, equipment, and materials of dual use (i.e., in both the military and civilian sector). The authors believe that this will allow the reduction of the respective R&D expenditures by three-to-fivefold. As foreign experience shows, however, dual-use technologies have a narrow field of implementation.

---

[14]E.B. Kapstein, "From Guns to Butter in the USSR," Challenge, Sept.–Oct. 1989.

[15]W.W. Kaufmann, Glasnost, Perestroika and US Defense Spending, Washington, The Brookings Institution, 1990, Table I.G.

4. MANAGEMENT OF CONVERSION

High quality and competitiveness of equipment and consumer goods can be achieved only in fierce competition. The administrative and command system has not been able to achieve this result, since this country lacks competition. There are no competitive markets, no equilibrium of supply and demand, nor winners and losers.

In the near future, conversion will be centrally managed in accordance with an overall program. The program was elaborated on the basis of "The Methodological Instructions for Social and Economic Planning," published by Gosplan of the USSR in the prereform period. According to this methodology, Gosplan elaborates plans for industrial defense ministries on the basis of the demand of the Ministry of Defense for the production and procurement of military equipment and the demand of foreign trade organizations for export. The plans stipulate the levels of military output, civilian output, including consumer goods, capital investment, supplies of material resources, expenditures for military and civilian R&D. On the basis of these plans, the industrial defense ministries construct a list of enterprises eligible for conversion, assign the levels of military and civilian output to them, and take care of necessary supplies. Then the enterprises elaborate detailed conversion plans for 1991–1995.

P. Potasov, corresponding member of the Soviet Academy of Sciences and chief military designer, writes that the Communist Party bodies interfere in conversion and impose inappropriate output assignments on enterprise.[16]

Such methods of planning doom the conversion program to failure. Though there is a section on the economic mechanism in the program, economic agents have no incentives to implement it.

The program leads to further monopolization and concentration. In the shortage economy, enterprises have to reduce the number of unreliable supplies and to expand to technologically adjacent sectors, hence increasing their scale. Ministries support concentration, since it is easier to manage a small number of large enterprises than a large number of small ones. The share of the defense sector rises due to the rapid growth in it of civilian capital investment, output, and R&D. The growth of the defense sector strengthens the command and administrative system. All this hinders economic reform.

Thus, reform of management is in even greater need in the converted sector than in other ones. Its main prerequisite is a nonmonopolized consumer market without shortages. The steps in this direction should include decentralization and change of property rights in the defense sector.

Given that the work on the conversion program should continue, what should the program look like?

A new management mechanism of conversion should be based on the assumption that the center is responsible only for decisions on military spending and individual military programs. The state conversion program should include the financial plan presenting the state budget allowances to, and revenue from, the defense sector.

The composition and quality level of output and R&D will be defined by firms experiencing market fluctuations. Firms know better about available R&D, equipment, and personnel. That knowledge is crucial for market adjustment. Higher economic agencies should warn firms about reductions in military orders, say, one year in advance. Firms can start working on their conversion programs

---

[16]*Literaturnaya gazeta*, May 9, 1990, p. 15.

before those warnings, since according to foreign experience, such programs need up to two years for full operation.

Conversion programs of firms should have many versions depending on the depth of conversion and should take into consideration anticipated amounts of military orders, loans, and budget allowances.

The state conversion program should not fix levels of detailed civilian output in a market economy. These levels should adjust to domestic and foreign market demand.

The conversion program must be dynamic and consider high-tech development as the main long-run guiding line. Since such development is not required by markets, the government should provide necessary support. In light of this, the state conversion program should include a section on R&D, high tech, competitiveness, and computerization.

The program must also include steps to ensure necessary social benefits and environmental protection to eliminate social tension.

Defense budget cuts and the conversion program are not likely to facilitate economic growth in the next 5 to 7 years. They also do not promise fast solutions to social problems, although they should improve the quality of growth. However, basing our viewpoint on positive Japanese and German and negative American experience, we believe that conversion can yield both short-run and long-run effects and provide a decisive impact on economic and social development.

* * *

While meeting with the delegation of the Institute of Economics, Nobel Laureate P. Samuelson mentioned his experience with the U.S. Commission on Conversion, which started working in 1941 to prepare postwar conversion. Many conclusions of the Commission proved to be wrong. For example, the Commission forecasted postwar depression and high unemployment due to the drop in military spending. But there was strong growth of investment activity, consumption, and high employment. P. Samuelson believes that such mistakes prove the value of timely conversion planning and forecasting.

Conversion in the USSR carried out under conditions of economic reform is a complex process with both achievements and social tensions. Though mistakes in the conversion process seem to be unavoidable, we should go ahead, analyzing the experience gained and correcting the program with the aim of increasing its effectiveness.

REFERENCES

Belonogov, I.S. (1989), Pravda, August 28.

Bischak, G. (1989), "Economic Conversion and Diversification Strategies for the Nuclear Weapons Complex," The New Economy, Vol. 1, No. 1, August–September.

Faltsman, V. (1989), "The Economic Concept of Conversion," Voprosy Ekonomiki, No. 9.

388

Grenier, P. and E. Stubbs, (1989), <u>A Farewell to Arms</u>, (New York: Council on Economic Priorities), April.

Kapstein, E.B. (1989), "From Guns to Butter in the USSR," <u>Challenge</u>, September–October.

Kaufmann, W.W. (1990), <u>Glasnost, Perestroika and U.S. Defense Spending</u>, (Washington, D.C.: The Brookings Institution) table I.G.

<u>Literaturnaya Gazeta</u> (1990), May 9, p.15.

Palankai, T. (1990), <u>Conversion: The Hungarian Case, Prospects and Problems in the Late 1980s and Early 1990s</u>, (Budapest).

<u>Pravda</u>, 05. 09. 1990.

Smyslov, I.V. (1990), <u>Izvestia</u>, February 28.

<u>Trud</u>, 02. 02. 1990.

Veterans Affairs, Department of (1989), <u>Facts and Figures</u>, (Washington, D.C.: Department of Veterans Affairs).

<u>Voprosy Ekonomiki</u> (1989), No. 6, p. 52.

<u>Voprosy Ekonomiki</u> (1990), No. 1, p. 6.

25. SUMMARY BY PROFESSOR JOHN HELLIWELL OF SESSION 4: "RESTRUCTURING OF SOCIALIST ECONOMIES AND THE IMPACT OF DISARMAMENT ON THE WORLD ECONOMY"

In this session, the discussion of the four chapters was combined with the general discussion at the end of the session, and was introduced by the comments of the designated discussants, Professor Ohtsu and Professor Sato.

Professor Ohtsu concentrated his comments on the Levine, Niwa, and Faltsman chapters. Starting with the Levine chapter, his first point related to the disharmony between the pace of economic and political reforms. The Soviet Union, from his observations during a recent visit to Moscow, had been already much democratized, and these political changes were the focus of all discussion, while economic reforms were not yet happening. He contrasted this with the situation in China, where, at least until the time of Tienanmen Square, the pace of economic reform had been rapid, while the political reforms had been slow. Why has the pace of economic reform been so relatively slow in the USSR?

In answer to this question, Professor Levine noted that the entire structure of the economic system was in question, and with this scope of change one did not rush in if one was prudent. That said, the general view, both within and outside the Soviet Union, was that the time for major changes had come, and in some eyes was overdue. He noted a Russian tendency to be apocalyptic; his view was that there was still time, and that production levels and inflation rates were not out of control.

Professor Ohtsu's second comment related to the issues that the current situation was posing at the enterprise or industrial level. He noted the recent departure from an instrument company of the chief accountant and the chief engineer, both frustrated with their inability to cope with changing targets and continuing demands to prepare dual accounts. Professor Levine replied that the marketization was taking place in the growing cooperatives, despite the tensions with the bureaucracy and with state firms. Perhaps the experts in the instrument-making state firm left not only because things were difficult there, but also because they could double their wages by working in a cooperative. In the process of marketization, the downside of capitalism may appear before the upside. That is, monopolies, whether territorial or sectoral, and criminal activities are appearing in the process, none of which are unknown in the history of capitalist economies.

Professor Ohtsu queried the nature of the 500 billion rouble figure used in Professor Niwa's chapter, as being so much larger than current or projected government deficit figures. Professor Niwa explained that the figure, drawn from a Russian study, related to accumulated excess purchasing power, mostly held in the form of cash balances.

Professor Ohtsu then noted the very small amount of transfers to the Soviet Union assumed in the simulations by Professor Pauly. In reply, Professor Pauly noted that his figures were very uncertain, but appeared to reflect the current state of affairs, in which there had only been $600 million earmarked for the Soviet Union (out of a total of $12 billion provisionally allocated by the European Reconstruction Fund). He has assumed another $1.5 billion of public money going to the USSR, which might be an optimistic assumption given the apparently low demand and supply.

Turning to the Faltsman chapter, Professor Ohtsu found himself impressed with the quality of analysis and depressed by the message, which emphasized the difficulty and expense of converting the Soviet military industry to peaceful uses. Professor Ohtsu also emphasized the housing and employment issues posed when the soldiers who had been released from the military (more than one quarter million by the end of 1989) remained where they were posted but without good prospects for employment in the local communities. Similar problems would exist with respect to the more than 600,000 Russian military posted overseas, who would be likely to return to the Moscow metropolitan labor market, posing enormous adjustment problems in the labor and housing markets.

In reply, Professor Faltsman estimated that there would be about 4 million people involved in the conversion of the military. The degree of support likely to be available for these individuals during the transition is greater for the ex-soldiers than for defense industry workers. It would be especially important to safeguard and transfer the knowhow and expertise in the military and its related industries. He noted that there were draft laws for the support of individuals during the transition, although at levels apparently far less than in other countries. He saw promise in encouraging foreign private capital investment in Soviet resource and energy industries, since these are better poised to be able to make use of the skills being released from the defense industries.

The second discussant, Professor Sato, started by stating his agreement with Professor Levine's apparent rejection of Polish-type shock therapy, which Professor Sato thought inappropriate for application in the Soviet Union, Czechoslovakia, and Hungary. Professor Sato saw a middle ground between the shock therapy and piecemeal approaches to economic reform. He described it as a "step-by-step approach but with a package of measures," similar in nature to the "radical-moderate" approach described by Professor Levine. The idea is to design an integrated package of mutually consistent and drastic reforms that are then introduced in a phased step-by-step manner.

Turning to the issue of monetary overhang emphasized by Professors Levine, Faltsman, and Niwa, Professor Sato argued that no transition to a market economy would be possible without some means of absorbing this overhang. Professor Sato doubted whether the privatization program, as described by Professor Levine, would be sufficient to absorb the huge monetary overhang. Although people might be prepared to buy real properties, or bonds that guarantee access to cars or other consumer goods, they would probably not be prepared to buy shares of enterprises because of their uncertain performance, profitability, and expected dividends. He thought that the Shatalin plan overemphasized the likely benefits of privatization and underestimated the degree of shocks likely to accompany price liberalization. He feared that there was a kind of soft-landing illusion in the Shatalin plan. Similar issues arose with the rather similar Gorbachev Plan, thus leading Professor Sato to adopt a "wait and see" approach. In reply, Professor Levine noted that there are both stock and flow aspects in the monetary overhang. The flow aspect, or the annual increase in the overhang, has to be dealt with by macropolicies, while the stock overhang has to be gradually reduced by a mixture of policies, mainly on the supply side.

The first contribution to the open discussion was by Professor Eaton, who suggested that the Latin American experience should make lenders skeptical about lending public money in the expectation of structural reforms that might then not take place. In the Latin American case, the borrowing tended to enable the postponement of the reforms rather than force them to take place. He favored official concentration on the structural reforms themselves, with private investment then flowing in as the reforms take place.

Dr. Higgins also took up the matter of the most appropriate forms for Western economic assistance to aid transformation. Professor Niwa had referred to financial support and cooperation, while Professor Pauly had referred to a combination of technical assistance, conceptual advice, and financial support, before concentrating on the latter for modeling purposes. Which type of assistance is likely to be most fruitful? In reply, Professor Levine noted that the most urgent form of aid from the United States was likely to be of food, and of assistance with food distribution. Second, there was much scope for facilitating movements of skilled individuals to provide on-the-ground expertise, a sort of peace corps under another name. Professor Niwa, from the Japanese perspective, suggested that economic cooperation based on the Japanese tough free enterprise system would appear to offer the best prospects of success. Professor Pauly thought that technical assistance and conceptual advice belonged as part of a comprehensive package with financial transfers, but there is as yet too little research to determine their relative importance.

Professor Klein referred first to the problems of converting the military, noting that Germany would bear part of the costs of repatriating Soviet troops from Germany, and that more such support was possible. With respect to Soviet reforms, he thought that some support for these might be available through conditions attached to Soviet membership in the GATT, the IMF, and the World Bank. Turning to Professor Pauly's results, Professor Klein noted that although the international macroeconomic effects of the transfers and increasing trade seemed small, they were only aspects of a process that promised much larger indirect gains from the reductions in international tensions and the lowering of risks of future international disturbances. As for the distinction between private and official capital lending, he noted that private capital would be inclined to go where the facilities and conditions looked favorable, while the official capital would reflect political attitudes rather than economic factors. Finally, he asked Professor Niwa if there were not financial fragilities in the Japanese situation that might lead him to qualify his optimistic assessment of the Japanese situation. In reply, Professor Niwa noted the perception, both inside and outside Japan, that post-1987 Japanese development has been marked by a succession of bubbles of real estate values, of stock prices, and so on. He preferred to emphasize the importance of an underlying real adjustment process involving mutually sustaining growth in Japan and the Asian NIEs.

Professor Onituka asked about the conceptual approach to the market system in Eastern Europe. Did it differ between the USSR and the other Eastern European countries? Were there legal systems, market ethics, and individual incentives sufficient to support a market system in the Soviet Union? After 70 years without a market economy, will there be a lack of entrepreneurship? Many Russian emigres to the United States apparently want to return to the Soviet Union, finding themselves unable to adjust psychologically to the dynamic competitive society they found in the United States. If this is so, will there not be problems in establishing such a system within the Soviet Union? In reply, Professor Levine noted that over the last three decades there has been remarkable urbanization that has created a well-trained middle class. The insecurities posed by the market system will indeed cause problems, perhaps best solved by an Adam Smithnykov to expound the longer-term benefits of a market system.

Professor Monsod doubted that a substitution of foreign savings for structural reform was likely in Eastern Europe, as suggested by Professor Eaton, despite the similarities between the Latin American and Eastern European situations. The Latin American debt buildup in the 1970s was made possible by the extreme eagerness of the private lenders, and that element is lacking today. Thus lenders will be more anxious to ensure that their lending neither anticipates nor postpones the necessary adjustments. She then asked Professor Niwa whether monetary reform could be readily accomplished under a democratic process, given that the earlier examples of Stalin in 1948 and Baron Shidehara in 1946 were accomplished under an authoritarian form of government. In reply, Professor Niwa acknowledged the issue raised, while noting that Japan was fully democratized in 1946, although the role of General MacArthur's administration in the currency reform was substantial.

Professor Nerb asked Professor Pauly for some estimate of the time horizon over which the proposed sequence of public lending, private lending, and then repayment would take place. He wondered whether the slow pace of official lending might make advisable an alternative sequence in which private funds were drawn in sooner. In reply, Professor Pauly agreed that it would be desirable to establish as soon as possible an environment in which the major element of Western investment was on the private side. The problem, however, is that in most of the countries the institutional arrangements are not developed enough for private investors to find them attractive. This problem does not exist for the GDR, and Poland and Hungary are both becoming more attractive to private investors. But the Soviet Union, at the present time, does not have the institutional arrangements to make it attractive for private investment. There is perhaps not yet even an awareness in the Soviet Union of how crucial some of these issues, e.g., currency convertibility, are to the ability of the country to attract foreign investment.